First and
Second Timothy
and Titus

First and
Second Timothy
and Titus

CHRISTOPHER R. HUTSON

Baker Academic
a division of Baker Publishing Group
Grand Rapids, Michigan

Published by Baker Academic
a division of Baker Publishing Group
PO Box 6287, Grand Rapids, MI 49516-6287
www.bakeracademic.com

Printed in the United States of America

Library of Congress Cataloging-in-Publication Data
Names: Hutson, Christopher R., author.
Title: First and Second Timothy and Titus / Christopher R. Hutson.
Description: Grand Rapids : Baker Academic, a division of Baker Publishing Group, 2019. | Series: Paideia : commentaries on the New Testament | Includes bibliographical references and index.
Identifiers: LCCN 2019017292 | ISBN 9780801031939
Subjects: LCSH: Bible. Pastoral Epistles—Commentaries.
Classification: LCC BS2735.53 .H88 2019 | DDC 227/.8307—dc23
LC record available at https://lccn.loc.gov/2019017292

ISBN 978-1-5409-6241-6 (casebound)

Unless otherwise indicated, all Scripture quotations are the author's translation.

19 20 21 22 23 24 25   7 6 5 4 3 2 1

In memoriam

Abraham J. Malherbe

Contents

Figures

Foreword

Paideia: Commentaries on the New Testament is a series that sets out to comment on the final form of the New Testament text in a way that pays due attention both to the cultural, literary, and theological settings in which the text took form and to the interests of the contemporary readers to whom the commentaries are addressed. This series is aimed squarely at students—including MA students in religious and theological studies programs, seminarians, and upper-division undergraduates—who have theological interests in the biblical text. Thus, the didactic aim of the series is to enable students to understand each book of the New Testament as a literary whole rooted in a particular ancient setting and related to its context within the New Testament.

The name "Paideia" (Greek for "education") reflects (1) the instructional aim of the series—giving contemporary students a basic grounding in academic New Testament studies by guiding their engagement with New Testament texts; (2) the fact that the New Testament texts as literary unities are shaped by the educational categories and ideas (rhetorical, narratological, etc.) of their ancient writers and readers; and (3) the pedagogical aims of the texts themselves—their central aim being not simply to impart information but to form the theological convictions and moral habits of their readers.

Each commentary deals with the text in terms of larger rhetorical units; these are not verse-by-verse commentaries. This series thus stands within the stream of recent commentaries that attend to the final form of the text. Such reader-centered literary approaches are inherently more accessible to liberal arts students without extensive linguistic and historical-critical preparation than older exegetical approaches, but within the reader-centered world the sanest practitioners have paid careful attention to the extratext of the original readers, including not only these readers' knowledge of the geography, history, and other contextual elements reflected in the text but also their ability to respond correctly to the literary and rhetorical conventions used in the text. Paideia commentaries pay deliberate attention to this extratextual repertoire in order to highlight the ways in which the text is designed to persuade and move its readers. Each rhetorical unit is explored from three angles: (1) introductory matters; (2) tracing the train of thought or narrative or rhetorical flow of the argument; and (3) theological issues raised by the text that are of interest to the contemporary Christian. Thus, the primary focus remains on the text and not its historical context or its interpretation in the secondary literature.

Our authors represent a variety of confessional points of view: Protestant, Catholic, and Orthodox. What they share, beyond being New Testament scholars of national and international repute, is a commitment to reading the biblical text as theological documents within their ancient contexts. Working within the broad parameters described here, each author brings his or her own considerable exegetical talents and deep theological commitments to the task of laying bare the interpretation of Scripture for the faith and practice of God's people everywhere.

Mikeal C. Parsons
Charles H. Talbert
Bruce W. Longenecker

Preface

I grew up in a family that was at church every time the doors were open, which was at least three times per week. I grew up knowing that our church was organized just like the Bible said. Our congregation had elders and deacons who were married men with faithful children, just as we read in 1 Tim. 3 (with a glance at Titus 1). Women never spoke in the worship assembly, just as we read in 1 Tim. 2. When I was a teenager, our minister organized a "Timothy Class" to teach boys how to lead worship, and when we did, I was the preacher. My dad was a deacon. My mom taught Sunday school. And I was one of four faithful children. That was all I knew about the Letters to Timothy and Titus, and all I needed to know, or so I thought.

My academic interest in these letters began in a Greek exegetical seminar led by Abraham J. Malherbe, who later directed my doctoral dissertation (Hutson 1998). Malherbe and Wayne Meeks were enormously influential for my understanding of exegesis and how to think about cultural context. Richard Hays and Leander Keck also influenced my understanding of Paul and how to think theologically about the New Testament.

This commentary is the result of some twenty-five years of thinking and writing about the Pastoral Epistles. I have read through these letters multiple times in Greek with students at Hood Theological Seminary and Abilene Christian University. I have benefited from conversations with colleagues in the Disputed Paulines Section of the Society of Biblical Literature, among whom I am especially grateful for the support and encouragement of Jerry L. Sumney.

I've discussed these letters with faithful people in a lot of churches. I know more about the Pastoral Epistles now than I did as a teenager, and I see them differently. I still think these letters are important for the church, and I believe people who think the church is important should study them closely.

I wish to thank Susan R. Garrett, who recommended me for this project. Thanks to the editorial staff at Baker Academic—James Ernest (now with Eerdmans) for patience when I blew past my deadline, and Bryan Dyer for encouragement and guidance as I brought this book to completion. Thanks to the series editors, Mikeal C. Parsons, Bruce W. Longenecker, and Charles H. Talbert, for their confidence in me. Thanks also to Wells Turner and the editorial staff at Baker Academic for their care and attention to detail in bringing this book to completion.

I am thankful for friends and colleagues who read drafts of various sections and gave valuable feedback, including Ayodeji Adewuya, Aaron G. Brown, Kenneth L. Cukrowski, Philip LeMasters, Sheila Sholes-Ross, Jason Vickers, and especially my faithful friend James P. Ware. Each of these helped me identify flaws and contributed to making this a better book.

This commentary is dedicated to the memory of Abraham J. Malherbe. For eight years I studied with him and worked with him in a local congregation. I learned from his scholarship and from his and Phyllis's examples of service to the church. When I began writing this commentary, Abe was working on his own for the Hermeneia series. Despite the wealth of his scholarship on these letters, his commentary was never realized. This is not the commentary he would have written, but he made this book possible.

Abbreviations

General

acc.	accusative case	Lat.	Latin
aka	also known as	lit.	literally
AME Zion	African Methodist Episcopal Zion	n.d.	no date
		no.	number
aor.	aorist tense	NT	New Testament
BCE	before the Common (Christian) era	OT	Old Testament
		par.	parallel
CE	Common (Christian) era	PE	Pastoral Epistles
cent.	century	pl.	plural
cf.	*confer*, compare	p(p).	page(s)
dat.	dative case	pref.	preface
diss.	dissertation	PRyl	papyrus of John Rylands Library
ed(s).	editor(s), edited by, edition	ps.-	pseudo-
e.g.	*exempli gratia*, for example	pt.	part
Eng.	English	repr.	reprinted
Ep.	*Epistles*, with specific author named	rev.	revised
esp.	especially	ser.	series
ET	English translation	sg.	singular
et al.	*et alii*, and others	SJ	Society of Jesus
etc.	*et cetera*, and the rest	Sr.	Senior
frag(s).	fragment(s)	St.	Saint
gen.	genitive case	s.v.	*sub verbo*, under the word
Gk.	Greek	trans.	translator(s), translated by
i.e.	*id est*, that is	v(v).	verse(s)
inscr.	inscription	var.	variant
Jr.	Junior	vol(s).	volume(s)

Bible Texts and Versions

א	Codex Sinaiticus (4th cent.)
א²	Codex Sinaiticus, second corrector
ASV	American Standard Version
B	Codex Vaticanus
CEB	Common English Bible
CEV	Contemporary English Version
CJB	Complete Jewish Bible
CSB	Christian Standard Bible
DRA	Douay-Rheims, American edition (1899)
ESV	English Standard Version
GNV	Geneva Bible
GW	*GOD'S WORD* Translation
HCSB	Holman Christian Standard Bible
ISV	International Standard Version
KJV	King James Version
LXX	Septuagint, Greek Old Testament
MT	Masoretic Text of the Hebrew Bible
NA²⁸	*Novum Testamentum Graece.* 28th rev. ed. Edited by [E. and E. Nestle], B. and K. Aland, J. Karavidopoulos, C. M. Martini, and B. M. Metzger. Stuttgart: Deutsche Bibelgesellschaft, 2012.
NABRE	New American Bible, revised (2010) edition
NASB	New American Standard Bible
NCV	New Century Version
NEB	The New English Bible
NET	The NET Bible (New English Translation)
NIV	New International Version
NLT	New Living Translation
NRSV	New Revised Standard Version
𝔓³²	a third-century papyrus; sample reference to a numbered papyrus
𝔓⁴⁶	Chester Beatty Papyrus II, of about 200 CE
Phillips	J. B. Phillips, *The New Testament in Modern English*
RSV	Revised Standard Version
TLB	The Living Bible
WYC	Wycliffe Bible
YLT	Young's Literal Translation

Ancient Corpora

OLD TESTAMENT

Gen.	Genesis
Exod.	Exodus
Lev.	Leviticus
Num.	Numbers
Deut.	Deuteronomy
Josh.	Joshua
Judg.	Judges
Ruth	Ruth
1–2 Sam.	1–2 Samuel
1–2 Kings	1–2 Kings
1–2 Chron.	1–2 Chronicles
Ezra	Ezra
Neh.	Nehemiah
Esther	Esther
Job	Job
Ps(s).	Psalm(s)
Prov.	Proverbs
Eccles.	Ecclesiastes
Song	Song of Songs
Isa.	Isaiah
Jer.	Jeremiah
Lam.	Lamentations
Ezek.	Ezekiel
Dan.	Daniel
Hosea	Hosea
Joel	Joel
Amos	Amos

Obad.	Obadiah
Jon.	Jonah
Mic.	Micah
Nah.	Nahum
Hab.	Habakkuk
Zeph.	Zephaniah
Hag.	Haggai
Zech.	Zechariah
Mal.	Malachi

DEUTEROCANONICAL BOOKS

Bel	Bel and the Dragon
1–2 Esd.	1–2 Esdras
Jdt.	Judith
1–4 Macc.	1–4 Maccabees
Sir. (Ecclus.)	Sirach (Ecclesiasticus)
Sus.	Susanna
Tob.	Tobit
Wis.	Wisdom of Solomon

NEW TESTAMENT

Matt.	Matthew
Mark	Mark
Luke	Luke
John	John
Acts	Acts
Rom.	Romans
1–2 Cor.	1–2 Corinthians
Gal.	Galatians
Eph.	Ephesians
Phil.	Philippians
Col.	Colossians
1–2 Thess.	1–2 Thessalonians
1–2 Tim.	1–2 Timothy
Titus	Titus
Philem.	Philemon
Heb.	Hebrews
James	James
1–2 Pet.	1–2 Peter
1–3 John	1–3 John
Jude	Jude
Rev.	Revelation

OLD TESTAMENT PSEUDEPIGRAPHA

Apoc. Mos.	Apocalypse of Moses
2 Bar.	2 Baruch (Syriac Apocalypse)
1–2 En.	1–2 Enoch
4 Ezra	4 Ezra
Jos. Asen.	Joseph and Aseneth
Jub.	Jubilees
Let. Aris.	Letter of Aristeas
Mart. Ascen. Isa.	Martyrdom and Ascension of Isaiah
Odes Sol.	Odes of Solomon
Pss. Sol.	Psalms of Solomon
Sib. Or.	Sibylline Oracles
T. Ab.	Testament of Abraham
T. Ash.	Testament of Asher
T. Dan	Testament of Dan
T. Gad	Testament of Gad
T. Iss.	Testament of Issachar
T. Jos.	Testament of Joseph
T. Jud.	Testament of Judah
T. Levi	Testament of Levi
T. Naph.	Testament of Naphtali
T. Reu.	Testament of Reuben
T. Sim.	Testament of Simeon

DEAD SEA SCROLLS

CD	Cairo Genizah, Damascus Document
1QH^a	Qumran, Cave 1, Hodayot Scroll, Thanksgiving Hymns^a
1QM	Qumran, Cave 1, War Scroll
1QpHab	Qumran, Cave 1, Pesher on Habakkuk
1QS	Qumran, Cave 1, Community Rule
4Q481	Qumran, Cave 4, scroll frag. 481
11QPs^a	Qumran, Cave 11, Psalms Scroll, frag. a
11QT	Qumran, Cave 11, Temple Scroll

RABBINIC TRACTATES

Letters preceding the names of Mishnaic tractates indicate sources: Mishnah (*m.*), Tosefta (*t.*), Babylonian Talmud (*b.*), and Jerusalem/Palestinian Talmud (*y.*).

Arakh.	Arakhin
Avot	Avot
Ber.	Berakhot
Ned.	Nedarim
Sanh.	Sanhedrin
Shabb.	Shabbat
Sotah	Sotah
Yad.	Yadayim
Yevam.	Yevamot

OTHER RABBINIC WORKS

Gen. Rab.	Genesis Rabbah
Lev. Rab.	Leviticus Rabbah
Sifre Num.	Sifre Numbers

APOSTOLIC FATHERS

Barn.	Barnabas
1–2 Clem.	1–2 Clement
Did.	Didache

Diogn.	Diognetus
Herm. Mand.	Shepherd of Hermas, Mandates
Herm. Sim.	Shepherd of Hermas, Similitudes
Herm. Vis.	Shepherd of Hermas, Visions
Ign. Eph.	Ignatius, To the Ephesians
Ign. Magn.	Ignatius, To the Magnesians
Ign. Phld.	Ignatius, To the Philadelphians
Ign. Pol.	Ignatius, To Polycarp
Ign. Rom.	Ignatius, To the Romans
Ign. Smyrn.	Ignatius, To the Smyrnaeans
Ign. Trall.	Ignatius, To the Trallians
Mart. Pol.	The Martyrdom of Polycarp
Pol. Phil.	Polycarp, To the Philippians

GNOSTIC WRITINGS

Gos. Phil.	Gospel of Philip
Treat. Res.	Treatise on the Resurrection

Ancient Authors

ARISTOTLE/PSEUDO-ARISTOTLE

Eth. Nic.	Nicomachean Ethics
Oec.	Oeconomica (Household Management)
Pol.	Politics
Probl.	Problems
Rhet.	Rhetoric

ATHENAEUS

Deipn.	Deipnosophistae

AUGUSTINE

Bapt.	On Baptism against the Donatists
Leg.	Contra adversarium legis et prophetarum (Against the Enemy of the Law and the Prophets)

CICERO

Cael.	Pro Caelio (In Defense of Caelius)
Mur.	Pro Murena (In Defense of Murena)

Off.	De officiis (On Duties)
Sen.	De senectute (On Old Age)

CLEMENT OF ALEXANDRIA

Paed.	Paedagogus (Christ the Educator/The Instructor)
Protr.	Protrepticus (Exhortation to the Greeks)
Quis div.	Quis dives salvetur (Salvation of the Rich)
Strom.	Stromata (Miscellanies)

CYPRIAN

Hab. virg.	De habitu virginum (On the Dress of Virgins)

DIO CHRYSOSTOM

Or.	Orations

DIOGENES LAËRTIUS

Lives	Lives of Eminent Philosophers

EPICTETUS

Diatr.	Diatribes
Ench.	Enchiridion

EUSEBIUS

Hist. eccl.	Historia ecclesiastica (Ecclesiastical History)
Praep. ev.	Praeparatio evangelica (Preparation for the Gospel)

GALEN

Animi mores	Quod animi mores corporis temperaturam sequuntur (That the Habits of the Soul Follow the Tempers of the Body)
Bon. mal. suc.	De bonis malisque sucis (On Good and Bad Humors)
PHP	De placitis Hippocratis et Platonis (On the Doctrines of Hippocrates and Plato)

GREGORY OF NYSSA

Hom. Cant.	Homilies on Song of Songs
Hom. Eccl.	Homilies on Ecclesiastes
Macr.	Life of St. Macrina
Vit. Mos.	De vita Mosis (Life of Moses)

HIPPOCRATES

Aph.	Aphorisms
Nat. hom.	De natura hominis (On the Nature of Man)
Vict. salubr.	De ratione victus salubris (Regimen in Health)

IAMBLICHUS

VP	Vita Pythagorica (The Pythagorean Way of Life)

IRENAEUS

Epid.	Epideixis tou apostolikou kērygmatos (Demonstration of the Apostolic Preaching)
Haer.	Adversus haereses (Against Heresies)

ISOCRATES/PSEUDO-ISOCRATES

Demon.	To Demonicus (Oration 1)
Soph.	Against the Sophists (Oration 13)

JOHN CHRYSOSTOM

Hom. 1 Tim.	Homilies on 1 Timothy
Sac.	De sacerdotio (On Priesthood)

JOSEPHUS

Ag. Ap.	Against Apion
Ant.	Jewish Antiquities
J.W.	Jewish War

JUSTIN MARTYR

1 Apol.	First Apology
Dial.	Dialogue with Trypho

LIVY

Ab urbe	Ab urbe condita (From the Foundation of the City)

LUCIAN/PSEUDO-LUCIAN

Am.	Amores (Affairs of the Heart)
Cal.	Calumniae non temere credendum (Slander)
Fug.	Fugitivi (The Fugitives or The Runaways)
Demon.	Demonax
Dial. mort.	Dialogi mortuorum (Dialogues of the Dead)
Peregr.	The Passing of Peregrinus
Somn.	Somnium (The Dream)

LYSIAS

Or.	Orations

ORIGEN

Cels.	Against Celsus
Comm. Jo.	Commentary on the Gospel of John
Comm. Matt.	Commentary on Matthew
Fr. 1 Cor.	Fragments of Commentaries on 1 Corinthians
Hom. Jes. Nav.	Homilies on Joshua Son of Nun
Hom. Luc.	Homilies on Luke

PHILO

Aet.	De aeternitate mundi (On the Eternity of the World)
Abr.	On the Life of Abraham
Agr.	Agriculture
Alleg. Interp.	Allegorical Interpretation of the Laws

Cher.	On the Cherubim
Conf.	On the Confusion of Tongues
Congr.	De congressu eruditionis gratia (On Preliminary Studies)
Contempl. Life	On the Contemplative Life
Creation	On the Creation of the World
Decal.	On the Decalogue
Deus	Quod Deus sit immutabilis (That God Is Unchangeable)
Dreams	On Dreams
Embassy	Embassy to Gaius
Flaccus	Against Flaccus
Gig.	De gigantibus (On the Giants)
Joseph	On the Life of Joseph
Names	On the Change of Names
Opif.	De opificio mundi (On the Creation of the World)
Praem.	De praemiis et poenis (On Rewards and Punishments)
Prelim. Studies	On the Preliminary Studies
QG	Questions and Answers on Genesis
Sacr.	The Sacrifices of Cain and Abel
Somn.	De somniis (On Dreams)
Spec. Laws	On the Special Laws
Virt.	De virtutibus (On Virtues)
Worse	That the Worse Attacks the Better

PHILODEMUS

Oec.	De oeconomia (On Property Management)
Parr.	Peri parrhesias (On Frank Criticism)

PINDAR

Nem.	Nemeonikai (Nemean Odes)

PLATO

Prot.	Protagoras

PLINY THE ELDER

Nat.	Natural History

PLINY THE YOUNGER

Ep. Tra.	Epistulae ad Trajanum

PLUTARCH/PSEUDO-PLUTARCH

Adol. poet. aud.	Quomodo adolescens poetas audire debeat (How a Young Man Ought to Listen to Poetry)
Adul. amic.	Quomodo adulator ab amico internoscatur (How to Tell a Flatterer from a Friend)
Aem.	Life of Aemilius Paullus
Amat.	Amatorius (Dialogue on Love)
Caes.	Life of Caesar
Cic.	Life of Cicero
Cohib. ira	De cohibenda ira (On Controlling Anger)
Comm. not.	De communibus notitiis contra stoicos (On Common Notions, against the Stoics)
Comp. Lyc. Num.	Comparison between Lycurgus and Numa
Conj. praec.	Conjugalia praecepta (Advice to Bride and Groom)
Curios.	De curiositate (On Curiosity)
Cupid. div.	De cupiditate divitiarum (On Love of Wealth)
Inim. util.	De capienda inimicis utilitate (How to Profit from One's Enemies)
Lib. ed.	De liberis educandis (On the Education of Children)
Luc.	Life of Lucullus
Lys.	Life of Lysander
Mor.	Moralia
Praec. ger. rei publ.	Praecepta gerendae rei publica (Precepts of Statecraft)
Pyth. orac.	De Pythiae oraculis (On the Phythian Oracles)
Quaest. conv.	Convivial Questions (Table Talk)
Quaest. rom.	Roman and Greek Questions
Rect. rat. aud.	De recta ratione audiendi (On Listening to Lectures)
Superst.	De superstitione (On Superstition)
Tu. san.	De tuenda sanitate praecepta (Advice about Keeping Well)

Virt. prof.	*Quomodo quis suos in virtute sentiat profectus* (*Progress in Virtue*)	*Marc.*	*Against Marcion*
		Mon.	*Monogamy*
		Praescr.	*Prescription against Heretics*
PSEUDO-CRATES		*Prax.*	*Adversus Praxean* (*Against Praxeas*)
Ep.	*Epistles*	*Pud.*	*De pudicitia* (*On Modesty*)
		Ux.	*Ad uxorem* (*To His Wife*)
PSEUDO-DIOGENES		*Virg.*	*On the Veiling of Virgins*
Ep.	*Epistles*		

PSEUDO-CRATES

Ep.   *Epistles*

PSEUDO-DIOGENES

Ep.   *Epistles*

PSEUDO-MELISSA

Cl.   *To Cleareta*

PSEUDO-MYIA

Phyl.   *To Phyllis*

PSEUDO-THEANO

Eu.   *To Euboule*
Call.   *To Callisto*
Nik.   *To Nikostrate*

SENECA

Ben.   *De beneficiis* (*On Benefits*)
Ep.   *Moral Epistles*
Helv.   *Consolatio ad Helviam* (*Consolation to Helvia*)

TERTULLIAN

Apol.   *Apology*
Bapt.   *De baptismo* (*On Baptism*)
Carn. Chr.   *De carne Christi* (*On the Flesh of Christ*)
Cult. fem.   *De cultu feminarum* (*On the Apparel of Women*)
Exh. cast.   *Exhortatione castitatis* (*Exhortation to Chastity*)

Marc.   *Against Marcion*
Mon.   *Monogamy*
Praescr.   *Prescription against Heretics*
Prax.   *Adversus Praxean* (*Against Praxeas*)
Pud.   *De pudicitia* (*On Modesty*)
Ux.   *Ad uxorem* (*To His Wife*)
Virg.   *On the Veiling of Virgins*

THEODORE OF MOPSUESTIA

Comm. 1 Tim.   *Commentary on 1 Timothy*
Comm. 2 Tim.   *Commentary on 2 Timothy*
Comm. Titus   *Commentary on Titus*

VERGIL

Aen.   *Aeneid*

XENOPHON

Anab.   *Anabasis*
Eq.   *De equitande ratione* (*On the Art of Horsemanship*)
Mem.   *Memorabilia*
Oec.   *Oeconomicus* (*The Household Manager*)

ANONYMOUS WORKS

Cynic Epistles   see Malherbe 1977
Pythagorean Letters to Women   see Huizenga 2013

Series, Collections, and Reference Works

ABD	*The Anchor Bible Dictionary.* Edited by D. N. Freedman et al. 6 vols. New York: Doubleday, 1992
AGRW	*Associations in the Greco-Roman World.* Edited by R. A. Ascough, P. A. Harland, and J. S. Kloppenborg. Waco: Baylor University Press, 2012.
ANF	*The Ante-Nicene Fathers: Translations of the Writings of the Fathers down to A.D. 325.* Edited by Alexander Roberts and James Donaldson. Revised by A. Cleveland Coxe. 10 vols. New York: Christian Literature, 1885–87. Reprint, Peabody, MA: Hendrickson, 1994.

BDAG W. Bauer, F. W. Danker, W. F. Arndt, and F. W. Gingrich. *A Greek-English Lexicon of the New Testament and Other Early Christian Literature*. 3rd ed. Chicago: University of Chicago Press, 2000.

BDF F. Blass, A. Debrunner, and R. W. Funk. *A Greek Grammar of the New Testament and Other Early Christian Literature*. Chicago: University of Chicago Press, 1961.

BGU *Aegyptische Urkunden aus den Königlichen/Staatlichen Museen zu Berlin, Griechische Urkunden*. 15 vols. Berlin, 1895–1983.

ChDog *Church Dogmatics*. By K. Barth. 4 vols. Edinburgh: T&T Clark, 1957–69.

CIG *Corpus Inscriptionum Graecarum*. Edited by A. Boeckh. 4 vols. Berlin, 1828–77.

CIJ *Corpus Inscriptionum Judaicarum*. Edited by J. B. Frey. 2 vols. Rome: Pontificio Istituto di Archeologia Cristiana, 1936–52.

CIL *Corpus Inscriptionum Latinarum*. Berlin: Reimer, 1862–.

DK H. Diels and W. Kranz. *Die Fragmente der Vorsokratiker*. 6th ed. Berlin, 1952.

ILS *Inscriptiones Latinae Selectae*. Edited by H. Dessau. 3 vols. in 5. Berlin: Weidmann, 1896–1916.

JIWE *Jewish Inscriptions in Western Europe*. Vol. 2, *The City of Rome*. Edited by D. Noy. Cambridge: Cambridge University Press, 1995.

LCL Loeb Classical Library

LSJ H. G. Liddell, R. Scott, and H. S. Jones. *A Greek-English Lexicon*. 9th ed. Oxford: Clarendon, 1996.

MM J. H. Moulton and G. Milligan. *The Vocabulary of the Greek Testament: Illustrated from the Papyri and Other Non-literary Sources*. Grand Rapids: Eerdmans, 1930.

NewDocs *New Documents Illustrating Early Christianity*. Edited by G. H. R. Horsley and S. Llewelyn. North Ryde, Australia: Ancient History Documentary Research Centre, Macquarie University, 1976–.

NPNF[1] *A Select Library of Nicene and Post-Nicene Fathers of the Christian Church*. 1st series. Edited by Philip Schaff. 14 vols. New York: Christian Literature, 1886–89. Reprint, Peabody, MA: Hendrickson, 1994.

OED *Oxford English Dictionary*. 2nd ed. Oxford: Clarendon, 1997.

OTP *The Old Testament Pseudepigrapha*. Edited by J. H. Charlesworth. 2 vols. Garden City, NY: Doubleday, 1983–85.

PhCT *The Philokalia: The Complete Text, Compiled by St. Nikodimos of the Holy Mountain and St. Makarios of Corinth*. Translated and edited by G. E. H. Palmer, P. Sherrard, and K. Ware. 4 vols. London: Faber & Faber, 1979–95.

POxy *The Oxyrhynchus Papyri*. 81 vols. London: Egypt Exploration Society, 1898–.

PTebt *The Tebtunis Papyri*. 5 vols. London: Egypt Exploration Society, 1902–2005.

SBL Society of Biblical Literature

SEG Supplementum Epigraphicum Graecum

SIG *Sylloge Inscriptionum Graecarum*. Edited by W. Dittenberger. 3rd ed. 4 vols. Leipzig, 1915–24.

TDNT *Theological Dictionary of the New Testament*. Edited by G. Kittel and G. Friedrich. Translated and edited by G. W. Bromiley. 10 vols. Grand Rapids: Eerdmans, 1964–76.

TDOT   *Theological Dictionary of the Old Testament.* Edited by G. J. Botterweck and
       H. Ringgren. Translated by J. T. Willis et al. 15 vols. Grand Rapids: Eerdmans,
       1974–2006.

TLNT   *Theological Lexicon of the New Testament.* By Ceslas Spicq. Translated and ed-
       ited by James D. Ernest. 3 vols. Peabody, MA: Hendrickson, 1994.

WPh   *Writings from the Philokalia on Prayer of the Heart.* Translated by E. Kad-
       loubovsky and G. E. H. Palmer. London: Faber & Faber, 1951.

General Introduction
to the Pastoral Epistles

This is a book about ministerial formation. Specifically, it is a commentary on a collection of letters for young ministers about how to be effective ministers of Christ Jesus.

Literary Characteristics

Author

The author identifies himself as Paul, and historically most Christians have assumed they were reading letters from the real Paul to his protégés. Within the academy, however, the identity of the author has been hotly contested for the past two centuries, and the prevailing position has been that "Paul" is a pseudonym for a writer in the late first or the second century, who recast Paul for his own time.

P. N. Harrison (1921) speculated that a pseudonymous editor compiled the PE from fragments of authentic notes from Paul. In support of that theory, James D. Miller (1997) suggests the PE represent an expansion of Pauline tradition after the manner of Jewish pseudonymous expansions of prophetic and apocalyptic traditions. We might even consider the possibility that *all* the Pauline letters received some editorial retouching as they were compiled into a collection (O'Neill 2004; W. Walker 2004). But I am not so confident as Harrison or Miller as to which bits of the PE are supposedly from Paul and which from an editor. This commentary will argue that each of the PE is thoughtfully composed rather than stitched together (Van Neste 2004; cf. Hutson 2005b).

More commonly, scholars read the PE as transparent forgery, not intended to deceive but to honor the ascribed author. Ancient students composed speeches and letters emulating the thinking and style of great orators and philosophers (Metzger 1972, 8–10; see also "Philosophical Training Regimen" below). Pythagorean philosophers traditionally attributed their treatises to Pythagoras, because they viewed him as the fountainhead of their thinking (Iamblichus, *VP* 157–58, 198). In pondering whether Luke's Gospel should be ascribed to Paul, Tertullian said, "It may well seem that the works which disciples publish belong to their masters" (Tertullian, *Marc.* 4.5, trans. Coxe, *ANF* 3:350). There is no a priori reason why any conventional mode of literature, including fiction and fictional authorship, could not have been used to convey the apostolic witness and included in the canon (Metzger 1972, 19–23).

In recent years, some scholars have considered the question of authorship letter by letter, leaving open the possibility that some but not necessarily all three could be authentic (Prior 1989; Murphy-O'Connor 1991; Johnson 2001, 55–99; Aageson 2008). An extreme example is the notion that in 1 Timothy and Titus two different authors take anti-Marcionite and pro-Marcionite positions against one another (T. Martin 2000). I find the arguments in favor of separate authorship strained and am convinced that the same author produced all three letters (Hutson 1998, 36–50; Ehrman 2013, 199–222). The PE share a distinctive vocabulary and style (see "Vocabulary and Style" below), distinctive epistolary openings (1 Tim. 1:1–2; 2 Tim. 1:1–2; Titus 1:1–4) and closing benedictions (1 Tim. 6:21; 2 Tim. 4:22; Titus 3:15), and obvious similarities in content.

In this commentary, I refer to the author as "Pastoral Paul" (following Fatum 2005; Kartzow 2009, 5). By this I mean to refer to the author of the so-called Pastoral Epistles, who calls himself "Paul," whether that was his real name or a pseudonym. Most commentators take a firm position on authorship and leave the impression that one cannot understand the PE correctly without first adopting that position. There is sometimes an insinuation that scholars who take the opposite position are not quite reasonable, either arrogant academics or pious dogmatists. But I would rather you follow me through the argument of these letters than agree with me about who wrote them. There are good reasons for wondering whether Pastoral Paul was the same Paul who wrote the undisputed letters. On the other hand, it is easy to exaggerate differences and downplay similarities. If the PE are pseudonymous, the author certainly meant them to be read as if from Paul.

I shall focus on the logic of the argument in each letter without forcing a prior commitment to a theory of authorship. In this general introduction and throughout the commentary, I shall point out details that show affinity with Paul's thought and details that suggest disparity or a later context. No one detail will settle the issue, but perhaps by the end you will gain some clarity on how you think about "Pastoral Paul." If you already have an assumption about authorship, you will likely think I am giving too much credit to the other side. Whether or not you change your mind by the end, it would be well to avoid an artificial binary between a supposedly "real Paul" of the undisputed letters and a "fake Paul" of the PE and other disputed letters (Krause 2016, 205). Early church leaders included the PE in the canon because they understood that the picture of Paul would have been incomplete without them (Wall 2004). No matter who (we think) wrote them, the PE are canonical Paul.

Addressees

Among the Pauline letters, the PE are distinctive in that they are addressed to individuals rather than to churches. Even the Letter to Philemon, also written in the second-person singular, is formally addressed not only to Philemon but "also to Apphia, . . . Archippus, . . . and the church in your [sg.] house" (Philem. 2). The PE, however, are addressed strictly to individuals. Still, each of these letters ends with a curious benediction in the plural, "Grace be with you [pl.]" (1 Tim. 6:21; 2 Tim. 4:22) or "grace be with you *all*" (Titus 3:15). These benedictions hint that the author has in mind some secondary audience beyond the named addressees, which leads most interpreters to read them as instruction sent through Timothy and Titus to the churches. Ministers usually read them as guidelines for organizing and evaluating churches.

I wish to stand that reading on its head by arguing that these letters are guidelines for forming and evaluating ministers. They represent communications from an aging apostle to his protégés, who are "youthful" (1 Tim. 4:12; 2 Tim. 2:22; Hutson 1998, 15–17) and whose peers are "younger men" (1 Tim. 5:1–2; Titus 2:6–8). Of course, "youth" is a relative term, but ancient Greeks and Romans had a clear conception of a period between puberty and marriage, the "summer of life" when young men were maturing physically, emotionally, and intellectually, often engaged in advanced education and training that would prepare them for marriage and civic leadership (Hutson 1998, 79–151). This would be the period from ages 14 to 28 years, according to Solon (as quoted in Philo, *Opif.* 104).

Aristotle was first to profile the character of youth (see sidebar), but the stereotype is widely reflected in Greek and Latin literature (Hutson 1998, 152–228). Ancient people did not know about hormones, but the theory of "humors" (bodily fluids; see comments at 1 Tim. 5:23) explained that an excess of yellow bile (*cholē*) made young men "choleric," or hot-tempered and passionate. Youth tended to excessive indulgence of appetites and desires. They were prone to lust, drunkenness, and gluttony; vain about appearance, spendthrifts, and rash. Because of inexperience, they were idealistic, but sexually naive, liable to be manipulated or exploited financially or politically, and educationally gullible in the hands of unscrupulous teachers.

Ancient stereotypes of youth shed light on much of the rhetoric in the PE. These letters have a lot to say about "lusts" (*epithymiai*) for sex, wine,

3

Aristotle on the Character of Youth

"The young [neoi], as to character, are prone to lusts [epithymētikoi] and inclined to do whatever they lust after. Of the bodily lusts they chiefly obey those of sexual pleasure, and these they are powerless against.... They are passionate, quick-tempered, and inclined to follow through on their anger, and unable to control their passion; for owing to their love of honor [philotimia] they cannot endure to be slighted, and become indignant when they think they are being wronged.

"They are lovers of honour, but more so of victory.... And they are both of these more than they are lovers of money [philochrēmatoi], to which they attach only the slightest value, because they never yet experienced want....

"They are not ill-natured but naïve, because they have never yet witnessed much depravity; trusting [eupistoi], because they have as yet not been often deceived. And they are hopeful, for they are naturally very hot [diathermoi], just as those who are drunk with wine, and besides they have not yet experienced many failures. For the most part they live in hope, for hope is concerned with the future as memory is with the past.... And they are easily deceived ... for they readily hope.

"And they are more courageous, for they are full of passion and hope, and the former of these prevents them fearing, while the latter inspires them with confidence. ... And they are sensitive to shame.... They are magnanimous, for they have not yet been humbled by life nor have they experienced the force of necessity....

"All their errors are due to excess and vehemence and their neglect of the maxim of Chilion [Chilion of Sparta said, "Nothing in excess; all good things come in due time," Diogenes Laërtius, Lives 1.41; Seneca, Ep. 94.43; Euripides, Hippolytus 265], for they do everything to excess, love, hate, and everything else. And they think they know everything, and confidently affirm it, and this is the cause of their excess in everything." (Aristotle, Rhetoric 2.12 [1388b–89b, trans. Freese, LCL, modified])

and money, and about trust, honor, and well-placed hope. They also say a lot about bad teachers, but not much about false doctrine (see "Opponents" below). Pastoral Paul instructs youth on how to distinguish between ethical and unethical teachers and how to set good examples for others to emulate.

Acts does not say how old Timothy was when he joined Paul on his travels (Acts 16:1–3). He was old enough that Paul could send him back to Thessalonica alone after he himself fled that city under duress (Acts 17:13–14; 1 Thess. 3:1–6). The common scholarly assessment, based on the Gallio Inscription, is that Paul arrived in Thessalonica in 49 and was in Corinth in approximately 50–51. On that chronology, Timothy would have been at least 30 if Paul wrote to him in the early 60s. And whatever his exact age, he had 12–15 years of experience as Paul's closest associate (Phil. 2:19–24), trusted to handle the most delicate situations (1 Thess. 3:1–10; 1 Cor. 4:16–17; Hutson 1997). The same was true for Titus (2 Cor. 8:16–17; Gal. 2:1), who similarly finds his peer group among the "younger men" (Titus 2:6–8).

In short, the characterization of Timothy and Titus as youthful in the PE has an air of artificiality about it. Pastoral Paul wrote to them as vehicles *through* whom to reach any "Timothy" or "Titus" in future generations. Throughout the commentary, I shall point out details that would have resonated particularly with young men in antiquity.

Genre

In content, the PE resemble letters of philosophical moral exhortation, or *paraenesis* (Fiore 1986; Quinn 1990b; Harding 1998, 107–46). Paraenesis is not instruction in new information but exhortation toward proper behavior in particular circumstances along with rationales, reminders of previous instruction, and examples to follow.

While all three PE are paraenetic in content, they differ in form. Since the publication of critical editions of the *Didache* in 1883 and the *Didascalia apostolorum* in 1929, scholars have tended to think of 1 Timothy and Titus as "church order" (e.g., Koester 2000, 304–5). But I shall argue in the introductions to the specific letters that 1 Timothy and Titus resemble administrative letters, while 2 Timothy has many features of a testament.

The PE as a letter collection. In recent decades a growing minority of scholars has argued that we should read the PE as three individual letters, each addressing specific issues (e.g., Prior 1989; Murphy-O'Connor 1991; Johnson 2001; Aageson 2008; Richards 2002; Herzer 2008). There is, however, no consensus on whether they were written by one, two, or three different authors or whether Paul wrote any or all of them. While I respect the integrity and coherence of each letter, I think we should read them as a collection, in part because Christians have always read them that way. In the history of Pauline letter collections, the PE appear together or not at all (see "Evidence from the Church Fathers" below).

It appears that the PE were part of a later, expanded collection of letters that came together after Paul's death (Dahl 1978; Trobisch 1994; Wall 2004). Whether the PE were composed as a set or edited into a set, it appears that early Christians did not read any one of them apart from the other two. From a canonical perspective, "the early catholic church canonized a thirteen-letter Pauline corpus and for theological reasons: *only in consideration of this thirteen-letter whole, and not a fraction thereof, is a complete understanding of the Pauline regula fidei possible for Christian nurture*" (Wall 2004, 36, emphasis original).

Still, scholars have struggled to explain how the PE cohere as a set of three letters addressed to two different addressees in different locations and taking different forms. Some have suggested that the PE resemble an epistolary novel

(Quinn 1990a; Pervo 1994; Häfner 2007; Zamfir 2013, 5–10). For Richard I. Pervo (1994), the best analogy is posed by the letters of Chion of Heraclea, but those letters have a clear plot, which is difficult to discern in the PE. Gerd Häfner (2007) argues for the sequence 1 Timothy→Titus→2 Timothy, which tracks Paul's geographical movements from east to west, ending in Rome, though Paul's movements from Ephesus to Macedonia and back (1 Tim. 1:3; 3:14) do not fit into a simple east-to-west scenario.

A more satisfactory sequence would be Titus→1 Timothy→2 Timothy based on formal features and internal logic (Hutson 1998, 50–53, 363–471; Pervo 1994). The Muratorian Canon suggests that some early Christians read them in this order. Formally, the epistolary opening to Titus has a surprisingly long author self-identification, which makes sense if the letter opens the collection by introducing Paul to secondary readers who did not know him. To Titus, Pastoral Paul comments on bad Christian teachers and seems concerned that Christians make a good impression on outsiders. Then 1 Timothy expands on ideas introduced in Titus, again commenting on rival teachers with more detail about social criticism from non-Christians. In 2 Timothy the pressure is ratcheted up to official censure with arrest and threat of execution. This last letter presents an aged Paul facing death and passing the torch to his "beloved child." The epistolary novel idea is intriguing, and the sequence Titus→1 Timothy→2 Timothy has its merits.

The traditional canonical order 1 Timothy→2 Timothy→Titus is arbitrary, apparently arranging the letters from longest to shortest (Trobisch 1994). Even so, it is the order in which most Christians have read the PE, and this commentary will follow that order. The PE have a cumulative effect, regardless of the sequence in which we read them. That cumulative effect is the same in other collections of paraenetic letters. There are, for example, interesting correspondences between the PE and a collection of five ancient Pythagorean letters from women to women (Huizenga 2013).

In my opinion, however, the best analogy for the PE is Seneca's *Moral Epistles* (Hutson 1998, 57–68). In the mid-60s, having retired to his villa on the Bay of Naples, Seneca wrote some 124 letters to his friend Lucilius, who was governor of Sicily at the time, a senior administrator contemplating retirement. But Seneca wrote to him as a beginning philosophy student, almost as if he were a teenager (Seneca, *Ep.* 4.2; 16; 26.7). Seneca planned to publish the whole collection as a kind of course in Stoic philosophy. While he wrote to Lucilius, he also wrote through him to future generations of students (Seneca, *Ep.* 8.1–2; 21.2–5; 79.13–17), who would typically be young men (Seneca, *Ep.* 108.12, 27; *Helv.* 10.10; 18.8).

In a similar way, the PE are paraenetic letters that function as a curriculum for training a young minister (cf. Hanson 1983, 23, "handbook for church leaders"). Could Paul, like Seneca, have constructed his addressees, writing to coworkers as if they were young in hopes of reaching later generations of young ministers? Or should we assume that a pseudonymous author constructed both Paul and his addressees, imagining what Paul would have said to protégés?

Philosophical training regimen. A distinctive feature of this commentary is my reading of the PE as an epistolary program in ministerial formation. Guidance in the PE resembles the exercises that ancient philosophy teachers assigned in the formation of young philosophers (Hutson 1998, 294–326; 2007). Typical exercises included (a) reading in one's own and other traditions; (b) writing to imitate the style and thought of seminal thinkers; (c) doctrinal instruction, including lectures on the seminal texts of the tradition; (d) meditation on what one had read and learned, contemplating implications and applications in various circumstances; and (e) physical exercise. These activities aimed to cultivate habits of mind and body, turning theory into practice. The one exercise not mentioned in the PE is writing. Proponents of pseudonymity might consider whether the PE are examples of such writing exercises. In the commentary, I shall point out where these elements appear throughout the PE, with the heaviest concentration at 1 Tim. 4:6–16.

Doctrines and precepts. A key point for understanding the PE is the philosophical distinction between core teaching and application. In *Ep.* 94–95, Seneca explains that "doctrines" (Lat. *decreta*) were the fundamental tenets of a philosophical school, while "precepts" (Lat. *praecepta*) were corollaries that applied those doctrines in particular circumstances (Hadot 1995, 59–61). In Greek the distinction was between *dogmata* ("doctrines," also called "axioms" or "theories") and *paraenesis* ("moral exhortation"; on the vocabulary, Gummere 1925, 451–52). The doctrines of a school were not open for debate, because they expressed how that school defined the supreme good (Seneca, *Ep.* 94.2). Plato thought the good lay in the practice of virtue (*aretē*). For Epicurus, the criterion for distinguishing between good and bad was seeking pleasure (*hēdonē*, hence hedonism) and avoiding pain. For a Stoic, the guiding principle was to live "according to Nature" (Seneca, *Ep.* 94.5). And so on. The doctrines were so central to the thought of each school that to change was to switch to a different school. But philosophers debated "precepts" about how to apply their doctrines in various circumstances (Seneca, *Ep.* 94.1; 95.37–56). According to Seneca, precepts are weak because they change with circumstances; but doctrines, because they are universally applicable, are strong and more valuable (*Ep.* 95.12).

The fundamental doctrine. It is the story of Jesus Christ that grounds the paraenesis in the PE, a story that is presumed throughout but not told (see "Not telling the story" below). The PE take for granted prior instruction. Without arguing *for* it, they argue *from* it (Hutson 2012). The story is reflected in "trustworthy sayings" (1 Tim. 1:15; 3:1; 4:9; 2 Tim. 2:11; Titus 3:8) and quotations of traditional material (e.g., 1 Tim. 2:5–6; 3:16; 6:15–16; 2 Tim. 1:9–10; 2:11–13; Titus 3:4–7). Pastoral Paul urges Timothy to "remember"

Christ Jesus (2 Tim. 2:8). He calls to mind what "we know" about the nature of Torah (1 Tim. 1:8–11) and prior instruction from Paul (1 Tim. 3:10–11; 2 Tim. 3:10–17). He addresses Titus as one who shares a "common faith" (Titus 1:4) and frequently refers to "the teaching" and "healthy words." The addressees are young ministers who know the basic doctrines and need practical guidance on applying them.

Date

Scholars have debated when the PE were written and have proposed dates ranging from the 50s to the 150s. This section considers how the PE might fit into a chronology of Paul's life, external evidence from manuscripts and church fathers, and internal evidence from vocabulary and style, theology, relation to the Gospels, and descriptions of opponents.

Chronology of Paul's Life

Those who assume that Paul wrote the PE must wrestle with fitting them into the chronology of his life. According to Acts, Paul spent over two years in Ephesus (Acts 19:8–10), then went to Macedonia, accompanied by Timothy (Acts 20:1–4). We know nothing about a Pauline mission in Crete. Though a few have dated the PE in the 50s (e.g., Robinson 1976, 67–85; P. Walker 2012a; 2012b), it is difficult to correlate them with Paul's movements as described in Acts or the undisputed letters. But since no sources tell us all of Paul's movements, a simpler theory is that these letters fill in some otherwise unknown gaps (Johnson 2001, 65–68).

The most common theory among proponents of Pauline authorship is that the PE reflect a post-Acts mission. In the late first century, Clement of Rome referred to Paul's travels in "the extremity of the west" (*1 Clem.* 5.7), but did he know or simply assume that Paul realized his goal of evangelizing Spain (Rom. 15:24)? From the late second (or fourth?) century, amid legendary lore about various Bible books, the Muratorian Canon notes that Paul left Rome and "journeyed to Spain." In the fourth century, Eusebius recorded an oral tradition—"it is said"—that Paul was acquitted after Acts, engaged in a further mission, and was again imprisoned in Rome, from which he wrote to Timothy (*Hist. eccl.* 2.22). So the theory of a post-Acts mission to Spain has tenuous support in tradition, but the PE describe Paul moving around the eastern Mediterranean. Furthermore, while it fits the portrayal of Paul as an old man in 2 Timothy, the post-Acts mission theory does not fit with the portrayal of Timothy and Titus as youthful (see "Addressees" above). Ultimately, chronology is indeterminate because it requires some speculation (Porter 2013, 88). Date and authorship must be decided on other grounds.

Manuscript Evidence

The earliest complete copies of the three letters are in the fourth-century Codex Sinaiticus (ℵ). The earliest fragments are two third-century papyri, one containing Titus 1:11–15; 2:2–8 ($\mathfrak{P}^{32}$), and the other 1 Tim. 3:13–4:8 (POxy 5259).

The PE are missing from some important manuscripts. The fourth-century Codex Vaticanus (B) lacks the PE, Philemon, and Revelation. But that codex breaks off at Hebrews 9:14, and it is impossible to know how many pages are missing or what was on them (Epp 2002, 503). Then there is $\mathfrak{P}^{46}$ (Chester Beatty Papyrus II; Kenyon 1936), dated around 200, which contains a collection of Paul's letters in this order: Romans, Hebrews, 1 Corinthians, 2 Corinthians, Ephesians, Galatians, Philippians, Colossians, and 1 Thessalonians, with some pages missing from the beginning and end. Because the codex was a single quire with numbered pages, we know how many pages are missing and how much text the scribe was putting on each page. At the end, there was not enough space to include all three PE but more than enough for 2 Thessalonians and Philemon, so we cannot say what was on those pages (Duff 1998; Epp 2002, 495–502). Codex Vaticanus and $\mathfrak{P}^{46}$ may provide evidence for early collections of Pauline letters that did not include the PE. Ancient manuscripts prove that the PE were circulating in the third century. Other evidence indicates that they were circulating earlier.

Evidence from the Church Fathers

Church fathers were using the PE in the late second century. Around 180, Irenaeus drew heavily on them in his critique of Gnosticism (B. White 2014, 142–58). About the same time, Clement of Alexandria (*Strom.* 2.11) quoted 1 Tim. 6:20–21 against gnostics, whom he condemned for not accepting the letters to Timothy. A little later, a presbyter from Asia composed the *Acts of Paul*, which included the pseudonymous 3 Corinthians (*Acts of Paul* 8), ostensibly written by Paul to condemn gnostic ideas and drawing heavily from the PE (B. White 2014, 116–21). When the forgery was discovered, the presbyter lost his office, and Tertullian condemned him for suggesting that Paul would have approved of women like Thecla teaching and baptizing (*Acts of Paul* 3; Tertullian, *Bapt.* 17). But Tertullian expressed no suspicion about the authorship of the PE. Like Clement, Tertullian criticized Marcion for not including in his canon "the two epistles to Timothy and the one to Titus, which all treat of ecclesiastical discipline" (Tertullian, *Marc.* 5.21, trans. Holmes, ANF 3:473). So by the late second century, the PE were widely accepted as Pauline and apparently read as a set. Yet Marcion provides circumstantial evidence that some Christians did not use and perhaps did not know about the PE.

F. C. Baur (1835) argued that Marcion did not know the PE because they did not yet exist and that they were composed precisely to confound Marcion.

That theory has waxed and waned over the past two centuries and is still argued by some (A. Collins 2011; Koester 2000, 305–10). Around 135 Marcion came to Rome from Pontus. Sometime around 138–40, he began promulgating an anti-Jewish form of Christianity. After he was defrocked in 144, he continued to propagate his doctrine in Asia Minor. Around 140, he was the first to draw up a canon of Christian writings, which for him included ten letters of Paul, omitting the PE. If the PE were anti-Marcionite compositions, they must have been written around 145–50, after the rise of Marcion but early enough that Irenaeus and Tertullian could assume that they were widely known.

Were the PE known before the time of Marcion? Tertullian and Clement of Alexandria thought Marcion should have known them, but it is possible that Marcion was using a standard Pauline collection of his day that did not include the PE. Before the time of Marcion, scattered words and phrases in the Apostolic Fathers call to mind passages in the PE, but there are no clear references or certain allusions, except in the epistle of Polycarp.

When Polycarp, bishop of Smyrna, wrote to the Philippians in the early second century, he assumed that they had a collection of Pauline letters (Pol. *Phil*. 3.2). We do not know how many letters were in that collection, but Polycarp quoted at least from Romans (*Phil*. 6.2), 1 Corinthians (*Phil*. 5.3), 2 Corinthians (*Phil*. 6.1), Galatians (*Phil*. 3.3; 5.3), Philippians (*Phil*. 9.2), and Ephesians (*Phil*. 1.3), with additional probable quotations in the parts of the letter that survive only in Latin (*Phil*. 10–12, 14). And several other statements resemble the PE (see sidebar).

Scholars interpret the similarities between Polycarp and the PE in various ways. Some dismiss every alleged quotation as common Christian parlance (e.g., "the present age," Pol. *Phil*. 9.2//2 Tim. 4:10) or quotations (e.g., Pol. *Phil*. 5.2//1 Tim. 6:7; 4.1//2 Tim. 2:12). Polycarp and Pastoral Paul, they argue, drew from the same sources. But not only does Polycarp's phrasing suggest allusions to the PE; his choices of topics also indicate a literary relationship (see sidebar). Some have thought the similarities so great that Polycarp must have written the PE (Campenhausen 1963; Koester 2000, 308–10), but it is simpler to suppose he was reading them (Pervo 2015, 145; 2016, 85; Merz 2004, 114–40). His quotation formula "knowing that" in *Phil*. 4.1 (cf. 1.3; 5.1; 6.1) suggests he assumed that the Philippians were familiar with 2 Timothy. And the way he intersperses references to the PE among references to undisputed Pauline letters indicates that he thought Paul wrote them (Berding 1999).

Scholars also debate the integrity and date of Polycarp's letter (Dehand-schutter 2010). Polycarp says he had received a letter from Ignatius (*Phil*. 13, referring to Ign. *Pol*.) but had not yet heard about Ignatius's fate. Yet elsewhere he seems to assume that Ignatius is dead (*Phil*. 9). But the relevant sentence in Pol. *Phil*. 9 is vague, and the one in Pol. *Phil*. 13 survives only in a Latin translation that seems somewhat loose (Dehandschutter 2010, 120–21). According to Eusebius (*Hist. eccl.* 3.36), Ignatius died during the reign of Trajan (98–117),

---

Did Polycarp Know the Pastoral Epistles?

These selections from Polycarp's *Letter to the Philippians* show wording similar to the Pastoral Epistles. Especially close parallels are marked with italic.

2.1 "empty talk" (cf. 1 Tim. 1:6; Titus 1:10)

2.1 "who will come as judge of the living and the dead" (cf. 2 Tim. 4:1)

3.3 "following after . . . leading on" (cf. 1 Tim. 5:24)

4.1 "And the beginning of all miseries is devotion to money" (cf. 1 Tim. 6:10)

4.1 *"We brought nothing into the world, and neither are we able to carry anything out"* (1 Tim. 6:7)

4.2 moral exhortations regarding wives (cf. 1 Tim. 2:8–15; 3:11; Titus 2:3–5)

4.3 moral exhortations regarding widows (cf. 1 Tim. 5:5–14)

5.2 moral exhortations regarding deacons (cf. 1 Tim. 3:8–13)

5.2 "in the present age" (1 Tim. 6:17; cf. 2 Tim. 4:10)

5.2 *"We shall reign with him"* (2 Tim. 2:12)

5.3 moral exhortations regarding younger men (cf. Titus 2:6–8)

6.1 moral exhortations regarding elders (cf. 1 Tim. 3:2–7; 5:19–22; Titus 1:6–9)

6.3 "zealous concerning the good" (cf. Titus 2:14)

9.2 "For they did not *love the present age*" (cf. 2 Tim. 4:10)

12.3 "Pray for kings" (cf. 1 Tim. 2:2)

---

so the traditional assumption is that Polycarp wrote between 108 and 115. Some have dated Ignatius to the reign of Hadrian (117–38), questioning Eusebius's reliability (Dehandschutter 2010; Pervo 2010, 134–39). P. N. Harrison thought the Polycarp letter we have is really two letters, one written soon after Ignatius's death (*Phil.* 13–14) and the other written in the late 130s to combat Marcion (*Phil.* 1–12; Harrison 1936; Quasten 1950, 79–80). But Pol. *Phil.* 7 is understandable as decrying the sort of docetism reflected in the Johannine Letters (1 John 4:2–3; 2 John 7) and Ignatius (*Smyrn.* 1–6; *Trall.* 10). Most scholars accept the integrity of Polycarp's letter (Hartog 2002).

Whenever Polycarp wrote, the PE had been in circulation long enough that he could assume the Philippians knew them. If Polycarp wrote around 110 (Lightfoot 1889–90, II.1, 578–603; II.3, 313–20; Holmes 2006, 132–33) or 115 (Hartog 2002, 169), the PE must have been written by the end of the first century. If he wrote in the 130s (Pervo 2016, 2010), the PE could have been written as late as 120.

No matter when he wrote, Polycarp was an early adopter of the PE. Merz (2004, 141–94) has challenged scholarly consensus by arguing that Ignatius also knew the PE. If so, that would further suggest that the PE were written in the first century, and it might also suggest they first circulated in the province of Asia. But whenever they were written, the PE apparently were not widely used until the late second century. They became popular later perhaps in part because theologians found in them ammunition against Gnosticism and Montanism. Still, external evidence suggests that they were written before the heyday of those movements, before 120 and likely before 100. If the PE were plausibly written in the first century, is there anything about them to indicate that Paul could not have written them?

Vocabulary and Style

P. N. Harrison (1921) made the most robust case for the pseudonymity of the PE on the basis of variation from the undisputed Pauline letters in vocabulary, grammar, and style (on the history of linguistic arguments since 1792 regarding the authorship of the PE, see van Nes 2018, 7–110). Many words that are thematic for the PE do not appear in the undisputed letters, including these: "avoid" (*paraiteomai*, 1 Tim. 4:7; 5:11; 2 Tim. 2:23; Titus 3:10); "manifestation" (*epiphaneia*, 1 Tim. 6:14; 2 Tim. 1:10; 4:1, 8; Titus 2:13; cf. 2 Thess. 2:8); "was manifested" (*epephanē*, Titus 2:11; 3:4); "myths" (*mythoi*, 1 Tim. 1:4; 4:7; 2 Tim. 4:4; Titus 1:14; cf. 2 Pet. 1:16); "piety" (*eusebeia*, 1 Tim. 2:2; 3:16; 4:7, 8; 6:3, 5, 6, 11; 2 Tim. 3:5; Titus 1:1); "speculations" (*ekzētēseis*, 1 Tim. 1:4; *zētēseis*, 6:4; 2 Tim. 2:23; Titus 3:9); "deposit" (noun: *parathēkē*, 1 Tim. 6:20; 2 Tim. 1:12, 14; verb: *paratithēmi*, 1 Tim. 1:18; 2 Tim. 2:2).

Thematic phrases in the PE are not found in the undisputed letters, including: "knowledge of the truth" (1 Tim. 2:4; 2 Tim. 2:25; 3:7; Titus 1:1); "trustworthy saying" (*pistos ho logos*, 1 Tim. 1:15; 3:1; 4:9; 2 Tim. 2:11; Titus 3:8; cf. Titus 1:9); and "when the times were right" (1 Tim. 2:6; 6:15; Titus 1:3). Although the use of "snare" in 1 Tim. 6:9 resembles that in Rom. 11:9, the distinctive phrase "snare of the devil/slanderer" is peculiar to the PE among the Pauline letters (1 Tim. 3:7; 2 Tim. 2:26). The PE make distinctive use of medical imagery as metaphors for treatment that leads to spiritual "health" (Malherbe 1980; 1989, 121–36; 2010, 388–92). These metaphors reflect the ideas of Epicureans (Philodemus, *Parr.* frags. 56–70; Konstan et al. 1998, 20–23, 64–75) and especially Cynics and Stoics (Dio Chrysostom, *Or.* 77/78.43–45; Seneca, *Ep.* 75). The philosophers saw themselves as physicians of the soul who endeavored to "cure" people from the "disease" of irrational thinking that allowed them to be mastered by passions and desires. In the PE, self-indulgence is a kind of mental illness (1 Tim. 6:3–5; 2 Tim. 3:8), but "healthy teaching" (1 Tim. 1:10; 2 Tim. 4:3; Titus 1:9; 2:1) and "healthy word(s)" (1 Tim. 6:3; 2 Tim. 1:13; Titus 2:8) make one "healthy in the faith" (Titus 1:13; 2:2). In vocabulary and style, the PE are similar to each other and distinct from the other Pauline letters.

Some scholars critique the method of analysis used by Harrison and others regarding vocabulary and style. Employing increasingly sophisticated analysis, scholars find it difficult to identify any feature of vocabulary or syntax in the PE that shows statistically significant variation from the undisputed Pauline letters (van Nes 2013; 2018). Further, they explain why the PE differ from other Pauline letters by pointing to sociolinguistic factors other than authorship—factors such as differences in addressees, the age of Paul, influence of coauthors and secretaries on various letters, the emotional state of an author in relation to addressees and subject matter, and so on (van Nes 2018; Pitts 2013). Pitts, for example, points to differences in context and target audience. Nevertheless, he notes that the PE "diverge *together*" (Pitts 2013, 148). In the minds of many, the cumulative force of numerous linguistic features still supports Harrison's basic argument for pseudonymity (Ehrman 2013), but it is a matter of possibilities and probabilities. The vocabulary and style of the PE mark them as a distinctive group within the Pauline corpus, but the case against Pauline authorship of the PE on linguistic grounds is by no means certain.

Theology

The PE are distinct among the Pauline letters also on such theological points as Christology, ecclesiology, eschatology, and soteriology. Whether the differences are degrees of emphasis or contradictions is a matter of subjective judgment. In the commentary I shall notice points of continuity and divergence, and readers may assess whether a given point sounds like Paul or a departure from Paul.

Relation to the Gospels

It is possible but not certain that the PE allude to the Gospels. Most plausibly, "ransom" (1 Tim. 2:6; Titus 2:14) may allude to Mark 10:45. It is possible that "all turned away from me" (2 Tim. 1:15) alludes to Mark 14:50. More speculatively, the hymn in 2 Tim. 2:11–13 might allude to Mark 8:34–38 (N. T. Wright 2003, 269–70). Recently Michel Gourgues (2016) has proposed that 1 Timothy might allude to the Fourth Gospel. Possibilities include the "trustworthy saying" that Jesus "came into the world" (1 Tim. 1:15//John 18:37) and the statement that Jesus "testified" (*martyreō*, a thematic word in John) before Pilate (1 Tim. 6:12–13//John 18:34–36). If any of these allusions is right, it has implications for how we date the PE and/or the Gospels.

Opponents

Interpreters overemphasize false doctrine in the PE. Philip H. Towner (1989, 21) is typical: "The heresy reflected in the Pastoral Epistles is the most important aspect of the background of these letters." Many have labored to identify one or more second-century movements against which to read the PE (Marcionism/Gnosticism, Montanism, some apocryphal *Acts*), and they date the letters accordingly. But any identification is tenuous (Sumney 1999a,

13

253–302; Zamfir 2013, 165–78). I am not persuaded that the PE are opposing any movement that would require a mid-second-century date. References to false doctrines are vague, because correcting false doctrine is not what the PE are about. Pastoral Paul offers almost no doctrinal arguments refuting others or defending "healthy teaching." The only exception is the argument against dietary restrictions (1 Tim. 4:3–5), but even there the text is vague and ambiguous. In sum, descriptions of bad teachers do not force a decision on the date.

It is more productive to consider different types of opponents reflected in the PE. The letters envision three types of opposition: factionalism within the community, social criticism from without, and official persecution (Hutson 2012, 171–77).

Factionalism within the Christian community. All three letters indicate factionalism. In 1 Timothy we read that "certain persons" who "teach otherwise" (1:3; cf. 6:3) have "swerved" and "turned aside" (1:6; 6:20) and "shipwrecked their faith" (1:19), some of whom were once under Paul's authority (1:20). In 2 Timothy rival teachers have abandoned Paul (1:15; 4:10), including Hymenaeus and Philetus (2:17) and perhaps Alexander the bronze-smith (4:14). In the Letter to Titus we find "many disorderly, . . . whose mouths must be stopped" (1:10–11) and whom Titus is to "reprove unceasingly" (1:13).

The letters indicate internal debates regarding marriage (1 Tim. 4:3), diet (1 Tim. 4:3), eschatology (2 Tim. 2:18), and the interpretation of Jewish Scriptures (1 Tim. 1:4, 7; 4:7; Titus 1:10, 14). Pastoral Paul disapproves "speculations" (1 Tim. 1:4) and refers intriguingly to "the antitheses of what is falsely called knowledge" (1 Tim. 6:20). The PE may reflect multiple doctrines and movements, and the commentary will speculate on their identities. Nevertheless, from these vague references we cannot with certainty identify any specific doctrinal positions. It is likely that social stratification within the community rather than doctrinal differences created some of the problems that the letters seek to correct (Countryman 1980; Kidd 1990). The emphasis is on the ethical misconduct of bad teachers rather than on their doctrine.

Social criticism from outsiders. Romans viewed new religions as strange, deviant, or subversive (Wilken 1984). Romans who misunderstood such Christian practices as the *agapē* meal, Eucharist, and "holy kiss" accused Christians of moral outrage (Tacitus, *Annals* 15.44), superstition (Pliny, *Ep. Tra.* 10.96.7), cannibalism, and orgies (Minucius Felix, *Octavius* 9.5–6). One major aim of the PE is to help deflect suspicion that Christianity is socially disruptive or politically subversive (D. MacDonald 1983; M. MacDonald 1988, 160–202). The paraenetic style (see "Genre" above) is well suited to this concern, since paraenesis functioned to foster the honor of a good reputation and avoid the shame of a bad reputation (ps.-Libanius, *Epistolary Styles* 52).

Pastoral Paul worries about outsiders who criticize Christian *mores.* An overseer must be "irreproachable" and have "a good testimony from outsiders" (1 Tim. 3:2, 7). An overseer must be able "to reprove those who speak against"

(Titus 1:9). Younger widows should "give no occasion to the opponent to revile us" (1 Tim. 5:14). Younger men should practice "healthy speech that is not condemned, so that one from the opposition might be put to shame, having nothing mean to say about us" (Titus 2:8). Slaves should behave so "that the name of God and the teaching not be slandered" (1 Tim. 6:1).

Official persecution. Only in 2 Timothy do we read about persecution from political authorities. Paul is a prisoner (1:8) in chains (1:16) as a wrongdoer (2:9), who has already faced one trial (4:16). He has a history of persecution in Antioch, Iconium, and Lystra (3:11). We know those persecutions from Acts 13–14. In Antioch Paul attracted the interest of "the whole city" (13:44) and of "devout women of high standing and the leading men of the city" (13:50). In Iconium, "most of the city was divided" over the Christian newcomers (14:4), and Paul's mission generated anger from gentiles and Jews "along with their rulers" (14:5). In Lystra, "the Jews" persuaded "the crowds" to stone Paul (14:19). In other words, what began as a doctrinal dispute within the synagogue in Antioch grew into a public furor that rolled from town to town, feeding on popular prejudices and attracting the notice of the civil authorities. The PE as a collection suggest a similar development.

Finally, "Alexander the bronze-smith did me much harm" and is liable to cause trouble for Timothy (2 Tim. 4:14–15). If this is the same Alexander mentioned in 1 Tim. 1:20, he was a rival teacher who turned against Paul. The "harm" might have been blasphemy (1 Tim. 1:20), which would imply slander from rival teachers (1 Tim. 6:4; 2 Tim. 3:2) or from outsiders (1 Tim. 1:13; 6:1; Titus 2:5). If Alexander discredited the community among non-Christians, there is a progression from rival teachers who turn against Paul (1 Timothy) to Paul in prison as a wrongdoer (2 Timothy).

Summary regarding Date and Authorship

In my opinion, the evidence from Polycarp indicates that the PE were written before 120 and likely before 100. At the earlier end of the date range, the question is whether Paul wrote the PE. A confirmed allusion to a Gospel would call Pauline authorship into question. Otherwise, only a subjective assessment of the cumulative weight of evidence from a linguistic and theological perspective, along with consideration of how the PE fit within their historical and cultural context, can decide the matter.

In the commentary, I point out details that bear on date and authorship. Whatever your assumptions, I encourage you to hold them lightly and keep asking, "What if I'm wrong?" By the end, the cumulative evidence may confirm your view or push you to reevaluate. Either way, my hope is that every reader will better appreciate what these letters say about Christian ministry.

The PE presume correct doctrine and focus on ethics. Bad teachers exemplify the types of misconduct a good minister should avoid. Pastoral Paul reminds his protégés of the good behavior they should model. He offers direction on how a minister devoted to the household of God could cope with bad Christian teachers, social criticism from outsiders, and the prospect of persecution from authorities.

Postcolonial Interpretation of the Pastoral Epistles

Postcolonial theory explores how marginalized groups negotiate space for themselves within the ideological constraints of a dominant society. Early Christianity was a marginal movement, with no legal standing in the empire apart from its origins in the oft-despised Jewish ethnic minority. Homi Bhabha's phrase "sly civility" is an apt description of Pastoral Paul's attitude (Hoklotubbe 2017, 57n2). The PE "strategically imitate the discourse associated with the imperial cult" and "adopt recognizably compliant postures toward imperial power" (Hoklotubbe 2017, 78).

Pastoral Paul embraces some of the ideals of Roman elites, such as piety, decorum, and temperance, and he repudiates Christian teachers who violate those ideals. He avoids attacking the establishment directly and counsels prayer for rulers and obedience of enslaved people. But he does not swallow Roman ideology whole. He brings Jewish monotheism, apocalypticism, and a Jewish experience of how to keep a non-Roman religion alive in Roman society. His ethics are christological and eschatological. He is in the Greco-Roman world but not of the Greco-Roman world.

James Scott and "Infrapolitics"

Helpful is James C. Scott's theory of "infrapolitics" (politics from below), how marginalized groups function in relation to dominant cultures (J. Scott 1990, 2013). According to Scott, for marginalized populations,

> the luxury of relatively safe, open political opposition is both rare and recent. The vast majority of people have been and continue to be not citizens, but subjects. . . . The strategic imperatives of infrapolitics make it not simply different in degree from the open politics of modern democracies; they impose a fundamentally different logic of political action. No public claims are made, no open symbolic lines are drawn. All political action takes forms that are designed to obscure their intentions or to take cover behind an apparent meaning. Virtually no one acts in his own name for avowed purposes, for that would be self-defeating. Precisely because such political action is studiously designed to be anonymous or to disclaim its purpose, infrapolitics requires more than a little interpretation. Things are not exactly as they seem. (Scott 1990, 199–200)

James Scott argues that the "public transcripts" of both elites and subjects inevitably reflect elitist viewpoints. But what subjects say in private does not necessarily match their public transcripts. Even in public, the subjects find ways of challenging elite perspectives in veiled language that avoids recriminations. Scott looks for "hidden transcripts," expressions of alternatives to the dominant ideologies. Recent scholars have applied Scott's theory to the NT to understand how early Christians negotiated their place in the empire (Horsley 2004; N. Beck 2010).

The Household of God

In the PE, a leading metaphor for the church is the "household of God" (1 Tim. 3:15). One fruitful line of inquiry has been to compare blocks of instruction in the PE with the so-called Household Code. The typical Household Code dealt with three axes of power, with the male head of household as the dominant pole in each axis: husband/wife, father/children, master/enslaved (Seneca, *Ep.* 94.1; cf. Col. 3:18–4:1; Eph. 5:21–6:9; Crouch 1972). The Household Code was part of a larger topos on Household Management that included discussion of the proper acquisition and use of wealth (Balch 1981). This topos originated in ancient political theory, especially in the correlation between a well-ordered household and a well-ordered state (Aristotle, *Pol.* 1253b, 1260b; *Eth. Nic.* 8.10 [1160b–61a]; cf. Plato, *Republic* 433c–d; *Laws* 690a–d; Judge 1960, 30–39; Balch 1981, 23–62).

The PE do not contain a Household Code per se, but we see aspects of the topos in 1 Timothy and Titus, to which D. C. Verner (1983) applies the looser term "Station Code." Although there is no explicit discussion of father and children, overseers and deacons should be good fathers (1 Tim. 3:4–5, 12), and Timothy should treat elders like fathers (1 Tim. 5:1–2). There is much attention to the proper behavior of wives, though not husbands (1 Tim. 2:9–15; [3:11?]; 5:3–16; cf. 2 Tim. 2:6–7; Titus 2:4); of slaves, though not masters (1 Tim. 6:1–2; Titus 2:9–10); and of subjects, though not rulers (1 Tim. 2:1–7; Titus 3:1–2). And there is concern about the proper use of wealth (1 Tim. 6:6–10, 17–19).

Because the Household Management topos was pervasive, outsiders could adapt it to show that they fit in. For example, in a context in which mystery cults drew suspicion of undermining social order (Plutarch, *Conj. praec.* 19 [*Mor.* 140d]), a cult of Dionysus in Philippi advertised their social conformity to squelch rumors about their secret meetings (*SIG* 3.985; Standhartinger 2000, 126–27). Similarly, Jewish writers used the topos to show that Torah was consistent with prevailing social order (Philo, *Decal.* 165–67; *Spec. Laws* 2.225–27; *Joseph* 38–39; Josephus, *Ag. Ap.* 2.199; Balch 1981, 52–56). In the NT, 1 Peter adapts the topos in negotiating a Christian identity within a hostile environment (Balch 1981, 81–116). But 1 Peter empathizes with the plight of aliens, abused wives, and slaves, whereas Pastoral Paul appears to approach the problems from the viewpoint of wealthy, slave-owning, male heads of household. But that appearance may also be part of a defensive strategy.

Cynthia Briggs Kittredge (2004) suggests that traditional interpretations of Ephesians are too quick to embrace Greco-Roman social values of patriarchal families as normative for Christianity. Christian feminists could profitably "read Ephesians as a public transcript that is in itself 'resistance' to the Greco-Roman household model by its christological modification of the motifs of marital, parental, and slave subordination" (Kittredge 2004, 151). In other words, we must recognize the family model that Ephesians assumes as typical of the surrounding society and distinguish it from the ways Ephesians modifies that model christologically.

Gail Streete sees a "technique of resistance" in the emphasis on self-discipline in the PE. These letters champion "a completely disciplined community of 'households' within a household (the church) in which one . . . obeys the rules that promote the survival of the church." Such a community "does not withdraw to create its vision of a good society, but instead presents its vision as an achievable transformation of the existing society 'of the present age' (*tō nyn aiōni*, 1 Tim. 6:17)" (Streete 1999, 299, 313; cf. Streete 2009, 155). It is "consonant with the prevailing social order," precisely in order "to achieve transformation within a dominant culture" (Streete 1999, 300).

The Subordination of Women

The PE are central to debates about whether women should be ordained and to what ministries. Most Christian leaders, men themselves, have applied the PE to reinforce male dominance in the church. The most important text is 1 Tim. 2:11–12, traditionally translated, "Let a woman learn in silence with all submissiveness. I permit no woman to teach or to have authority over men; she is to keep silent" (RSV). The commentary discusses problems with the traditional translation and application of these verses, but for now suffice it to say that this text is the chief cornerstone of a wall between men and women in the church. Patriarchalist wall builders have found additional bricks in passages that reflect traditional domestic roles for women (1 Tim. 2:8–15; 5:3–16; Titus 2:3–5), imply the instability of women (1 Tim. 2:14; 2 Tim. 3:6–7), and portray church leaders as analogous to male heads of household (e.g., 1 Tim. 3:1–13; Titus 1:5–9).

There have always been alternative voices for female leadership in Christianity, even if they have usually been dismissed or suppressed. But the twentieth century saw a new rise in such voices. Martin Dibelius staked out what came to be the dominant position of the twentieth century: the PE represent a shift from Paul's countercultural community, living in expectation of Christ's imminent return, to a community accommodated to the dominant culture, awaiting Christ's return in some distant future (Dibelius and Conzelmann 1972, 8–10, 39–41). Elisabeth Schüssler Fiorenza (1983) applied a "hermeneutics of suspicion" that critiqued the androcentric bias in biblical texts written by men and largely for men. David Horrell (1993) argued that what began as a "potentially subversive faith" in the undisputed Pauline letters became in the PE "a religious ideology which supports and legitimates the forms of domination upon which Graeco-Roman society depended." More recent scholars have argued that the PE were intended to tame any liberating impulses that might have arisen from Pauline Christianity (e.g., J. Marshall 2008; Mitchell 2008; Zamfir 2013, 19–36; Krause 2016). Ironically, many feminists agree with traditional patriarchalists that the intention of the author is to inscribe the subordination of women in the church. Typical are the following:

> In keeping with his ideal of patriarchal order, male social control, and the hier-archic transparency of church organization, the immediate goal of the author is to establish an outwardly recognizable household order for the whole church on the unabridged model of the *paterfamilias*-institution. . . . To reach this goal he endeavors, with Paul's help, to transfer to his church the hierarchic structure of the ideal household, including, of course, marriage and procreation as the necessary and normative foundation also of the Christian *oikonomic* orga-nization. (Fatum 2005, 179–80)

> The PE develop an ideal of ecclesial and social hierarchy based on traditional values, in an attempt to impose in the community and in the *oikos* an order thought to embody divine will. (Zamfir 2013, 19, cf. 69)

In my opinion, this approach is backward. Pastoral Paul is not embracing Greco-Roman social *mores* as normative; rather, he is injecting Christian theo-logical commitments—monotheism, Christology, apocalyptic eschatology—into a Roman social context.

Seeing What Is Hidden

In using James Scott's theory, we must not claim too much, projecting wishful thinking onto the text (Zamfir 2013, 12–19). A "hidden transcript" is, after all, hidden. The PE are a public transcript, designed to avoid antagoniz-ing dominant social and political expectations. How can we read between the lines to reconstruct what Pastoral Paul said offstage in private?

Direct challenge. Pastoral Paul's challenge to Roman sensibilities is not always hidden. He is unequivocal in his stand for monotheism (1 Tim. 2:1–7), and much of what he says in these letters can be understood as advice on how to keep marching forward, holding aloft the flag of monotheism, which is likely to draw fire.

Not telling the story. Meanwhile, Pastoral Paul lowers his Christology flag. The overt transcript is about the "manifestation" (*epiphaneia*) of a God, who "educates us" to live by virtues that any Greek or Roman would espouse—piety, temperance, and justice (Titus 2:11–12). What we don't read is how that God was "manifested" in the flesh of a Jewish peasant who was crucified for alleged insurrection.

The Jesus story is essential to the letters, but it is offstage. In liturgical fragments and "trustworthy sayings," we read allusions but not the story. We recognize allusions only because we know the story already. We read about a divine manifestation (1 Tim. 1:15; 3:16; 2 Tim. 1:9–10; Titus 2:11; 3:4) and a hint of a physical birth (2 Tim. 2:8). We don't read how Jesus died, but there are hints of self-sacrifice (1 Tim. 2:6; Titus 2:14), that Pilate was involved (1 Tim. 6:13), and that it was shameful (2 Tim. 1:8). There is one mention of Jesus's resurrection (2 Tim. 2:8), but we could not make sense of the hymn in 1 Tim. 3:16 without resurrection. We read about an exaltation (1 Tim. 3:16; 2 Tim. 2:11; 4:1) and anticipated coming (Titus 2:13; cf. 2 Tim. 1:18; 2:11; 4:1, 8). Pastoral Paul assumes that readers know he is anchoring his ethics in that story, not in Greek philosophy or Roman ideology.

Living Roman, writing Greek, thinking Jewish, acting Christian. Pastoral Paul lives in a Roman ideological world and uses Greek terminology. When he calls for piety, temperance, and justice, he uses the vocabulary of the power brokers, but the content of his vocabulary is informed as much by the Septuagint as by any philosophical treatise. The PE also display an apocalyptic expectation (Kidd 1990; Harding 2017). Monotheism, the resurrection of Christ, and hope in the age to come ground the ethics of these letters. Pastoral Paul asserts the supremacy of the one God and adapts Jewish practices of resistance to the imperial cult (1 Tim. 2). His discussion of honor and wealth undermines Greco-Roman assumptions about privilege and power (1 Tim. 5–6). The incarnation and parousia of Christ inform Christian ethics in the present age (Titus 2–3). The minister's struggle is spiritual warfare oriented toward life in the age to come (2 Tim. 1–2). Pastoral Paul's context is Greco-Roman, but his religious thinking is Jewish, and his call to action is Christocentric.

Deliberate ambiguity. Pastoral Paul frames social issues in terms amenable to the perspective of male Roman citizens, but we should not assume that he shares their perspectives. In 1 Tim. 6:1–2 he admonishes slaves in words that are deliberately ambiguous, so that unbelieving masters will hear what they want to hear, and the enslaved can hear what they need to hear.

Choosing between acceptable alternatives. When it comes to the attire and behavior of women in 1 Tim. 2:9–10, Pastoral Paul does not embrace Greco-Roman culture uncritically. There were different ways of being Roman, and he considers which way is more compatible with Christian ideals. He grounds directives in a theological narrative different from that of the dominant culture. Throughout this commentary we shall observe points at which the PE preserve a "hidden transcript" that is countercultural.

How to Use This Commentary

If you are reading a commentary on the PE, you are a hard-core Bible student. I hope seasoned scholars and ministers will find insights here, but these letters are especially for ministerial students. In the commentary I point out details that were apt for youth in antiquity. In "Theological Issues," I offer my own exhortations to young ministers, tapping 2,000 years of Christian tradition about spiritual and ministerial formation. I encourage you to explore your own and other traditions more thoroughly. As a minister, you must expound the gospel amid new cultural trends and philosophical questions. You will speak more effectively when you can bring to bear the weight of two millennia of deep thinking from spiritual ancestors who faced similar questions in the past.

I assume that many readers are students who may not yet be highly familiar with the ancient literature and material evidence from which scholars understand the cultural context of the NT. I have tried to be generous in quoting texts and identifying who wrote them, where, and when. For those who wish to dig deeper, the parenthetical notes offer additional resources. For those who read or are learning Greek, I sometimes comment on vocabulary, grammar, and textual variants. For those who wish to understand the cultural context more fully, I frequently cite additional primary and secondary sources.

My task is to guide readers through a scholarly forest. A commentary of this size tends to stick to the main path, pointing out landmarks, pitfalls, side paths, and alternate routes, but not analyzing every beetle and lichen. I sometimes indicate where previous hikers camped or hacked their initials into favorite trees. I try to pick up some rubbish they dropped, but if they had not passed through, I myself would not have a sense of this forest. I have tried to be fair in describing where scholars have taken different routes. When I think one pathway is superior, I argue for it. But often I point out more than one legitimate option and leave readers to choose. Sometimes I eliminate a weak position and leave other options open. When I do not force a decision, readers may judge whether the text is genuinely ambiguous or my thinking is cloudy.

In the end, I hope that, for hiking it with me, you will understand better this patch of forest known as the Pastoral Epistles. Whether or not you follow my recommendation at every turn, I hope you will gain a stronger understanding of early Christian ministry in the first two centuries and will consider how Christian ministers might lean into the twenty-first century.

1 Timothy

Introduction to 1 Timothy

Genre

In content 1 Timothy is paraenesis, or moral exhortation (see "Genre" in the general introduction). In form, 1 Timothy resembles ancient administrative letters, such as from a king to a governor or an official to an assistant, of which numerous examples survive (Welles 1934; J. White 1986, §§5–26; Stirewalt 1993, 6–10; 2003, 25–55; Klauck 2006, 77–101; Johnson 2001, 137–42; Kidson 2014; and cf. Mitchell 2002, who critiques the use of some papyrus evidence). Such letters were generally brief. After the opening address, a typical *proem* describes the circumstances that led to the letter. The letter body begins with a statement of the purpose of the letter, often introduced by "therefore" (Welles 1934, xliv, §36.17; §37.7; §44.18). The purpose might be simply to inform ("that you may know," J. White 1986, §7.8; §9.10–11), or to issue some directive(s) (Welles 1934, §36.17ff.; J. White 1986, §10.6, 12; §13.6–7; §19.7ff.). First Timothy is longer than most administrative letters. The longest letter in Welles's collection runs 108 lines of Greek text (Welles 1934, §3/4; cf. PTebt 27, a dossier of 110 lines), similar in length to Titus. Paraenetic letters sometimes ran longer. Several of Seneca's *Moral Epistles* are longer than 1 Timothy. In sum, 1 Timothy is an administrative letter containing moral exhortation from an older mentor to a younger protégé (similarly, Kidson 2014).

Addressee

Timothy was one of Paul's closest and most trusted coworkers (Hutson 1997, 60–61). According to Acts, he joined Paul on his second and third journeys (Acts 16–20; cf. 2 Cor. 1:19; Rom. 16:21). Paul trusted him to handle difficult pastoral assignments (1 Thess. 3:1–6; 1 Cor. 4:17; 16:10–11), called him "soul mate" (Phil. 2:20), and credited him as coauthor of four letters (1 Thessalonians, 2 Thessalonians, 2 Corinthians, and Philippians). His appearance in this letter as a "youth" (4:12; 5:1–2), then, does not square with the common theory that Paul wrote this letter during a post-Acts mission in the early 60s, by which time Timothy would have been at least 30 years old and well seasoned in ministry (see "Chronology of Paul's Life" in the general introduction). In light of this, we might try to date this letter much earlier in the 50s (Robinson 1976, 67–85; P. Walker 2012a; 2012b) and/or consider the aims of the author in constructing an addressee who was at least in part artificial (see "Addressees" and "The PE as a letter collection" in the general introduction).

Ephesus

The letter addresses Timothy in Ephesus (1:3; see "Chronology of Paul's Life" in the general introduction). Some have labored to read the letter in the context of the Artemis cult and/or specific history and culture of Ephesus (e.g., Padgett 1987; Kroeger and Kroeger 1992; Baugh 2005; Hoag 2015). In my opinion, the arguments of the letter are generically applicable in any Greek-speaking context of the eastern Roman Empire, certainly including but not limited to Ephesus.

Outline of 1 Timothy

Letter opening (1:1–2)

Proem: First charge to Timothy (1:3–20)

Circumstances of the charge (1:3–7)

Digression on the nature of Torah (1:8–11)

Thanksgiving prayer (1:12–17)

The charge proper (1:18–20)

First set of directives concerning the church (2:1–3:13)

Exhortation to pray for all people (2:1–7)

Proper comportment for prayer (2:8–10)

Digression on women teaching (2:11–3:1a)

Pastoral leadership (3:1b–13)

Overseers (3:1b–7)

Deacons (3:8–13)

Second charge to Timothy (3:14–4:16)

The foundation of the truth (3:14–16)

Doctrines of demons (4:1–5)

Training for piety (4:6–16)

Proper diet (4:6–7)

Exercise (4:8–11)

Practice (4:12–16)

Second set of directives concerning the church (5:1–6:2a)

Elder and younger (5:1–2)

Widows (5:3–16)

Honor for real widows (5:3)

Offspring should care for widows (5:4–8)

Enrolled widows (5:9–10)

Younger widows (5:11–15)

Women should care for widows (5:16)

Elders (5:17–25)

Honor for teaching elders (5:17–18)

Adjudication of charges against elders (5:19–21)

Ordination of elders (5:22–25)

Slaves (6:1–2a)

Third charge to Timothy (6:2b–21)

Those who teach otherwise (6:2b–10)

Exhortation to flee . . . pursue (6:11–12)

Exhortation to keep the commandment (6:13–16)

The rich in this age (6:17–19)

Exhortation to guard the deposit, and the letter closing (6:20–21)

1 Timothy 1:1–2

Letter Opening

Introductory Matters

The standard opening of an ancient Greek letter included (a) the name of the author, (b) the name of the addressee(s), and (c) a greeting. All three parts of this opening receive theological embellishment more elaborate than one expects in a private letter. The self-introduction of the author seems odd for a private letter to an intimate associate, but administrative letters typically included the formal titles of the writer and/or addressee and sometimes included a term of endearment for the addressee (Kidson 2014, 106). The elaborate self-identification here suggests that this letter was aimed at a secondary audience who did not know Paul (see comment at 6:21). My suggestion is that the targeted secondary readers are youthful ministers analogous to the "youthful" Timothy portrayed in this letter.

> **1 Timothy 1:1–2 in the Rhetorical Flow**
>
> ▶ Letter opening (1:1–2)

Tracing the Train of Thought

1:1–2. The author identifies himself as **Paul, apostle of Christ Jesus, in accordance with the command of God our Savior and Christ Jesus our hope** (1:1). Paul was commissioned as an "apostle of Christ Jesus" (Gal. 1:1, 15–16). The phrase "in accordance with the command [*kat' epitagēn*] of God" (Rom. 16:26; 1 Cor. 7:6) reflects a standard formula for obedience to the command of a ruler (1 Esd. 1:16 LXX [= 1:18 Eng.]) or deity (*NewDocs* 2:§49; MM 247, s.v. *epitagē*). "God our Savior" introduces a motif central to the theology of this letter and Titus (2:3; 4:10; cf. Titus 1:3; 2:10; 3:4; Sumney 1999b). An ancient pagan would apply the epithet "Savior" to any deity who delivered from death. A Jewish reader would have no trouble applying this language to the God of Israel. Two details place this reference in a distinctly Christian context. The correlation between "God our Savior" and "Christ Jesus our hope" hints at, but does not explicitly declare, a high Christology (cf. Titus 2:13; 3:4), and the word "hope" conveys an eschatological connotation (cf. Titus 1:2; 2:13; 3:7).

The letter is addressed **to Timothy, a true child in faith** (1:2a). The appellation "true child" (cf. Titus 1:4) is not found in the undisputed Pauline letters, but it reflects how Paul related to his converts as a "father" to "children" (1 Cor. 4:15; 2 Cor. 6:13; Gal. 4:19; 1 Thess. 2:11–12). The word translated "true" (*gnēsios*) originally designated a "legitimate" child, but it came to apply in various contexts to anything genuine, honorable, or sincere (MM 128–29, s.v. *gnēsios*). Here it is a term of affection for a close protégé.

The opening greeting is **grace, mercy, and peace be to you from God [our] Father and Christ Jesus our Lord** (1:2b). Whereas the typical Greek letter opened with a simple "greetings" (*chairein*, James 1:1; Acts 15:23; Klauck 2006, 17–21), Paul routinely made it a pun with the word "grace" (*charis*). He usually combined this with the Jewish greeting "peace" (e.g., *2 Bar.* 78.3). The greeting in 1:2 is typically Pauline, except for the insertion of "mercy" (*eleos*), the usual LXX translation for the Hebrew *hesed*, God's "gracious love" or "faithful and merciful help" (R. Bultmann, *TDNT* 2:479–82). Although "mercy" appears in no other Pauline greeting except 2 Tim. 1:2 (and Titus 1:4 var.), it does appear in the benediction of Gal. 6:16 and in some epistolary greetings outside the Pauline corpus (2 John 3; Jude 2). So this greeting is atypical for Paul but consistent with Paul's Jewish theological orientation. Rhetorically, "mercy" anticipates the thanksgiving prayer (1:13, 16).

Theological Issues

The identity of any human writer who bears witness to God is an interesting historical question, but it is secondary to the question of the content of that testimony about who God is and what God is doing. Whatever your judgment about the identity of the author (see "Author" in the general introduction), the fundamental theological question in this letter from an "apostle of Christ Jesus" (1:1) to a "minister of Christ Jesus" (4:6) is how the story of Christ Jesus defines the minister and the minister's message.

Even though the PE fit comfortably into Greco-Roman cultural contexts, the language of "grace, mercy, and peace" indicates that their underlying theology stems from Jewish roots. Pastoral Paul does not inculcate Greco-Roman values as normative for Christian practice so much as describe how to function as a "good minister of Messiah Jesus" in a Greco-Roman social context.

1 Timothy 1:3–20

Proem: First Charge to Timothy

Introductory Matters

After the epistolary opening, ancient letters typically included an introductory section called a proem, often employing clichés and stock formulas that prepared readers for the letter body (Klauck 2006, 21–23, 31–33). Letter writers commonly included prayers for the addressees, sometimes in the middle or end of the letter, but often in the proem (Arzt 1994; Reed 1996). The proem of a Pauline letter usually takes the form of a thanksgiving prayer. In a letter from Paul, therefore, we expect a thanksgiving in verse 3 and do not find it. It is incorrect to say this letter lacks a thanksgiving prayer (Murphy-O'Connor 1995, 60–61); rather, the prayer is "interjected" (Prior 1989, 62; cf. Rom. 7:25) into a larger proem that has four parts:

1. Circumstances of the charge (1:3–7)
2. Digression on the nature of Torah (1:8–11)
3. Thanksgiving prayer (1:12–17)
4. The charge proper (1:18–20)

This proem also serves as the opening bracket of a larger *inclusio* around the whole letter with the idea of a "commission" or "deposit" (1:18; 6:20). Several correspondences between the opening and closing sections (1:3–20 and 6:2b–21) frame the letter (Bush 1990).

The threefold use of "charge" in chapter 1 corresponds to its appearance twice in chapter 6. And if we take *parangelia/parangellō* as brackets around the whole letter, then inside this larger *inclusio* we find the theme repeated: "charge

Parallels between 1 Timothy 1:3–20 and 6:2b–21

1 Timothy 1:3–20	1 Timothy 6:2b–21
just as *I exhorted* you (1:3)	Teach and *exhort* these things (6:2b)
that *you might charge* certain ones (1:3) the goal of *the charge* is love (1:5) this *charge* I deposit with you (1:18)	*Charge* those who are rich (6:17) *I charge* you (6:13)
not to *teach otherwise* (1:3)	if anyone *teaches otherwise* (6:3)
which lead to *speculations* (1:4)	about *speculations* (6:4)
the goal of the charge is *love* . . . and a good conscience and sincere *faith* (1:5)	pursue righteousness, piety, *faith, love*, steadfastness, long-suffering (6:11)
faith from which some, *having deviated* (1:6)	some *deviated* concerning the faith (6:21)
turned aside to empty talk (1:6)	*turn aside* from empty speech (6:20)
not understanding what they are talking about (1:7)	knowing nothing (6:4)
to the healthy teaching (1:10)	to the healthy words . . . and the teaching . . . (6:3)
so that Christ Jesus might display in me (1:16)	which he will display . . . (6:15)
doxology: king . . . immortal, invisible, only . . . honor . . . forever, amen. (1:17)	doxology: only . . . king . . . only, having immortality . . . whom no one has seen . . . honor . . . forever, amen. (6:15–16)
this charge I deposit with you (1:18)	guard the deposit (6:20)
fight . . . the good fight (1:18)	struggle the good struggle (6:12)

[*parangelle*] and teach these things" (4:11); "charge [*parangelle*] these things" (5:7); and "charge [*parangelle*] the rich" (6:17). The entire letter, therefore, entails Timothy's marching orders: Paul charges Timothy to charge others.

Tracing the Train of Thought

Circumstances of the Charge (1:3–7)

1:3–7. The description of the circumstances of the letter begins with **just as I urged you** (*kathōs parekalesa se*, 1:3). We expect "so also" to complete the thought, but instead we find a digression on the nature of Torah (1:8–11), followed by a prayer (1:12–17). Only in 2:1 do we find the resumption of the thought, "I urge, therefore, first of all." This confirms that all of 1:3–20 is the proem, and the body begins in 2:1. The circumstance of the directives is the previous charge Paul gave Timothy when he assigned him to Ephesus.

> **1 Timothy 1:3–20 in the Rhetorical Flow**
>
> **Letter opening (1:1–2)**
>
> ▶ **Proem: First charge to Timothy (1:3–20)**
>
> **Circumstances of the charge (1:3–7)**
>
> **Digression on the nature of Torah (1:8–11)**
>
> **Thanksgiving prayer (1:12–17)**
>
> **The charge proper (1:18–20)**

It is not clear when Paul might have urged Timothy **to remain in Ephesus** while he himself was **going into Macedonia** (see "Chronology of Paul's Life" in the general introduction). Porter argues that this could also be rendered "when I was about to go," indicating Paul's intent at the time but not necessarily his actual movements (Porter 2013, 67, 70). In any case, the reminder "just as I urged you" assumes previous oral instructions. We might compare the admonition of King Ptolemy IV (?) in a letter to a provincial governor in the late third century BCE, "Now I think that when you were with me I gave you an order on this subject . . ." (Welles 1934, 136–40 [§30.10–11]). The verb "urge" (*parakaleō*) is a polite request, common in paraenesis. The exhortations in this letter are not new instruction but reminders of what Timothy has already been taught.

Paul encouraged Timothy to **charge certain ones** (1:3), and the content of that charge takes the form of antithetical statements: not that (1:3b–4), but this (1:5); not that (1:6–7), but this (1:8–11). The charge **not to teach otherwise** (*heterodidaskalein*) implies that Timothy has been taught a specific doctrine. That doctrine is not expounded, although it is reflected in quotations of traditional material scattered throughout the PE (see "The fundamental doctrine" in the general introduction). "Certain ones" were deviating from it. We could understand the deviation as error (1 Tim. 4:3) or as disputes over minor issues that miss the main point of the gospel.

This passage is vague about the doctrine Pastoral Paul is opposing (Sumney 1999a, 253–302). All we can say at this point is that the other teachers are within the Pauline circle, subject to a charge from Paul via Timothy. **Myths and endless genealogies** (1:4) could describe any texts from a Jewish apocalypse like *1 En.* 8 and 69.1–15 to a gnostic text like *The Secret Book of John*.

Our passage brushes aside speculation in favor of **God's *oikonomia*, which is in faith** (1:4). The term *oikonomia* is multifaceted, and English translations are all over the map. Such translations as "godly edifying" (KJV) and "divine training" (NRSV) miss the point, while "God's work" (NIV) is vague. The root idea is **household management,** but the word could refer to administration of a household, city, empire, or, as Stoics applied it, to divine administration of the cosmos. In the second century, church fathers Christianized this Stoic concept, using the word as a theological technical term for God's "economy," meaning God's plan of salvation (Irenaeus, *Haer.* 4.14.2; Osborn 2001, 74–94; cf. Ign. *Eph.* 18.2; 20:1; Justin, *Dial.* 30.3; 31.1; 45; 87.5; 103.3; 120.1; cf. also Eph. 1:10; Reumann 1959). A translation such as "dispensation of God" (ASV) or "God's plan" (CSB), reflecting this technical, theological connotation, might explain how the PE were interpreted in the late second century, but it would be anachronistic for a first-century letter and invites metaphysical "speculation," which this verse explicitly rejects. The PE focus on the local church as God's "house" (1 Tim. 3:15; 2 Tim. 2:20) and the overseer as household manager (3:4–5; *oikonomos*, Titus 1:7; cf. Paul's ministry as *oikonomia*, 1 Cor. 9:17;

Eph. 3:2; Col. 1:25). A translation such as "stewardship from God" (ESV) or "God's household management" reflects this simpler understanding and seems preferable. The letter is concerned not with God's grand plan for the cosmos but with ministry in the local community.

In managing God's household, the **goal** of Timothy's **charge** is to foster ethical lives characterized by **love from a pure heart, good conscience, and sincere faith** (1:5). Timothy's goal is not to drill everyone on approved doctrinal phrases but to guide them toward ethical lives. Some have lost sight of this goal, and **having swerved, turned aside toward worthless talk** (1:6; cf. 6:21). In Titus 1:10–11, "worthless talk" characterizes those who teach "for shameful gain." "Deviate" (*astocheō*) and "turn aside" (*ektrepō*) reflect the "two ways" motif from Greek philosophy, which called for a decision between the paths of virtue and vice (Hesiod, *Works and Days* 286–92; Xenophon, *Mem.* 2.1.20–34; Cebes, *Tabula* 5.1; 15.1; Philo, *Sacr.* 20–42; cf. early Christian adaptations, *Did.* 1; *Barn.* 18–20; De Villiers 2003, 145–47). "Turning aside" suggests either an outright decision to pursue vice or a wavering in commitment to virtue.

Those who "teach otherwise" are **wanting to be Torah teachers, though understanding neither what they are talking about nor the things about which they make confident assertions** (1:7). In this context, "law teachers" (*nomodidaskaloi*) refers not to purveyors of pagan customs (Hoag 2015, 163) but teachers of Torah. Regardless of their ethnicity, they did not grasp the essence of Torah. We should heed Pastoral Paul's advice and avoid making "confident assertions" about the doctrine of these teachers (see comments at 4:3–5). Within gender-sensitive Greco-Roman culture, "myths," "empty talk," and "not knowing what they are talking about" were typically associated with women's speech (Rohrbaugh 2001; Kartzow 2009). We need not assume that any or all of the rival teachers were women (as does Payne 2009, 299–304), but such rhetoric may have had the effect of feminizing and dismissing them. Even so, the focus is on the teachers' misconduct rather than their doctrine.

Digression on the Nature of Torah (1:8–11)

1:8–11. After criticizing those who "want to be Torah teachers," Paul heads off any misconception that he has abrogated Torah. In language that echoes Rom. 7:12–13, the digression in 1:8–11 affirms that **Torah is good, if one uses it Torah-ly, knowing this: that Torah is not laid down for the just, but for the lawless** (1:8–9a). A proverbial statement (cf. Titus 1:15) describes the purpose of Torah to correct the "lawless." The vocabulary—law, lawfully, just, lawless (*nomos, nomimōs, dikaios, anomos*)—would have been understandable in a philosophical discourse on the nature of law and justice. Some interpreters take it that way and see the passage as non-Pauline (e.g., Easton 1948, 113). But the only one of these words that does not appear in the undisputed Pauline letters is the adverb "Torah-ly," usually rendered "lawfully." This adverb can refer to acting "according to the rules" (2 Tim. 2:5), but here the issue is interpretation of Torah. The problem is not that there is anything wrong with Torah but that those "wanting to be Torah teachers" (1:7) misuse Torah (cf. Rom. 7:12–13) by failing to discern its essential function as a moral guide. Read this way, our passage comes into conversation with Gal. 3, which discusses "the righteous one (*dikaios*, Gal. 3:11, quoting Hab. 2:4) in relation to the function of Torah (*nomos*). Torah was "added because of transgressions" (Gal. 3:19 KJV) and "became our pedagogue until Christ" (Gal. 3:24). So also here, Timothy must use Torah as Torah intended, to instill an ethical way of life and correct those who need correction.

Verses 9b–10 describe people who need correction. The vice list was a common rhetorical device in Greco-Roman moral exhortation (Malherbe 1986, 138–41; J. T. Fitzgerald, *ABD* 6:587–89). Vice lists appear elsewhere in the NT (1 Tim. 6:3–5; 2 Tim. 3:2–5; Titus 3:3; cf. Rom. 1:29–32; 13:13–14; 1 Cor. 5:9–13; 6:9–11; 2 Cor. 12:20–21; Gal. 5:19–21; Eph. 4:17–19, 31; 5:3–5; Col. 3:5–8). These lists do not follow a logical progression, but words are placed together for rhetorical effect based on sound. English translators try to replicate the effect by repeating prefixes (a-, un-) and suffixes (-less).

This vice list has been read as a polemic against the false teachers (Karris 1973, 553) or a list of crimes against the law (Harrill 2006, 139–44, citing Heraclitus, *Ep.* 7). Vilification rhetoric often employed exaggeration, implications of guilt by association, and impugning the motives of opponents. From such polemics we cannot assume that the false teachers were guilty of all, or any, of these crimes. The list functions to describe not the teachers but the purpose of Torah. The list begins with four pairs, but that arrangement breaks down as synonyms pile up.

In gentile contexts the first pair, **lawless and insubordinate** (1:9), could refer to any who flouted law and custom. Ancient Greeks and Romans assumed that the cosmos was orderly and that every person had a proper place: a slave was subordinate to a master, a wife to her husband, a free man to a more powerful man, and all people to the gods. The theme of subordination appears in chapter 2 with particular attention to women. But in Hellenistic Jewish contexts the "lawless" (*anomoi*) were flouting Torah (1 Cor. 9:21). Jewish Christians might hear a punning dig at the wannabe Torah teachers who are "Torah-less." It is also tempting to think of them as "insubordinate" to Pauline teaching, since this adjective describes the false teachers in Titus 1:9.

In the next pair, **impious** (*asebeis*) is the opposite of "pious" (*eusebēs*), a thematic idea for the PE. Impiety was neglect of religious duty to family and community (see comments at 2:2). **Sinners** is a generic word but in Hellenistic Judaism could describe people who were not Torah observant (e.g., "publicans and sinners"). The pair **irreverent and profane** refers to people who do not show respect for sacred matters, so it is roughly synonymous with the previous pair (Philo, *Spec. Laws* 1.327).

The words in the triad **patricides and matricides, murderers** obviously overlap in meaning. Murder of a parent was especially heinous (Aeschylus, *Eumenides* 210–12). These three are piled up for rhetorical effect, as is the case with various synonyms throughout this list.

The next three are related, **fornicators, pederasts, slave dealers** (1:10). "Fornicators" (*pornoi*) engage in any sort of unsanctioned sexual activity. But heterosexual promiscuity is often ignored in our churches, while homosexual promiscuity has become a battleground issue. An evangelist should stand equally against all fornication and should be clear on what this passage is and is not saying about same-sex behavior.

The word *arsenokoitai* (translated "pederasts") appears nowhere in Greek literature prior to Paul (1 Cor. 6:9). Some suppose that Paul coined the term, perhaps by combining the Greek words for "male" (*arsēn*) and "bed" (*koitē*, especially a "marriage bed" as a metaphor for sex). These two words appear in Lev. 18:22; 20:13 LXX. While the word seems to have a sexual connotation, it appears only in contexts of economic exploitation (*Sib. Or.* 2.56–77; *Acts of John* 36), so the precise cultural nuance escapes us (D. Martin 2006, 38–43; response in Jepsen 2006). That is, the word *arsenokoitēs* probably did not apply simply to any male-male sex but seems to have carried some connotation of a pimp or one who trafficked boys for sex.

We must avoid imposing our cultural categories onto the ancient context. In our culture, "homosexual" commonly designates people innately oriented to same-sex attraction, regardless of whether they act on those impulses. It is not clear to what extent ancient people had a notion of sexual orientation (but consider Plato, *Symposium* 189d–93d). It is likely that most men who had sex with other males were also—and more frequently—having sex with women.

At the same time, ancient Greeks and Romans understood some categories not operative in our culture. Specifically, some (not all) Greeks accepted the idea of a mature man engaging in sex with a youth as part of socializing him into the world of men. The Greek adult "lover" was a mentor, as illustrated in Socrates's (platonic!) relationship with his disciple Alcibiades (Plato, *Symposium* 212d–22b; Plutarch, *Lib. ed.* 15 [11e]; Cretan custom described in Strabo, *Geography* 10.4.21). Greeks and Romans knew variations on same-sex relations, to which they accorded varying degrees of approval or shame, depending on whether one's partner was slave or free, youth or adult, whether sex was freely given, coerced, or paid, and so on (MacMullen 1982, 491–92). Romans often scorned the Greek tradition of men having sex with boys (MacMullen 1982), although such practices were discussed more openly in the imperial period (MacMullen 1982, 490; Eyben 1993, 241–46). But even Greeks looked down on sex between adult men (Ruden 2010, 45–71, who overstates the case). Plutarch expresses indecision about a sexual relationship between mentor and protégé because he sees potential for both moral formation and exploitation.

He debates whether erotic love for boys is "the only genuine love" found "in the schools of philosophy, . . . searching for young men whom it cheers on with a clear and noble cry to the pursuit of virtue," or whether it is "ashamed and afraid. . . . So it pretends friendship and virtue" (Plutarch, *Amat.* 4–5 [751a–52a], trans. Helmbold, LCL; cf. Plutarch, *Lib. ed.* 15–17 [11d–13c]; ps.-Lucian, *Am.* 19–53). If we are shocked that philosophers seriously discussed such a question, this illustrates the degree to which we often fail to consider what categories were operative in first-century culture. When we argue about same-sex relationships, we are often not discussing exactly the same things they were discussing.

Finally, Plutarch's anxiety about this practice reflects concern for boys who were freeborn citizens, not foreigners, and certainly not slaves. Enslaved people were presumed to be available for sexual exploitation. The translation "pederasts" (boy-lovers) respects the ancient cultural context and carries overtones of exploitation and coercion. If this translation is close to correct, then Pastoral Paul reflects a Roman and Jewish bias against a Greek practice, especially in exploitative manifestations. But we should be wary of confident assumptions about the vice named here.

The term **slave dealers** (*andrapodistai*, 1:10) appears only here in the NT. Slave dealers were a stock feature of Greek polemical rhetoric because they were notoriously unscrupulous and frequently engaged in sex trafficking (Harrill 2006, 119–44; Glancy 2006, 79–80). With its overtones of sexual exploitation and dishonesty, "slave dealers" fits neatly between sexual vices and vices of dishonesty.

The terms **liars and those who forswear** are related. To "forswear" could mean either to swear falsely that something is true—perjury—or to renege on a sworn promise. Both ideas make sense here (Fitzgerald 1995). Both were religious offenses, since most oaths entailed invocation of a deity, much as today one might take an oath on the Bible. Oath breaking was considered impious and irreverent (e.g., Plutarch, *Quaest. rom.* 44 [275d]; Fitzgerald 1995, 169, 173–75), which brings us back to the top of the list. The vice list as a whole describes a breakdown in moral order expressed in terms of intertwined religious and social obligations.

The list ends with **and if there is anything else that is contrary to the healthy teaching** (1:10), which indicates that it is not an exhaustive list but illustrative. References to "the healthy teaching" occur throughout the PE (2 Tim. 4:3; Titus 1:9; 2:1; cf. "healthy word(s)," 1 Tim. 6:3; 2 Tim. 1:13; Titus 2:8; "healthy in the faith," Titus 1:13; 2:2). This is one of several medical metaphors in the PE (Malherbe 1980; see "Vocabulary and Style" in the general introduction). If the vices in 1:9–10 are "contrary to the healthy teaching," we may think of the "goal" of "love from a pure heart and a good conscience and sincere faith" (1:5) as good spiritual health. Timothy is charged to promote health in his hearers, and a physician does not shrink from treating those he loves just because the treatment is unpleasant (cf. Paul's treatment of Hymenaeus and Alexander, 1:20). The distinction between healthy and unhealthy teaching is whether it nourishes virtue. Healthy is as healthy does.

The criterion for evaluating what is "contrary to the healthy teaching" is **the glorious gospel of the happy God** (1:11). The content of that gospel appears in liturgical quotations scattered through the letter (1:15; 2:5–6; 3:16; 6:15–16). "Glorious gospel" is a Hebraic idiom (lit., "gospel of glory"; BDF §165; cf. 2 Cor. 4:4). On the other hand, "happy" (*makarios*; cf. 6:15) is a very un-Jewish way to describe deity (F. Hauck, *TDNT* 4:362–70). Jews, including Paul, ordinarily described God as "blessed" (*eulogētos*, Rom. 1:25; 2 Cor. 1:3; 11:31; H. Beyer, *TDNT* 2:754–65) and people as "happy, fortunate" (*makarios*, Matt. 5:3–11). This phrase reflects the mind of a Jewish Christian comfortable with Greco-Roman idioms.

A Prayer of Thanksgiving for Forgiveness

"I [thank Thee, O Lord],
 for Thou hast enlightened me through Thy truth.
In Thy marvelous mysteries,
 and in Thy loving-kindness to a man [of vanity,
 and] in the greatness of Thy mercy to a perverse heart
 Thou hast granted me knowledge.
Who is like Thee among the gods, O Lord,
 and who is according to Thy truth?
Who, when he is judged,
 shall be righteous before Thee?
For no spirit can reply to Thy rebuke
 nor can any withstand Thy wrath.
Yet Thou bringest all the sons of Thy truth
 in forgiveness before Thee,
[to cleanse] them of their faults
 through Thy great goodness,
and to establish them before Thee
 through the multitude of Thy mercies forever and ever.
For Thou art an eternal God;
 all Thy ways are determined forever [and ever],
 and there is none other beside Thee.
And what is a man of Naught and Vanity
 that he should understand Thy marvelous mighty deeds?"
     (1QHᵃ, Hymn 16, trans. Vermes 1997, 276–77)

With which I was entrusted (1:11). Paul was "entrusted" (cf. 2:7; 2 Tim. 1:11; Titus 1:3; Gal. 2:7; 1 Thess. 2:4) with a sacred obligation to tell the story. This letter honors that trust by equipping Timothy to transmit the story to the next generation. This phrase evokes stories of Paul's prophetic call (Gal. 1:11–16; 1 Cor. 15:8–11) and anticipates the thanksgiving prayer that follows.

Thanksgiving Prayer (1:12–17)

1:12–17. The prayer begins with thanks (1:12) and ends with eschatology ("forever and ever," 1:17). David W. Pao (2010) argues against any typical Pauline thanksgiving form, but he does find consistent theological themes in Paul's thanksgiving prayers. They are God-centered, focus on the cross and the parousia, and recognize an eschatological "between time." This prayer offers thanks to Christ rather than God (1:12), although the doxology is directed to God (1:17). Also, whereas Paul usually gives thanks for qualities valued in his addressees, this prayer gives thanks for God's mercy. It includes a veiled reference to the first coming of Christ (1:15) but not the second. There is a sense of a future "eternal life" (1:17) but not of living between the times (as is clear in Titus 2:11–14). The idiom "I am thankful" (lit., "I have thanks" [*charin echō*], 1:12) was a common way of expressing gratitude (Rom. 6:17; Luke 17:9; Josephus, *Ant.* 4.316; Epictetus, *Diatr.* 4.7.9), but among Pauline prayers it is peculiar to the PE (cf. 2 Tim. 1:3). Finally, this prayer is embedded within a larger charge to Timothy, and it is the only Pauline thanksgiving that ends with a doxology (Sanders 1962, 357). In sum, this prayer resembles thanksgiving prayers in the undisputed Pauline letters, but it also differs from them in form, style, and content.

The autobiographical elements in this prayer and the praise for deliverance from sin resemble some "Thanksgiving Hymns" (*hodayoth*) from Qumran (Richards 2002, 170–74; Sanders 1962, 358). Richards may go too far in suggesting that the entire prayer is a liturgical tradition. It is plausible to think Pastoral Paul incorporated traditional elements—a "faithful saying" and a doxology—in composing his own prayer (Yarbrough 2009, 66–75; cf. Sanders 1962, 362). But the comparison with the *hodayoth* illustrates his Jewish sense of devotion to God.

The prayer is artfully arranged in two parts, with the "faithful saying" (1 Tim. 1:15ab) at the center:

> Thanksgiving (1:12)
>> Description of Paul's former contemptible life (1:13a)
>> "But I was shown mercy" (1:13b)
>> "Because . . ." (1:13c–14)
>>> Faithful saying about Christ (1:15ab)
>> Description of Paul's former contemptible life (1:15c)
>> "But I was shown mercy" (1:16a)
>> "So that . . ." (1:16b)
> Doxology (1:17)

The expression, **I am grateful to** (lit., "I have thanks to," *charis* + Gk. dat., 1:12) has a double meaning, since the word "thanks" (*charis*) anticipates the contents of this prayer celebrating God's abundant "grace" (*charis*, 1:14). Pastoral Paul is grateful **to Christ Jesus our Lord, who strengthened me** (1:12a; cf. 2 Tim. 4:17; cf. 2 Tim. 1:7 on the correlation between strengthening and "grace"). He is grateful **because he considered me trustworthy in appointing me to ministry** (1:12b). Although he is an "apostle" (1:1), he thinks of his ecclesial role as "ministry" (*diakonia*), not oversight (*episkopē*), so he models for Timothy what it means to be a good minister (4:6).

In the first part of the prayer, Pastoral Paul describes himself as **formerly a blasphemer, a persecutor, insolent** (1:13a), descriptions that assume knowledge of Paul's pre-Christian life. That story is not told, which makes sense in a letter to a protégé. If the letter is pseudonymous, the author presumes that his readers know the stories from Acts or elsewhere (cf. 2 Tim. 3:11). There is no attempt to whitewash Paul. "Blasphemer" suggests slanderous *speech*, especially against religious opponents (e.g., against Artemis, Acts 19:37). "Persecutor" has to do with hostile *actions*. And "insolent" (*hybristēs*) suggests an arrogant *attitude*.

The prayer expresses two reasons why **I was shown mercy** (1:13b–14). The first reason, **because I acted ignorantly,** may sound like making excuses, since the conjunction "because" (*hoti*) usually indicates a cause, why something happened (BDAG 732, s.v. ὅτι 4.a)—"The plane crashed because a bolt broke." But "because" (*hoti*) can also indicate how a thing is known ("inferring this from that," BDAG 732, s.v. ὅτι 4.b; e.g., 1 Cor. 4:9; 1 John 3:14)—"Fred is dead, because I saw on the news that his plane crashed." The second usage applies here. Paul can only explain God's mercy toward him "because" he knows he did nothing to cause such a response. Acting **in unbelief** describes his earlier actions from the vantage point of his current trust in Christ. In that earlier time, he would have said he was acting in faith, but his incomprehension of God only perverted faith into a self-serving effort, bullying others into agreeing with his limited understanding.

The center of the prayer is a christological statement deemed **trustworthy** and **worthy of all acceptance** (1:15). This is the first of five "trustworthy sayings" in the PE (cf. 1 Tim. 3:1; 4:9; 2 Tim. 2:11; Titus 3:8). Scholars debate how to understand these "trustworthy sayings" (Campbell 1994b). The designation sometimes precedes and sometimes follows the saying itself. Here the saying is **that Christ Jesus came into the world to save sinners**, which sounds like a paraphrase of the Jesus story (Luke 19:10; John 12:46–47, etc.; Knight 1992, 99–102). Llewelyn observes that the expression "trustworthy saying" appears in ancient religious contexts to legitimate what a human prophet says about a deity (*NewDocs* 9:§5, "Faithful Words" [an inscription on marble], pp. 9–14). For Pastoral Paul, then, a "trustworthy saying" is an element of tradition that is settled and unquestionable.

Of whom I am foremost revisits Paul's contemptible, pre-Christian state and introduces the second half of the prayer (1:15c–16). It also locates Paul explicitly among the **sinners** in the vice list (1:9). For the second time we read **but I was shown mercy,** now adding the purpose of that mercy, **so that . . .** Just as he was **foremost** of sinners (1:15; cf. 1 Cor. 15:9; Gal. 1:13; Acts 8:3; 9:1–2, 21; 22:4, 19; 26:10–11), so now he is the "foremost" exemplar of one shown mercy: **so that in me foremost Christ Jesus might exhibit all his forbearance** (1:16a). It was Paul's appalling badness that made him a vivid exhibit of mercy. Paul serves **for an example for those who would believe on him** [Christ] **for eternal life** (1:16b). Paul is an example first for Timothy, and also for future generations "who would believe on him."

The doxology (1:17) reflects Greek patterns of praise for a god. Ancient Greek prayers used such negative epithets as **immortal, invisible** to distinguish gods from mortals, and they ascribed uniqueness (**only**) as a standard element of praise (Neyrey 2005a, 65–68, 77–78). At the same time, the phrase **to the king of the ages** sounds very Jewish. Although this expression is little attested in Greek before the NT period (Tob. 13:7; Rev. 15:3 var.), its Hebrew equivalent (*melech ha-'olam*) would become the standard epithet for God in Jewish prayers. Both "king of the ages" and **forever and ever** (lit., "for the ages of the ages") reflect an apocalyptic perspective that views time in terms of "this age" and the "age to come" and affirms God's sovereignty over all. "While the form derives from Israelite/synagogue practice, the bulk of [the] contents are distinctively Greco-Roman modes of god-talk" (Neyrey 2005a, 85). This prayer expresses Jewish ideas in categories accessible to Greco-Roman readers.

The Charge Proper (1:18–20)

1:18–20. This section ties together and completes the proem. Here Paul formalizes the charge, the ethical goal of which he described earlier (1:5). Craig A. Smith (2006, 152–53; cf. 2 Tim. 4:1–8) identifies five formal elements of a charge:

1. Charge verb: "I commit" (1:18)
2. Person charged: "to you, child Timothy" (1:18)
3. Authority phrase: "in accordance with . . . the prophecies" (1:18)
4. Content of the charge: "fight . . . good conscience" (1:18–19)
5. Implications of the charge: ". . . certain ones have made shipwreck" (1:19–20)

The word "charge" or "command" frames the entire section: "that you charge [*parangeilēis*] certain ones . . ." (1:3) and "this charge [*parangelia*] I commit to you" (1:18). It also appears within the section: "the goal of the charge [*parangelia*]" (1:5).

The verb **I commit** (*paratithēmi*) indicates a deposit of some item of value with another person in sacred trust for safekeeping (cf. Tob. 4:1, 20). The corresponding noun "deposit" (*parathēkē*) appears at 6:20 to form brackets around the whole letter, which constitutes Timothy's marching orders. The verb "I commit" also picks up an idea from the preceding prayer, where Paul says God "appointed [*themenos*, 1:12] me for ministry." The letter passes along to Timothy the commission that Christ had given to Paul (cf. 2 Tim. 2:2).

Pastoral Paul commits **to you, child Timothy** (see comments at 1:2) **the prophecies that were previously pronounced over you** (1:18), referring to Timothy's ordination by the presbytery (4:14; cf. Acts 13:1–3). **With them** refers to those earlier prophecies, and **that you should fight the good fight** indicates the purpose of those prophecies to sustain Timothy as a spiritual warrior (see comments and "Theological Issues" at 2 Tim. 1:7). Philosophers described the philosophical life as a "battle" against passions and desires (Malherbe 1989, 79–89; cf. 6:12; 2 Tim. 4:7). The charge is not simply *that* Timothy should fight but *how* he should fight, **having faith and a good conscience** (1:19). Timothy, like Paul, should model the behaviors he is charged to instill in others (cf. 4:12). His manner of fighting should reflect the qualities he is trying to inculcate, the "goal of our instruction" (1:5).

Faith and a good conscience are the factors, **which certain ones have rejected and thereby have made shipwreck of the faith** (1:19). Plutarch cautioned that a banquet could be "shipwrecked" if the director did not exercise "proper oversight" (*paedagōgias orthēs*), permitting disgraceful and abusive jokes to prevail over gracious, good humor (Plutarch, *Quaest. conv.* 1.4 [622B]). Our topic is more serious than a dinner party. What is at stake is "the faith," which can be shipwrecked by a teacher who is not trustworthy and ethical, exercising "faith and a good conscience." This letter emphasizes the immorality of bad teachers and the desirable conduct of Christian leaders.

Hymenaeus and Alexander (1:20) are negative counterexamples to Paul's positive example in 1:12–17. **I have handed them over to Satan** conjures up the image of Satan as the prosecutor in the heavenly court (Job 1–2; Zech. 3:1). Hymenaeus and Alexander face what we might call a pretrial diversion (cf. 1 Cor. 5:5). Excommunication is a drastic measure, intended to be disciplinary. The aim is **that they might be trained not to blaspheme.** The verb "train" (*paideuō*) could be understood in the sense "educate" (Titus 2:12), which would address the problem of lack of understanding (1:7; cf. 6:5; 2 Tim. 3:8), or in the sense "train, discipline, correct," which would imply a goal of correction, like a pedagogue supervising the behavior of a child (cf. Gal. 3:24; Plutarch, *Quaest. conv.* 1.4, quoted above). Either connotation would make sense.

Theological Issues

Christ Came into the World to Save Sinners

To begin, everything depends on Christology, here expressed succinctly in the "faithful saying." Linda L. Belleville (2013, 325) underscores the centrality of this simple statement: "Salvation is the result of Christ's entrance into history. This makes Christology and soteriology inseparable both here in 1:15 and throughout the Pastorals." She makes an interesting suggestion about the word order of "Christ Jesus," implying "Christ the Saving One," rather than the usual "Jesus Christ," implying "Jesus, the Anointed One" (as in 1 Tim. 6:3, 14; 2 Tim. 2:8; Titus 1:1; 2:13; 3:6; Belleville 2013, 322). A "good minister of Christ Jesus" (4:6) must attend to the story of Christ and its relation to salvation.

Sinners, of Whom I Am First

An effective minister is self-critical. If you cannot look honestly at the vice list of 1:9–10 and see yourself in it, you are not ready to comprehend the mercy of God or engage in the discipline and redemption of troublemakers. As blasphemers, Hymenaeus and Alexander are not so different from what Paul once was (1:13, 20). So also, you share with your nemesis the potential for extraordinary grace and extraordinary damage. The proper place to begin your ministry is self-examination and confession, gratitude for God's mercy, and prayer for your most cantankerous opponents. This goes against the tendency to read a vice list judgmentally by picking out whichever sins do not tempt us (or our donor base) and decrying them as reprehensible. "It's the oldest religious shortcut in the book," says Rachel Held Evans, "the easiest way to make oneself righteous is to make someone else a sinner" (2015, 81).

The Goal of Our Instruction

Following Paul's charge to Timothy, your charge is to foster ethical behavior. To that end, you must consider what habits you seek to cultivate and the best ways to cultivate them (J. Smith 2016). Your goal is to engender love from a pure heart, good conscience, and sincere faith. If you would read Scripture properly, attend to the *ethical* demands of the texts. Help people see how the text challenges and corrects behavior, and put your understanding into practice yourself. No sophisticated theology will matter if people cannot see how it makes a difference in your life. One who begins by nurturing ethical habits is likely to grow into deeper contemplation of God and appreciate more fully the subtleties of Scripture. But even one who never moves to deep theological exploration may nevertheless attain the goal of a life well lived in love and faith.

Speculations and Empty Talk

The negative example of those who "teach otherwise" warns against beginning with any arrogant certainty that you have comprehended the meaning of Scripture, much less Deity, so as to expound the deep things to your hearers. It is ironic that the cryptic references to "myths and endless genealogies" (1:4) and would-be "Torah teachers" (1:7) have led to so much scholarly speculation on the identity of the false teachers. Proving the point about useless speculations, scholars make confident assertions, as if we could demonstrate our own orthodoxy by naming the false doctrine in view. But Pastoral Paul does not identify a specific false doctrine that we can use as the heretical dart board on which to demonstrate our theological dexterity. Rather, the "otherwise" teachers illustrate our own tendency to enter the pulpit confident that we know the answers because we have read a few books or had a flash of insight in a late-night kaffeeklatsch. Never mind those other teachers. We who desire to be Scripture teachers are liable to be the greater problem for the churches.

Is this anti-intellectual? Shall we close the seminaries and stop reading commentaries like this one? The PE promote deep study and reflection (see comments at 4:12–16). But it is a question of where one begins. The prayer is an expression of Paul's gratitude for mercy. His own appalling actions, he now sees, were grounded in ignorance and faithlessness. But against that he offers no doctrinal statement. He offers praise and applies his new and deeper knowledge and faithfulness in changed behavior.

The Immortal, Invisible, Only God

This leads to a consideration of the nature of God. Pastoral Paul praises the only God by describing what God is *not*. This way of contemplating deity led to the apophatic tradition (from Gk. *apophasis*, "denial"), which recognized in every statement about God a claim that is somehow false, diminishing, or misleading. Gregory of Nyssa presents the paradox of Moses seeing God on Mount Sinai as an allegory for how the mind contemplates deity:

> For leaving behind everything that is observed, not only what sense comprehends but also what the intelligence thinks it sees, it [the mind] keeps on penetrating deeper until by the intelligence's yearning for understanding it gains access to the invisible and the incomprehensible, and there it sees God. This is the true knowledge of what is sought; this is the seeing that consists in not seeing because that which is sought transcends all knowledge, being separated on all sides by incomprehensibility as by a kind of darkness. . . . When, therefore, Moses grew in knowledge, he declared that he had seen God in the darkness, that is, that he had then come to know that what is divine is beyond all knowledge and comprehension, for the text says, "Moses approached the dark cloud where God was [Exod. 20:21]." (Gregory of Nyssa, *Vit. Mos.* 2.163, trans. Malherbe and Ferguson 1978)

The patristic theologian who wrote under the pseudonym Dionysius the Areopagite also commented on 1 Tim. 1:17:

> He is described as invisible [1 Tim. 1:17], infinite, ungraspable, and other things which show not what he is but what in fact he is not. . . . God is in no way like the things that have being and we have no knowledge at all of his incomprehensible and ineffable transcendence and invisibility. (Ps.-Dioynsius, *Celestial Hierarchy* 2.3 [140d], trans. Luibheid 1987)

God, who transcends human understanding, cannot be defined in human terms because any terms we use are too limited and therefore misleading. If you wish to explore this apophatic tradition, consider ps.-Dionysius, *The Divine Names* 5.4 [817d]; Gregory of Nazianzus, *Oration* 45.4, 9 (also Armstrong 2009, chap. 2; Rollins 2006).

We who assay to lead God's people must begin by acknowledging that we do not know God fully and open ourselves to rebirth. Engaging issues from a posture of false certainty is likely to result in fruitless debate. But if we engage issues as opportunities to reexamine our assumptions, we may discover new dimensions to faith.

1 Timothy 2:1–3:13

First Set of Directives concerning the Church

After the opening charge, a transitional "therefore" (*oun*, 2:1) marks the beginning of the body of the letter. This paragraph contains the first of many directives in the form of exhortations (2:1; cf. 1:3–4), wishes (2:8, 9; 5:14), commands (2:11; 4:7, 11–16; 5:1–2, 3–4, 7, 9, 11, 20, 21, 22, 23; 6:1, 2, 11–12, 13–14, 17, 20; cf. 1:18), requirements ("It is necessary that . . . ," 3:2, 15; implied at 3:8, 11), and conditions (4:6; cf. 3:1, 5). The letter body opens with instructions about prayer. The first directive expounds the aim of prayer, supported by a theological rationale (2:1–7). The second directive deals with the proper comportment of men and of women when they pray (2:8–10), followed by a digression on the subordination of women (2:11–15 [or to 3:1a]). After that, there are directives concerning the qualifications of overseer (3:1b–7) and deacons (3:8–13).

1 Timothy 2:1–7

Exhortation to Pray for All People

Introductory Matters

The exhortation to pray not *to* but *for* rulers reflects traditional Roman sensibilities. According to Cassius Dio, the emperors Augustus, Tiberius, and Claudius all demonstrated their modesty in that they forbade Roman citizens to offer sacrifices *to* them (Dio, *Roman History* 51.20.6–9; 58.8.4; 60.5.4). Such sacrifices could be cause for condemnation (Cassius Dio 58.7.2; 8.4; 11.2) and became a mark of megalomania in the emperor Caligula (Cassius Dio 59.4.4). Philo dramatically describes how Caligula, when informed of the Jews' "impiety" (*asebeia*) toward him, challenged a delegation of Jewish petitioners, "Are you the god-haters who do not believe me to be a god?" When the Jews protested that they had offered grand public sacrifices on his behalf, the emperor pressed his point, "True, you have sacrificed, but *to* another, even if it was *for* [*hyper*, on behalf of] me; what good is it then? For you have not sacrificed *to* me" (Philo, *Embassy* 353–57, trans. Colson, LCL, emphasis added). This was not the normal expectation of Roman emperors, and numerous Greek inscriptions attest the common practice of offering sacrifices for (*hyper*) the emperor (Price 1980, 29–33; Galinsky 1996, 322). For example, when Caligula acceded to the throne in 37 CE, a decree of the city of Assos in the Troad listed five prominent citizens who traveled to Rome and, "while offering prayers on behalf of [*hyper*] the Savior Gaius Caesar Augustus Germanicus, made sacrifice to Zeus Capitolinus in the name of the city" (*SIG* 797, lines 31–33, trans. Hutson). The same inscription records that the city council and assembly, in consultation with local Roman businessmen, passed an ordinance requiring all citizens to take a loyalty oath:

We swear by Zeus Savior and the god Caesar Augustus and the ancestral Holy
Virgin [i.e., Athena Polias] to be well disposed toward Gaius Caesar Augustus
[i.e., "Caligula"] and to his entire household, and to consider as friends those
whom he favors and as enemies those whom he rejects. If we so swear, may it
be well with us, and if we forswear, the opposite. (*SIG* 797, lines 20–24, trans.
Hutson; for similar oaths, see *ILS* 190, 8781; Danker 1982, §53; Sørensen 2015)

Such an oath illustrates how business and political leaders could pressure
people to support their interests. Even if Jews and Christians were not citizens
and so were exempt from the oath, they might feel social pressure. But how
much more if they were citizens? Jews and Christians who refused to take the
oath because of their commitment to monotheism would need to be scrupulous
about presenting themselves as loyal citizens and supporters of social order.

As Philo illustrates, the distinction between praying *to* and praying *for* a
ruler fits the thought world of Judaism under pagan domination, beginning
with Jeremiah's advice for Jews in Babylonia to "seek the welfare of the city
where I have sent you into exile, and pray to the LORD on its behalf, for in its
welfare you will find your welfare" (Jer. 29:7 NRSV). After the exile, their
strict monotheism precluded faithful Jews from praying *to* any earthly rulers
as divine, but Jews regularly prayed *for* whatever authorities were over them. In
the second century BCE, the high priest offered sacrifices *for* King Ptolemy in
Egypt (*Let. Aris.* 45). And even at the height of the Maccabean revolt, priests
offered sacrifices in the temple *for* King Antiochus (1 Macc. 7:33). Likewise in
the Roman period, prayers and sacrifices were presented daily in the temple for
the emperor (Josephus, *J.W.* 2.197; cf. 2.409–10; *Ag. Ap.* 2.74–77; Philo, *Embassy*
157, 317; cf. 356–57; *m. Avot* 3.2); and Jews in Alexandria offered prayers for
rulers (Philo, *Flaccus* 49; Winter 2015, 94–123; Williams 1998, 91–92).

In response to charges that Christians were unpatriotic because they did not
pray to the emperor (Origen, *Cels.* 8.65), early Christians followed this Jewish
practice of praying *for* their rulers (*1 Clem.* 60.3–61.1; Tertullian, *Apol.* 39.2;
Origen, *Cels.* 8.73). We should not underestimate the degree to which monotheism challenged the ideology of the Roman Empire. The Jewish tenet that
"God is one" carried with it the corollary that all other gods and pretensions
of divinity were false, and that included the Roman emperor. Kavin Rowe has
argued that the Christian claim of monotheism was "destabilizing" to Roman
political order and brought with it a "potential for cultural collapse" (Rowe
2009, 24, 46; cf. Hoklotubbe 2017, 68–79; Wilken 1984, 117–25). Cassius Dio
summed up imperial policy on foreign religions. His account of Maecenas's
speech in 29 BCE, urging the young Octavian to abandon pretensions of de-
mocracy and embrace the role of monarch, includes the following advice
about religion:

Those who attempt to distort our religion with strange rites you should abhor
and punish, not merely for the sake of the gods (since if a man despises these

An Early Christian Prayer for Rulers

"Yea, Master, shine your face upon us in peace for good, so that we may be guarded by your mighty hand and delivered from all our sins by your upraised arm. And may you deliver us from those who hate us unjustly. Grant concord and peace both to us and to all who dwell on the earth, just as you granted to our ancestors, when they called upon you religiously in faith and truth, because they were obedient to your almighty and all-virtuous name, [and grant these] also to our rulers and governors upon the earth. You, Master, have granted to them the right of kingship through your magnificent and indescribable might, in order that we who know that glory and honor have been granted to them by you may be submissive to them, not opposing your will. Lord, grant them health, peace, concord, stability, in order that they may conduct unfailingly the government that was granted to them by you. For you, Heavenly Master, King of the Ages, having granted to the children of men glory and honor and the right of ruling over the earth, may you, Lord, direct their council in accordance with what is good and well pleasing in your sight, so that, as they exercise with piety, in peace and humility, the authority that was granted to them by you, they may find you to be well disposed toward them. You alone are able to do these and more good things for us. We acknowledge you through the High Priest and Protector of our souls, Jesus Christ, through whom to you be glory and majesty both now and through all generations forever and ever. Amen." (*1 Clem.* 60.3–61.3, trans. Hutson; cf. Pol. *Phil.* 12.3; Justin Martyr, *1 Apol.* 17; Tertullian, *Apol.* 30)

he will not pay honour to any other being), but because such men, by bringing in new divinities in place of the old, persuade many to adopt foreign practices, from which spring up conspiracies, factions, and cabals, which are far from profitable to a monarchy. Do not, therefore, permit anybody to be an atheist or a sorcerer. (Cassius Dio, *Roman History* 52.36.2, trans. Cary, LCL)

From Dio's perspective, "our religion" was the Roman state religion, while Jews and Christians would have been "atheists" because they denied the Roman gods. Furthermore, Roman critics of Christianity accused Jesus of practicing sorcery (Origen, *Cels.* 1.6). In Dio's account, although Maecenas also advised Octavian not to permit temples to himself (Cassius Dio, *Roman History* 52.35.4), that very year Octavian authorized the provinces of Asia and Bithynia to erect temples to his father the "divine" Julius Caesar in Ephesus and Nicaea as well as temples to himself in Pergamum and Nicomedia (Cassius Dio, *Roman History* 51.20.6–9). These were the first of what would become numerous such temples instigated by local magistracies, competing with one another for imperial favors (Price 1984; Galinsky 1996, 288–331; Friesen 2001; Hardin 2008; Rowe 2009, 17–51).

In such a context, refusal to honor the emperor as divine could be hazardous, especially if one espoused a new or foreign religion. Our letter adapts Jewish strategies for surviving in such a religious and political climate. The advice in 1 Tim. 2:1–7 takes this reality into consideration (Portefaix 2003, 149–51; cf. also 1 Pet. 2:13–16). This section is not a "liturgical call for alliance with civil authority" (Krause 2016, 211) but a call for Christians to imitate Jews in shielding themselves from the civil authorities as they live out their own obedience to God.

In two respects, however, our passage departs from typical Jewish practice. First, the prayer is grounded not only in Jewish monotheism (2:5a; cf. *Let. Aris.* 45) but also in Christology (2:5b–6). Second, the prayer is not merely a survival strategy (2:2b; cf. Philo, *Embassy* 353–57; Josephus, *J.W.* 2.195–97) but also takes on an evangelistic tone (2:4, 7). This directive offers Christians a way of living in harmony with the Roman imperial ideal of piety (*eusebeia*; see comments at 2:2) while maintaining a Jewish understanding of true piety as "fear of YHWH" (Prov. 1:7; Isa. 11:2) and a monotheistic commitment to the God of Israel. At the same time, it shifts the stance from a posture of defensiveness in the face of a threatening world to one of advancement into the world with the "knowledge of truth." N. T. Wright's (2013, 734) observation about 1 Cor. 8:6 is equally true of 1 Tim. 2:5–6, that for Paul "monotheism is . . . an *agenda*."

Another formal feature of this section is the quotation of traditional liturgy (2:5–6; Yarbrough 2009, 79–86). These verses comprise a self-contained unit of short, balanced lines containing dense expressions of central tenets of the faith. The symmetrical arrangement of terse lines calls to mind a creed arranged for liturgical use.

> For God is one (5a),
> And one the mediator between God and humans (5b),
>> A human, Christ Jesus (5c),
>> Who gave himself, a ransom for all (6a),
> The testimony when the times were right (6b).

It is not clear whether this quotation consists of four lines or five, that is, whether 2:6b is part of the quotation. If 2:6b is the beginning of the comment on the quotation, then the quotation consists of a pair of couplets (Yarbrough 2009, 85–86). Or, if 2:6b is the end of the quotation, then we could read the statement as a couplet and a triplet, or as five lines with "a human, Christ Jesus" at the center.

The main theme of this section is the universal will of God. An exhortation to pray for "all people" (2:1) is based on the understanding that God "wants all people to be saved" (2:4). The theological warrant for this is a creedal tradition that begins with an affirmation of monotheism (2:5) and continues with a christological statement (2:6). This is the gospel for which Paul was commissioned as a "teacher of gentiles" (2:7). We must understand the various details in the pericope in relation to the theme that God wills the universal salvation of all people.

Tracing the Train of Thought

2:1–7. The phrase **first of all** (2:1) could indicate first in sequence or in importance, and probably it is both. Obviously, it is sequentially the first directive in the letter, but it is also "the single most significant change Timothy can effect" (Mounce 2000, 78). The essential point "first of all" (2:1) is that monotheism ("God is one," 2:5) implies universalism ("all people," 2:1, 4; "all," 2:6; "gentiles," 2:7). There is only one God and creator of all people, and whatever God does has implications for all people. The unstated corollary is that the claims of all other gods are false. But denying the gods of Rome does not entail a call to overthrow the government. It is a call to view reality through a different lens—looking to the one God for orientation and not to any human power. The rest of chapters 2–3 provide guidance on how early Christians could be seen as promoters of peace and concord in a well-ordered society, despite their denial of the Roman gods (cf. Titus 3:1; 1 Pet. 2:13–17).

> ### 1 Timothy 2:1–7 in the Rhetorical Flow
>
> **Letter opening (1:1–2)**
>
> **Proem: First charge to Timothy (1:3–20)**
>
> **First set of directives concerning the church (2:1–3:13)**
>
> ▶ Exhortation to pray for all people (2:1–7)

The terms **supplications, prayers, intercessions, and thanksgivings** (2:1) overlap. "Supplications" (*deēseis*) express need. "Prayers" (*proseuchai*) is a generic term for any type of prayer. "Intercessions" (*enteuxeis*) are entreaties on behalf of another but can be another generic word for prayer (1 Tim. 4:5). The term "thanksgivings" (*eucharistiai*) calls to mind psalms of thanksgiving, as well as the prayers near the beginnings of most Pauline letters (e.g., 1 Tim. 1:12–17). Together, the four terms suggest all types of prayers.

Regarding prayers **on behalf of rulers** (2:2), see "Introductory Matters," above. Under the Roman Empire, **kings** included the emperor, who was more or less a military dictator, as well as client-kings and governors of conquered territories. Whether traditional, hereditary rulers or shrewd political manipulators, they all governed at the behest of the emperor. Our passage is nonspecific: **all those who are in authority.**

The conjunction **that** (*hina*) normally introduces a purpose clause, translated "so that." Understood this way, the purpose of the praying is **so that we** [Christians] **may lead a tranquil and quiet life** (2:2). As discussed above in

"Introductory Matters," prayers *for* rulers were part of the survival strategy of monotheistic Jews, to deflect suspicion about their alleged disloyalty or rebelliousness. Several details in this letter indicate that Christians were liable to draw criticism from pagan neighbors (e.g., 3:7; 5:14; 6:1; cf. Titus 1:9; 2:5, 8), and elsewhere the PE reflect persecution from the governing authorities (e.g., 2 Tim. 2:9; 3:11; 4:16). Prayers for rulers signaled that Christians were not "public enemies" (Tertullian, *Apol.* 35).

On the other hand, the conjunction **that** (*hina*) could also indicate the content of the prayers (i.e., *hina* in the sense of *hoti*, with verbs of praying or requesting, as in 1 Tim. 5:21; 1 Cor. 1:10; 14:13; Eph. 1:17; cf. BDAG 476, s.v. ἵνα 2.a.γ). Understood this way, the content of the prayers is **that we may lead a tranquil and quiet life.** The exhortation is that Christian prayers should appropriate key words from Roman political discourse. The word "quietness" (*hēsychia*) could mean "silence" (Ign. *Eph.* 15.2), but in a context of political or community relations it represents the opposite of civil unrest, party strife, or factionalism, as when the Jerusalem mob calmed down to listen to Paul (Acts 22:2; cf. Josephus, *J.W.* 1.201). Plutarch suggested that the state is like a beehive in that it thrives not so much when it is noisy and swarming as when it is marked by *hēsychia* and gentleness (Plutarch, *Praec. ger. rei publ.* 32 [824F]). He discussed the cardinal civic virtues of concord (Gk. *homonoia*) and peace, arguing that a good statesman cultivates quietness (*hēsychia*) and concord among the people (Plutarch, *Mor.* 824e). Roman rulers were hypersensitive to any hint of social disturbance or unrest (Acts 19:31–32; 21:30–32). A "tranquil and quiet life" echoes the Roman civic virtues of concord and quietness (*hēsychia*). From this perspective, "that we may lead" could refer not only to "we" Christians but more broadly to "we" subjects of the empire. Such prayers might become prayers for general peace within the empire and for the strength of the empire as a guarantor of peace and stability in the world (cf. Tertullian, *Apol.* 32).

The phrase **in all piety and solemnity** (2:2) reflects Roman social virtues, how one expressed devotion to the gods by honoring obligations to family and city. This word "piety" is thematic for the PE (see sidebar; see comments at 1 Tim. 4:8; 2 Tim. 3:5; Titus 2:12).

As monotheists (2:5) who honored neither family idols nor the gods of the state, Christians faced suspicion of impiety, disrespecting the state, and/ or lacking family values (Hoklotubbe 2017, 13–54; Zamfir 2013, 27–33). To counter such suspicions, Pastoral Paul endorses a "quiet and tranquil life," neither causing nor inviting trouble. He urges Christians to be "pious," representing good social order, but he is not endorsing pagan values. He captures and redefines the language of the dominant society. Christians live "in all piety," but they understand that word in relation to the God of Israel rather than to any pagan gods.

The nearest possible antecedent to **this** (2:3) is the clause "that we may lead a tranquil and quiet life" (2:2b). No doubt, such a life **is acceptable before God,**

Piety as Religious and Ethical Ideal

The translation "godliness" obscures the cultural context of the word "piety" (Gk. *eusebeia* = Lat. *pietas*; Hoklotubbe 2017; I. H. Marshall 1999, 135–44; Quinn 1990a, 282–91). *Eusebeia* was devotion to the gods expressed in ritual observances and ethical obligations (Isocrates, *Demon.* 13). Numerous inscriptions from Ephesus document *eusebeia* as the correlation between civic duties and devotion to Artemis and/or the Imperial Cult (Hoklotubbe 2017, 111–48; Hoag 2015, 167). The city of Rhodes honored a magistrate Eratophanes for his "piety" toward Emperor Claudius, who was a "god" and "savior and benefactor of all humanity," because he funded civic programs and "sacrifices to the Gods and to the Augusti" (Danker 1982, §34).

Piety also included devotion to family. A favorite illustration of Roman *pietas* was the Trojan hero Aeneas (D'Angelo 2003, 142–43). In Vergil's vivid depiction (*Aen.* 2), as the Greeks were sacking Troy, Aeneas placed the family gods in his father's hands, hoisted the old man on his shoulders, grasped his young son by the hand, commanded his wife to follow, and fled the burning city. Alas, his wife was lost in the melee. But the hero valiantly saved three generations of men and his family gods. He sailed off to become the noble ancestor of the Roman people. The image of *Pious Aeneas* fleeing with son, father, and gods became emblematic of the Roman civic virtue of piety, popularized in literature, sculpture, paintings, jewelry, and coins.

Hellenistic Jews co-opted the word *eusebeia* but thought of it in terms of Torah observance and Jewish monotheism (Quinn 1990a, 288; W. Foerster, *TDNT* 7:179–81; I. H. Marshall 1999, 138–41). Piety is related to the God of Israel (*eusebeia* translates "fear of the Lord" in the LXX of Prov. 1:7; Isa. 11:2; 33:6) rather than the gods of Olympus or Rome.

Similarly for Pastoral Paul, *eusebeia* is related to "God our Savior" (1 Tim. 2:2–3), the Christ story (1 Tim. 3:15–16; cf. 2 Tim. 3:12), and eternal life (1 Tim. 4:8). It is taught by Christ (Titus 2:12) and entails care for family (1 Tim. 5:4). Thus "piety" becomes an "all-encompassing ethical ideal" (Sumney 1999b, 121; cf. cautionary remarks in Mitchell 1999, 130).

especially as the means to the larger end of allowing believers to spread the news of God's salvation to "all people" (Oberlinner 1994, 68). But as soon as we interpret the thrust of the "tranquil and quiet life" as evangelistic, then we realize that the pronoun "this" refers to the directive to "pray for all people" (2:2a). The reason that prayer for all people **is acceptable before God our Savior** is that God **wants all people to be saved** (2:4). So in the larger context, the antecedent of "this" is the directive to pray, though we could say that it also points to the entirety of verses 1–2.

Sumney (1999b, 108) identifies the claim that God is "our Savior" (2:3) as "the fundamental and *operative* theological conviction of 1 Timothy." Once again, such a claim goes against the grain of Greco-Roman culture. "Savior" (*sōtēr*)

had long been a common epithet of any god honored as
preserver or protector, and
it also applied to the Roman
emperors and other officials in
recognition of their benefactions to cities or provinces (W.
Foerster, *TDNT* 7:1004–12;
Winter 2015, 71–74; Neyrey
2005b, 472–73; Nock 1951).
But, regardless of the sense in
which any god or human ruler
could be called "savior," this
letter looks to the one God as
"our Savior," who **wants all
people to be saved and come
to knowledge of the truth**
(2:4; cf. 4:10). This language
calls to mind the vision of
Isa. 45, which describes the
creator God as the one and
only "savior" (Isa. 45:15, 21),
to whom "all the ends of the
earth" will turn (45:22), and
the universal sovereign, to
whom "every knee shall bow"
(45:23). Salvation in our passage is not preferential treat-

Figure 1. Terra-cotta image of Aeneas escaping from Troy, carrying his father, Anchises, on his shoulders and giving his hand to his son, Ascanius (first cent. CE).

ment for a particular city or nation but is universal, for "all people." And it
is associated with knowledge of the truth claimed in the creedal statement of
2:5–6.

The conjunction **for** (2:5) introduces the theological grounding of the exhortation in 2:1–4, which appears to be a quotation of an early Christian
tradition. Verses 5–6 show affinity with 1 Cor. 8:6, so we could read them as
"one of Paul's typically compressed christological-soteriological statements"
(Johnson 2001, 191) or as a reworking of a Pauline text by a later author
(Mitchell 2008, 54–55). In any case, 1 Cor. 8:6 similarly emphasizes "one God
the Father" and "one Lord Jesus Christ," who are respectively the creative
source "from whom" and the creative agent "through whom" are "all *things*."
In our passage, by contrast, Christ is the "ransom of all *people*."

The affirmation **God is one** (*heis theos*, 2:5a) was common in Greek religious
contexts (Peterson 2012, 375–557). On a popular level, Greeks might have
heard it as a kind of syncretism that viewed various gods as manifestations

of one single god (e.g., Apuleius, *Metamorphoses* 9.14; 11.2; cf. MacMullen 1981, 83–84). Alternately, *heis theos* might affirm the supremacy of one god over all others (e.g., *NewDocs* 3:§7; Peterson 2012, 534–35). Peterson identifies six inscriptions that honor Apollo as the supreme god over all other gods.

But Christians and Jews could appropriate pagan affirmations of the supremacy of one deity to express their own monotheistic tradition. For example, when Xenocrates of Colophon referred to "one god [*heis theos*], greatest among gods and men, resembling mortals in neither stature nor thought" (DK, frag. 23), Clement of Alexandria thought he must have gotten his idea of God from the Hebrews (*Strom.* 5.14.109). Similarly, Philo approvingly cited the Pythagorean Philolaus, "For there is one god [*theos heis*], governor and ruler of all, who is eternal, unitary, immoveable, unique to himself, and different from others" (*Creation* 100). Michael Frede has gone so far as to argue that the philosopher Antisthenes held a view of deity that could be described as true monotheism in the Jewish sense (Frede 2010). Even if Frede is right about Antisthenes, most gentiles certainly did not understand "God is one" as affirming the existence of only one God. On the other hand, Jews and Jewish-Christians would have no difficulty co-opting a pagan affirmation *heis theos* and using it to express their own monotheism. What, then, did Jews in antiquity mean when they said "God is one"?

The expression *heis theos* is not quite a biblical quotation. The closest parallels are a rhetorical question affirming the kinship of all Israelites (Mal. 2:10), and an affirmation of the oneness of God in heaven (Dan. 3:17). In the Second Temple period, *heis theos* became an affirmation of monotheism (Philo, *Creation* 171; cf. *Alleg. Interp.* 3.105; *Cher.* 83; *Dreams* 1.229; *Spec. Laws* 1.30; Josephus, *Ant.* 3.91; 4.201; 5.97). The expression also appears in the NT (Rom. 3:30; Gal. 3:20; 1 Cor. 8:6; James 2:19) and other early Christian literature (*Acts of John* 42.7; *Acts of Paul* 1.17–18; Clement of Alexandria, *Protr.* 6.72; 7.74; 8.80; 12.120; *Paed.* 1.4.10; 2.1.10, 14; *Strom.* 1.24.164; 4.15.97; 5.3.18.8 [quoting Rom. 3:30]; 5.14.113.2; 5.14.115.3).

For our purposes, three points are significant. First, *heis theos* was shorthand for the Shema (Deut. 6:4), which became a standard expression of monotheism (N. T. Wright 2013, 179–83, 619–25). In rabbinic tradition, reciting the Shema was tantamount to taking upon oneself the "yoke of the kingdom of heaven" (*m. Ber.* 2.5). Second, the universalistic implications of monotheism are found in the psalms (e.g., Pss. 2; 96–98) and Isaiah, especially chapters 56 and 66 (Kaminsky and Stewart 2006). The idea may be found throughout the OT that Israel is the vehicle through whom God reaches all nations (Kaiser 2000; Willis 2003). That is, if there is only one God, then that God is creator and sovereign of all peoples. Third, Paul uses the same shorthand with similar universalizing implications in Rom. 3:30; Gal. 3:20 (N. T. Wright 1992, 170–71); and 1 Cor. 8:6 (N. T. Wright 2013, 661–70). So also in our passage, an allusion to the Shema launches the creedal statement in 2:5–6.

The proposition of the **one mediator between God and humans, a human, Christ Jesus** (2:5) also has a Jewish ring to it. Moses was the mediator of the covenant at Sinai (Gal. 3:20; N. T. Wright 1992, 157–74). At the same time, in Jewish tradition an "angel of the presence" assisted Moses in writing the Torah (*Jub.* 1.27, 29; 2.1), just as in the Bible angels are intermediaries delivering messages from God to humans. In this sense, we might think of Jesus as the "mediator" who communicates God's will to humans. Anthony T. Hanson (1968, 56–64) sees here an allusion to Job's wish for a "mediator" between God and a "human like me" (Job 9:32–33). He thinks that allusion tends toward an Arian understanding of Jesus as a creature, but an allusion to Job could as well be understood in terms of the incarnation of Jesus. Tertullian took "mediator" as a description of the two natures of Christ, divine and human (Tertullian, *Prax.* 27).

Who gave himself, a ransom for all (2:6) is a concise reference to the passion of Christ. The word for "ransom" (*antilytron*) appears nowhere else in the NT, although other words based on the root *lytr-* do appear. Two passages are noteworthy. First, in a related text, Titus 2:14 refers to Christ, "who *gave himself* for us so that he might *ransom* us from all lawlessness," juxtaposing two ideas that appear in our verse. Second, Jesus's passion prediction in Mark 10:45 (//Matt. 20:28) ends with "to *give* his life a *ransom* for many [*lytron anti pollōn*]," juxtaposing self-giving and ransom. Perhaps our verse alludes to that saying of Jesus. If so, it is notable that Jesus's "ransom for *many*" has been changed to "ransom for *all*," heightening the universal implications of Jesus's sacrifice.

The stem (*lytr-*) of the word "ransom" (*antilytron*) refers to the price for release of a captive, such as a prisoner of war or a slave. Paul uses the related word "act of ransoming" (*apolytrōsis*, Rom. 3:24; 8:23; 1 Cor. 1:30), as well as the synonyms "purchase" (*agorazō*, 1 Cor. 6:20; 7:23; cf. 2 Pet. 2:1; Rev. 5:9; 14:3–4) and "buy back" (*exagorazō*, Gal. 3:13; 4:5) as metaphors for the work of Christ. In the LXX, the Greek stem *lytr-* commonly translates the Hebrew "redeem" (*gā'al*), often used as a synonym for "ransom" (*pādâ*). Both words are metaphors for deliverance, whether from the power of death (Hosea 13:14), from slavery (Isa. 35:9–10), or from enemies (Ps. 69:18 [68:19 LXX]). "Redeemer" is an epithet for God in deutero-Isaiah (H. Ringgren, *TDOT* 2:355, citing Isa. 41:14; 43:14; 44:6; 47:4; 48:17; 49:7, 26; 54:5; 60:16; cf. Ps. 19:14 [18:15 LXX]; 78:35 [77:35 LXX]). Similarly, we could understand "ransom" as a generic metaphor for rescue. D. Francois Tolmie (2005, 266) suggests that, at its "barest essence," redemption points to a "radical status reversal." For Paul, this reversal was relational in that the ransomed person moved from the household of one owner to that of another (Tolmie 2005, 255–56, 267). This idea is suggestive for understanding 1 Timothy, since this letter views the community of believers as "the house of God" (3:15).

In sum, the concept of "ransom" shows continuity with Paul's thought and reflects a Hebrew metaphor for divine rescue. Our creedal statement does not say to whom Christ paid a ransom (though cf. Titus 2:14), and we should not overextend the metaphor (see "Theological Issues," below). The creed focuses on the object of the ransom, "for all," reinforcing the point of verse 4 by expressing the universalizing implications of monotheism.

It is not clear whether 2:6b is the last line of the creedal statement or the beginning of the comment on that statement. The word **testimony** (*martyrion*) normally refers to some concrete object or action that serves as testimony or proof (Mark 6:11//Luke 9:5; James 5:3). Paul uses the word in this sense when he refers to the "testimony [*martyrion*] of our conscience," which is equivalent to how "we conducted ourselves in the world" (2 Cor. 1:12).

On the other hand, although *martyria* was the usual word for testimony about one's personal knowledge of a matter (e.g., 1 Tim. 3:7; John 1:7, 19), our word *martyrion* sometimes had that connotation (e.g., 2 Thess. 1:10; Acts 4:33). Most commentators take the "testimony" of 2:6 in this second sense to refer to what someone says *about* Jesus. Some ancient scribes in the sixth century and later inserted words into verse 6b to resolve the ambiguity in favor of this understanding: "*of whom* (or *of which*) the testimony *was given*." But even without those inserted words, it is possible to separate 2:6b from the creedal statement and read it as the beginning of the comment about Paul's apostolic commission: "the testimony to which, when the times were right, I was appointed . . ." (cf. Titus 1:3).

Nevertheless, there are reasons to include 2:6b as part of the creedal statement, restating verse 6a. Jesus giving himself as a ransom for all was itself the concrete action that served as Jesus's own testimony. While it is possible to understand *martyrion* as something said *about* Jesus, it is also possible to understand it in its more basic sense of a concrete action—namely, Jesus's self-sacrifice—as his own testimony (e.g., 1 Cor. 1:6; 2 Tim. 1:8). This reading makes sense of the odd phrase **when the times were right** (*kairois idiois*). That phrase appears in 1 Tim. 6:15, another semi-poetic, creedal passage, where it refers to the anticipated "epiphany of our Lord Jesus Christ," at the close of the age (6:14–15). Similarly in Gal. 6:9, the singular "when the time is right" refers to the eschatological "harvest" as a metaphor for the judgment (Martyn 1998, 553–54; cf. 1 Cor. 7:29). So it makes sense to read 2:6b as focusing on Jesus's self-sacrifice as the eschatological moment, the dawn of the age to come, rather than on the period when Paul preached about Jesus.

Regardless whether one includes 2:6b, the point of the quotation is that Christ "gave himself, a ransom for all" (2:6a). The word "all" is the explicit verbal connection to verses 1 and 4, and the creedal statement supports the proposition that God's salvific purpose is universal in scope.

The vehement affirmation, **I am telling the truth; I am not lying** (2:7) is familiarly Pauline. Margaret M. Mitchell (2008) has suggested that the echo of Rom. 9:1 invites us to explore intertextual echoes between our passage and all of Rom. 9–11. She considers how this text adapts Rom. 9–11 and "represents Paul as the champion of prayer . . . for Gentile unbelievers" (Mitchell 2008, 53–54). It is odd that Paul would insist so strongly on the nature of his apostolic commission when writing to a longtime, trusted associate. Such an affirmation would make more sense in a pseudonymous letter written a generation or two later to readers who did not know Paul (J. Marshall 2008, 789). In any case, the point on which the text insists is not the mere fact that Paul was **appointed a herald** (cf. Rom. 10:8–15) **and apostle** (Rom. 1:1; 11:13; 1 Cor. 1:1, etc.), but the scope of his commission as a **teacher** (cf. 1 Cor. 4:17) **of gentiles** (Rom. 11:13; Gal. 3:14). The antecedent of the pronoun **which** (2:7) is the message that Paul was appointed to proclaim, a message summarized in 2:4 and in the supporting creedal statement of 2:5–6.

In sum, 2:1–7 highlights the universal concern of the one God for all people. The community should reflect this universalism in their prayers. This pushes for the survival of the people of God in a world dominated by false gods and rulers who claim to be divine. It also pushes the church to move out of a bunker mentality and go on the offensive with an evangelistic program that aims at all peoples. These two impulses—for survival in a hostile environment and for effective evangelism—apply to various issues throughout the letter.

Theological Issues

The fundamental Christian doctrines presumed in this letter include monotheism and Christ as mediator and ransom. Pastoral Paul applies these doctrines in his precept concerning prayer for all people.

The Sovereignty of God

Christians who follow an Augustinian or Calvinist doctrine of predestination with emphasis on the sovereignty of God may struggle with this text. If God predestines some to be saved and others lost, then why should we pray for all people, and how can we assert that God "wants all people to be saved"? And if God wants all people to be saved, and they are not saved in the end, then is God sovereign? Does the sovereignty of God imply that God will ultimately find a way to save all people? Does God's will preclude the free will of the creatures?

In considering such questions, a good starting place is the document *Nostra Aetate*, the declaration of Pope Paul VI on the relation between the church and non-Christian religions (1965), which begins with the tenet that God is the creator and "final goal" of all people. We might also consider that Calvin himself encouraged prayer for all people in light of this very text (McKee 2009), although in his commentary on 1 Timothy he interpreted the text as if it said "all peoples," thus "no nation of the earth and no rank of society is excluded from salvation, . . . he is speaking of classes and not of individuals" (Smail 1964, 208). If it seems that Calvin bent the passage to fit into a preconceived theological schema, then one could say that our text is an example of the inscrutability of God that we discussed with reference to 1 Tim. 1:19.

The text is less problematic, however, for Christians who stand in the traditions of Erasmus, Arminius, and Wesley, emphasizing human freedom to accept or reject God's grace. Here is an excerpt from Erasmus's commentary on 1 Tim. 2:

> We have no way of knowing whether this or that ungodly worshipper of statues will presently accept the gospel. Hence Christian charity prays for the salvation of all. Jew loves Jew, proselyte another proselyte, Greek loves Greek, a brother loves a brother, a kinsman another kinsman. This is not evangelical love; evangelical love is that love which loves the godly for the sake of Christ and loves the ungodly so that they may someday come to their senses and repent. . . . The pagans sacrifice to demons and invoke evil upon you. You, however, are following closely in the footsteps of Christ. . . . One must pity their blindness rather than retaliate with their own malice. Otherwise, they will not become better persons, and we shall cease to be Christians. (trans. Bateman 1993)

Erasmus saw that the passage pushes us to rise above group prejudices and seek the good of our persecutors, to act on the implications of our belief in the universal sovereignty of God.

At the same time, this text illustrates what it means to be both loyal to and detached from an earthly government. A Christian's primary allegiance is to the reign of God. But it is easy to confuse loyalty to God with loyalty to one's native country. Because political rhetoric employs religious terminology, it can lull us into thinking there is no competition between earthly governments and the kingdom of heaven for our allegiance.

This point is crucial in a world torn by political tensions and rival religions. Even monotheism can be co-opted (Volf 2011, 219–38). Nevertheless, monotheism is an essential resource for believers who wish to engage political pluralism, and committed monotheists understand that "the correlate of 'one God' is 'all people.' Nothing could be more inclusive than monotheism" (Volf 2011, 223).

Already in the late second century, Tertullian (*Apol.* 30–32) argued that Christians benefited from the peace and security that Rome provided, and therefore they should pray for the strength and stability of the empire. Although we might see in his writings the seeds of what would blossom after the rise of Constantine in the fourth century, when political leaders began to think of the state as an expression of God's reign, Tertullian still distinguished between the church and the empire, and he knew where his allegiance lay.

The assertion of God's desire for "all people" challenges imperialism, nationalism, ethnocentrism, and elitism. Politicians and socialites flatter themselves that they enjoy divine favor. On one level, Pastoral Paul's message to "pray for rulers" may seem to accommodate the Roman Empire, and no doubt rulers have always been happy to read it that way. But on another level, the message that God wants "all people" subverts the presumed privilege of Romans over barbarians, citizens over noncitizens, free over enslaved.

The Atonement as Ransom

As a description of the self-sacrifice of Jesus, we should use the "ransom" metaphor with caution. Pastoral Paul does not say to whom a ransom was paid. Paul wrote about bondage to Sin and Death (Rom. 5–7; cf. Athanasius, *Incarnation* 21.7; 25.3–4). Pastoral Paul speaks of ransom from "lawlessness" (Titus 2:14). Later, Irenaeus (e.g., *Haer.* 3.23.1; 5.21.3; *Epid.* 37–38) argued that Christ's death conquered the enemy who tyrannized humankind and spoke of that enemy as "sin," "powers of evil," "death," and "the devil," using those terms interchangeably (Aulén 1969, 16–35). Over the centuries, "the devil" tended to squeeze out the other terms. Eventually, Anselm of Canterbury rejected the "ransom" metaphor altogether in his influential *Cur Deus Homo?* (*Why Did God Become Human?*). He argued that it would challenge any understanding of the sovereignty of God to suggest that God needed to pay off the devil to free people from his clutches (Anselm, *Cur Deus Homo?* 1.7; cf. Gregory of Nazianzus, *Oration* 45.22; on the phrase "snare of the devil," see comments at 1 Tim. 3:7). Laboring to explain God's absolute justice, Anselm became stuck on an overly literal understanding of the "ransom" metaphor (Aulén 1969, 84–92). But the biblical metaphor of "ransom" emphasizes liberation from bondage (see comments at 2:6). Instead of focusing on the identity of the captor, the present passage emphasizes the means of the ransom ("gave himself," cf. "blood . . . of Christ," 1 Pet. 1:18–19) and the scope of the ransom ("for all"; on the implications for universalism, see "Theological Issues: Universalism" at the end of the comments on 4:6–16).

The Quiet Life

From Orthodox tradition we may learn the value of hesychasm (stillness, quietness), or practicing the quiet life (Deseille 2008, 93–153). This tradition offers a broader perspective on the prayer, "that we may live a peaceable and quiet life" (*hesychios bios*). The spiritual practices associated with hesychasm are found in the *Philokalia*, an anthology of writings of Orthodox fathers from the fourth century to the fifteenth. The *Philokalia* was compiled in the late eighteenth century on Mount Athos in Greece by the monks Nikodimos of the Holy Mountain and Makarios of Corinth (*PhCT*) and was perpetuated in Slavonic by Païsy Velichovsky (*WPh*). Consideration of similar practice in Western traditions might begin with the *Rule of St. Benedict* 6, "On Keeping Silent."

In the nineteenth century the *Philokalia* challenged the rising tide of scientism that grew out of the Western Enlightenment. It reasserted the value of metaphysics, contemplation, and symbolism over against a Western emphasis on empiricism, reason, and literal meaning (Sherrard 1989, 420–27; Ware 2012, 9–13). With its focus on contemplative prayer, the *Philokalia* asserts the primacy of the Greatest Commandment, "Love the LORD thy God," over the Second Commandment, "Love thy neighbor as thyself," which is to say that, to be truly transformative, love for neighbor must be grounded in love for God (Sherrard 1989, 427–28). The writings in the *Philokalia* show how the monks in each generation restated the essentials of spiritual formation.

Hesychasm is a quest for inner stillness, a cultivation of spiritual discipline, accepting the vicissitudes of earthly fortune while living according to heavenly principles, including repentance, humility, struggle against all passions and desires, and charity toward others. Strictly speaking, hesychasm is the practice of a monk living in solitude and contemplative prayer under the direction of a spiritual director, endeavoring to avoid worldly distraction and focus wholly on God. The hesychast repeats a prayer, which could be a verse from a psalm or any simple prayer. A common, simple prayer, so formulated by the desert monk Abba Philemon in the sixth century but based on earlier tradition, is "O Lord Jesus Christ, Son of God, have mercy on me" (*Discourse on Abba Philemon*, *PhCT* 2.347; St. Simeon the New Theologian, *On Faith*, *WPh* 145; Callistus and Ignatius, *Directions to Hesychasts* 19, 49 [*WPh* 192, 222], etc.). This prayer is commonly shortened, "Lord, have mercy" (*kyrie eleēson*; *Discourse on Abba Philemon* [*PhCT* 2.345]) or simply "Lord Jesus!" (Diodochos of Photiki, *On Spiritual Knowledge* 59 [*PhCT* 1.270]; Hesychius of Jerusalem, *WPh* 300, etc.). This simple prayer could serve as a meditation to focus the mind from distraction, or a confession, or a plea for help in the struggle against sin, or a form of communion with God (Cunningham 2012). The hesychast repeats it continually throughout the day until it infiltrates all thoughts and actions.

Whereas the Orthodox practice of hesychasm originated in monastic life, its principles are adaptable to broader community, and perhaps by publishing the *Philokalia* Nikodimos intended for lay Christians to learn from it (Ware 2012, 25–27). Hesychasm is a resource for helping believers relate to the wider, unbelieving world. It has sustained Orthodox faith under the Roman Empire, Islamic domination, Nazi occupation, and Communist regimes. Hesychasm is not simply a passive desire that the authorities leave us alone; rather, it is a way of intentional living so as to bear witness to the faith. In the context of prayer for rulers in 1 Tim. 2:2, a "quiet life" (*hēsychios bios*) begins with an acknowledgment of the lordship of Jesus above all others. The Christian confession "Jesus is Lord" trumps a loyalty oath to any earthly lord.

As our world is nationalistic, we find ourselves joining in noisy, patriotic enthusiasm. Our churches may honor heroes of the world—soldiers who killed and died for honor and country, while ignoring the heroes of the faith—martyrs who refused to kill and died for the glory of God. Our prayer for rulers and authorities is a way of setting aside our personal, political preferences and aligning ourselves with the will of God, who desires the salvation of *all* people.

Similarly, as our world is commercial, we import management techniques into church organization, and we count heads and dollars. But who can quantify the value of prayer, contemplation, deep study, and fellowship? How do we measure the gain when we spend our resources on the poor? The quiet pursuit of a spiritual agenda set by the Lord Jesus as a counterpoint to worldly agendas will be the most effective witness to our noisy, nationalistic, and profit-centered world. Read this way, the prayers in 1 Tim. 2:2 are less about passive deliverance from worldly powers and more about an active quest for God.

Hesychasm refuses to allow the world to set the agenda for the church. When Christian ministers are captivated by noisy methods of evangelism—television, internet, a creative logo, a better church band, or razzle-dazzle sermon props—they find themselves chasing the next gimmick that will attract people already jaded by last month's hip performance. In a world addicted to noise, we find ourselves ever striving for something new and sensational, more amplification to make ourselves heard above the din. We might consider how the *hesychios bios* does not attempt to shout down the noisemakers of the world; rather, in simple words and simple actions, with a still, small voice and a steady hand, it repeats the basic tenets and practices of the faith. The pastor who wishes to present a quiet but forceful leadership might well consider the impact of repeated doctrinal formulas in the worship assembly, whether in the form of a hymn or liturgy or a simple prayer. One should choose those liturgical formulas carefully, repeat them frequently in private devotion and public worship, and set an example for the flock by living them out in an intentional way.

1 Timothy 2:8–10

Proper Comportment for Prayer

Introductory Matters

The instruction in 2:1–15 (or to 3:1a) falls into two parts. On the surface, the whole seems to be about prayer: the proper content and purpose of prayer (2:1–7), and proper comportment of men and women when praying (2:8–10), followed by a digression on women teaching (2:11–15 [or to 3:1a]). But at a deeper level, this unit constitutes advice about survival in a hostile environment. If Christians commit to monotheism (2:1–7)—refusing to worship the emperor or the emperor's gods—they must conduct themselves so as to show that they are neither fostering sedition against the political order nor unraveling the fabric of society. The instruction about the behaviors of men and women in worship follow logically from the previous instruction about prayer for all people and should be read as an extension of it.

This instruction reflects the cultural shift in attitudes about women in the early Roman Empire. Upper-class Roman women in the late Republic had more legal rights and freedoms than their predecessors, even though public rhetoric continued to uphold traditional images of domestic bliss, including marital fidelity (Pomeroy 1975, Fantham et al. 1994, 280–93; Winter 2003, 21–31; Nevett 2002). But some influential men identified the new freedoms of women with moral decay. The first century BCE had been a time of social turmoil, as civil wars ground the Roman Republic into a military dictatorship, and a younger generation challenged social conventions. Poets of the Augustan era—including Catullus, Horace, Juvenal, Ovid, and Propertius—played the political and domestic changes against one another. They associated the collapse of the old order with the "New

Woman," whom they criticized for having a public life, pursuing education, flaunting attention-grabbing attire, and practicing sexual promiscuity (e.g., Horace, *Odes* 3.6; Juvenal, *Satires* 6; Fantham et al. 1994, 280–93; Winter 2003, 17–38). The early Roman Empire saw a cultural backlash, led by Augustus himself, whose propaganda machine portrayed him throughout the realm as champion of law and order and traditional piety (Lat. *pietas* = Gk. *eusebeia*). Augustus's wife Livia was often portrayed with her *palla* (woman's outer garment, corresponding to a man's toga) pulled up over her head, the traditional symbolic attire of a Roman married woman of piety and modesty—a paragon of decorum. It became fashionable to depict Roman women this way, as models of domestic virtue, even though aristocratic women could be heavily involved in public affairs (D'Ambra 2007, 143–66; see comments at 2:9).

Roman hypersensitivity about the behavior of women created problems for Christian women. Pagans often misunderstood such innocent practices as men and women assembling and dining together, the use of familial language ("brother," "sister"), and predawn prayer meetings (Wilken 1984). Such practices spawned suspicion and slander, and Christian women were easy targets (M. MacDonald 1996, 49–126). To the extent that women were leaders in Pauline churches (Kraemer 1992, 174–76; Cotter 1994; Hutson 1996), including prophets (1 Cor. 11:5; cf. Acts 2:17–18; 21:9), deacons (Rom. 16:1–2; 1 Tim. 3:11), and teachers (Rom. 16:3, 6–7, 12), they were liable to be smeared with the broad brush of critics who associated liberated women with sexual promiscuity. Our letter advises on how to deflect such criticism.

Christian apologists in the second century described Christians as a distinct people who were not disrupting society but creating an alternative and more virtuous way of living in the world. One such apologetic work is the *Epistle to Diognetus* (see sidebar). Chapter 5 of this anonymous work brings together several themes found in 1 Tim. 2. Christians desire to be good citizens (*Diogn.* 5.4, 10), while they take a universalizing view of the world (*Diogn.* 5.5), claiming ultimate citizenship in heaven (*Diogn.* 5.9). Christians conform to local customs in dress and marriage, but only insofar as those customs are consistent with their own highest ideals (*Diogn.* 5.6–8). Christians are routinely misunderstood and persecuted, even though they repay good for evil (*Diogn.* 5.11–17; cf. Ign. *Eph.* 10; Ign. *Trall.* 8.2). All of 1 Tim. 2–3 is a precursor to the *Epistle to Diognetus* in offering advice for Christians about how to survive under threat of persecution.

Romans portrayed themselves as bringers of law and order into places of social unrest and civil discord, champions of concord and harmony. They also viewed households and associations as microcosms of the larger society, so that good order and decorum within such small groups reinforced proper order in the whole society, while disorder in the household portended social instability (Zamfir 2013, 60–159). Pastoral Paul approaches social harmony

---

Epistle to Diognetus 5.4–11, 15

"But while [Christians] live in both Greek and barbarian cities, as each one's lot was cast, and follow the local customs in dress and food and other aspects of life, at the same time they demonstrate the remarkable and admittedly unusual character of their own citizenship. They live in their own countries, but only as nonresidents; they participate in everything as citizens, and endure everything as foreigners. Every foreign country is their fatherland, and every fatherland is foreign. They marry like everyone else, and have children, but they do not expose their offspring. They share their food but not their wives. They are in the flesh, but they do not live according to the flesh. They live on earth, but their citizenship is in heaven. They obey the established laws; indeed in their private lives they transcend the laws. They love everyone, and by everyone they are persecuted. . . . They are cursed, yet they bless; they are insulted, yet they offer respect." (trans. Holmes 2006)

---

first from the perspective of the larger society (2:1–7), and then from that of the household (2:8–15). The emphasis on order or decorum helps thwart suspicions about Christians (Portefaix 2003, 152–58).

Finally, we should observe that the points in this section are presented as "exhortation" (*parakalō*, 2:1) and "wish" (*boulomai*, 2:8). Such expressions are consistent with the paraenetic nature of the letter. The specific advice deals with how men and women should behave in the context of Greco-Roman culture and ideology. But "lifting holy hands" (2:8) and the arguments from Genesis (2:12–15) indicate that this community is still close to its Jewish roots, and the underlying principles come from Jewish theology ("God is one," 2:5), shaped by a christological perspective (1:15; 2:5–6; 3:16; 6:13). Just as 2:1–7 incorporates survival tactics learned from diaspora Jews who preserved their right to maintain their religious identity by making public displays of loyalty to the government, so also 2:8–15 is akin to ancient rabbinic attitudes about how dress reflects religious identity (Cohn 2014). Pastoral Paul urges Christians to comport themselves in ways that reflect Christian ethical ideals as well as the best ideals of a larger society that was often misinformed, suspicious, or downright hostile to them (Wilken 1984). For a similar survival tactic, see 1 Pet. 2:11–12.

---

1 Timothy 2:8–10 in the Rhetorical Flow

Letter opening (1:1–2)

Proem: First charge to Timothy (1:3–20)

First set of directives concerning the church (2:1–3:13)

   Exhortation to pray for all people (2:1–7)

▶ Proper comportment for prayer (2:8–10)

Tracing the Train of Thought

2:8–10. Therefore I want the men in every place to pray, lifting reverent hands (2:8). "Therefore" marks a logical connection between the general exhortation to prayer for all people (2:1–7) and specific exhortations regarding the prayers of men and women (2:8–10). The conduct of Christian men and women deflects criticism and advances the evangelistic concern to be vehicles through whom knowledge of truth and salvation come to all people.

The word "men" in verse 8 is the specific term for males (*andres*). This verse probably reflects the emergence of early Christian communities from diaspora Judaism. In the synagogues, men always prayed, but women were exempt from certain commandments because menstrual uncleanness precluded their attendance at the place of prayer (Ilan 1996, 177–80). Of course women did pray (e.g., Acts 16:13). Verse 8, therefore, is not a directive that only men should pray. It reflects the reality that it was more typical to see men praying in a synagogue.

"In every place" refers to places where people worship God (cf. 1 Thess. 1:8; *Did.* 14). Jewish inscriptions refer to the place where a synagogue met as a "holy place" (*hagios topos*; L. White 1990, 178n39). "Every place" applies to all the house churches in a city (1 Cor. 1:2; Ferguson 1991).

"Lifting hands" was an OT posture of prayer (J. Willis 2001, 89–96), standing with palms turned upward as if to receive from God (1 Kings 8:22, 54; Pss. 28:2; 141:2; 143:6 [27:2; 140:2; 142:6 LXX]; Isa. 1:15) or with palms forward to pronounce praise or blessing (Lev. 9:22; Neh. 8:6; Ps. 63:4 [62:5 LXX]; Luke 24:50). That posture resembled a cross: "I extend my hands and approach my Lord, because the stretching out of my hands is his sign" (*Odes Sol.* 42.1, trans. J. H. Charlesworth, *OTP* 2:770). The posture appears in early Christian art (Torjesen 1998, 43–44). The classic Greek posture for supplication was grasping the knees of the person or idol being supplicated. The typical Roman gesture was to touch the altar of the deity being supplicated (Vergil, *Aen.* 4.219; cf. altar of the temple of the genius of Augustus [aka Temple of Vespasian] in Pompeii). This is not a mandate to adopt a particular posture for prayer; rather, it reflects how early Christians typically followed the Jewish custom of praying with hands raised (*1 Clem.* 29.1; Tertullian, *Apol.* 30). "Hands" is a metonym for the worshiper approaching God. "Reverent hands" represent the attitude one brings to worship (cf. "pure hands," Mal. 1:9–11 LXX), approaching God with integrity, having nothing to hide (Willis 2001, 98–102).

The intent of the advice is **without anger or argument** (2:8), a development from the exhortation to pray "that we may lead a tranquil and quiet life . . ." (2:2). In *Precepts of Statecraft*, Plutarch makes a similar move. Having argued that the greatest blessings to a state include "peace" and "concord," he says statesmanship begins with establishing concord and friendship among neighbors, removing strife and discord, settling quarrels, so the whole state may enjoy concord and quiet (*Praec. ger. rei publ.* 32 [824a–e]). Origen (*Cels.* 3.30) said the church (*ekklēsia*) of God was superior to the political assembly (*ekklēsia*) in any city to the extent that its leaders exhibited meekness and stability rather than indolence and sedition.

An early second-century letter from Egypt expresses a similar sentiment (POxy 3057 = *NewDocs* 6:§25). The writer Ammonius acknowledges a delivery of clothing and other items from his "brother" Apollonius and refers to a quarrel over a missing key. Ammonius prays that Apollonius and his "brothers" will live in concord (*homonoia*) and mutual affection and "be at peace and not give to others opportunities against you [pl.]." Scholars debate whether Ammonius and Apollonius were Christians, but either way, Ammonius appeals to the Roman civic virtue of concord and expresses concern about how an internal conflict might affect or be affected by outsiders. When Christians pray "without anger or argument," they demonstrate the internal harmony of the Christian community and model the "tranquility and quietness" that they pray will prevail in the wider society (2:2).

The verse can also be read as countercultural. Bruce J. Malina (1993, 34–37) describes how in ancient Mediterranean culture every social interaction could imply a competition (*agōn*) for honor (see comments at 6:11–12). No matter the points of dispute—doctrine, office, preferred seating, whatever—when men come to the assembly, they should check their competitive urges. The same point applies "likewise" to women. Among Greco-Roman elites, women's clothing, hairstyles, and jewelry often functioned in a competition for status (D'Ambra 2007, 111–28; Bartman 2001; Batten 2009). At the same time, the way a woman decorated her body was presumed to reflect her moral character (Huizenga 2011, 263). Our text focuses on the behavior of women with a concern to deflect outsider criticism (cf. 5:14). As with the men, the behavior of the women should be consistent with their moral values.

Although translators sometimes punctuate **likewise the women** (2:9) as the beginning of a new sentence or even a paragraph, in fact 2:8–10 is one sentence in Greek, with one verb, "I want," in verse 8 (cf. 3:2, 8, 11). The sentence begins, "Therefore I want . . ." (2:8), and the contents of that want are two infinitives, "to pray" (2:8) and "to adorn themselves" (2:9b). The question is what Pastoral Paul advises women to do "in orderly apparel" (2:9a). We must fill in the blank from context (Zamfir and Verheyden 2008).

The first option infers "to adorn themselves" from the subsequent clause, so that there are two items of advice: "I want (a) men to pray lifting reverent hands . . . , (b) **likewise the women in orderly apparel, with modesty and temperance to adorn themselves.**" This option has the beauty of simplicity and was generally preferred by early church fathers (e.g., Clement of Alexandria, *Paed.* 3.11.66; John Chrysostom, *Hom. 1 Tim.* 8; Gregory of Nyssa, *Hom. Cant.* 15.220).

The second option infers "to pray" from the previous clause, so that there are three items of advice: "I want (a) men to pray lifting reverent hands . . . , (b) **likewise the women** [to pray] **in orderly apparel,** (c) **with modesty and temperance to adorn themselves.**" Note that the second option requires us to keep intact the adverbial phrase "with modesty and temperance." Splitting that phrase would create a grammatical impossibility in Greek (Cukrowski 2006).

The second option makes better sense as a development from the previous paragraph, in that 2:1–7 deals with the contents of prayer, and then 2:8–10 deals with the behavior of believers when they pray. Also, the second option is consistent with Paul's advice about women's attire when they pray and prophesy (1 Cor. 11:5). Indeed, some see this passage as a more restrictive reinterpretation of 1 Cor. 11 (Merz 2004, 339–43; Zamfir and Verheyden 2008).

"Temperance" (*sōphrosynē*, 2:9, 15) was one of the four cardinal virtues in classical antiquity, an expression of the Greek ideal of moderation. Plato compared "*sōphrosynē* in the soul with *kosmos* or *taxis* (order, arrangement) in the physical universe" (*Gorgias* 506–8; North 1966, 162). Xenophon compared a woman wearing makeup with a man who cooks his account books so he will appear richer than he really is. He preferred to see a woman's natural beauty (Xenophon, *Oec.* 10.1–13). The concepts of order and temperance were so closely associated that the expression "decent and respectable" (*kosmios kai sōphrōn*) was a Hellenistic commonplace (North 1966, 243). In the Roman period, *sōphrosynē* expressed frugality, temperance, and chastity (North 1966, 258–311). Stoic philosophers treated orderliness (*eutaxia*) and decorum (*kosmiotēs*) as subdivisions of temperance (*sōphrosynē*; Malherbe 2007, 54).

The logic of the paragraph depends in part on a wordplay that is difficult to translate into English. The Greek word *kosmos* (Eng. "cosmos") is often translated "world," or "creation," but the basic idea is "order" (H. Sasse, *TDNT* 3:867–98), as opposed to chaos. Greeks and Romans thought a properly "ordered" society or household or individual was in harmony with the proper "order" of the world, meaning the *kosmos*. Our passage turns on a pun in verse 9, between the "orderly/decorous" (*kosmios*) apparel of women and the verb "adorn/decorate" (*kosmeō*), with its overtones of arranging in proper "order/decorum."

The Pythagorean letter of Melissa to Cleareta illustrates the idea. It was preserved on a third-century papyrus from Roman Egypt, a copy of a letter from an unknown date, probably pseudonymous, composed as early as the third century BCE (Pomeroy 2013, 102). It is one of five similar letters, often found together in manuscripts, that collectively provide an epistolary handbook for philosophical women (Huizenga 2013, 25–27; Pomeroy 2013, 99–116). Pseudo-Melissa's advice is similar to that in 1 Tim. 2:9–10 (cf. comments at Titus 2:4). The translation provided here (see sidebar) highlights the themes of temperance, decorum, and orderliness that are central to our passage.

A Woman of Decorum

"Melissa to Cleareta, greetings.

"It appears to me that on your own accord you have most good attributes. For your earnest wish to hear about a wife's decorum [eukosmia] offers a good hope that you are going to grow old in accordance with virtue. So, then, the temperate [sōphrōn] and married woman must belong to her lawful husband, adorned with quietness [hēsychia], dressed in clothing that is whitened, clean and simple, but not very expensive [polytelē] or excessive. For she ought to avoid garments of purple cloth, and those that are shot through with purple and gold, since that sort is useful for the courtesans [hetairai] in their hunting of many men. But the decor [kosmos] proper to the woman who is well pleasing to only one man, her own, is her character and not her clothing. For the married woman must appear fair of form to her own husband, but not to neighbors.

"You should have a blush as a sign of modesty on your face instead of rouge, and goodness and the height of decorum [kosmiotēs] and temperance [sōphrosynē] instead of gold and emeralds; for the temperate [sōphrōn] woman should be enthusiastic not for the expense [polyteleia] of clothing and of the body but for the management [oikonomia] and preservation [sōtēria] of her household. And she should please her own husband by completing his desires, since the wishes of her husband ought to be an unwritten law to the woman of decorum [kosmiai gynaiki], according to which she must live. And she must consider that, along with herself, her orderly behavior [eutaxia] has been offered as her best and greatest dowry. She must trust in the beauty and wealth of her soul rather than that of her looks and possessions; for jealousy and sickness take away from the latter, but the former are present in good decorum [eukosmia] even to the point of death." (trans. Huizenga 2013, 59–61 modified; cf. Huizenga 2010, 387; Malherbe 1986, 83; *NewDocs* 6:§2)

Pseudo-Melissa advocates a wife's subordination to her husband as a matter of domestic order, and she associates expensive clothing and makeup with illicit sexuality (cf. Plutarch, *Quaest. conv.* 6.7 [693]).

Associations between adornment and sexuality appear also in ancient Jewish culture (Esther 2:9, 12; Jdt. 10:3–4; Philo, *Virt.* 34–40; *Sacr.* 21). Although the rabbis did not question women's adornments except on the Sabbath (*m. Shabb.* 6), they dealt with an adulterous woman by challenging the modesty of her attire (*m. Sotah* 1.5–7; *t. Sotah* 3.1–5; Cohn 2014, 29–32). By contrast, a Jewish funerary monument from Rome describes a woman named Regina in Latin verse, celebrating her "piety" (*pietas*), "chaste life" (*vita pudica*), and attention to her marriage (*JIWE* 2:103 = *CIJ* 1:476; Chester 2013, 115, 128). The inscription cites Regina's "observance of law," a delightfully ambiguous phrase that would appeal equally but with different connotations to any Jews or gentiles who happened to read it. Such inscriptions portraying members of their community as exemplary citizens helped to deflect prejudice against the Jews.

Such prejudice accrued also to Christians, whose weekly communal meals, including the Lord's Supper, were out of sync with prevailing dining etiquette. In traditional Greco-Roman society, men dined together, joined perhaps by courtesans but not decent women. Although in Roman society, the ideology of the "New Woman" permitted wives to dine with their husbands, such liberated women could attract criticism regarding their morality (Corley 1993, 24–75). So it is not surprising to hear insinuations of Christian orgies from pagan critics (Minucius Felix 8.4–12.5; Corley 1993, 75–79). In their attire it was essential that Christian women represent the ideals of modesty and decorum.

"Clothing of decorum" entails **not with braids and gold or pearls or expensive garments** (2:9; cf. 5:6; 1 Pet. 3:3–4). Statuary, paintings, and literature portrayed respectable women wearing all these items as markers of social status, though not without risk of censure (Zamfir 2013, 366–84; Batten 2009). Ostentatious displays of wealth could be criticized as "foreign" (Upson-Saia 2011, 15–17), as amorous allurements (Epictetus, *Ench.* 40; Cyprian, *Hab. virg.* 12; Martial, *Epigram* 9.37), or as threats to social order (Juvenal, *Satire* 6.457–73; Tacitus, *Annals* 3.52–54; Plutarch *Conj. praec.* 30 [142c]; Athenaeus, *Deipn.* 12.518–44; Wallace-Hadrill 2008, 315–55). Pearls were a mark of oriental luxury (Rev. 17:4; 18:12; Pliny the Elder, *Nat.* 9.54–59; 37.14–17; Clement of Alexandria, *Paed.* 2.13; Tertullian, *Cult. fem.* 1.6; Batten 2014), and Roman law restricted pearls to women who had borne at least three children or were at least forty-five years old (Batten 2014, 247–48). Pliny the Elder, a powerful man with a lavish lifestyle, decried displays of luxury among lower classes and pined for the good old days, when only men of equestrian rank wore gold rings (*Nat.* 33.7–8). In a highly class-conscious society, when immigrants, freedmen, or slaves donned dress associated with high social status, they upset elite sensibilities (Wallace-Hadrill 2008, 352).

The antithesis of luxury was traditional modesty, as represented in this anecdote:

> The Sicilian despot [Dionysius] sent clothing and jewelry of the costly kind to the daughters of [the Spartan general] Lysander; but Lysander would not accept them, saying, "These adornments will disgrace my daughters far more than they will adorn them." . . . It is not gold or precious stones or scarlet that makes her such, but whatever invests her with that something which betokens dignity, good behavior, and modesty. (Plutarch, *Conj. praec.* 26 [141d–e], trans. Babbitt, LCL; cf. Seneca, *Helv.* 16.3–4)

Plutarch's anecdote squares nicely with our text: **but with good deeds, which is fitting for women who profess piety toward God** (2:10). "Good deeds" are acts of charity (Acts 9:36, 39), such as would characterize a "real widow" (1 Tim. 5:10).

The instruction in 2:9–10 aims at people of relatively high status (cf. Acts 17:4, 12). Women typically grew hair long but wore it tied up, "restrained" as a marker of sexual restraint (Huizenga 2011, 266). Elaborate braids required leisure time and stylists and so advertised status (Thompson 1988, 106–13; Stephens 2008; Bartman 2001), as did jewelry (Petronius, *Satyricon* 67) and expensive clothing (Huizenga 2011, 267). For a woman of decorum our text does not identify specific clothing but emphasizes the decorations of "modesty and temperance" and "good deeds" (2:9–10), implying marital chastity and charity (cf. Xenophon, *Oec.* 7.43; 10.2–13; ps.-Crates, *Ep.* 9 to Mnasos [Malherbe 1977, 60–61]).

Romans alternated between two competing attitudes toward women's dress. Fancy clothing and adornments could represent "feminine excess that was leading Rome into a state of moral decline," or they could advertise "the wealth and prestige of Rome's leading families, according honor especially to their male relatives" (Upson-Saia 2011, 19; cf. Livy, *Ab urbe* 34.1–8).

Two portraits illustrate the alternatives, both carefully composed. A Roman-Egyptian mummy portrait from the early second century shows a woman whose attire matches 1 Tim. 2:9. We do not know whether she is wearing her best pearls, sentimental favorite pearls, her only pearls, borrowed pearls,

Figure 2. Flaunting wealth. This mummy portrait of a woman (100 CE) is attributed to the Isidora Master (Romano-Egyptian, active 100–125).

Figure 3. Flaunting virtue. This is a sculpture of Livia Drusilla, wife of Emperor Augustus. Museo Arqueológico Nacional in Madrid.

or pearls imagined by the artist. All that remain of her identity are the name Isidora on the shoulder of the mummy wrappings and this portrait, in which elaborately braided hair with gold crown, a gold necklace set with emeralds and amethyst, pearl earrings, and lavender clothing project wealth and status. By contrast, a statue of Livia from Spain projects a different image. As the wife of Augustus, Livia was enormously wealthy and powerful, but the statue projects none of that. The artist sculpted an image of unadorned virtue—a Roman wife with simple hairstyle, no jewels, and simple clothing with head veiled to project modesty and temperance.

Respectable Roman women appeared in public flaunting wealth or flaunting virtue. Given those choices, Pastoral Paul urged that Christian values were in line with the Roman rhetoric of modesty but not the Roman practice of status competition. Far from capitulating to Roman values, this argument for the apologetic value of clothing anticipates Diognetus (*Diogn.* 5.4). We can plot a trajectory from 1 Tim. 2 through the third and fourth centuries, as Christians developed clothing traditions that demonstrated Christian values to the wider society (Upson-Saia 2011, 33–58).

There is nothing inherently sinful about braids or gold. Christians should behave in ways that reflect modesty and temperance where they live. This is all the more true where Christianity is not well known or lacking secure legal status. But what hairstyle, jewelry, or clothing constitutes "decorum" or "extravagance" varies, from culture to culture and from century to century. We should not expect Christians in all times and places to conform to the societal norms of the early Roman Empire, but Christians should consider how their attire reflects Christian values.

1 Timothy 2:11–3:1a

Digression on Women Teaching

Introductory Matters

This digression is closely linked to what precedes, and readers should take into account the "Introductory Matters" for 1 Tim. 2:8–10. Scholars debate nearly every word and phrase in this battleground passage. The opposing camps are known as "patriarchalist" and "feminist" or as "complementarian" and "egalitarian." Male church leaders (patriarchs) have traditionally used these verses to establish a "stained-glass ceiling" in the church—a level above which women are not permitted to rise. They quibble about how relatively high or low that ceiling should be, but they insist that God gave different and complementary roles to men and women. By contrast, Christian feminists or egalitarians insist that both male and female are created in the image of God and that God calls and gifts both men and women for all sorts of ministries and leadership. One way to think theologically about the debate is to consider the difference between the present age (creation) and the age to come (new creation). Such thinking is thoroughly Pauline:

	Creation / Present Age	New Creation / Age to Come
Romans 5	Adam	Christ
Romans 5–7	tyranny of sin/death	reign of grace/righteousness
Romans 8	flesh	Spirit
1 Corinthians 15:20–28	Adam / reign of death	Christ / reign of God
Galatians	"present evil age" (1:4)	"new creation" (6:15)

In what follows, I shall attempt to represent the text as literally as possible and the debate fairly, but it will be clear that I view social rules as human constructions that are profoundly affected by the fallenness of the present age, and I look toward God's glorious future in the age to come as the vision that should orient Christians' behavior in the present age. The traditional complementarian arguments are well known and widely available for those who wish to see more on the other side (Moo 2006 and Schreiner 2005 are representative).

1 Timothy 2:11–3:1a in the Rhetorical Flow

Letter opening (1:1–2)

Proem: First charge to Timothy (1:3–20)

First set of directives concerning the church (2:1–3:13)

Exhortation to pray for all people (2:1–7)

Proper comportment for prayer (2:8–10)

▶ Digression on women teaching (2:11–3:1a)

Tracing the Train of Thought

2:11–12. Let a woman learn in quietness, in full subordination; but I do not permit a woman to teach or presume authority over a man, but to be in quietness (2:11–12). These are the key verses in this battleground text, so we must proceed with caution. A compelling reading should make sense of the concern about decorum (2:8–10) and the theological warrants (2:13–15).

To begin, the text assumes that it is appropriate for women to learn. Though a few in antiquity deplored education for women (Juvenal, *Satires* 6.434–56; *m. Sotah* 3.4), there was a philosophical tradition in favor of it (Huizenga 2013, 1–17; Estep 2011). Plato argued that people should be trained for leadership on the basis of ability, not sex (*Republic* 451e, 453e–56a, though elsewhere he takes more patriarchal views). Similar views held among Cynics (ps.-Crates, *Ep.* 28–33; Malherbe 1977, 78–79) and Pythagoreans (Iamblichus, *VP* 267; Huizenga 2013, 107–8). Even those who maintained that men and women belonged to separate spheres still argued that educated women were better prepared to train children and manage the household (Musonius Rufus, *Fragments* 3, 4; Plutarch, *Conj. praec.* 48 [145b–d]; Pliny the Younger, *Ep.* 4.19; Quintilian, *Institutes* 1.1.6–7). This passage restricts women from teaching, not from learning.

The restriction on women teaching is surprising in light of the evidence that Paul named women "coworkers" on his teams (Hutson 1996; Cotter 1994), including Prisca (2 Tim. 4:19; Rom. 16:3). It is also surprising in that the OT refers to women prophets (Exod. 15:20–21; Judg. 4:4; 2 Kings 22:14//2 Chron. 34:22; Isa. 8:3; Joel 2:27–29) and a judge (Judg. 4–5), while the NT refers to women teachers (Acts 18:26), prophets (Luke 1:41–43; 2:36–38; Acts 2:17–18; 21:8–9; 1 Cor. 11:5), and an apostle (Rom. 16:7; Belleville 2005a; Eisen 2000, 47–49; Epp 2005; Lampe 2003, 165n39, 177–78). Female false prophets in the Bible are censured not for their sex but for their teaching (Neh. 6:14; Ezek.

13:17–23; Rev. 2:20–23). Early Christian literature and inscriptions attest to women evangelists (*Acts of Paul* 3), prophets (*1 Clem.* 12.8; Eisen 2000, 63–87), apostles (Eisen 2000, 49–52), elders (*Acts of Philip* 1.12.8–9 [Codex Xenophontos]; Eisen 2000, 116–42; Madigan and Osiek 2005, 163–202), and bishops (Eisen 2000, 199–216).

The question is why Pastoral Paul restricts women teaching. One possibility is that he is addressing a specific local problem in first-century Ephesus. Some argue that the English "I do not permit" conveys a false sense of universal application, whereas the Greek should be rendered, "I am not permitting"—that is, in this specific situation (Payne 2009, 320–25). Alan Padgett describes that situation as involving wealthy women under the influence of false teachers who preyed on them for money (2 Tim. 3:2–7; Titus 1:11). He argues that these women were unduly influential in spreading the false doctrine (Padgett 1987; cf. Estep 2011; Payne 2009, 299–304). On this reading, Pastoral Paul directs those women to learn "in full subordination" to the healthy doctrine. Alternatively, Gary G. Hoag (2015) argues that Pastoral Paul is warning wealthy Ephesian women to stop adorning themselves in imitation of Artemis. Some such reconstruction is necessary if one assumes that this is a real letter addressing a specific situation in Ephesus.

Another possibility is to read this restriction within the broader social context of the first century. The poet Horace blamed social disorder and instability on the demise of traditional Roman religion and the moral laxity of women. Horace's *Ode* 3.6 opens with a reference to the civil wars, for which he says the Romans will continue to pay "till you've restored the temples, and the tumbling shrines of all the gods." A few lines later he expounds on the moral failures of women: "Our age, fertile in its wickedness, has first / defiled the marriage bed, our offspring, and homes / disaster's stream has flowed from this source / through the people and the fatherland" (trans. Kline 2003). In such terms imperial propaganda addressed the social uncertainties of the time. Politically, emperors styled themselves as the "saviors" of countries they conquered, champions of order, justice, and concord. Domestically, new laws promoted marriage and legitimate children, and public discourse celebrated piety and marital fidelity.

In this context, 1 Tim. 2 offers advice about how Christians could deflect suspicion by upholding their own ethical values, especially where they coincided with the stated values of the dominant culture. Even though Christians denied the gods of the empire, their lives demonstrated concord and decorum.

"Quietness" (*hēsychia*) brackets this directive. The noun *hēsychia* has been translated "silence" (KJV), which gives the false impression that this verse is saying the same thing as 1 Cor. 14:34 ("let them be silent," *sigatōsan*). But "quietness" stems from the same root as the adjective "quiet" (*hēsychios*) in 2:2, where it corresponds to "peaceable." Women should live untroubled by others and not causing trouble (cf. 1 Pet. 3:4). If *hēsychia* was appropriate for a woman of decorum when her husband cheated on her (ps.-Theano, *Nik.* 2.13;

Huizenga 2013, 160–61; cf. 1 Pet. 3:1), how much more appropriate should it be in the context of study?

The center of the directive is "not to teach [*didaskein*] or have authority over [*authentein*] . . ." Reading this as two prohibitions makes both seem absolute. In practice, this text has blocked women from being ordained ministers, whether or not they were accepted as lay exhorters and teachers, and from being ordained elders or bishops, whether or not they were ordained deacons or teachers. In other words, this verse is the slender column that supports the entire stained-glass ceiling above which women are not allowed to rise in many churches.

It seems preferable to read 2:12 as one prohibition expressed in *hendiadys*, a literary figure communicating a single idea using two related expressions, usually joined by "and" or "nor" (BDF §442[16]; Rom. 3:10; 9:16; 1 Cor. 2:6; 5:1; 11:16; Gal. 1:16–17; Josephus, *Ant.* 7.127; Payne 2009, 337–53; Osburn 2001, 223). In Pauline usage, the second expression in a hendiadys often makes the first more specific: "Charge certain ones not to teach otherwise *nor* to give attention to myths and endless genealogies" (1 Tim. 1:4).

But if "to presume authority" (*authentein*) specifies the manner in which a woman is "not to teach," then much depends on the meaning of *authentein*. This verb occurs only here in the NT, so its precise meaning is debatable (Baldwin 2005; Osburn 1982). The generic sense, "to govern, control" (Origen, *Frag. 1 Cor.* 74; Knight 1992, 141–42), was a post-Pauline usage (Payne 2009, 373–80). The pejorative translation, "to dominate or domineer," is more plausible (Belleville 2005b, 216; Osburn 2001, 224). Philip B. Payne (2009, 361–97) translates this as "assume authority" for an action that has not been delegated (cf. Baldwin 2005, 47–48, usages 3 and 3b). This usage is attested in a first-century BCE letter from Egypt, in which a man takes it upon himself to order another's slave to pay a ferryboat fee (BGU 1208.38; Payne 2009, 365–70, with other examples, 385–94). In our passage, "I do not permit a woman to teach on her own authority." That is, a woman should learn "in full subordination" (2:11) and teach in subordination to the ordained leadership of the church (Padgett 1987, 24).

Andreas J. Köstenberger (2005) contests this reading, arguing that the two terms in a hendiadys must both be positive, "teach . . . have authority," or both negative, "teach [error] . . . domineer." And because "to teach" is a positive value in this context, he argues that *authentein* must also be positive, "to have authority." But Payne (2009, 356–59) shows that at least seven of Köstenberger's examples are cases in which the conjunction "nor" (*oude*) joins a positive and a negative term (e.g., 2 Cor. 7:12; Sir. 18:6 LXX). A mixed positive-negative translation would be, "to teach in a domineering way" (Belleville 2005b; Osburn 2001) or better, "to teach on one's own authority" (Payne 2009). Our passage restricts women, but interpreters have applied it more severely than Pastoral Paul intended.

Another issue is whether 2:12 restricts a woman in relation to any man or only her husband. Instead of the specific nouns "husband" (*gametēs*) and "wife" (*gametē*), Pastoral Paul uses the generic "man" (*anēr*) and "woman" (*gynē*), which often have the sense "husband/wife," depending on context. A severe reading requiring every woman to "be in subordination" to every man does not fit the first-century cultural context. Jewish women could be leaders in synagogues (Brooten 1982; Kraemer 1985; 1992, 117–27; van der Horst 1988, 198–99). Greco-Roman cities included affluent women who were influential within the power structures of the day (Winter 2003, 173–211), such as Mamia and Eumachia of Pompeii (A. Cooley and M. Cooley 2004, 96–101), Junia Theodora of Corinth (Kearsley 1999, 191–98; Winter 2003, 183–93, 205–10; Friesen 2014), Claudia Metrodora of Chios in Asia (Kearsley 1999, 198–201), and Julia Severa of Acmonia in Phrygia (*AGRW* §145; Schürer 1986, 30–32; Trebilco 1991, 58–59; Kahl 2010, 240–41). Coins and inscriptions indicate that women held civic offices and priesthoods in Ephesus in the first and second centuries (Friesen 1999; Baugh 2005, 28–33). In short, "It is simply not reasonable to claim that women's life was limited to the home" (Crook 2009, 607; cf. Zamfir 2013, 289–337; MacMullen 1980). A woman's social prominence did not necessarily violate either a Jewish or a Greco-Roman sense of decorum.

Even if ancient standards of decorum did not require every woman to be in subordination to every man, there remained a presumption that each woman would be under some specific man. A Roman woman traditionally had a male legal guardian (Cicero, *Mur.* 27), normally her father or husband. The old Roman king Numa legislated that women were not to speak in public unless their husbands were with them (Plutarch, *Comp. Lyc. Num.* 3.5; cf. *Conj. praec.* 31 [142d]). But in the early empire, the most common marriages were "without hand" (Lat. *sine manu*), which meant a woman's husband did not become her *paterfamilias*. She remained under her father's authority, and if she bore at least three children, she could win the legal right to be free from the oversight of a man (Gaius, *Institutes* 1.194; *NewDocs* 4:§24, "Aurelia Tapammon," pp. 100–103; Rawson 1986, 18–20).

Nevertheless, regardless of her legal status, a woman usually needed the social protection of some man. That was typically her husband, though it could be another male relative (e.g., grandson, POxy 261; foster-father, *NewDocs* 4:§24) or guardian. Similar customs pertained with variations in different provinces (Ng 2008). Origen understood that ". . . let them ask their men at home . . ." (1 Cor. 14:35) did not refer only to the "husbands" of married women, because even an unmarried virgin or a widow should defer to some close male family member (Origen, *Frag. 1 Cor.* 74).

The point of 2:11–12 is that a woman should maintain decorum by learning "in full subordination" to the ordained leaders of the church, and she should not "presume authority" to teach in the assembly without approval of church leaders and whatever man was legally responsible for her. Such deference demonstrated "modesty and temperance" (2:9) as much as clothing. A woman who flouted those conventions could bring criticism on herself and the church.

2:13–15. In support of the directive, our text offers two arguments based on traditional Jewish readings of Genesis. The first supporting argument, **for Adam was formed first, then Eve** (2:13), derives from Gen. 2, as is clear from the emphasis on the sequence of creation, the verb "formed" (*eplasthē*; cf. Gen. 2:15, 19 LXX), and the name "Adam" (Gen. 2:15–16; the LXX translates Heb. *'adam* into the Gk. *anthrōpos* ["human"] in 2:15 but treats it as a proper name "Adam" in 2:16). The argument from sequence of creation assumes that priority implies superiority (Zamfir 2013, 235–39, numerous examples). But that logical fallacy flies in the face of empirical evidence and biblical theology (Gen. 25:23; 1 Sam. 16:6–13). Paul himself, having mounted that argument in 1 Cor. 11:8–10, rejected it as not valid "in the Lord" (1 Cor. 11:11–12). But some ancient rabbis used it to justify the social inequality of women to men on the basis of Eve's "natural" inferiority to Adam (Baskin 2002, 44–62), and some early Christians followed their lead.

The second supporting argument—**Adam was not deceived; but the woman, having been thoroughly deceived, fell into transgression** (2:14)—derives from Gen. 3, as is clear from the reference to "the woman" and the verb "deceived" (*apataō*). But our text reinterprets Genesis by exonerating Adam as "not deceived" and amplifying the deception of the woman as "thoroughly deceived" (*exapataō*). This use of Gen. 3 to blame the woman is another Jewish tradition: "From a woman sin had its beginning, and because of her we all die" (Sir. 25:24 NRSV). The Jewish reading of Gen. 3 as the seduction of Eve (4 Macc. 18:6–8; Philo, *QG* 1.33; 1.47, *Alleg. Interp.* 3.59–61; *Apoc. Mos.* 22; 2 *En.* 31; Hanson 1968, 65–77; Bassler 1988) was also familiar to Paul (2 Cor. 11:3, 14).

But Paul knew another traditional way to read Gen. 3, emphasizing Adam as the first transgressor with no mention of Eve (Rom. 5:14–19; 1 Cor. 15:21–22; cf. 4 *Ezra* 3.21; 2 *Bar.* 54.15). Furthermore, Jewish tradition offered a third way to read Gen. 3, blaming it all on the devil (Wis. 2:23–24; cf. Josephus, *Ant.* 1.40–43). So if blaming Eve is not the only traditional Jewish reading of Gen. 3, and not the only Pauline reading of it, why is it preferred in this letter?

This reading fits the needs of the present argument. Just as reading Adam as the first transgressor served Paul's Adam-Christ typology (Rom. 5 and 1 Cor. 15), so here reading "the woman . . . thoroughly deceived" serves to press an ethical point within a patriarchal social order. In other words, Pastoral Paul does not read Gen. 2–3 and deduce that a woman should "not teach or presume authority over a man." Rather, he reads the cultural context of his time and argues that Christians should present themselves as nonthreatening. His two arguments from Gen. 2–3 offer a nominally biblical rationale for his directive, much as Gen. 2 provided a nominally biblical rationale for women to cover their heads while praying or prophesying (1 Cor. 11:8–9).

The two arguments from Genesis lead to an aside, **but she will be saved through childbearing, if they remain in faith and love and holiness with temperance** (2:15; the following summarizes Hutson 2014). This is one of the most puzzling verses in the NT in terms of grammar (Who is "she," and who are "they"?) and theology (How could "saved through childbearing" square with Paul's "saved by grace"?). Efforts to untie the knot have led to three lines of interpretation.

The first line of interpretation reads the verse as figurative. The most popular figurative interpretation reads "the woman" as a type for Mary and takes the Greek phrase "through *the* childbirth" as an allusion to the birth of Jesus (Payne 2009, 417–41; Knight 1992, 215; Witherington 2006, 229–30). Some patristic texts do refer to an Eve-Mary typology (Ign. *Eph.* 18–19; Justin, *Dial.* 100; Tertullian, *Carn. Chr.* 17; and Irenaeus, *Haer.* 3.22; 5.19); but they do not tie that typology to 1 Tim. 2:15, so the patristic support for this interpretation is illusory. Alternatively, focusing on the plural pronoun "they," Kenneth L. Waters Sr. suggests that the four virtues are the woman's figurative children, citing virtues as Noah's "offspring" in Philo (*Deus* 117–18; *Gig.* 5; Waters 2004). Waters has not found much support, but his reading could be compatible with the second or third lines of interpretation.

The second line of interpretation reads "childbirth" and the virtues as endorsements of the traditional, domestic ideals associated with women (John Chrysostom, *Hom. 1 Tim.* 9; Huizenga 2013, 355–56; Zamfir 2013, 260–64). Since Greeks and Romans viewed procreation as the purpose of marriage (Lacey 1968, 15–16; Rawson 1986, 8–12; Zamfir 2013, 264–77), some argue that 2:15 and 5:14 together rebut those who forbid marriage (4:3). Some suggest that "they" (2:15b) are husband and wife, both of whom should manifest Christian virtues (Bird 1940, 262). More commonly, however, interpreters take "they" as a reference to the children, whose virtues are evidence that a woman was a good mother (John Chrysostom, *Hom. 1 Tim.* 9; Lois and Eunice in 2 Tim. 1:5). The Pythagorean ps.-Phintys said, "The best adornment [*kosmos*] and foremost glory of a free woman is that her temperance [*sōphrosynē*] toward her husband is testified to through her children, if they bear the image of the likeness of the father who begot them" (Stobaeus, *Florilegium* 4.23.61a [591.11–12], trans. Huizenga 2013, 178). Conversely, bad children are evidence of bad mothering (ps.-Theano, *Eu.*; Huizenga 2013, 319–20; see comments at 1 Tim. 2:9 and Titus 2:4).

But this second line of interpretation stumbles on the meaning of "saved." It is true that in the PE "save" normally refers to eschatological salvation (1 Tim. 1:15; 2:4; 2 Tim. 1:9; 4:18; Titus 3:5). And it is also true that the idiom "to be saved through x" (*sōthēnai dia* + gen.) often refers to the means of salvation (Titus 3:5; 1 Cor. 1:21; cf. 1 Cor. 15:2; Eph. 2:5), as also in classical, Jewish, and early Christian texts (Aristotle, *Pol.* 1313b.30; 1330b.36; 2 Kings [4 Kingdoms] 14:27 LXX; Philo, *Cher.* 130.4; *Abr.* 145.5; Josephus, *Ant.* 5.26; *Acts of Paul* frag. 1.16; *Acts of John* 22.18). Yet, to imagine that a woman will be saved to eternal life by means of bearing children requires tortuous logic indeed. Commenting on this passage, John Calvin illustrates the difficulty as he argues that, although women are "the whole ruin of the human race," there is "the hope of salvation offered them" who accept "servitude to their husbands" and endure "the many severe troubles that have to be borne both in bearing children and in bringing them up" (Smail 1964, 218–19). Apart from the chauvinism, this seems awfully like justification by works.

The third line of interpretation takes the verb "save" in its nontheological sense of "preserve safe," "rescue," or "heal," a usage also attested in the PE and elsewhere in the NT (see comments at 4:16). Further, the idiom "to be saved through x" (*sōthēnai dia* + gen.) could describe the ordeal through which one was safely delivered (1 Cor. 3:15, "brought safely through fire"; Xenophon, *Anab.* 5.5.8, an army "through many dreadful troubles . . . came safely"; cf. the verb *diasōzō* in Acts 27:44; 28:1, 4; 1 Pet. 3:20). This is a minority reading (Barrett 1963, 56–57; Keener 1992, 118–20; Ames and Miller 2011; Hutson 2014), but it makes sense as a continuation from 2:14, reflecting on Gen. 3, in which Eve's punishments include pain in childbirth (Gen. 3:16; cf. Josephus, *Ant.* 1.49).

According to rabbinic tradition, Eve's sin led to death in childbirth for women who did not observe specific commandments: "For three transgressions do women die in childbirth: for heedlessness of the laws of the menstruant, the Dough-offering, and the lighting of the [Sabbath] lamp" (*m. Shabb.* 2.6, trans. Danby 1933, 102). This text refers to "separation," abstaining from sex during the menstrual period (Lev. 15:19–24); "dough offering," the requirement that anyone who makes dough must offer a small portion "to the Lord" (Num. 15:17–21, 31); and "lighting the lamp" before sundown on Friday (Exod. 35:3). Torah neither identifies these commandments as pertaining exclusively to women nor requires a death penalty for violation. But rabbinic tradition did bind them on women and associated them with Eve's transgression and with death in childbirth (*y. Shabb.* 2.6.1–2; cf. *Gen. Rab.* 17.8; *t. Shabb.* 2.10; *b. Shabb.* 2.6 [31B–32A]). The logic is similar to that of explaining a tragedy as punishment for sin. Even though there is no simple correlation between sin and personal tragedy, the pious tend to think God will protect virtuous people from harm.

Our verse makes sense in the context of rabbinic discourse about death in childbirth. The switch from singular "she" to plural "they" is an immaterial quirk of the author's style (2:11–12; Titus 1:5–6). The verse is an aside on the experience of women in light of the story of Eve, underscoring the Christian virtues of "faith, love, and holiness." The fourth virtue is set apart, "with temperance." Both holiness and temperance imply sexual fidelity, holiness being the preferred Jewish term and temperance (*sōphrosynē*) the quintessentially feminine virtue in Greco-Roman society (Malherbe 2007; Huizenga 2010; 2013, 169–220, 334–37; Pomeroy 1984, 70; Kent 1966, no. 128; Meritt 1931, no. 86). "Temperance" also connects this aside back to the main argument (2:9). This verse suggests that Christian women should take virtuous behavior with deadly seriousness, as an important witness to the non-Christian world.

Before we use 1 Tim. 2:11–12 to silence or subordinate women, we have a burden to explain the logic of 2:13–15. It is not enough to say, "Paul said so in 1 Tim. 2:11–12." That same Paul gave his reasons in 2:13–15. If those reasons seem murky, we should be wary of wielding 1 Tim. 2:11–12 against women who say God has called them to serve, and we should consider other NT references to women.

3:1a. Trustworthy is the saying (3:1a). Keeping in mind that chapter and verse divisions were added in the Middle Ages and are often arbitrary (Handy 1997, 41–43), we might ask whether the chapter division makes sense here. Elsewhere the expression "trustworthy saying" highlights either what precedes (cf. 4:9) or what follows (cf. 1:15). Does it highlight the preceding statement about salvation (John Chrysostom, *Hom.* 9 on 1 Tim. 2:11–15; footnotes in CEV, CSB, NRSV) or the subsequent statement about desire for oversight? I take it with 2:15, but either way the comment seems awkwardly placed. The decision is not theologically significant, only a matter of emphasis.

Theological Issues

Under "Doctrines and Precepts" in the general introduction, we saw the ancient philosophical distinction between doctrines and precepts. The fundamental Christian doctrines presumed in 2:5–6 include monotheism and Christ as mediator and ransom. In 2:1–7, Pastoral Paul sets forth the universalizing implications of monotheism. In 2:8–3:1a, he develops precepts about decorum that have both apologetic and missional functions: decorum deflects criticism and creates space for the community to influence a larger society that is suspicious of new, foreign religions. But precepts that make sense in one social context do not necessarily make sense in every social context (Calvin, *Institutes* 4.10.27–31; Douglass 2009, 141–43). Most modern Christians would have trouble following the advice of Clement of Alexandria that a Christian woman "of decorum" (*kosmiōs*) should wear a burka, "completely covered" (*Paed.* 3.11.79.4 [*ANF* 2:290]; cf. 2.11–13; Dio Chrysostom, *Or.* 33.48). Even if Clement's idea of decorum made sense in Egypt in the second century, it does not work in every cultural context. A good minister must understand the fundamental doctrines and apply them in precepts appropriate to new contexts.

We should set aside two extreme positions. One extreme, patriarchalism, emphasizes fathers as rulers. Patriarchalists would use this text to perpetuate presumptions of privilege in all areas of society. Elisabeth Schüssler Fiorenza coined the word "kyriarchalism" (from Gk. *kyrios*, "lord," and *archein*, "to rule") to emphasize the interconnectedness of all forms of "lordship" or domination (Schüssler Fiorenza 2014, 9–14). Attitudes regarding male domination intersect with attitudes about slavery, tyranny, racism, colonialism, and any other claim that some categories of people have a God-given right to dominate other categories. Read superficially, the Bible often becomes a tool of oppression rather than of liberation and redemption. Against such claims, we must consider how any given passage relates to the theological center of the biblical narrative about the sovereignty of God as understood through the death and resurrection of Jesus.

At the other extreme, secular feminism would dismiss this passage as hopelessly mired in misogynistic, patriarchalist ideology, an antique text written by men for men and irrelevant for modern societies. Kathryn Greene-McCreight (2000) has criticized some feminist theologians who replace the biblical narrative with a narrative drawn from secular theory. If secular feminism is willing to throw out the baby with the bathwater, fundamentalist patriarchalism continues to bathe each new generation in centuries-old bathwater. Neither approach is likely to result in theologically healthy children.

For most Christians the debate is between these extremes, entailing two moderate positions, the so-called "complementarian" and "egalitarian" views. (On the four positions and the debate between the two middle positions, Osburn 2001; critique by Hutson 2005a). These two views take the Bible seriously as foundational for Christian faith and practice and try to apply it in ways that make room for changing social *mores*.

Complementarians reject abuse of women and are open to female leadership in business, education, government, medicine, and so forth, but they argue that the Bible assigns different and complementary roles to men and women. We might not like it, they say, but we are following the Bible. Complementarians take restrictive readings of 1 Tim. 2:11–12 and 1 Cor. 14:34–35 as the lenses through which to view all Bible teachings about women. This is looking through the wrong end of a telescope, when what is needed is a wide-angle lens that comprehends these two passages in the light of everything the NT says about women (Hutson 1996).

The complementarian position is ancient. Origen was aware of the women prophets Miriam, Deborah, Huldah, Anna, and Philip's daughters, but he dismissed all their prophetic utterances as "not in the assembly" (cf. 1 Cor. 14:34) or directed only at other women (Origen, *Frag. 1 Cor.* 74). Yet Origen also referred to two women prophets of the second century, Priscilla and Maximilla, which indicates that his interpretation was in part a polemic against the Montanist movement. Yet, "it was not the *fact* or *mode* of their prophesying which concerned him, but rather that their activity was unacceptably *public*" (Trevett 1996, 174). Origen had no problem in referring to the Samaritan woman at the well as an "apostle" who "evangelized the Samaritans about the messiah" (Origen, *Comm. Jo.* 13.28 [169, 165] on John 4:26; cf. 13.29 [173]; 13.30 [179] on John 4:28–29). Still, complementarians can point to texts like Origen's commentary on 1 Corinthians as evidence that their view is traditional.

This brings us to the fourth view. Egalitarians, or biblical feminists, would begin with a broad understanding of the gospel as challenging all forms of domination and oppression (e.g., Purvis 1993) and approach texts like 1 Tim. 2:11–12 and 1 Cor. 14:34–35 as anomalies. Those who espouse the ordination of women have been a minority in the history of Christianity, though they also have ancient precedent. The Montanists, whom Origen opposed, embraced women evangelists (Kraemer 1992, 157–73). The PE predated Montanism, although some argue that similar movements existed as early as the time of Ignatius (Ford 1971; Trevett 1996, 37–42; Pietersen 2004, 97–106). Montanism illustrates how a theological emphasis on the Spirit could lead to a very different perspective on women as Christian leaders.

Montanus and his followers Priscilla and Maximilla (Eusebius, *Hist. eccl.* 5.16.13) lived in a rural village in Asia Minor (Phrygia?). Around 170 CE, they began to deliver a "New Prophecy," which opponents characterized as "pseudo-prophecy" (Eusebius, *Hist. eccl.* 5.16–19). Despite the abuse heaped on them later, it is difficult to identify any doctrine of Montanus that was heretical (Trevett 1996, 155). Irenaeus defended them (*Haer.* 3.11.9; A. Collins 2016, 214). Montanus's Christology and theology were orthodox, even if followers seem to have taken some of his ideas in quirky directions regarding the Holy Spirit and the Trinity (Tabbernee 2007, 119–22, 156–64). The Montanists' eschatology was also quirky in that they expected a return of the Messiah in Phrygia (Eusebius, *Hist. eccl.* 5.18.2; Tabbernee 2007, 115–18). But Montanist ethics were impeccable, with emphasis on fasting and sexual abstinence (Tabbernee 2007, 147–53), and that is what inclined Tertullian to join them about 208.

Alistair Stewart-Sykes suggests that opposition to Montanism was fueled by prejudice against rural, uneducated leaders (1999, 9–18), which, ironically, was also a prejudice against Peter and John (Acts 4:13). He concludes that the earliest opponents had two objections. First, Montanists legitimated their prophetic oracles by ecstatic speech, or glossolalia (Eusebius, *Hist. eccl.* 5.16.7–8; Stewart-Sykes 1999, 14–15; Tabbernee 2007, 92–101), which affronted Catholic sensibilities about apostolic succession (A. Collins 2016, 215–24). Second, Montanists accepted ecstatic prophecy as a legitimation of poor, uneducated, rural leaders, whereas mainstream churches in Asia tended to choose leaders who were educated property owners, heads of urban households (Stewart-Sykes 1999, 18–20). As Christine Trevett (1996, 155) puts it,

"Exorcism [of women prophets only, not of men] here should be seen not least as an attempt at social control."

The model of church leadership in the PE corresponds not only to Stewart-Sykes's description of mainstream churches in Asia in the second century but also to that in mainline churches in industrialized Western countries today, with their historic preference for an educated, male clergy. At the same time, the Montanists' way of doing things and the scorn heaped upon them calls to mind the modern Holiness and Pentecostal movements, with their original base among poorer and less educated people, the Holiness movement emphasizing rigorous ethical demands, and the Pentecostals emphasizing the Holy Spirit and glossolalia.

Like ancient Montanists, when modern Pentecostals look for legitimate Christian prophets and teachers, their first question is not gender but whether one is "filled with the Spirit" (Eusebius, *Hist. eccl.* 5.18.3; Trevett 1996, 185–97, esp. 195). To be sure, many modern Pentecostals operate with patriarchalist assumptions (Powers 2001; Clifton 2009), and ancient Montanists were not entirely egalitarian (Trevett 1996, 196–97). Nevertheless, these groups illustrate the potential effect on how the church regards the giftedness of women when they look at the question through the wide-angle lens of the whole NT rather than squinting through the peephole of 1 Tim. 2:11–12. When one understands the Spirit as an equal-opportunity gifter (Acts 2), passages like 1 Cor. 14:34–35 and 1 Tim. 2:11–12 appear as exceptions for specific contexts but not the general rule (Wood 2001). Apostles, prophets, evangelists, pastors, and teachers are gifts bestowed by the Spirit for building up the body of Christ (Eph. 4:11–12). Should we spurn such gifts when they come wrapped in bodies that do not meet our expectations?

All this raises a crucial question: How do we distinguish the core message of the gospel from the cultural package in which it was wrapped before it was handed on to us? It is useful to make a list of all the specific instructions in 1 Tim. 2 and ask which are binding for all Christians in all times and places, and which simply reflect the cultural context of an eastern province in the early Roman Empire. Should we ignore the latter as irrelevant, or should we represent the principles in ways that are understandable in our cultural context?

Before we use 1 Tim. 2:11–12 to silence or subordinate women, we must explain the basis on which we decide which instructions in 1 Tim. 2 are rigidly binding and which are culturally determined and can be flexed to fit new contexts. The Anglican Book of Common Prayer includes prayers for the monarch (1 Tim. 2:2), but the liturgy of the Episcopal Church in the USA includes prayers for the president, congress, justices, and so on, even though no biblical writer imagined a constitutional democratic republic with three branches of government. Some Christians in Anabaptist and Holiness traditions apply instructions about hair, jewelry, and clothing (2:9–10) not only to women but also to men as bearing witness to their countercultural values, while most Christians in other traditions have no qualms about gold, pearls, braids, or expensive clothing, and they sometimes interpret "modesty" quite loosely. In evangelical circles, women as well as men "lift reverent hands" while singing, even though our passage specifies this gesture only for men during prayer, and even though the common practice of lifting one hand high above the head is unlike the ancient posture for prayer (see comment at 2:8). So Christians routinely recognize that some aspects of 1 Tim. 2 are specific to the ancient cultural context, and they ignore or adapt them without doing violence to the gospel.

One way of getting at the distinction between what is central/binding and what is peripheral/adaptable is to place the cross at the center and ask why Jesus died. Did Jesus die so men would adopt a particular posture when they prayed? Or so women would avoid certain hairstyles? Or so women would not preach about him? These matters are the baggage of a specific cultural context. According to our passage, Jesus died as a "ransom for all" (2:5), to free all people from bondage to some larger power. The Paul of Rom. 5–7 would call that power "Sin" and "Death" (for a nontechnical discussion, see R. Beck 2014). Pastoral Paul writes about being ransomed from "lawlessness" (Titus 2:14). Jesus's death is associated with the proposition that there is only one God, who is sovereign and savior of all people. The precepts in 2:8–15 suggest how ancient Christians could represent this doctrine effectively to a society that saw them as a threat.

In terms of "infrapolitics" (see under "James Scott and 'Infrapolitics'" in the general introduction), 1 Tim. 2 is "ideological and symbolic dissent . . . pressing against the limit of what is permitted on stage" (J. Scott 1990, 196). Far from kowtowing to Roman ideology, Pastoral Paul is picking his battles within a larger offensive strategy. When Christians asserted that God is "Savior," against the common designations of various gods and rulers as "savior," how could they avoid charges of sedition? By following the Jewish practice of praying *for* but not *to* the emperor, modeling the Roman ideal of concord in their own community, and scrupulously observing matters of decorum that marked them as members of a well-ordered society. This text "straddles the dual positions of exhibiting a reverent deference toward imperial power and of offering its own counter narrative about the true location of piety and global mission of 'God our Savior' and Jesus the one mediator—a theological position that benefited from its discreetness or camouflage of *pietas* before the imperial gaze" (Hoklotubbe 2017, 77).

We might think about the apparel in 1 Tim. 2:9–10 as a matter of donning the costume of the dominant society in order to infiltrate and influence it. But choosing a costume calls for shrewdness. The power elites of the Roman Empire recognized two types of costume: the quiet and modest demeanor of domestic tranquility and the ostentatious display of status and privilege. Given those options, Pastoral Paul advises Christians to seize the home-court advantage by playing to the ideals of modesty and temperance. Tertullian similarly advised modest clothing, arguing that ostentatious attire smacked of idolatry (Daniel-Hughes 2016). Marginalized people can undermine an ideology by exposing how it fails to live up to its own ideals. "Every publicly given justification for inequality thus marks out a kind of symbolic Achilles heel where the elite is especially vulnerable. . . . One reason [attacks on this Achilles heel] are particularly hard to deflect is simply because they begin by adopting the ideological terms of reference of the elite" (J. Scott 1990, 105). The Achilles heel of Roman Imperial ideology was their claim that they were people of decorum (*kosmios* people) who brought order (*kosmos*) to the peoples they conquered. By emphasizing decorum, Pastoral Paul called the bluff of Roman elites, embracing neither their flaunted wealth nor their oppressive power. He advised Christian women to demonstrate how their own values and practices made them more "orderly" than the Romans.

Finally, consider whether there are contexts today for which the instruction in 1 Tim. 2:8–15 seem reasonable. Consider the specific cultural context in which *you* are now living. Is Christianity legal where you live? Is it a minority religion? If your congregation prohibits a woman to "teach or presume authority over a man," does that have a positive or negative impact on how non-Christians in your town view Christianity? Do they view Christianity as a promoter or a corrector of Western decadence? Do they view Christianity as an agent of liberation and uplift or of Western imperialism? In your town, is it legal for women to drive? Is it acceptable for women to wear pants? Do people assume that a legitimate religious teacher has a beard? Depending on where in the world you live and your answers to such questions, the tactics of 1 Tim. 2 can seem very relevant. The effectiveness or even the survival of your church may depend on your willingness to respect local laws and customs. Christians should adhere to Christian standards of holiness, piety, faith, love, and temperance, as defined by their affirmation of the one God and the crucified Messiah. And they should do so in ways that the society around them can recognize those values.

1 Timothy 3:1b–13

Pastoral Leadership

Introductory Matters

The shift from prayer to church leadership seems abrupt, but in an administrative letter an itemized list of topics is sufficient (e.g., PTebt 703), and we should not expect a polished, literary style. On the other hand, we have seen that the instructions in chapter 2 have an apologetic function. The impeccable reputation of Christian leaders serves that same function, as is explicit in 3:7. "The bishop is leader of a community in danger of experiencing slander, and as the head of this household he has the crucial role of embodying its standing in society" (M. MacDonald 1996, 157). A similar list appears in *Didache* 15.1, which says overseers and deacons should be, "gentle, not devoted to money [*aphilargyros*], true, and tested [*dedokimasmenos*]." Likewise, honorific inscriptions of diaspora Jews sought to portray their leaders as exemplary citizens so as to blunt anti-Jewish prejudice (Chester 2013, 130, 141).

The chapter invites us to consider what models informed early Christian community organization. The first-century Platonist philosopher Onasander lists eleven qualities of an ideal general (*On the Office of General* 1.1–17; text in Dibelius and Conzelmann 1972, 158–60). This is interesting for understanding Greco-Roman ideals of leadership in general, but Pauline churches were hardly organized along military lines. Scholars have debated whether early Christian communities were organized on the model of a city-state, a voluntary association, household, synagogue, or philosophical school (Judge 1960 [2008, 10–34]; Meeks 1983, 75–84). The largest consensus is that the voluntary association and the household are the models most relevant to the PE.

A voluntary association (Lat. *collegium*) was a relatively small group with voluntary membership, sometimes including both men and women, free and enslaved. *Collegia* had regular meetings, usually monthly, at which they typically ate together. Associations were of all sorts: craft guilds, fire brigades, devotees of a particular deity, and so forth. Some were household based (*AGRW* §§52, 121, 323, etc.). A diaspora synagogue might be legally recognized as a *collegium* (Josephus, *Ant.* 14.213–16; *AGRW* §46). Each *collegium* had rules for membership and behavior, a treasury, and officers, such as "president" (*prostatēs*, *AGRW* §§94, 300, etc.; cf. 1 Tim. 3:4–5; 5:17; Rom. 16:2), "supervisor" (*epimeletēs*, *AGRW* §§11, 12, 14, 132, 133, etc.; cf. 1 Tim. 3:5), and "attendant" (*diakonos*, *AGRW* §§29, 36, 38, etc.; cf. 1 Tim. 3:8–13).

Pastoral Paul's list of desirable qualities for an overseer would have resonated with well-to-do heads of households in antiquity, who were often patrons of *collegia* (Countryman 1980, 149–82; similarly for synagogue leaders, Chester 2013, 126). L. William Countryman argues that the PE are attempting to co-opt local elites into leadership (1980, 167), but it is unlikely that they needed to be co-opted. They would have emerged as officers anyway, on the basis of education, experience, patronage, and leisure time to devote to the *collegium*. More likely, the list was intended "to help rich Christians understand their place in the household of God and to help the church, in turn, learn how to make room for such people" (Kidd 1990, 155). Pastoral Paul recognizes the presumptions of power that pertain to free, male, wealthy householders, but he ameliorates those with a theological understanding of the church as *God's house*. The rhetorical effect is "a subtle transformation of the benefactor ideal" (Kidd 1990, 139; cf. Neyrey 2005b on God as "benefactor"; Hoklotubbe 2017, 111–48; Malherbe 1983, 92–112).

In 1 Timothy the dominant metaphor for the church is "household of God" (3:4, 12, 15; Verner 1983; Horrell 2001; Malherbe 2012; Zamfir 2013, 60–159; for critique of this view, Herzer 2008). If God is the householder, then the overseer (*episkopos*) is "God's household manager" (*oikonomos*, Titus 1:7), the equivalent of a "foreman" (Gk. *epitropos*, Gal. 4:2; Lat. *vilicus*, *CIG* 963; *CIL* 3.447; Anderson 1937, 20; D. Martin 1990, 15–22, 169–73). The household manager was sometimes a freedman but usually enslaved (Young 1994, 99–102). He was not the master (*despotēs*), a title reserved for the *paterfamilias* (cf. 2 Tim. 2:21), but he represented the master's will to other slaves in the household (Harrill 2006, 86–87).

In his dialogue *Oeconomicus* (*Household Manager*), Xenophon discusses the duties of a foreman (*epitropos*) in classical Athens. Xenophon's *Oeconomicus* was popular among Roman aristocrats in the late Roman Republic and early Empire (Pomeroy 1994, 69–73). Cicero translated it into Latin (Cicero, *Sen.* 59; *Off.* 2.87). In this dialogue, the wealthy landowner Ischomachus explains two qualities of a good foreman: loyalty to the householder (Xenophon, *Oec.* 12.5) and being careful (*epimeleisthai*, 12.9). The latter is a major theme in the dialogue, where it connotes both attention to detail (e.g., 11.17; 12.4; cf. 1 Tim. 3:5) and practice in specific skills (e.g., 11.13, 22–23; cf. 1 Tim. 4:14–15).

In choosing a foreman, Ischomachus says he avoids those who lack self-control regarding wine (*oinou akrateis*, *Oec.* 12.11), who lack self-control in general (*akrateis*, 12.12), are infatuated with sexual desire (12.13), or are infatuated with profit (*erōtikōs tou kerdainein*, 12.15). Men besotted with sexual infatuation "are incapable of being taught by or giving careful attention to anyone else" (12.13; cf. 1 Cor. 7:32–35). On the other hand, those distracted by profit can be redirected to understand that carefulness (*epimeleia*) is profitable (*kerdaleon*, 12.15; cf. 1 Tim. 6:5–6). Finally, Ischomachus praises foremen who are careful about the right things: "I praise and try to honor [*timan*] them" (12.16; cf. 1 Tim. 5:17).

Viewed from the outside, a Christian community resembled a voluntary association. But our passage does not endorse the social expectations of patrons in a *collegium*. Instead, the text incorporates household terminology as the way to think theologically about a Christian community. If the church is God's household, this chapter describes the household staff.

The discussion of pastoral leaders falls into two lists of desirable qualities for overseer (3:1–7) and for deacons (3:8–13), connected by the adverb "likewise" (3:8). In similar lists in 5:9–10 and Titus 1:6–9 we find some of the same terms, some synonymous terms, and some variations. Each list is representative and suggestive.

Tracing the Train of Thought

Overseers (3:1b–7)

3:1b–7. If anyone craves oversight, he desires a good deed (3:1). "Craving" (*oregomai*) and "desire" (*epithymeō*) often carry negative connotations (Epictetus, *Diatr.* 4.4.1). This very letter warns about those who are "craving" (*oregomenoi*) money (6:10) and associates love of money with "foolish desires" (*epithymiai*, 6:9; cf. 2 Tim. 2:22; 3:6; 4:3; Titus 2:12; 3:3). But "craving" and "desire" are neutral. What is important is the object of desire. Epictetus encouraged students to pay attention to what they desired and avoided (*Diatr.* 1.4.11). "The one making progress," he said, has "learned from the philosophers that craving [*orexis*] is for good things, and disinclination is toward bad things" (*Diatr.* 1.4.1; cf. "crave justice," ps.-Isocrates, *Demon.* 38). Philo described followers of the "holy word" as "lovers" (*erastai*) of temperance, decorum, modesty, self-control, and so forth (Philo, *Somn.* 1.124). Such are the proper objects of "desire," as opposed to worldly desires for influence (1 Tim. 1:7; 6:9–10) and physical pleasures (2 Tim. 2:22). Spiritual cravings can be trained. "The church—the body of Christ—is the place where God invites us to renew our loves, reorient our desires, and retrain our appetites" (J. Smith 2016, 65).

It is common to think of Timothy as a bishop evaluating candidates for office. But he is Paul's envoy (Mitchell 1992; Johnson 2001, 94–97) and a prototypical young minister in training. Whereas the stereotypical youth would "crave" sex, wine, appearance, and money (Hutson 1998, 143–90; "youthful lusts," 2 Tim. 2:22), Pastoral Paul redirects youthful passions toward nobler aspirations, so that 3:1b–7 becomes a list of qualities that a youth should cultivate in order to become the sort of person who could hold that office.

It is necessary, therefore, that an overseer be . . . (3:2). The English word "bishop" is an Anglicized form of the Greek word for "overseer" (*episkopos*). Here is the historical problem: the plural "overseers" (*episkopoi*) appears only once in the Pauline letters (Phil. 1:1), referring to local congregational leaders, a synonym for "elders" (cf. Acts 20:28; Lightfoot 1868, 95–99). In the early second century, however, Ignatius describes each church as organized with a single bishop (*episkopos*) and a plurality of elders and deacons (Ign. *Pol.* 6.1; cf. *Trall.* 7.2; *Phld.* inscr.; 7.1; *Smyrn.* 8.1; 12.2). Ignatius took for granted that every church had this organization (Ign. *Eph.* 2.2; 20.2; *Magn.* 2.1; 6.1) with one bishop over each city (Ign. *Eph.* 4.1; 5.3; *Trall.* 2.1; 7.1; *Phld.* 7.2; *Smyrn.* 9.1; Pol. *Phil.* 5). The question is whether the descriptions of the "overseer," "elders," and "deacons" in the PE reflect an organization more like that in Philippians, or like that assumed by Ignatius, or something between (Aageson 2008, 127–31; Young 1994, 97–121; for a possible intermediate polity, *Herm. Vis.* 3.5.1).

Some take the singular "overseer" (3:1b; Titus 1:7) with the plural "deacons" (1 Tim. 3:8) and "elders" (5:17; Titus 1:5) as reflecting monepiscopacy, a single bishop overseeing multiple elders. That reading depends on dating the PE as post-Pauline and reading Titus 1:5–9 as distinguishing between the plural "elders" and the singular "overseer."

But the text would also make sense in a first-century context before the development of monepiscopacy. Pastoral Paul sometimes uses a singular in a distributive sense, so "an overseer" could mean "any and every overseer" (cf. "a woman," 1 Tim. 2:11–12; "a widow," 5:3, 9). Also, he sometimes shifts carelessly between singular and plural (e.g., 2:15; 5:3, 9, 11, 14; 5:19–20). And "overseers" and "elders" could be synonymous (see comments at Titus 1:5–9). While this letter assumes a church organization, it does not explain the functions of or relations between the offices. Debates about church polity miss the point of the passage, which is desirable ethics of church leaders.

89

After the introductory statement (3:1b), the list begins with **unimpeachable** (3:2) and ends with **a good testimony from outsiders** (3:7). These negative and positive ways of saying the same thing form rhetorical brackets (*inclusio*) around the list. "Unimpeachable" is the umbrella term, of which the other qualities are representative examples. The behavior that gets the most attention is how the overseer functions as head of household (3:4–5), and the household context colors the other qualities in the list.

The phrase **husband of one wife** (3:2) has been much misunderstood. Naive, commonsense assumptions about the English phrase are highly misleading. A proper understanding must make sense of all three occurrences of the Greek idiom in the letter ("husband of one wife," 3:2, 12; "wife of one husband," 5:9) and must make sense in the cultural context of the early Roman Empire.

One mistake is to take "husband of one wife" against opponents who "prevent to marry" (4:3) as a requirement that an overseer be married (Pietersen 2004, 111). It would be nonsensical if "wife of one husband" (5:9) were a requirement that a "real widow" be married. Also, it is illogical to suppose that a letter written by or in the name of Paul construes congregational leadership so as to disqualify Paul himself (or Jesus!) on the basis that he was not married. In light of Paul's recommendation of celibacy (1 Cor. 7:8, 25–38), it would be strange to discover here that celibacy was a disqualifier for leadership rather than an asset (see comments at 2 Tim. 2:4–7). Pastoral Paul emphasizes sexual control, framed as "temperance" (*sōphrosynē*, 1 Tim. 2:15; 3:2; Titus 2:4, 5, 6, 12), "purity" (*hagneia*, 1 Tim. 4:12; 5:2, 22; Titus 2:2), and criticism of "lusts" (*epithymiai*, 2 Tim. 2:22; 3:6; Titus 2:12; 3:3).

A second mistake takes "husband of one wife" as a requirement that an overseer be male. In fact, women served as presbyters in the early centuries (Madigan and Osiek 2005, 163–202; Kraemer 1992, 183–87; Ramelli 2010a). For comparison, the term *paterfamilias* (father of the family) originated in an old, agrarian society in which the typical head of household was a free, male estate owner with wife and children. The corresponding *materfamilias* (mother of the family) referred to his wife, who managed the domestic slaves. But Richard P. Saller shows that by the time of the empire the terms took on new meanings in legal and popular contexts. "The good *paterfamilias* was a responsible estate owner, with or without children and wife, and the good *materfamilias* was a chaste, sexually respectable woman, married or widowed, with or without children" (Saller 1999, 196). Because *materfamilias* did not designate an estate owner, a woman estate owner could be called a *paterfamilias* in legal contexts, where "use of a word in the masculine is usually extended to cover both sexes" (Ulpian, *On the Edict* 46; Justinian, *Digest* 50.16.195, quoted in Saller 1999, 185). The term *paterfamilias* reflected the social reality that typical estate owners were male, but it did not prescribe that they be male. Similarly, the command to pray for "kings" (2:2) reflects the social reality that monarchs were typically male, and no one would argue that Christians should not pray for a queen. We might compare such English words as "landlord" and "governor." The feminine "landlady" is quaint, and no one would be surprised or confused to read a lease that identified a woman as "landlord." It would be insulting and inaccurate to call the chief executive of a state a "governess." "Husband of one wife" reflects the social reality that early Christian overseers were typically male and does not require that they be male.

In "husband of one wife," the emphasis is on "one." It's about marital fidelity. This would, of course, preclude polygamy, but Greeks and Romans repudiated polygamy as barbarian (Euripides, *Andromache* 213–20; Caesar, *Gallic War* 6.19). Jews recognized polygamy as according to Torah (Josephus, *Ant.* 17.14), but they rarely practiced it in the Roman period (Page 1993, 107–8), and strict Jews condemned it (CD 4.30–5.6; 11QT 57.15–19; Instone-Brewer 2002, 59–72). The common problems in Greco-Roman society were infidelity (Page 1993) and serial monogamy. A double standard denounced women for infidelity but turned a blind eye to men who cheated or divorced for trivial reasons.

Our text reflects a Greco-Roman ideal that only a few interpreters have appreciated (Spicq 1969, 430, 533; Verner 1983, 128–31). Ancient Greeks and Romans idealized lifelong fidelity to a single spouse—no adultery, divorce, or remarriage after the death of a spouse. While remarriage was accepted, even expected, lifelong fidelity to a single partner garnered high admiration. Such a person was a "man of one woman" or a "woman of one man" (Lightman and Zeisel 1977; Fantham et al. 1994, 231–32, 276–77; cf. Livy, *Ab urbe* 10.23; Plutarch, *Quaest. rom.* 50 [289a–b]).

Most examples of this ideal were women. The poet Propertius mourned the death of Augustus's stepdaughter Claudia with this epitaph: "Read it on this stone, she was wedded to one alone" (*Elegies* 4.11, trans. Kline 2008). The ideal of lifelong fidelity to a single spouse persisted in Greek romances (e.g., Xenophon of Ephesus, *Ephesian Tale* 1.11; 2.7; 4.3), and Jewish examples included Judith (Jdt. 16:22) and Anna (Luke 2:36–38).

Men who lived up to this ideal were less common but similarly admired. In the first century BCE a Roman freedman butcher erected a memorial to his wife, praising her chastity and tooting his own horn by referring to her as "my only wife" (*CIL* 1.1221; D'Ambra 2007, 82–83). Another husband from Pisa inscribed his wife's tombstone, "To the gods of the underworld. To Scribonia Hedone, with whom I lived 18 years without a quarrel. At her wish, I swore that after her I would not have another wife" (*CIL* 11.1491 = *ILS* 8461; Lefkowitz and Fant 1992, 206).

Most early Christians did not censure members for remarrying, but they valued widows who remained celibate (*Herm. Mand.* 4). Clement of Alexandria saw no sin in a widower remarrying but asserted, "He does not fulfill the heightened perfection of the gospel ethic. But he gains heavenly glory for himself if he remains as he is, and keeps undefiled the marriage yoke broken

---

Tertullian, *To His Wife* 1.7

"We have been taught by the Lord and God of salvation that continence is a means of attaining eternal life, a proof of the faith that is in us, a pledge of the glory of that body which will be ours when we put on the garb of immortality, and, finally, an obligation imposed upon us by the will of God. . . . Therefore, when God wills that a woman lose her husband in death, He also wills that she should be done with marriage itself. Why attempt to restore what God has put asunder? Why spurn the liberty which is offered you by enslaving yourself once more in the bonds of matrimony? Art thou bound in marriage? Scripture says, seek not to be loosed. Art thou loosed from marriage? Seek not to be bound. For, though you sin not in remarrying, yet, according to Scripture, tribulation of the flesh will follow if you do. . . .

"The law of the Church and the precept of the Apostle show clearly how prejudicial second marriages are to the faith and how great an obstacle to holiness. For men who have been married twice are not allowed to preside in the Church nor is it permissible that a widow be chosen unless she was the wife of but one man." (trans. Le Saint 1951, 19–21)

---

by death, and willingly accepts God's purpose for him, by which he has become free from distraction for the service of the Lord" (*Strom.* 3.12.82, trans. Oulton and Chadwick 1954).

Whereas Clement saw the potential for fruitful ministry in celibate widowhood, others required it. Tertullian insisted on it even before he joined the Montanists (Tertullian, *Ux.* 1.7 [see sidebar]; cf. Tertullian, *Exh. cast.* and *Mon.*). Origen argued, "Not only fornication, but also a second marriage, excludes someone from office in the church. Anyone twice married may be neither a bishop nor a presbyter nor a deacon nor a widow" (*Hom. Luc.* 17.10, trans. Lienhard 1996, 75).

This expectation not to remarry after the death of a spouse might seem to contradict the emphasis elsewhere on marriage and children (1 Tim. 2:15; 4:3; 5:14; Page 1993, 112–13), but Pastoral Paul assumes that overseers, deacons, and real widows have been married and produced children (1 Tim. 3:4, 12; 5:10). Having done that, they *also* manifest the highest ideal of marital fidelity (e.g., Publia in Theodoret, *Ecclesiastical History* 3.14; see comments at 1 Tim. 5:9, 14).

In sum, "husband of one wife" places a premium on sexual chastity. Outsiders might have been skeptical of this new religion, but they had to admire Christian leaders who so exhibited the highest ideals of Greco-Roman society.

The next three qualities are related. **Sober** (*nēphalios*, 3:2) overlaps with "not given to wine" (3:3), though it can have broader applications (see comments at 2 Tim. 4:5). **Temperate** (*sōphrōn*, 3:2) often appears in contexts relating to sex but may relate to other desires, so it overlaps with several qualities in verses 2–3 and with the previous paragraph (2:9). We have seen how **person of decorum** (*kosmios*, 3:2) connoted temperance and self-control, not flaunting status or sexuality (2:9). "Decorum" is not for women only. A male leader is a moral agent responsible for his own actions, not the victim of a courtesan who "hunts" him (ps.-Melissa, *Cl.* 1 [see sidebar at 2:9]; ps.-Theano, *Nik.* 1).

The overseer should be **devoted to strangers** (*philoxenos*, hospitable, 3:2; cf. 5:10; Titus 1:8). Hospitality was an important virtue (Rom. 12:13; Heb. 13:2; 1 Pet. 4:9; *TDNT* 5:17–24, s.v. ξένος). Christian missionaries depended on hospitality for lodging and support (Matt. 10:11–15; Acts 16:15, 40; 18:2–3, 7; Rom. 16:23; Philem. 22; 3 John 5–8), even if some abused the privilege (*Did.* 11.3–6; Lucian, *Peregr.* 16). Local churches depended on members with means to provide houses in which to meet (Acts 2:46; Rom. 16:5; Col. 4:15; Ign. *Smyrn.* 13.2; Countryman 1980, 157–60; L. White 1990, 111–23; 1997, 121–257), even if some abused their prerogatives (3 John 9–10; Malherbe 1983, 92–112). It is likely that a person who was able to show hospitality to missionaries and/or a house church was financially stable or relatively wealthy.

The word **didactic** (*didaktikos*, 3:2; cf. 2 Tim. 2:24) is rare. The adjectival suffix –*ikos* (Smyth 1956, §858.6; BDF §113[2]) could indicate ability, as in *archikos* (capable of ruling), *graphikos* (skilled at writing), and *mousikos* (musical). Or it could indicate orientation, as in *barbarikos* (barbaric), *keramikos* (made of clay), and *sōmatikos* (fleshly). An overseer should be associated with teaching, but how? Most translators take *didaktikos* as "skilled at teaching" (CEB), "apt to teach" (KJV; cf. NASB, NIV, ESV), just as "the prudent is teacher [*didaktikos*] of the imprudent" (Sextus Empiricus, *Against the Mathematicians* 245, 248). A primary responsibility of a father was to attend to the education of his children (ps.-Aristotle, *Oec.* 1.3.6 [1344a]; Plutarch, *Lib. ed.*). If *didaktikos* describes a duty of an overseer, we might think not only of an expert delivering eloquent discourses (5:17; Titus 1:9) but also of a parent as moral guide to children (1 Thess. 2:11–12; cf. Plato, *Prot.* 325c–d). Read this way, however, *didaktikos* stands out as the only duty in the list. On the other hand, Philo distinguishes virtue acquired through study (*didaktikē aretē*) from virtue acquired through disciplined practice (*askētikē aretē*, Philo, *Names* 84, 88; *Prelim. Studies* 35; *Praem.* 27). If *didaktikos* describes a characteristic, we might think of a "studious" overseer who continues to learn, as modeled by Timothy (4:13). Augustine admired Cyprian as a bishop who "was not only learned, but also patient of instruction," and he concluded that a good overseer should both "teach with knowledge" and "learn with patience" (Augustine, *Bapt.* 4.5.8, trans. *NPNF*[1] 4:449).

An overseer must be **not a drunkard, not violent, but fair, not combative** (3:3). "Not a drunkard" echoes "sober" (3:2). It would be easy to take "not violent, but fair, not combative" (cf. 2 Tim. 2:24) as the way an overseer responds to doctrinal differences, whether he is argumentative (cf. "word battles," 1 Tim. 6:4; 2 Tim. 2:14) or able to listen to all sides and respond with gentleness (Titus 3:2). But, given the analogy to a head of household (3:4–5), we should also consider these four qualities as describing a family man. Epicureans disavowed corporal punishment of slaves and urged gentle correction (Fiore 2004, 274). One who abuses his wife, children, or slaves is not fit to oversee the house of God.

The quality **not devoted to money** (*aphilargyros*, 3:3; cf. Heb. 13:5; "shameful gain," Titus 1:7, 11) could be associated with "apt to teach." Ever since Plato challenged Protagoras, suspicion of profit motives fell on "sophists," rhetoricians who purported to teach virtue for a fee (Plato, *Protagoras*; Diogenes Laërtius, *Lives* 9.52). The "Second Sophistic" movement brought a parade of hucksters who peddled pseudo-philosophy (Lucian, *Pregr.* 3, 11; *Fug.* 12–21; Dio Chrysostom, *Or.* 77/79.34–36; Malherbe 1989, 38–39; Winter 2002). This letter warns against those who teach for "profit" (6:5). A father does not take payment from his children but teaches them freely and provides good teachers for them. A bad father puts "devotion to money" (*philargyria*) ahead of educating his children (ps.-Plutarch, *Lib. ed.* 7 [4–5]). His "devotion to wealth" (*philoploutia*) corrupts his children, who inherit his avarice along with his money (Plutarch, *Cupid. Div.* 7 [526b–27a]).

An ancient commonplace was the correlation between **well maintaining his own household** (3:4) and public leadership (Zamfir 2013, 70–85). "The future statesman," wrote Philo, "needed first to be trained and practiced in household management (*oikonomia*); for a household is a city compressed into small dimensions" (Philo, *Joseph* 8.38, trans. Colson LCL). The Roman general Agricola was successful in governing Britain in part because he "first contained his own house" (Tacitus, *Agricola* 19.1–2).

We should beware of projecting our own cultural assumptions onto the text, so that church and family come to resemble monarchies ("ruleth well," KJV) or corporations ("manages well," NRSV, NASB, NIV, etc.). Such translations encourage authoritarian views of leadership. The verb translated "maintain" is literally "stand before" (*proïstēmi*), a flexible word, depending on who is standing before whom to do what. A soldier "protects" (Herodotus, *Histories* 9.107; cf. 1 Macc. 5:19), a political leader "presides" (Plutarch, *Quaest. rom.* 57 [*Mor.* 304a]; POxy 239.11), and so on. The translation "maintaining" suggests leadership without autocracy.

Two connotations are significant for Paul's usage of *proïstēmi* in terms of a family model of leadership (3:4–5, 12, 15; Malherbe 2012, 78–80; Clark 2006). First, *proïstēmi* connotes a teaching function in 1 Thess. 5:12, sandwiched between "labor" (metaphor for evangelism, cf. 1 Tim. 4:10) and "admonish." In our letter, "elders who preside [*proestōtes*] well" are those who "labor in word and teaching" (5:17). This connotation jibes with "apt to teach" (3:2). Second, *proïstēmi* connotes financial support in Rom. 12:8, sandwiched between

> ### How God Is Like a Father
>
> *"For God made all mankind to be happy, to be serene. To this end He gave them resources, giving each one some things inherent and others not inherent. The things that are subject to hindrance, deprivation, and compulsion are not inherent, but those which cannot be hindered are inherent. The true nature of the good and the evil, as was fitting for Him who watches over and protects us like a father* [patrikōs proïstamenon], *He gave to mankind to be among their inherent possessions."* (Epictetus, *Diatribes* 3.24.3, trans. Oldfather, LCL modified)

"donate" and "give alms" (cf. the related noun "patroness," *prostatis*, Rom. 16:2). This connotation jibes with "not devoted to money" (3:3). These ideas of teaching and financial support apply to a parent in relation to children (on the duties of a *paterfamilias*, Balch 1981, 23–80; Neyrey 2003, 81–82). In describing God (Zeus) as "father" of humans (see sidebar), Epictetus taught that things over which one has no control are not "inherent." What is "inherent" is the ability to make moral choices, which is a "resource" provided by God, who "protects/provides for [*proïstēmi*] us like a father." The translation "maintain" connotes a nurturing and supportive parent. The overseer should "be a good family leader" (NCV).

The next two qualities, **having children in subjection, with all dignity** (3:4), expound on "maintaining." The phrases are consistent with expectations about the duties of children toward parents and vice versa (1 Tim. 5:4–8; Eph. 6:1–4; Col. 3:20–21; cf. Exod. 20:12; Deut. 5:16). Children owe respect to parents, and a good parent is worthy of respect (cf. "dignified," 1 Tim. 3:8, 11).

In verse 4, the ideal overseer protects and provides for the church family, which prepares us for the analogy to one who **will care for** [*epimelēsetai*] **the church of God** (3:5; see discussion of Xenophon in "Introductory Matters," above). The analogy will not work if we think of the overseer as a ruler with authority to act on a whim. The overseer is one of the slaves, bound by the policies of the divine householder.

The qualification **not a neophyte** (3:6) is important in the context of patronage. In Greco-Roman society, a wealthy person who joined a voluntary association and made a large donation could expect a significant office or at least an honorary title (Countryman 1980, 157). But rushing to reward a donor with an office can backfire, as the church in Rome learned when they ordained Marcion as bishop. Marcion was a generous patron, but his teaching was so disastrous that the Roman church excommunicated him, and church leaders in other countries repudiated him as a heretic (Clement of Alexandria, *Strom.* 3.3–4; Tertullian, *Marc.*; Irenaeus, *Haer.* 1.27; 4.8, 34).

The aim of all this is **so that he might not be puffed up and fall into judg-ment of the slanderer. And it is also necessary to have a good testimony from outsiders, so that he might not fall into reproach and a snare of the slanderer** (3:6–7). The word translated "slanderer" (*diabolos*) is traditionally rendered "devil." A reference to the "snare of the devil" (3:7) reflects a Jewish idea that temptations come from the devil (1 Chron. 21:1; 1 Pet. 5:8) or Satan (Job 1–2; Mark 1:12–13; cf. Pagels 1995, 35–62) or some evil spirit (1 Kings 22:19–23; 2 Tim. 1:7; often in *Testaments of the Twelve Patriarchs*). That reading would be consistent with the idea that some younger widows have "turned aside after Satan" (1 Tim. 5:15). On the other hand, *diabolos* has its generic sense "slanderer" in the immediate context (3:11; cf. 2 Tim. 3:3; Titus 2:3). Given that "unimpeachable" (3:2), "a good testimony from outsiders," and "re-proach" (3:7) all fall in the semantic domain of gossip (Rohrbaugh 2001), it makes sense to understand "slanderer" in 3:6–7 as referring to non-Christian "outsiders" who expressed "judgment" of the behavior of Christian leaders (cf. M. MacDonald 1988, 167). While "fall into a snare" is a metaphor for sinning, the snare is often set by other people (Ps. 57:6; Tob. 14:10; Sir. 9:3), even if they are doing the devil's bidding (2 Tim. 2:26). So we might take *diabolos* with a double meaning, both "slanderer" and "devil." In that case, "devil" would function within a hidden transcript of resistance by labeling opponents without naming them (N. Beck 2010, 79–80; cf. "James Scott and 'Infrapolitics'" in the general introduction above).

Deacons (3:8–13)

3:8–13. The desired qualities of deacons are tightly linked to those for an overseer. There are related concerns for reputation ("blameless," 3:10; cf. 3:2, 7) and family life (3:12; cf. 3:4–5). In a similar list Polycarp identifies the Lord Jesus as the archetypical deacon (Pol. *Phil.* 5.2).

Likewise, [it is necessary for] **deacons** [to be] **dignified, not duplicitous, not heavy users of wine, not after shameful gain, holding the mystery of the faith with a pure conscience. And they should be approved first, then they should serve, if they are blameless** (3:8–10). "Likewise" ties this list to the previous, and both lists depend on the same verb, "it is necessary . . . to be" (3:2; cf. 2:8–10). This prepares us to expect similar qualities that function in a similar way, to identify leaders whose reputations are impeccable to outsiders.

"Dignified" (*semnos*, 3:8) is the umbrella term. It was originally a religious word ascribed only to gods, but it came to be applied to humans of great stature (Plato, *Phaedrus* 257d). It was equivalent to the Latin *gravitas* (weight) to describe a person of strong moral fiber, prudence, and achievement, whose opinion merited consideration.

The adjective translated "duplicitous" (*dilogos*) is rare. The etymology suggests a person of "two words." Most interpreters take it in the sense of "speaking with forked tongue," and we might find motive for deception in "shameful gain." But that usage is not found before Paul. Alternatively, the related verb and noun (also rare) carry the sense of "repeat" and "repetition" (e.g., Xenophon, *Eq*. 8.2). So we might translate, "not repetitious," describing one who, lacking anything substantive to say, simply repeats himself (Demetrius, *On Style* 212).

There is no significant difference between "not a drunkard" (3:3) and "not heavy users of wine" (3:8). Wine was the typical beverage with meals, and a person of decorum drank in moderation, never to excess (Epictetus, *Diatr*. 3.13.20–21 [see sidebar at 4:12]; see comments at 5:23).

"Shameful gain" could describe money received illegally or by deception. The latter connotation often applied to merchants and those who sold their services as teachers when they were not qualified to teach (cf. 6:5; Titus 1:7, 11). The opposite of "shameful gain" is the integrity of a "pure conscience" (cf. 1:5, 19; 2 Tim. 1:3).

This passage envisions a teaching function for deacons (cf. Rom. 12:7; 1 Cor. 3:5; Eph. 3:7; Acts 6:4; 20:24; 21:19). The "mystery of the faith" refers to basic Christian doctrine, elsewhere called the "mystery of piety" (3:16) or "the faith" (1:19; 4:1, 6; 5:8; 6:10, 12, 21; 2 Tim. 3:8; 4:7; Titus 1:13). On the content of that "mystery," see comments at 3:16. The idea that deacons should be "approved" (3:10) refers to the need to test teachers.

Women likewise (3:11) is oddly placed in the middle of the section on deacons, and interpreters have debated its implications since antiquity. At issue is whether this refers to female deacons or the wives of male deacons. The Greek word *gynē* means "woman" and is normally translated "wife" only when there is a specific reference to her husband, as in the phrase, "the *gynē* of [name of man]," which is not the case in 1 Tim. 3:11 (Blackburn 1993, 308–9).

In the West, churches were ambivalent about ordaining women deacons. Ambrosiaster understood 1 Tim. 3:11 to refer to the wives of deacons, even though there is no corresponding mention of the wife of an overseer in 3:1–7. The Councils of Orange (441), Epaon (517), and Orléans (533) all sought to abolish or restrict women deacons, which indicates that churches were ordaining them. Inscriptions refer to women deacons, and Popes Gregory the Great (6th cent.) and Benedict VIII (11th cent.) affirmed the practice (Madigan and Osiek 2005, 141–49), and at least three tombstones of women deacons survive in Greece from the fourth and fifth centuries (Kraemer 1988, 221–23), though we should not assume that female deacons were always performing the same functions as male deacons.

In the East, churches ordained women deacons more commonly (Pliny the Younger, *Ep*. 10.96–97; *NewDocs* 2:§109; 4:§122; Madigan and Osiek 2005, 25–140, 150–62; Kraemer 1988, 221–23; cf. Witherington 1988, 199–201). Various patristic texts endorse the practice (Clement of Alexandria, *Strom*. 3.6.53 [which Stiefel 1995, 447, reads as a reference to 1 Tim. 3:11]; *Didascalia apostolorum* 16; John Chrysostom, *Hom. 1 Tim*. 11; Theodore of Mopsuestia,

Comm. 1 Tim. 128). The Eastern practice is consistent with the reference to Phoebe as a "deacon of the church" (Rom. 16:1–2), understood as an ordained office by ancient commentators, including Origen (3rd cent.), Theodoret (4th cent.) and others. Even so, some bishops restricted women deacons from presiding at the Eucharist (Epiphanius, *Panarion* 79.4). The most natural reading of verse 11 includes women in the group "deacons," following the Eastern tradition.

Still continuing the verb from 3:2 (cf. 3:8), [it is necessary for] women likewise [to be] **dignified, not slanderers, sober, faithful in all things** (3:11). "Dignified" (*semnē*) is a quality desired in older men (Titus 2:2) and deacons (3:8). "Not slanderers" (*diaboloi*; see comments at 3:6–7) reflects a stereotype of women (Kartzow 2009; cf. 4:7; 5:13). "Sober" is roughly similar to the requirement that deacons be "not heavy users of wine" (3:8) and applies also to older men (Titus 2:2), overseers (1 Tim. 3:2), and evangelists (2 Tim. 4:5). "Faithful" suggests fidelity to marriage vows and by extension to family (1 Tim. 5:16; 6:2a; Titus 1:6) and more broadly to Christ (2 Tim. 2:2). In that broadest sense, it describes any Christian (1 Tim. 1:12; 4:12; 5:16; 6:2a; Titus 1:6). Faithfulness to family and to God are interrelated (see comments on "piety" at 2:2; 4:7–8).

After the remark about women, Pastoral Paul resumes his description of male deacons. **Deacons should be husbands of one wife, presiding well over their children and their own households** (3:12). On "husbands of one wife," see comments at 3:2. In light of the mention of women deacons in verse 11, this is not a mandate that the deacons be male. It reflects the social reality that deacons were more typically male. On "presiding well over their children and their own households," see comments at 3:4. But here the implication is even more pointed that the analogy between deacon and *paterfamilias* does not imply domination. After all, a *diakonos* was a menial servant involved in the care of God's "household," including serving literal and spiritual food.

For those who serve well . . . (3:13). "Those who serve" (*diakonēsantes*) could be either literal or metaphorical servants. Deacons likely performed literal service, feeding the poor (5:3–16; cf. Acts 6:1–2; Rom.15:31; 2 Cor. 8:4; 9:1, 12–13, etc.). But "holding the mystery of the faith" (3:9) suggests that they were also teachers (cf. Acts 6:4; Rom. 11:13; 12:7; 2 Cor. 4:1; 5:18; 6:3–4; 11:8, etc.).

Good deacons **procure for themselves a good standing and much frankness in the faith that is in Christ Jesus** (3:13). The word "standing" (*bathmos*), which occurs only here in the NT, is an architectural term for a stair, used metaphorically for a progression in rank or status. Interpreters generally apply 3:13 internally to a deacon's "standing" in the church, a metaphor for rank (*TLNT* 1:250–51), as if a good deacon might be promoted to overseer. But such a hierarchical clergy system assumes a second-century context for the letter. More consistent with a first-century context, it could be a metaphor for reputation (e.g., Kelly 1963, 85). In my opinion, it makes more sense to apply this metaphor externally, referring to the reputation of deacons among outsiders, corresponding to a similar concern about an overseer (3:2, 6–7). In this vein, "frankness" (*parrhēsia*) is telling people the truth about themselves rather than flattering them (Philem. 8–9; Fredrickson 1996; *TLNT* 3:56–62). Benjamin Fiore (2004) applies this "frank speech" to the moral development of the Christian community. In the context of response to outsider criticism, however, we could read it as the boldness to speak truth in hostile situations (1 Thess. 2:2; Phil. 1:20; Acts 4:13, 29, 31; 28:31). Deacons must maintain impeccable reputations so they will have the moral standing to declare the faith frankly to skeptical outsiders.

Theological Issues

Church Polity

First Timothy 3 is like a Rorschach inkblot test for questions of church polity. Interpretations usually tell more about the traditions of the interpreters than the meaning of the text. All sides claim this passage, and the debates are unending (Ferguson 1968; Burtchaell 1992, 1–190). While Pastoral Paul seems to assume some church organization, he does not explain that organization, and his references are ambiguous. He focuses on the ethical character of leaders (Hutson 2012). So, whether you are committed to an episcopal, presbyterian, or congregational polity, it is appropriate to read 1 Tim. 3 at ordination services. But it is okay to say, "Our tradition interprets the text this way." You can embrace your tradition without thinking that all others are willfully perverting the text.

Christian Leadership

Although they use different terminology, many Western congregations organize themselves as corporations, each with its chief executive officer and board of directors. There were both monarchies and corporations in the first century, so those models were available, and the verb "preside" (*proïstēmi*) was adaptable to those contexts. But our passage describes an overseer or deacon like a parent rather than a monarch or business executive.

Your task as a minister is to help Christians become morally upright people and to help your congregation identify leaders who will be unimpeachable. The specific qualification "husband of one wife" may not be culturally meaningful today, but fidelity to a marriage vow certainly is. Churches need leaders who do not indulge desires but are self-controlled in matters of sexual conduct, alcohol, anger, and ego; who are attentive to the needs of others, starting with their own families. We need leaders whom non-Christians respect, even if they dismiss Christianity as hogwash.

1 Timothy 3:14–4:16

Second Charge to Timothy

This central section of the letter (3:14–4:16) turns from discussing ecclesial concerns in the third person (2:1–3:13) back to addressing Timothy directly in the second person, as in 1:3–20 and 6:2b–21. Here we find a string of imperatives (4:7, 11, 12, 13, 14, 15, and 16), including the key word "charge" (*parangelle*, 4:11). This central section contains a reason for the letter—"so that you may know how to conduct yourself" (3:15)—as well as the most detailed description of the exercises by which Timothy will become "a good minister of Christ Jesus" (4:6).

This section unfolds in three parts: first, a description of the church, supported by a quotation from early Christian tradition (3:14–16); second, a warning about apostates (4:1–5); and third, exhortations about training for ministry (4:6–16). The whole section describes the teachings that Timothy should and should not follow. Unifying themes include the coming of Paul (3:14; 4:13), Timothy's conduct (3:15; 4:12), and doctrine (*didaskalia*, 4:1, 6, 13, 16).

1 Timothy 3:14–16

The Foundation of the Truth

Introductory Matters

Some read 3:14–16 as recapping themes from the previous sections. "How to conduct yourself" recalls attention to behavior in chapters 2–3; "house of God" recalls 1:4; 3:4, 5, 12; "church of God" recalls 3:5; and "mystery of piety" recalls "mystery of the faith" in 3:9. Nevertheless, while the passage is transitional, there is a shift in focus at 3:14.

The poem in 3:16 appears to be another quotation of traditional material (cf. 1:15; 2:5–6), an early Christian liturgy (Ham 2000; Yarbrough 2009, 95–102), used here to express the "mystery of piety." Michael Goulder (1996, 250–56) reads the verse as a counterpoint to the supposed opponents' false Christology, but this seems misguided in light of the obvious poetic qualities of the text. There are six lines, each containing a passive verb (Gk. aor.) and a noun (Gk. dat.). The rhythmic language and compact imagery resemble an OT praise psalm (Hengel 1980). Furthermore, line 1 begins with a relative pronoun, "who," although some English translations omit it. The same pronoun begins other NT passages that appear to be hymnic (Phil. 2:6; Col. 1:15). For these reasons, most interpreters regard 1 Tim. 3:16 as an early Christ hymn (Gundry 1970; Gloer 1984). But they debate whether to read it as six lines, three couplets, or two triplets (on the possibilities, see below). For now, we should consider how this quotation functions within the argument.

In the mystery religions (e.g., cults of Demeter, Mithras, Isis), the "mystery" was a story presented during an initiation (Bremmer 2014, 37–83). Tertullian compared Christian baptism with initiatory rituals in the mystery religions (Tertullian, *Bapt.* 5.1; cf. Ign. *Eph.* 12.2). As a celebration of the foundational story of Christianity, this poem might have been appropriate at a baptism. But in our context, it is the opening bracket of an *inclusio* that closes with an allusion to Timothy's ordination (4:14). The whole of 3:14–4:16 functions as another charge to Timothy as a "good minister of Christ Jesus" (4:6), and 3:16 encapsulates the message he was ordained to proclaim.

In the mystery religions, the "mystery" was the foundational story of the cult, known only to initiates. The "mystery" in 3:16 expresses central doctrine in a way that is not obvious. Following James Scott's theories on the resistance strategies of marginalized groups, Neil Elliott has suggested that the reference to an inscrutable "mystery" (Rom. 11:25, 33) points to the "hidden transcript" in Pauline Christianity (Elliott 2004, 118; see "James Scott and 'Infrapolitics'" in the general introduction). In a similar way, this poem reflects the "hidden transcript" that grounded the community. It evokes the story for those who know it already.

> **1 Timothy 3:14–16 in the Rhetorical Flow**
>
> Letter opening (1:1–2)
>
> Proem: First charge to Timothy (1:3–20)
>
> First set of directives concerning the church (2:1–3:13)
>
> Second charge to Timothy (3:14–4:16)
>
> ▶ The foundation of the truth (3:14–16)

Tracing the Train of Thought

3:14–16. I am writing these things (3:14). Pastoral Paul regularly refers to "these things" by way of summary as he shifts to a new topic (cf. 3:14; 4:6; 6:2b; Titus 3:8; Malherbe 2010, 387). Here "these things" includes all of 2:1–3:13. But in this programmatic statement at the center of the letter, it could also refer to the whole letter, which is about Timothy's "conduct in the house of God."

The language **hoping to come to you soon, but if I am delayed** (3:14–15) is tantalizing but difficult to link to Paul's movements as we know them from the letters or Acts. Of course, there are many gaps in our knowledge of Paul's travels, but the following clause raises questions.

The reason for writing is **so that you may know how it is necessary to conduct yourself in the house of God** (3:15). The purpose is not generic ("how people ought to conduct themselves," NIV, ESV, NRSV) but specific to Timothy (Gk. subject of an infinitive is usually unexpressed when it is the same as the subject of the principal verb in the clause: Smyth 1956, §937). The principal verb is "that you may know," and the object of that verb is "how to conduct yourself" (KJV, CEB). Against common assertions that the purpose of the letter is to combat heresy, this verse indicates that the purpose is to instruct Timothy on his conduct. It seems odd that the real Timothy should have needed such instruction after serving as Paul's most trusted associate for so long (Hutson 1997, 60–61; see "Addressees" in the general introduction). This sentence, therefore, gives the impression that "Timothy" functions as a type for any young minister in training.

"House of God" was a common Jewish metaphor for the temple (2 Sam. 7:1–17; 1 Kings 8:19; etc.; Herzer 2008). It is theologically interesting to think of the community as a metaphorical "temple" (N. T. Wright 2013, 391–96), but we should not discard the domestic implications of the word "house." In reference to the temple, the metaphor "house" connotes familial relationship. When David sang, "I shall dwell in the house of the LORD forever" (Ps. 23:6 RSV), he was not thinking about the location of his cot but of being a member of God's family.

The church as "house of God" is Pauline (Gal. 6:10; Eph. 2:19), but the PE elaborate the idea (Verner 1983): **which is the church of the living God, a pillar and bulwark of the truth** (3:15). In the undisputed Pauline letters, "church" is a local congregation, and some read it that way here (Horrell 2001, 2008). The temple metaphor is also familiar from 1 Cor. 3:10–16, except that there Paul was building a local congregation on Christ as the foundation; whereas here the "pillar and bulwark of the truth" suggests something larger. We might discern an evolution in the metaphor from the church under construction on the foundation of Christ (1 Cor. 3:10–16; cf. 1 Pet. 2:5–6) to the church under construction on the foundation of the apostles and prophets, with Christ as the cornerstone (Eph. 2:19–22), to the completed church as the "pillar and bulwark" of the truth (1 Tim. 3:15). Especially if the PE are post-Pauline, this evolution suggests a trend over the course of the first century toward a "routinization of charisma" (Weber 1963, 60–79), greater institutionalization (M. MacDonald 1988; Horrell 2001), and higher ecclesiology (see below, "Theological Issues"). Luke Timothy Johnson (2001, 231–32, 237) reconciles the two ends of the spectrum by reading "pillar and bulwark" as a delayed appositional reference to "how it is necessary to conduct yourself." Timothy's proper conduct supports the truth. This reading could work if "Timothy" aspires to be an apostle, teacher, or prophet of the church (Gregory of Nyssa, *Vit. Mos.* 2.184). A young minister in training should be prepared to shoulder a great weight of responsibility. But in the end, the church collectively, not any individual, is the mainstay of the truth (Calvin on 1 Tim. 3:15).

The term "living God" (cf. 4:10) invokes the covenant God of Israel (Deut. 5:26; Ps. 42:2; Goodwin 2001, 15–41). In the postexilic period the "living God" came to be seen as the creator and universal sovereign. This verse echoes earlier expressions of monotheism (2:5) and the salvation of "all people" (2:4).

And confessedly great is the mystery of piety (3:16). The "mystery of piety" represents fundamental doctrine (cf. 2:5–6; see "Doctrines and Precepts" in the general introduction) that undergirds warnings about bad teachers (4:1–5) and instructions about ministerial formation (4:6–16). A proper Christian understanding of piety is grounded not in the story of Aeneas, a symbol of

Roman identity, nor in the story of Abraham, a symbol of Jewish identity, but in the story of Jesus Christ.

1 **Who was made evident in flesh,**
2 **Justified by the Spirit,**
3 **Seen by angels,**
4 **Proclaimed among the nations,**
5 **Believed in the world,**
6 **Taken up in glory.** (3:16)

Scholars debate the structure of the hymn. Some read it as six individual lines. To most interpreters, line 1 suggests the incarnation, and line 6 the ascension (cf. "taken up," Mark 16:19; Acts 1:2, 11, 22), so some have tried to read it as a linear narrative but without agreement on the six points of reference (Alford 1871, 333–35; Barrett 1963, 64–66; cf. D. J. MacLeod 2006). All attempts to extract a chronological narrative seem forced.

Others read the hymn as three couplets (e.g., Dibelius and Conzelmann 1972; Johnson 2001). For example, the first two lines give an impression of the dual nature of Christ as "flesh/spirit." Each couplet reflects a similar contrast between two realms, and the sequence contains a double inversion: A-B (flesh/spirit) B-A (angels/nations) A-B (world/glory). This leaves open how the three couplets are related to one another.

Still others read two triplets. Walter Lock reads lines 3 and 6 as parallel references to the Ascension: (1–3) the earthly Jesus seen and (4–6) the risen Christ proclaimed on earth (Lock 1924, 45; cf. Mounce 2000, 217–18). Robert H. Gundry argues for the structure ABB/CCD. He argues that line 1 (incarnation) and line 6 (ascension) form brackets that unify the hymn, with lines 2–3 referring to Christ's reception in the underworld, and lines 4–5 to his reception on earth (Gundry 1970).

Ultimately, whether the hymn is six lines, three couplets, or two triplets is not important, unless we wish to set it to music. Nor is it essential to identify each line with one specific referent, because poetic images are polyvalent. We need not insist on one "correct" interpretation. The poem is a collage that evokes the Christ story, with emphasis on resurrection.

Rather than telling the story, this poem invites reflection on its meaning. Line 1, **who was made evident in flesh**, alludes to the incarnation. Line 2, **vindicated by the Spirit**, alludes to the resurrection, by which the one condemned as a criminal in earthly court was vindicated. Yet the language could suggest the Holy Spirit at Jesus's baptism. Line 3, **seen by angels**, may allude to the ascension but could call to mind God's providential care (Mark 1:13) or Christ preaching to the spirits in prison (1 Pet. 3:18–19) or even the apostolic "messengers" who witnessed the resurrection ("was seen by x" in 1 Cor. 15:5–8; Barrett 1963, 64; Johnson 2001, 233). Line 4, **proclaimed among the nations,** and line 5, **believed in the world,** both express the universal implications of Christ's work, an important theme of this letter (2:1–7). Line 6, **taken up in glory,** probably alludes to the ascension but could suggest enthronement at the parousia (cf. "glory" in 2 Tim. 2:10; Titus 2:13).

This hymn expresses "the faith" on which Timothy is nourished (4:6) and from which "some will depart" (4:1). It expresses "the teaching" that Timothy has followed (4:6) and to which he should "hold fast" (4:16; see comments at 4:13). This hymn, associated with the "living God" (3:15), anticipates the "hope in the living God" that orients the minister's labor and struggle (4:10). The "mystery of piety" (3:16) anticipates the "piety" that is the aim of spiritual exercise (4:7) and of a minister's labor and struggle (4:10). Lines 4–5 reinforce the universal implications of the gospel (cf. 2:1–7; 4:10), while lines 3 and 6 anticipate an orientation toward the "life to come" (4:8; cf. 2 Tim. 1:16; 2:11).

Significantly missing is any explicit mention of the crucifixion. This hymn emphasizes the glorification of Christ rather than the suffering of Jesus.

Theological Issues

Ecclesiology

The church as the "pillar and bulwark of the truth" (3:15) speaks to the old "high church / low church" debate between Protestants and Catholics. In common parlance, "high church" and "low church" refer to styles of worship, whether liturgy and music are formal or informal. But the term "high church" originated in reference to ecclesial authority. In the wake of the Reformation and in the heat of debates about church polity, the term "high church" came to apply to Anglican theologians of the Oxford Movement as shorthand for an emphasis on the importance not only of ancient liturgies but especially of the apostolic succession of bishops, who were the locus of authority (e.g., Keble 1833). Protestants challenged the authority of the pope and bishops and developed a "high view of Scripture" as an alternative locus for authority. Both sides tended to push their views to extremes. In 1870, Vatican I (First Vatican Council) issued the dogmatic constitution *Pastor Aeternus*, affirming papal infallibility. Soon afterward, Protestant theologians at Princeton Theological Seminary articulated classic statements on the inerrancy of Scripture (Hodge and Warfield 1881; Warfield 1915). In retrospect, both sides were responding to the shifting socioreligious context, each in its own way being "reflective of classic modernity's desire for epistemic certainty" (Powell 2008, 196).

Both sides appeal to the PE. "High Scripture" advocates can cite 2 Tim. 3:16 to argue that the church must submit to Scripture. "High church" advocates can argue that the church existed before the NT, produced the NT, and according to 1 Tim. 3:15, is guarantor of proper interpretation of Scripture.

While 1 Tim. 3:15–16 does not entail a doctrine of apostolic succession, it does suggest a development toward the idea of a "rule of faith" (Lat. *regula fidei*). That is, the church interprets Scripture in accordance with the apostolic teaching of the story of Jesus Christ as a "rule" (Gk. *kanōn*, Gal. 6:14–16; Hutson 2004). In the second century, the story of Jesus served as the "canon," or yardstick, to define orthodoxy (e.g., Clement of Alexandria, *Strom.* 6.15; Irenaeus, *Haer.* 1.9.4; Tertullian, *Praescr.* 13; *Marc.* 1.21). The "canon" was not a creed, since it had no fixed wording. It was the church's consensus regarding the central ideas of apostolic teaching about Jesus Christ, as attested in Scripture.

I have outlined the "high church" and "high Scripture" positions in broad strokes. Upon reflection, we can see problems with both papal infallibility (Powell 2008) and scriptural inerrancy (Christian Smith 2011). Thoughtful theologians seek to avoid extreme positions by finding ways to value both the authority of Scripture and the authority of the church. For a high understanding of Scripture from a "high church" position, see the Vatican II (Second Vatican Council) dogmatic constitution *Dei Verbum* (1965). For a high understanding of the church from a "high Scripture" tradition, see Everett Ferguson (1996).

Incarnation

Jesus was "made evident in flesh." Flesh is not qualified. It is not "male flesh," not "Jewish flesh," not "freeborn flesh," just "flesh." When he entered into the human condition, Jesus took on the particular flesh of a freeborn, male, Jewish peasant from Galilee. But the incarnation is not about God's identity with a particular demographic; it is an identity with "flesh," the universal human condition.

The Resurrection as a Guide to Conduct

The hymn is not a creed that lists all the central tenets of the faith but a poem that views one idea through a kaleidoscope of shifting images. This hymn celebrates the resurrected Christ. Karl Barth even suggests that all six lines of 1 Tim. 3:16 refer to the resurrection, so we could use it as an Easter hymn (*ChDog* IV/3.1:291–92). Obviously, there would be no resurrection if Jesus had not died, but the important thing is that he did not stay dead. The meaning of Jesus's death is not in its gruesomeness but in the resurrection by which he "nullified death" (2 Tim. 1:10). In 1 Cor. 15, Paul merely mentions Jesus's death without specifying how he died (15:3), but he argues at length for the meaning of the resurrection (15:4–58). There is a reason why the holiest day on the Christian calendar is not Good Friday but Easter Sunday.

A good minister should ask: How does the resurrection inform my decisions and actions? "Do not be conformed to this age, but be transformed by the renewal of your mind" (Rom. 12:2). What does it mean to live in the present age with a mind oriented to the age to come? Such thinking pervades Paul's letters (e.g., N. T. Wright 2003, 109–398). It should pervade our preaching.

1 Timothy 4:1–5

Doctrines of Demons

Introductory Matters

This section is a counterpoint to the previous. The "teachings of demons" (4:1–5) contrast with the Christ hymn (3:16) as the wellspring of theology. "Latter times" (4:1) suggest recent innovations, in contrast with the well-established "pillar of the truth" (3:15). The text demands a decision between two options.

This is one of two passages in the PE (cf. 2 Tim. 2:18) that give any hint about specific false doctrines, although the details are vague. The polemic picks up the invective of 1:3–11. The language in verses 2 and 7 was typical of the abuse ancient rhetoricians heaped on one another (Karris 1973; Johnson 1989, 430–34). But the reference to spirits and demons (4:1) gives a Jewish cast (see comments at 2 Tim. 1:7; cf. John 8:48; 1QS 2.5–10; 3.18–21), which becomes more distinct in the rebuttal in verses 3–5. Pastoral Paul is a Jewish Christian engaged in a debate about the interpretation and application of Gen. 1. This fits with his earlier characterization of would-be Torah scholars who don't know what they are talking about (1:7).

Jewish polemic often represents demons as advocating self-indulgence. "Understand, my children, that in the last times your sons will abandon sincerity

> **1 Timothy 4:1–5 in the Rhetorical Flow**
>
> Letter opening (1:1–2)
>
> Proem: First charge to Timothy (1:3–20)
>
> First set of directives concerning the church (2:1–3:13)
>
> Second charge to Timothy (3:14–4:16)
>
>   The foundation of the truth (3:14–16)
>
> ▶ Doctrines of demons (4:1–5)

and align themselves with insatiable desire" (*T. Iss.* 6.1, trans. H. C. Kee, *OTP* 1:804; cf. *T. Reu.* 4.7, 11; *T. Jos.* 7.4; *Mart. Ascen. Isa.* 2.4–5). But in our passage the opponents "forbid marrying" (4:3), which hardly sounds like promoting promiscuity. This boilerplate invective signifies mainly "that someone *was* an opponent" (Johnson 1989, 433).

Tracing the Train of Thought

4:1–5. But the Spirit expressly says that in the latter times some will apostatize from the faith, giving attention to deceitful spirits and teachings of demons (4:1). "But" marks a contrast, and the text presents a choice. Rather than the story of the resurrected Christ (3:16), the apostates "give attention to deceitful spirits and teachings of demons." By contrast, Timothy should "give attention . . . to the teaching" (4:13). "Those who apostatize from the faith" function as negative examples of what a good minister should *not* be.

The "latter times" (cf. 2 Tim. 3:1; 4:3) reflects an apocalyptic understanding that things will get worse before the day of the Lord (cf. 2 Thess. 2:2–4). The Spirit's speech is a prophetic warning, much like Paul's speech to the Ephesian elders (Acts 20:22, 29–30; cf. 2 Tim. 4:3).

One question is whether "deceitful spirits and teachings of demons" are two different things or a hendiadys, two terms expressing one idea. According to Dale B. Martin (2010), in 1 Cor. 10:20–21 Paul follows OT usage by identifying demons with pagan idols (e.g., Deut. 32:17; Pss. 95:5 LXX; 105:37 LXX), but the equation of demons with unclean spirits is rare (only *Jub.* 10) until the late first century (e.g., Mark 5:1–20//Luke 8:26–39; Josephus, *J.W.* 6.47; *Ant.* 6.166, 168, 211, 214; 8.46–49), and it gains currency in Justin Martyr, Tatian, and Origen. Those who argue that Paul wrote this letter should read "spirits" and "demons" as two different species, whatever those might be. If we read "spirits" and "demons" as synonymous, then the phrase seems post-Pauline.

Pastoral Paul continues excoriating the apostates, **in hypocrisy of lies, their own conscience being seared** (4:2). "Hypocrisy" and "lies" were stock charges against teachers of rhetoric (Isocrates, *Soph.* 1, 7–8; Seneca, *Ep.* 108.35–37; Karris 1973, 552–53). Burning can be good, if one cauterizes a wound, but a seared conscience can no longer function reliably.

The false doctrine, **who prevent to marry** (4:3), is vague, with no indication as to why the teachers prevented marriage. In the second century, followers of Marcion renounced marriage and sex (Hippolytus, *Heresies* 7.18). The *Acts of Paul* re-presented Paul as requiring celibacy. Some suggest that the PE were written specifically to counter either Gnosticism (Dibelius and Conzelmann 1972, 65–67) or the apocryphal *Acts* (D. MacDonald 1983). Either of these positions would push us to date this letter in the mid-second century or later. But we cannot identify these marriage-renouncing opponents with certainty.

Another false doctrine, **to abstain from foods** (4:3), is grammatically ambiguous in that the verb "preventing" is followed by two infinitives describing what the false teachers prevented. A literal translation is "preventing to marry, to abstain from foods." What does this mean?

A. Most interpreters read 4:3 as a grammatical slip (*anacolouthon*) and supply an extra verb: "preventing to marry, [compelling] to abstain from foods." On this interpretation, the false teachers required ascetic practices regarding sex and diet. But from what foods did they abstain and why? Were they Montanists, who opposed marriage and required extra fasts (Eusebius, *Hist. eccl.* 5.18.2)?
   1. Perhaps the false teachers advocated a kosher diet. That would be consistent with "those who want to be Torah teachers" (1:7). But then were they Jewish Christians who wanted gentile converts to adopt Jewish practices? Or were they gentile Christians making a mess of Torah because they lacked a proper framework to understand it?
   2. Perhaps the false teachers brought dietary scruples from gentile backgrounds. Pythagoreans refused to eat animals, among other things (Iamblichus, *VP* 106–9), while Stoics recommended temporary dietary restrictions as a matter of practicing self-discipline (Seneca, *Ep.* 18.5–6; 123.3; Epictetus, *Diatr.* 3.13.21; Corrington 1992).
   3. In the second century, followers of Marcion adopted an ascetic diet (Tertullian, *Marc.* 1.14.5; cf. Hippolytus, *Heresies* 7.18; McGowan 2001). Some assume that the opponents represented some form of Gnosticism (Dibelius and Conzelmann 1972).

All variations on interpretation A may be manufacturing evidence by supplying the supposedly missing verb "compelling." Is it possible to understand 4:3 without "correcting" the text by adding words to it?

B. It might sound odd that the teachers would prevent believers from abstaining, but the Nicolaitans in Ephesus and Pergamum (Rev. 2:6, 15) apparently opposed those who abstained from idol meat, for they taught people to "eat food sacrificed to idols" (Rev. 2:14). And the "strong" in 1 Cor. 8–10 had no qualms about eating idol meat. Were the opponents in 1 Tim. 4 Nicolaitans and/or "strong" Corinthians (Schüssler Fiorenza 1998, 117–20; Trebilco 2008, 331–35)? If so, then on both marriage and diet, we could draw a line from 1 Cor. 7–10 to 1 Tim. 4. In both instances, false teachers took Paul's teaching to extreme positions that our letter now opposes. On both issues Pastoral Paul allows for abstinence without insisting on it (Rom. 14:14; 1 Cor. 10:25–33).

Interpretation *B* is attractive because it does not rely on inserting words into the text and offers a consistently Pauline position. Nevertheless, we cannot absolutely rule out all the variations of *A*. If the purpose of this letter were to combat false teaching, we would have to say that Paul was remarkably unclear in identifying the teaching he opposed.

Whatever the apostates thought about diet, Pastoral Paul was open to eating any foods, **which God created to be received with thanksgiving by those who are faithful and who know the truth. Because God's whole creation is good, and nothing is to be rejected, if it is received with thanksgiving; for it is sanctified through the word of God and prayer** (4:3b–5). This rationale for unrestricted diet alludes to the creation story: "and behold it was very good." Genesis 1:31 is the sanctifying "word of God." The "sanctifying prayer" is a thanksgiving (4:3, 4) for the food one is about to eat. The custom of giving thanks for a meal recalls both Paul (Rom. 14:6; 1 Cor. 10:30) and Jesus (Matt. 14:19; 15:36), both of whom reflected Jewish practice (*m. Ber.* 6–7). To say food is "sanctified" is to say it has "acquired a holy quality by its consecration to God; by being acknowledged as God's gift, and partaken of as nourishing the life for God's service" (Adewuya 2016, 150).

1 Timothy 4:6–16

Training for Piety

Introductory Matters

Although the PE as a whole reflect the training regimen of Greco-Roman philosophers (see "Philosophical Training Regimen" in the general introduction), this section is the most concentrated expression, touching on all the elements except writing exercises. It includes pedagogical language: "teach/teaching" (*didaskō, didaskalia*, 4:6, 11, 13, 16), "example" (*typos*, 4:12), "give attention" (*prosechein*, 4:13), "practice" (*meletaō*, 4:14–15), "progress" (*prokopē*, 4:15), and "attend" (*epechō*, 4:16). It employs the metaphors of exercise (*gymnasia*, 4:7–8) and struggle (*agōn*, 4:10). All this is in the context of the training of a "good minister of Christ Jesus" (4:6).

Becoming a good minister involves proper spiritual diet (4:6–7), proper exercise (4:8–11), and good habits (4:12–16). Timothy must study and practice so he can choose between the words of the faith (4:6), summed up in the hymn (3:16), and the teachings of demons (4:1–5), associated with apostates (4:1). This regimen will help Timothy develop spiritually healthy habits based on right doctrine and develop instincts for avoiding bad behaviors that stem from false doctrine.

**1 Timothy 4:6–16
in the Rhetorical Flow**

Letter opening (1:1–2)

Proem: First charge to Timothy (1:3–20)

First set of directives concerning the church (2:1–3:13)

Second charge to Timothy (3:14–4:16)

  The foundation of the truth (3:14–16)

  Doctrines of demons (4:1–5)

▶ Training for piety (4:6–16)

    Proper diet (4:6–7)

    Exercise (4:8–11)

    Practice (4:12–16)

Tracing the Train of Thought

Proper Diet (4:6–7)

4:6–7. By setting these things before the brothers, you will be a good minister of Christ Jesus, because you were nourished on the words of the faith and the good teaching, which you have come to follow (4:6). This letter represents Timothy as a "minister" (*diakonos*), not a bishop. Timothy will become a good "server" of the diet on which he himself was "nourished." The verb "nourished" (*ektrephomenos*, Gk. causal participle) became a generic term for the care and training of children (cf. 5:10), but its original sense of "nourish" fits this context. The sentence casts Paul as a parent (cf. 2 Tim. 3:10–17) who "nourished" Timothy on "the faith" from which others turn aside (4:1) and on "the good teaching" (cf. 2 Tim. 3:10; cf. "healthy teaching," 1 Tim. 1:10; 6:3). The recommended diet is "the faith" (e.g., 2:4–5; 3:16) that Paul taught and modeled (e.g., 1:12–17; cf. 2 Tim. 3:10–17).

The instruction, **but avoid profane and old wives' tales** (4:7), reflects ancient stereotypes of old women as gossips (Parkin 2003, 86; Kartzow 2009, 137–39). The educational context also calls to mind Plato's ideas on the education of children (*Republic* 376e–412b). Plato criticized poets for debasing the gods by characterizing them as full of vices. Children do not have the capacity to distinguish between literal and symbolic stories (*Republic* 378d), so the state should legislate which stories "nurses and mothers" might tell to "mold the souls" of young children (*Republic* 377c) and make them "pious toward the gods [*theosebeis*]" (*Republic* 383c; cf. 1 Tim. 2:10).

Our letter admonishes Timothy to "avoid profane and old wives' tales" associated with childhood. This does not mean women should not teach children (witness Lois and Eunice, 2 Tim. 1:5; 3:14–15). Nor does it mean that tales cannot be effective in teaching religion (Mbuwayesango 2014, 81–82, on folktales in teaching children). But Timothy is no longer a child. A youth (4:12) should set aside children's stories, begin learning to critique theologically misleading stories, and be nourished on "the words of the faith and the good teaching" (4:6).

Exercise (4:8–11)

4:8–11. It is not enough to commit good teaching to memory. The healthy student must put words into practice (Seneca, *Ep.* 75.7–8). The exhortation to **exercise yourself for piety** (4:7) points to the spiritual exercises spelled out in 4:12–16. The analogy between physical and spiritual health continues: **for bodily exercise is beneficial for a little, but piety is beneficial for everything** (4:8a). The philosophers valued physical exercise (*gymnasia*) as serving the larger goal of training the mind (ps.-Crates, *Ep.* 3; ps.-Diogenes, *Ep.* 31.4 [Malherbe 1977, 54, 136]). Diogenes the Cynic said there were two kinds of training (*askēsis*), mental and physical, and neither was complete without the other (Diogenes Laërtius, *Lives* 6.70). Epictetus taught that one should practice the principles of philosophy the way an athlete trains the body (Epictetus, *Diatr.* 1.4.13–17; 1.24.1–2; 2.17.29–33; 2.18.27; 3.23.2; 4.4.11–13; *Ench.* 29.4–7). Pastoral Paul argues in rabbinic style from the lesser to the greater. If physical exercise is beneficial, how much more the exercise of piety?

The goal of training is "piety" (*eusebeia*). Classic Stoic doctrine used the term "duty" (*kathēkonta*, Diogenes Laërtius, *Lives* 7.25, 108). "Duties" included, "being a good citizen, marrying, shaping children, piety toward God [*theon sebein*], caring for [*epimeleisthai*] parents" (Epictetus, *Diatr.* 3.7.25–26; cf. Cicero, *Off.* 1.160). But instead of the Stoic "duty," Pastoral Paul uses "piety" (*eusebeia*). He is co-opting philosophical language and turning it in a Judeo-Christian direction (see sidebar at 2:2; I. H. Marshall 1999, 141; Donelson 1986, 159–62).

Pastoral Paul turns his argument specifically toward eschatology. Piety is beneficial **because it holds a promise of life in the present and of life to come. Trustworthy is the saying and worthy of all acceptance** (4:8b–9). "Life to come" is consistent with the emphasis on resurrection (3:16; 2 Tim. 2:11; Titus 3:7; cf. Rom. 12; 1 Cor. 15; Phil. 3). The "trustworthy saying" underscores this point as an element of the tradition deposited with Timothy (see comments at 1:15).

Because for this we labor and struggle (4:10). The antecedent of "this" is "life to come" (4:9), which orients the labor of a "good minister" (4:6). "Labor" (*kopiaō*) is a Pauline metaphor for evangelism (1 Thess. 2:9; 3:5; 5:12; 1 Cor. 15:10; Gal. 4:11; Phil. 2:16).

The verb "struggle" (*agōnizō*) reflects the philosopher's "struggle" (*agōn*; cf. 6:12) against passions and desires, which in this context is associated with "piety" (4:7) and "purity" (4:12). Instead of "we struggle," some ancient manuscripts read, "we are reproached," which would connect this verse back to the "reproach of the slanderer" (3:7). But the verb "reproach" is not Pauline (only Rom. 15:3 quoting Ps. 69:9). On the other hand, "struggle" is Pauline (1 Cor. 9:25; cf. Col. 1:29; 4:12; Pfitzner 1967) and anticipates the exhortation in 1 Tim. 6:12 (cf. 2 Tim. 4:7).

Because we have come to hope in the living God, who is savior of all people, specifically [or especially] **of the faithful** (4:10). Jewish theology connected the "living God" (cf. 3:15) with the God of Sinai (Deut. 4:33 LXX; 5:26; 2 Macc. 15:4; Philo, *Decal.* 67) and the temple in Jerusalem (e.g., Ps. 84; 2 Kings 19//Isa. 37). Mark J. Goodwin (2001) has shown that Hellenistic Jews also associated the "living God" with hope for the restoration of Israel (Hosea 1:10 [= 2:1 LXX]), the eschaton (*Jub.* 1.24–25; 3 Macc. 6:28; *Jos. Asen.* 19.8), and God's universal sovereignty (Dan. 5:23 LXX; 6:27 LXX; Bel 5 [Theodotion]). "Savior of all people" recapitulates 2:4.

The adverb "specifically [or especially]" (*malista*) surfaces questions about universalism. The traditional "especially" (KJV; Poythress 2002; Kim 2004) implies that "the faithful" is a subset of the group "all people," suggesting

---

Epictetus on How a Youth Can Be an Effective Teacher

"Great power is always dangerous for the beginner. We ought, therefore, to bear such things according to our power—nay in accordance with nature… Practice [meletēson, cf. 1 Tim. 4:14–15] *sometime a style of living as one who is ill, so that at some other time you may live as one who is healthy* [cf. 1 Tim. 1:10; 6:3]. *Take no food; drink only water* [hydropotēson, cf. 1 Tim. 5:23]; *refrain sometime altogether from desire, so that at some other time you may desire rationally. And if you do so rationally whenever you have some good in you, you will desire well. 'No, but we wish to live as sages* [sophoi] *and to benefit* [ōphelein, cf. 1 Tim. 4:8] *people immediately.' What sort of benefit? Indeed, have you benefited yourself? But you wish to convert them. Indeed, have you converted yourself? Do you wish to benefit them? Show them in yourself what sort of people philosophy makes, and stop talking nonsense. As you eat, benefit those who eat with you; as you drink, benefit those who drink with you; as you yield to everybody, as you give place, as you carry yourself, benefit them in this way, and don't spray them with your own spittle."* (Epictetus, *Diatr.* 3.13.20–23, adapted from Oldfather, LCL)

---

that "the faithful" are the preferred but not exclusive objects of salvation. "Specifically" understands *malista* as connecting two designations for the same group, when the second is more specific than the first, so "all people, specifically, all faithful people" (cf. 5:8, 17; Skeat 1979 cites examples, of which the most compelling is POxy 3302). With this translation, God's desire to save "all people" will not be realized apart from their coming to faith. On the choice between these translations, see "Theological Issues," below.

Command and teach these things (4:11). "These things" summarizes the points just made, before shifting to a new topic (cf. 3:14; 4:6; 6:2b; Titus 3:8). Verses 8–10 express some of what Timothy should teach, but the new topic is habits he should cultivate.

Practice (4:12–16)

4:12–16. Let no one despise your youth (12). This admonition seems anachronistic as a description of the historical Timothy (see "Addressees" and "Chronology of Paul's Life" in the general introduction). But we could read "Timothy" as a vehicle through whom Pastoral Paul addresses young ministers, who needed to overcome the stereotype of youth as irresponsible and inexperienced. The following paragraphs advise how a young minister gains credibility.

But be an example for the believers in word, in conduct, in love, in faith, in purity (4:12). In philosophical education, a mentor set a good example (*typos*) for his protégés (Seneca, *Ep.* 6.5–6; Pliny the Younger, *Ep.* 8.14.4–10; Malherbe 1986, 135–38). Not only did Paul present himself as a model (1 Thess.

1:6; 2:14; 1 Cor. 4:16; 11:1; Phil. 3:17; Fiore 1986, 164–90), he also held up Timothy as a model (1 Cor. 4:16–17; Phil. 2:19–24). This letter encourages Timothy to cultivate himself as a model for his own followers. "Conduct" here is grounded in the hymn (3:15–16). "Conduct" is general, while "love, faith, and purity" are specific. The point resembles Epictetus's admonition that "for a beginner" the most effective teaching will be demonstrating "what sort of person philosophy makes" (see sidebar). But what was framed above in terms of Greco-Roman religion as "the mystery of piety" (3:15) is now framed in terms of Judeo-Christian ethics as "love, faith, purity."

Until I come (4:13) suggests that Paul expects to join Timothy shortly in Ephesus. It is impossible to correlate this with Paul's movements as reflected in the letters or Acts.

Western commentators almost universally take verse 13 as a description of the public duties of a minister, to teach, read, and exhort. But I shall argue that it is about Timothy's ministerial formation. **Give attention to the teaching** does not mean "teach." The expression "give attention to" (*prosechein* + dat.) points to the source of understanding (Heb. 2:1; 2 Pet. 1:19; Acts 9:6, 10, 11; 16:14). Bad teachers "give attention" to "myths and endless genealogies" (1:4; cf. 2 Tim. 4:4; Titus 3:9) and to "deceitful spirits and instructions of demons" (4:1).

To the reading (4:13). In this context of training and practice, Pastoral Paul is assigning Timothy to keep reading for himself. John Chrysostom commented tersely on this phrase, "Let us then be instructed not to neglect the study of the sacred writings" (*Hom. 1 Tim.* 13, *NPNF*[1]; cf. Origen, *Comm. Matt.* 10.15 on Matt. 13.52). Because this ancient interpretation goes against entrenched assumptions of modern, Western scholarship, it requires justification.

Many translations add words to the text: "give attention to the *public reading of Scripture*" (NRSV, NIV, ESV, etc.). It is true that the word "reading" (*anagnōsis*) is used elsewhere for the reading of Scripture (2 Cor. 3:14) and for public reading in a synagogue (Luke 4:16; Acts 13:15). But those passages explicitly identify specific texts (of the old covenant; Isaiah; Torah and Prophets) and synagogue settings (Nazareth; Pisidian Antioch). Most often in the NT, when people "read" (*anaginōskō*), they are reading Scripture, and it is common for them to do so in public settings (Luke 4:16; Acts 13:27; 15:21). But the word itself does not imply anything about the content or location of the reading. Sometimes a person reads for private study (Acts 8:28, 30, 32). Sometimes the focus is on the meaning of Scripture, while the setting is irrelevant (Matt. 12:3 par.; Matt. 12:5; 19:3; 21:16, 42 par.; 22:31 par.; Luke 10:26). Sometimes people read letters (Acts 15:31; 23:34; 2 Cor. 1:13; 1 Thess. 5:20; Eph. 3:4; Col. 4:16) or inscriptions (Matt. 27:37 par.). Depending on the context, "reading" could refer to reading any text in any setting. The present context has to do with the formation of Timothy into a "good minister of Christ Jesus" (1 Tim. 4:6).

A major aspect of ancient philosophical training was reading (*anagnōsis*) works of the founder(s) of the school. A budding philosopher should "give attention" (*prosechein*) to such texts (Plutarch, *Virt. prof.* 8 [79–80]). In addition to acquiring intimate familiarity with the foundational writings of one's own school, a philosopher should read the works of other schools. One should not presume to advise others how to behave before thoroughly digesting and applying the works of one's own school. Study was a lifelong habit (Seneca, *Ep.* 82.3; Dio Chrysostom, *Or.* 18.1; cf. Philo, *Contempl. Life* 28–30). An educated person's books were like a farmer's tools (ps.-Plutarch, *Lib. ed.* 10 [8b]).

When Seneca wrote to his friend Lucilius, a beginner in his study of Stoic philosophy, Seneca sent him books with passages marked (*Ep.* 6.5). He advised not to skim many books but to master one before continuing to another (*Ep.* 2), reading whole books and not merely excerpts from handbooks (*Ep.* 39.1–2). Reading for oneself was more profitable than hearing a book read (*Ep.* 41.3). Seneca offered himself as a model, often referring to his own study, much as Pastoral Paul models lifelong study in asking for scrolls (2 Tim. 4:13).

Epictetus cited numerous authors in his lectures and assumed that his students read widely (*Diatr.* 2.16.34; 2.19.6–15; 3.2.13; 3.26.3). He expounded texts line by line (*Diatr.* 1.10.8; 1.17.11–12), but he also expected students to read for themselves (*Diatr.* 2.19.10). He said that books are like teachers and role models (*Diatr.* 2.16.34–35; 1.17.13–19). Reading was "a kind of preparation for the act of living" (*Diatr.* 4.4.11, trans. Oldfather, LCL).

In sum, to become an effective minister, Timothy should "give attention to the reading." We should probably understand some or all of the Scriptures of Israel, as well as this letter, other letters of Paul, and perhaps other texts.

To the exhortation (4:13). It is true that exhortation is one of Timothy's duties (5:1; 6:2b; cf. 2 Tim. 4:2; Titus 2:6, 15), just as it is a duty of an overseer (Titus 1:9). In this context of training and practice, however, the definite article in "*the* exhortation" suggests that Timothy is supposed to "give attention" to some specific exhortation he received on a prior occasion (1:3; 2:1). The immediate context suggests the exhortation of the elders when they ordained Timothy as a minister (4:14).

To the instruction (4:13). Again, it is true that teaching is one of Timothy's duties (4:11). But "*the* instruction" refers in the PE to a body of doctrine passed down from Paul to Timothy (*hē didaskalia*, 1 Tim. 1:9; 6:1, 3; 2 Tim. 3:10; Titus 2:7, 10; cf. *hē didachē* in Titus 1:9). Also, the previous context associates "the good teaching" with "the words of the faith" on which Timothy was "nourished" (4:6; cf. 2 Tim. 3:10).

From a Cynic point of view, the mark of a false prophet was "saying nothing healthy" (*mēden hygies legein*; Lucian, *Dialogues of the Dead* 9 [28].447). Likewise in the PE, "the healthy teaching" is the standard (1 Tim. 1:10) to which bad teachers give no attention (2 Tim. 4:3). It is the standard by which a teacher measures his words (Titus 2:1). We see hints at Timothy's prior instruction in the "faithful sayings" (1:15; 3:1; 4:9) and the creedal traditions (2:5–6; 3:16; 6:15–16) scattered throughout the letter. By meditating on healthy teaching, Timothy will be better able to present himself as "an example for the believers" (4:12).

An important discipline for philosophers was meditation on prior instruction (Newman 1989). A student must spend time digesting new and complex ideas, working out implications, and putting them into practice. Epictetus likened assumptions unexercised (*agymnastoi*) to armor stored away and rusting. Therefore, "In wrestling or in writing or in reading, I am not satisfied with mere learning, but I turn over and over the arguments presented to me, and fashion new ones, and likewise syllogisms with equivocal premises" (*Diatr.* 4.6.14–15, trans. Oldfather, LCL; cf. 3.10.1–4). "Give attention to . . . the exhortation, the instruction" is a literal counterpart to the metaphorical spiritual diet of "the words of the faith and the instruction" (4:6).

Do not neglect the gift that is in you, that was given to you on account of prophecies with the laying on of hands by the eldership. Practice these things; be in them (4:14–15). The language of "neglect" (*ameleō*) and "practice" (*meletaō*) were typical of philosophical training. Book learning was not an end in itself but should inform practice. A student, having read, should, "go home at once and not neglect [*amelein*] his concerns," since the goal is "to practice [*meletan*] how he may rid his life of sorrows and lamentations " (Epictetus, *Diatr.* 1.4.22–23, trans. Oldfather, LCL, modified).

Pastoral Paul does not specify what "gift" (*charisma*) was in Timothy. Several gifts in various Pauline lists (Rom. 12:6–8; 1 Cor. 12:4–11, 27–31; Eph. 4:11–12) resonate with the thrust of this letter. Since Timothy is learning to be a "good minister" (*diakonos*, 4:6), the gift of ministry (*diakonia*, Rom. 12:7; 1 Cor. 12:5) would fit this context.

The "laying on of hands by the eldership" suggests an ordination. There were precedents in ancient Israel (Num. 8:9–10; 27:15–23) and parallels in rabbinic tradition (Ferguson 1960, 1992). Most English translators render the phrase *dia prophēteias* as "through prophecy" (Gk. gen. sg.), suggesting that the elders prophesied when they laid hands on Timothy. But elsewhere those who lay on hands do not prophesy; they pray (Acts 6:6; 13:3; Ferguson 1975, 5–6). So we might better translate it as "on account of prophecies" (Gk. acc. pl.), suggesting that the elders discerned some divine directive in choosing Timothy (cf. 1:18; Acts 13:2).

The point of practice is **so that your progress may be evident to all** (4:15). In philosophical jargon, "progress" described the path of a person who renounced vice and began striving toward wisdom (e.g., Philo, *Agr.* 157–60). Such a person was not yet "wise" (*sophos*) but a "lover of wisdom" (*philosophos*) who manifested understanding of his philosophy through behavior. Epictetus admonished students that studying Chrysippus was not an end in itself. The one who keeps and guards the teachings of Chrysippus in daily life—while bathing, while eating, doing anything—"this is the one who is progressing to truth" (*Diatr.* 1.4.18–21). Seneca exhorted Lucilius that, while he had not yet reached "perfect wisdom," he was making "progress" through continuous study, self-examination, and practice (*Ep.* 16.1–3; cf. 25.6; 75.8). Plutarch compared philosophical study with going to a physician: the first step in making progress toward health is recognizing the symptoms of illness and submitting to treatment (*Virt. prof.* 11 [81f–82a]). Indicators of progress included changes in conduct that result from close attention to the writings of philosophers (Plutarch, *Virt. prof.* 8 [79c–80a]), speech (*logos*) that has a positive impact on others (*Virt. prof.* 9 [80b–e]), and turning words into actions (*Virt. prof.* 14 [84b]).

Our passage resonates with the philosophical training regimen. This letter depicts Timothy making "progress," learning through constant reading, meditation on and practicing what he has been taught. At this stage, he should not overwhelm his flock with argument. He should "be an example for the believers" (4:12).

Give attention to yourself and to the teaching. Remain in them (4:16). This verse is a counterpoint to the warning in 4:1 and reiterates 4:13. Pastoral Paul encourages self-reflection (cf. Luke 12:1; 17:3; 21:34; Acts 20:28).

For by doing this you will save both yourself and those who hear you (4:16). In medical contexts the verb "save" (*sōzein*) means "heal" (Mark 5:23, 28, 34; 6:56; 10:52; Luke 7:50; 8:36, 48, 50; 17:19; 18:42; John 11:12; Acts 14:9, etc.). As physicians of the soul, philosophers "saved/healed" people from their moral "sickness" (Dio Chrysostom, *Or.* 32.10, 16–18; Philo, *Worse* 109–11; Malherbe 1989, 128–30; 2005, 340–43). This sense of "save" is Pauline (1 Cor. 7:16; 9:22; 10:33; Rom. 11:14; cf. Glad 1995, 78–79, 203, 252). Like Paul, Epictetus advised students that their exemplary behavior would "benefit" (*ōphelein*) both themselves and their hearers (*Diatr.* 3.13.23 [see sidebar at 4:12]; cf. "beneficial," *ōphelimos* in 1 Tim. 4:8). Philosophers spoke of "saving" people from enslavement to worldly passions into the freedom of the philosophical lifestyle (Plutarch, *Adol. poet. aud.* 1 [15a]; a "curative [*sōterios*] drug," Philo, *Worse* 110). Timothy's example (4:12) should lead to spiritual health and freedom from enslavement to appetites and desires.

In sum, 1 Tim. 3:14–4:16 describes Timothy's conduct in the house of God (3:15). As a young minister, he should choose carefully "the teaching" to which he will "give attention" (4:2, 6, 13, 16), rejecting unprofitable areas of study (4:7). He should be grounded in the celebration of Christ's resurrection (3:16) and in the hope of the life to come (4:8). He should "exercise" and "practice" a regimen that cultivates "piety" (4:8), regular reading and meditation on what he has been taught (4:13), that he might be a good "example" (4:12). In this way, Timothy will "save both himself and those who hear him" (4:16).

Theological Issues

Universalism

Verse 10 raises again the question of the extent of God's universal sovereignty (see "Theological Issues" at 2:1–7). If God is the savior of "all people" (cf. 1 John 4:14), then is faith necessary? If "the faithful" are a subset of "all people," then will God find a way to save everyone? Or if God saves only "the faithful," then is God's universal sovereignty being challenged by a rebellion among God's creatures?

And how should we think about the ultimate victory of Jesus? Should we understand Jesus's victory as a surgical strike to rescue a few faithful followers before destroying the majority of creatures? In that case, a "good minister of Christ Jesus" is merely trying to get a few hostages to an extraction point. Or should we understand victory as Jesus liberating all who are under the tyranny of Sin and Death, in order to reconcile them to God? In that case, the enemy is not the rebellious creatures but Death itself (1 Cor. 15:26, 54–55; 2 Tim. 1:10), and a good minister is engaged in a "ministry of reconciliation," as God is "reconciling the world to Godself" (2 Cor. 5:18–19).

One profound thinker on this point was the Reformed theologian Karl Barth, whose arguments are so subtle that all sides claim him as their champion. Barth did not endorse a doctrine of universalism per se. But he did ponder Christ as a type of Adam (Rom. 5:12–21), in whom humanity itself is elect. Barth absolutely refused to impose any limits on God's freedom to act as God chooses. So, rather than referring to God's election of the "totality" of all human beings, he preferred to think of God's election of the "limitless many" (*ChDog* II/2:421–22). Barth affirmed God's will that all people "should be brought subjectively to the truth" (*ChDog* IV/4:29). If the ways of God are inscrutable, the mission of the evangelist is not. The minister who has "hope in the living God" should not think anyone is so far given over to the "doctrines of demons" as to be unworthy of any effort to instill true piety. "For this we labor and struggle."

A Regimen for Spiritual Formation

I have argued that 4:6–16 reflects the language of education and training in Greco-Roman philosophical schools. This goes against the weight of Western tradition, which is heavily invested in reading this passage as a description of Timothy's duties as teacher. It is, however, consistent with Eastern Orthodox tradition.

Typical is *Directions to Hesychasts*, composed by two fourteenth-century monks, Callistus of Xanthopoulos and Ignatius of Xanthopoulos, and preserved in the *Philokalia* (on which, see "Theological Issues" at 1 Tim. 2:1–7). In section 45, Callistus and Ignatius list five daily disciplines for monks entering the quiet life: (1) prayer, especially the *kyrie eleēson*—"Lord, Jesus Christ, Son

119

Callistus and Ignatius, *Directions to Hesychasts* 45

"The five activities of preliminary, or introductory silence [hēsychia] *to be practiced by beginners, namely: prayer, psalmody, reading, thinking on Divine things and work with one's hands. A beginner just starting the practice of silence* [hēsychia] *should spend every twenty-four hours ... in five activities pleasing to God, namely: in prayer, that is, in constant remembrance of our Lord Jesus Christ, quietly led into the heart by way of breathing, as was described above* [§§19–25, WPh, 192–96], *and again led out, with closed lips, without any extraneous thought or imagining. ... In addition to this prayer, a beginner should spend his time in psalmody, in reading the holy Apostle, the Gospels, and the writings of the holy fathers, especially chapters on prayer and sobriety and other Divine words of the Spirit; in remembrance of his sins with heart-felt pain; in meditating on the day of judgment, or on death, or eternal torment, or on participation in eternal bliss and other such things, and to a small extent in work with his hands, to banish despondency."* (WPh, 219–20)

of God, have mercy on me, a sinner"—which monks pray with each breath throughout the day (*Directions to Hesychasts* 19, 48–49 [*WPh* 192–93, 222–25]); (2) chanting psalms from memory; (3) reading in Scripture and the church fathers; (4) "thinking on divine things," which in the subsequent exposition is divided into contemplation of one's sins and meditation on Christian doctrines; and (5) work with one's hands. Work should grow from and be informed by the other disciplines, if it is to be true devotion. This program resembles the philosophical regimen in attention to daily reading, meditation, and practice. It is distinctively Christian in its orientation to prayer and Scripture.

Orthodox tradition commonly reads 1 Tim. 4:13 as a note on spiritual formation. According to Hesychius of Sinai (7th cent.?), "As St Paul puts it, 'Pay attention, my child Timothy, to what you read'" (*On Watchfulness and Holiness* 13 [*PhCT* 1, 164]; cf. Hesychius of Jerusalem, *To Theodolus* 13 [*WPh* 282]). For those who concentrate on spiritual formation, the thrust of 1 Tim. 4:13 is that Timothy should engage in disciplined reading and meditation on the doctrines and precepts of the faith (Callistus and Ignatius, *Directions to a Hesychast* 27 [*WPh* 198], 37 [*WPh* 209]; Gregory of Sinai, *Texts on Commandments and Dogmas* 99 [*WPh* 57]).

Orthodox monks are hardly the only Christians who have thought reading was an important discipline. And without reference to 1 Tim. 4:13, most thinkers on spiritual formation include reading as an essential discipline (e.g., Gregory the Great, *Pastoral Rule* 2.11; Philipp Spener, *Pia Desideria* 5; John Wesley, Letter to John Trembath [see sidebar]; Bonhoeffer 1954, 76–89; Paulsell 2001). Some have understood 1 Tim. 4:13 to say Timothy's reading for himself

> **John Wesley, Excerpt from Letter to John Trembath, August 17, 1760**
>
> *"What has exceedingly hurt you in time past, nay, and I fear to this day, is want of reading. I scarce ever knew a preacher read so little. . . . Hence your talent in preaching does not increase. It is just the same as it was seven years ago. It is lively, but not deep; there is little variety; there is no compass of thought. Reading only can supply this, with meditation and daily prayer. . . . Whether you like it or no, read and pray daily. It is for your life; there is no other way: else you will be a trifler all your days, and a pretty, superficial preacher."*

should inform his exhortation and instruction to the people (Theodore of Mopsuestia, *Comm. 1 Tim.* 148–49; cf. John Chrysostom, *Hom. 1 Tim.* 13; Smail 1964, 246–47, on 1 Tim. 4:13). The Orthodox tradition is distinctive in associating 1 Tim. 4:13 with the disciplines of reading and meditation on one's own spiritual condition and on prior instruction.

Progress

The comments on 4:15 described "progress" as philosophical language. In classic Stoic doctrine, however, wisdom was an all-or-nothing affair, with no intermediate stage between virtue and vice (Engberg-Pedersen 2000, 71). Anyone who was not perfect (*teleios*) in wisdom was still a fool (Diogenes Laërtius, *Lives* 7.127). For the old Stoics, it made no difference whether a drowning man was eighteen inches under water or three thousand feet: he was still drowning (Plutarch, *Comm. not.* 9 [1063a–b]). But other philosophers applied the term "sage" to anyone who renounced vice and began making "progress" (*prokopē*) toward wisdom (Plutarch, *Virt. prof.*; R. Wright 2007). By the first century, Stoics like Seneca and Epictetus came around to this more commonsense attitude and emphasized the importance of "progress" toward wisdom (see comments at 4:15).

The evolution of the idea of "progress" in Stoic thought resembles the evolution of John Wesley's doctrine of sanctification, known popularly as "going on toward perfection." Wesley's seminal essay, "A Plain Account of Christian Perfection" (Wesley 1777), recounts a debate that ranged over some four decades as to whether a believer is sanctified, or reaches "perfection" (*to teleios*), only at the end of life or at some earlier point. Throughout "A Plain Account," Wesley assumed that most believers obtain "entire sanctification" in an instant shortly before they die, though he admitted that some reach this state of "perfection" earlier. Over time, he began to describe sanctification as a gradual process. In "A Plain Account," he wrote, "There is indeed an instantaneous, as well as a gradual, work of God in his children" (quoting the preface to his second volume of hymns from 1741). After a person is justified, "from that time a believer gradually dies to sin and grows in grace," and one should preach sanctification to those who are "pressing forward" (Phil. 3:14; quoting the minutes of the Second Conference, in 1745). Finally, he agreed, "(1.) That every one must be entirely sanctified in the article of death. (2.) That till then a believer daily grows in grace, comes nearer and nearer to perfection. (3.) That we ought to be continually pressing after it, and to exhort all others so to do" (quoting the minutes of the Fourth Conference, in 1747).

Holy living was central to Wesley's thought (Abraham 2009). He described sanctification as a process of spiritual and moral refinement associated with the work of the Holy Spirit in the believer. Although our passage does not use the word "sanctification," it alludes to the Holy Spirit: "the gift [*charisma*] that was given to you on account of prophecies" (4:14). We could think of Timothy's spiritual exercises as working out what the Holy Spirit had begun within him. They were a way of holy living.

A Good Example for Believers

Finally, we return to Orthodox Christianity for an illustration of the principle that an example is worth a thousand words (1 Tim. 4:12, 15). In the fourth century Abba Poemēn was a monk in the Egyptian desert. When a young monk was eager to share his spiritual training with newcomers who asked him to do so, the wise, old father admonished his brother not to explain anything to them but merely to set them an example. This is sound advice for anyone who aspires to become a "good minister of Christ Jesus."

Show, Don't Tell (Abba Poemēn, saying 174)

"A brother said to Abba Poemēn, 'Brothers stay with me. Do you counsel me to give them orders?' The elder said, 'No, but be the first to do good works, and if they want to have life, they will see by themselves what they have to do.' The brother replied, 'But they themselves want me to command them.' The elder replied, 'Do not do this at all. Be a model for them, not a legislator.'" (*Sayings of the Desert Fathers*, quoted in Deseille 2008, 106)

1 Timothy 5:1–6:2a

Second Set of Directives concerning the Church

Introductory Matters

The material in 5:1–6:2a is the second section of ecclesial concerns, after 2:1–3:13. Still presuming the fundamental doctrines of the faith, this section continues developing precepts that apply those doctrines in specific contexts (see "Doctrines and Precepts" in the general introduction). The section begins with general instructions about how Timothy should relate to older and younger (5:1–2), followed by more detailed instructions regarding older widows (5:3–10), younger widows (5:13–16), older men (5:17–25), and slaves (6:1–2a). Titus 2:1–10 discusses similar groups more briefly.

One issue is whether "elders" (*presbyteroi*) in 5:17–25 means generic older men (e.g., Malherbe 2008) or is a technical term for an office (e.g., Towner 2006, 361–63, 373–75). In favor of the former position, *presbyteroi* is clearly generic in 5:1. Also, if elders are officers, we need to account for the odd structure of the letter, since this passage is far removed from the discussions of overseer and deacons in chapter 3. In favor of the latter position are references to presiding and teaching functions (5:17), and the "laying on of hands" (5:22) suggests an ordination (cf. 1 Tim. 4:14; 2 Tim. 1:6; cf. Acts 6:6; 13:3). And some would add that "elders" and "overseer" are used interchangeably in Titus 1:5–9.

Perhaps we need not choose between these positions. In Jewish communities elders were "the senior men of the community, heads of the leading families within it, who as such exercise an authority that is informal, representative and collective. . . . [The term "elders"] neither denotes particular office-holders, nor excludes them. . . . 'The elders' does not so much denote an office as connote prestige" (Campbell 1994a, 65; cf. Trebilco 2008, 447–57). Similarly, in

123

**1 Timothy 5:1–6:2a
in the Rhetorical Flow**

Letter opening (1:1–2)

Proem: First charge to Timothy
(1:3–20)

First set of directives concerning the
church (2:1–3:13)

Second charge to Timothy (3:14–4:16)

▶ Second set of directives concerning
the church (5:1–6:2a)

    Elder and younger (5:1–2)

    Widows (5:3–16)

        Honor for real widows (5:3)

        Offspring should care for widows (5:4–8)

        Enrolled widows (5:9–10)

        Younger widows (5:11–15)

        Women should care for widows (5:16)

    Elders (5:17–25)

        Honor for teaching elders (5:17–18)

        Adjudication of charges against elders
        (5:19–21)

        Ordination of elders (5:22–25)

    Slaves (6:1–2a)

Greco-Roman society the "elders" (*presbyteroi*) were "a class of person to whom respect was instinctively felt to be due, not so much the leaders of the state or town, but *one's own elders* within family, clan or acquaintance" (Campbell 1994a, 95; cf. Young 1994, 120). Following R. Alastair Campbell, David G. Horrell sees the church in 1 Timothy as "more like a structured *oikos* [household] than an assembly of siblings" (Horrell 2008, 116; cf. Horrell 2001; Ramelli 2009; 2010b). Chapter 5 is about how Timothy should treat older women and men, some of whom are "enrolled" (5:9) or ordained (5:22) to specific ministerial functions for which they receive honoraria.

A second issue is how 6:1–2 coheres with 5:1–25. It appears that 6:1 begins a new topic not anticipated by the introductory admonitions at 5:1–2. C. K. Barrett (1963, 82–83) speculates that some of the elders were slaves, which makes sense theologically but is difficult to imagine in the social context. Still, certain details suggest that 6:1–2 is a continuation of chapter 5. The theme of "honor" (*timē*) connects widows (5:3), elders (5:17), and enslaved (6:1). The parallel passage in Titus 2:1–10 suggests that the paragraph on slaves is integral to the preceding material. The familial language bears some resemblance to the philosophical topos on household management that included four parts: proper order between husband/wife; father/children; master/slaves; and proper acquisition and use of wealth (Aristotle, *Pol.* 1253b; Balch 1981, 23–59; see "The Household of God" in the general introduction), which suggests that all of 5:1–6:21 is a coherent section.

Tracing the Train of Thought

Elder and Younger (5:1–2)

5:1–2. Do not chastise an elder man, but exhort him as a father, younger men as brothers, elder women as mothers, younger women as sisters in all

purity (5:1–2). In exhorting Timothy to treat members of the community as kin, Pastoral Paul resembles a Stoic philosopher (Ramelli 2009, 2010b).

"Chastise" (*epiplēssō*, lit., "beat up") is metaphorical, like the English idiom "tongue-lashing." This is one way youthful Timothy can set an example (4:12) for overseers, who should not be "violent" (*plēktēs*, 3:3; Titus 1:7). It also sets a tone for how he will adjudicate charges against an elder (5:19–21, 24–25). To "exhort/encourage" (*parakaleō*) is a gentler way to guide people. Just as Paul models "exhortation" to Timothy (1:3; 2:1), so Timothy should "exhort" others (6:2b; 2 Tim. 4:2; Titus 2:6, 15). The same imperative "exhort" is implied for all four groups in this sentence. The main concern of 5:3–25 is how Timothy will relate to elder women and men (Malherbe 2008).

Timothy's peer group is younger men, to whom he relates as "brothers." Because he is young (4:12), his behavior toward younger women will come under scrutiny. Timothy must model "purity" for the believers (cf. 4:12).

Widows (5:3–16)

A few have supposed that 5:3–8 and 5:9–16 deal with two different groups, but most interpreters view 5:3–16 as a unified treatment of widows. In early Christianity there was an order of widows who lived celibate lives in service to the church (*Apostolic Constitutions* 3.1–15; Davies 1980, 98–99; Thurston 1989). We read about widows in the early second century (Ign. *Smyr.* 13.1; Pol. *Phil.* 4) but not otherwise in the first. This passage is about financial assistance for indigent widows, and some assume it is about that alone (Aquinas, *Comm. 1 Tim.* 5.1.180–81 [Baer 2007]; I. H. Marshall 1999, 576–81; Johnson 2001, 269–76). But the qualifications (5:9–10) parallel those for overseer and deacons (3:1–13). For those who assume that Paul wrote this letter, an order of widows and vows of celibacy seem anachronistic, unless this passage created the order (Thurston 1989, 45). Those who favor a post-Pauline date are more likely to read this passage as regulating an order that already existed (Bassler 1984; 2003, 136, 141–46). Either way, the passage is about who should be "enrolled" (5:9–10) and receive an honorarium (5:3).

There are three criteria. First, enrolled widows must be "real widows," having no family (5:4–8, 16). Families are morally obligated to care for their own widows (5:4, 16). This passage sets guidelines for when the church assumes responsibility (Bassler 1984). Second, they must be of impeccable character and reputation (5:9–10). Third, they must be at least sixty years old (5:9, 11–15).

5:3. *Honor for real widows.* **Honor widows who are really widows.** (5:3). Popular culture ascribed honor to public acts such as victory in a battle or large donations. Here, however, "honor" goes not to benefactors but to indigent widows. The word translated "widow" (*chēra*) could apply to any woman of marriageable age who lived without a man (G. Stählin, *TDNT* 9:442), including a widow, a divorcée (ps.-Theano, *Nik.* 6.55; Huizenga 2013, 72, 158), or a woman who never married in the first place (Bassler 1984, 35). The breadth

---

Hierocles, How to Conduct Oneself toward One's Parents

"But we must begin with the assumption that the only measure of our gratitude [eucharistia] *to them is perpetual and unyielding eagerness to compensate their benefactions* [euergesias], *since, even if we were to do a great deal for them, that would be far too inadequate. . . . So, in order to choose our duties to them easily, we should have this summary statement at hand, namely, that our parents are the images of the gods, and, by Zeus, domestic gods, benefactors* [euergetai], *kinsmen, creditors, lords, and the warmest of friends. . . . They are lenders of the most valuable* [timōtatōn] *things, and they take back only things of which the repayment is again a benefaction* [euergesia] *to us. For what gain is so great to a child as to be pious* [eusebēs] *and grateful to his parents?"* (excerpt from Stobaeus, *Florilegium* 4.25.53, *NewDocs* 8:§7, p. 115, trans. J. R. Harrison, modified)

---

of the term explains how "virgin" and "widow" were used interchangeably to refer to celibate women, regardless of prior marital status (Ignatius, *Smyrn.* 13.1; Tertullian, *Virg.* 9.2–3; *Ux.* 1.6.4; *Acts of Peter* 29; Cyprian, *Hab. virg.*; Theodoret, *Ecclesiastical History* 3.14; Methuen 1997). Whatever the reason, an unmarried woman lost social status and financial security (Nadar 1991 describes the difficulties).

5:4–8. *Offspring should care for widows.* Greco-Roman society emphasized the reciprocal obligations of parents to care for their young children and adult children for their aged parents. **But if anyone has a widow or offspring, let one first learn to show piety toward one's own household and to give back compensation to one's parents, for this is acceptable before God** (5:4). Religious piety entailed a sacred obligation to care for parents, especially mothers, who risked their lives in childbirth (Parkin 2003, 205–17; see comments at 2:2; 4:8). This virtue is illustrated by the second-century Stoic philosopher Hierocles (see sidebar) and the third-century Neopythagorean philosopher ps.-Perictione (see sidebar at 5:8; cf. Xenophon, *Oec.* 7.19; ps.-Aristotle, *Oec.* 1.3.3; Tob. 4). Hierocles describes parents as "benefactors" who deserve "honor" from their children.

But the one who is really a widow and left all alone has placed her hope in God (5:5). The "real widow" was bereft of family and without means of support. Unmarried women were frequently reduced to poverty (Mark 12:40, 42; Luke 7:11–17; Acts 9:39; Thurston 1989, 9–17). That is why Ignatius instructed the bishop of Smyrna, "After the Lord, you be their caregiver" (Ign. *Pol.* 4.1; Ng 2008).

And continues in supplications and prayers night and day (5:5). Such a woman was Anna (Luke 2:36–37). Jewish widows were widely associated with prayer (Jer. 31:11; Luke 18:1–8; Thurston 1989, 26–28, 82). Karen Jo Torjesen (1998, 48–52) has suggested that early Christian portrayals of anonymous female figures in the posture of prayer (see comments at 1 Tim. 2:8) represent widows ordained to the ministry of prayer (Pol. *Phil.* 4.3; Tertullian, *Pud.* 13; Hippolytus, *Apostolic Tradition* 10.5; *Didascalia apostolorum* 15). Even pagans recognized Christian widows at prayer (Lucian, *Peregr.* 12).

But the self-indulgent is dead while she lives (5:6). This verse recalls warnings against ostentatious luxury in 2:9. Jerome cited it in exhorting Christians to renounce bodily pleasures and luxuries as things that drown the soul (Jerome, *Against Jovinianus* 2.9; Ramelli 2011, 160). The phrase "dead while she lives" (5:6) refers to her spiritual condition, as in 1 Cor. 11:30, where Paul associates ethical misconduct with spiritual "sickness" and "death" (Ramelli 2010b; 2011, 155–56; cf. Philo, *Congr.* 87).

Command these things also, so that they may be irreproachable (5:7). "Irreproachable" echoes the requirement for an overseer (3:2) and anticipates the list of desirable characteristics in verses 9–10.

But if any do not take forethought for their own, specifically, members of their household, they have denied the faith and are worse than unbelievers (5:8). I take "their own" and "household" as synonymous (see comments on *malista* at 4:10; 5:17). All the Greek pronouns and verbs in this verse are singular, but translating them as plurals preserves the more important idea that the Greek is gender neutral. The welfare of family members is not the exclusive domain of men (5:16).

Perictione Explains Piety toward One's Parents

"One must not speak evil of parents nor oppose them, but must obey parents in matters small and great, in every circumstance of mind and body, in matters private and public, in peacetime and wartime, in health and sickness, in plenty and poverty, in glory and humiliation, whether they are private persons or rulers. One must live amenably with them and never shirk, and obey with integrity and enthusiasm. For this is sensible and agreeable to those who are pious [eusebeis].

"And if anyone should despise her parents in any such evil manner, sin is ascribed by the gods to her who is dead even as she lives, and she is hated by people, and under the earth she would be punished forever along with the impious [asebeis] in the place reserved for such people, being wounded by Justice and by the gods of the underworld, who are ordained as overseers [episkopoi] of such matters." (Ps.-Perictione, *On the Harmony of a Woman*, in Stobaeus, *Florilegium* 4.25.50, trans. C. R. Hutson in consultation with Annette Huizenga)

"Forethought" is part of the vocabulary of benefaction. It is the concern of the strong for the weak (Dio Chrysostom, *Or.* 3.50; *NewDocs* 8:§7, pp. 109–16). "Worse than unbelievers" reflects the social obligation of care for parents (5:4), as illustrated by Hierocles (see sidebar at 5:3) and ps.-Perictione (see sidebar; cf. Pomeroy 1984, 68–71). One should care for relatives, especially when they are fellow believers (Campbell 1995), but the verse redefines responsibility beyond blood kin to spiritual family. The hospitality of an overseer could be expressed as providing shelter and support for widows and orphans (*Herm. Sim.* 9.27 [104]; Ign. *Pol.* 4.1). This assumes not that the overseer was rich but that he administered the church's treasury.

5:9–10. *Enrolled widows.* **Let a widow be enrolled** (5:9). One question is how these restrictions in 5:9–15 relate to the care of destitute unmarried women in 5:3–8, 16. Christian women who never married were liable to bring suspicion on the church for disrupting the social order (D. MacDonald 1983; M. Mac-Donald 1996; Upson-Saia 2011). Pastoral Paul created restrictions around this order of widows that affirmed traditional conventions of feminine domesticity, because outsiders were looking critically at ordained Christian leaders, including widows (Thurston 1989, 39, 48; Portefaix 2003, 152–57; Bassler 2003).

Who is not less than sixty years old (5:9). Only about 6–8 percent of the population of the empire was above age 60, and only around 2 percent above 70 (Parkin 2003, 49–50, 281). This age restriction severely limited the number of eligible widows. The third-century church order known as the "Teaching of the Apostles" followed 1 Tim. 5 closely but adjusted the restriction to age 50 (*Didascalia apostolorum* 14), which was traditionally viewed as the upper limit of menopause.

The phrase **a woman of one man** (5:9) reflects the culture wars of the first century, which brought both new freedoms for women and a backlash against those freedoms (Winter 2003). In this context, the "one-man woman" (Lat. *univira*; *JIWE* 2:324; see comments at 3:2) came to symbolize traditional family values: "In Roman thinking the *univira*, who had slept with only one man and never remarried after the loss of her husband, was most honored as the sexual ideal; but the ideal was in conflict with both the widow's need for a social protector and society's need for children; there would come a time when it was overridden by legislation" (Fantham et al. 1994, 232). Just as in 3:2, 12, the high ideal of the *univira* addresses a concern "to give the opponent no occasion for reviling" (5:14; see comments at 3:7, 13). But fidelity to a deceased spouse stood in tension with imperial legislation that provided tax incentives for bearing children. Our passage shows a similar tension between this ideal and the preference for younger widows to marry and bear children (5:14).

Attested for good deeds, if she reared children, if she was hospitable to strangers, if she washed the feet of saints, if she came to the aid of the afflicted, if she followed every good work (5:10). The idea of "good deeds" forms an *inclusio* at the beginning (*kalois ergois*) and end (*ergō agathō*) of verse 10, with representative examples between these brackets. The specific "good deeds," or acts of charity (2:10; 2 Cor. 9:8), pertain to the domestic roles of women. A widow who "reared children" had complied with Augustan marriage laws that incentivized procreation (Fantham et al. 1994, 303–6). The verb "reared" is literally "nourished." We could think not only of physical food but also of spiritual diet (see comments at 4:6; cf. 2 Tim. 1:5; 3:14–15; and ps.-Myia, *Phyl.* on a mother's role in moral formation).

Hospitality was important in ancient, Mediterranean cultures, a virtue expected also in an overseer (3:2). "Hospitable to strangers" and "washed the feet of saints" are roughly synonymous, if we think of traveling evangelists (Osiek and Balch 1997, 208). There may have been women, even widows, who provided such hospitality (Ign. *Smyrn.* 13.2). A woman with a house large enough to host guests would not be an indigent "real widow," but 5:10 describes the widow's past service, even if she is no longer able to perform such functions. Alternatively, if we understand "strangers" in its broadest sense, the virtuous widow has a reputation for hospitality to all in need. "Afflicted" might describe the poor, sick, imprisoned, grieving, and so on. We recall Tabitha's good deeds and almsgiving (*ergōn agathōn*, Acts 9:36, 39; 2 Cor. 9:8). This list of "good deeds" challenges the Roman patronage system. Even though giving money is a "good deed" (6:18), honor goes not to large donors but to indigent women who have devoted their lives to serving children, strangers, and the sick (see comments at 5:17).

5:11–15. *Younger widows.* **But avoid younger widows, for when they have wantonly turned away from Christ, they wish to marry, having condemnation because they have made void their first pledge** (5:11–12). Stories abound in antiquity of widows who "behaved wantonly" after their husbands died (Winter 2003, 128–34; Kartzow 2009, 160–66). Petronius recounts the salacious tale of a widow in Ephesus, who, while keeping vigil over the body of her husband, was seduced by a soldier, abandoned the corpse, and ran off with her new lover (Petronius, *Satyricon* 111–12; Cicero, *Cael.*).

The "first pledge" (CSB, NIV, NRSV) suggests a vow of celibate service to the church (Tertullian, *Mon.* 13; Gregory of Nyssa, *Macr.* 381.15 = Lefkowitz and Fant 1992, 328). As we saw above, the word translated "widow" (*chēra*) could refer to any unmarried woman. This verse could apply to women who opted for celibacy as teenagers, later regretted that "first pledge," and "wished to marry" for the first time (Methuen 1997, 290–91; Bassler 2003, 138). The apocryphal Acts attest that some Christians in the second and third centuries renounced marriage (see comments at 4:3; Davies 1980). But the "first pledge" could also refer to a first marriage vow. Either way, celibacy could be a struggle for a young widow, as John Chrysostom describes in the case of his own mother (*Sac.* 5).

If we ask what might have drawn young women to celibacy, three movements come to mind: Montanism, Gnosticism, and the women in the apocryphal Acts.

First, many gnostic groups held that God is both male and female, with the result that they welcomed women as equals of men (Pagels 1979, 48–69). Catholic Christians were appalled to hear of gnostic female priests and bishops, and they accused gnostic women of immodesty and sexual indiscretion (Irenaeus, *Haer.* 1.13.3–6; Tertullian, *Praescr.* 41; Hippolytus, *Heresies* 6.35). Second, Montanism began with a robust notion of the Holy Spirit as equally active among men and women, with the result that Montanists recognized women prophets (see "Theological Issues" at 1 Tim. 2:8–15). Third, the apocryphal Acts recount stories of celibate women who devoted their lives to Christian ministry and evangelism (Davies 1980). The stories include reports of violent reactions against these women for upsetting the social order, precisely because they did not marry (D. MacDonald 1983; M. MacDonald 1996, 154–82). It does not matter which of these movements might have been in view, since the text makes no mention of their doctrine, but defenders of Pauline authorship should seek evidence that at least one of these movements had antecedents in the first century. Even though the focus here is on behavior, it is possible to trace two competing trajectories from Paul, one leading toward celibate women prophets and evangelists and the other toward married women in traditional domestic roles (Fatum 2005, 195–96, 202–4). Being enrolled among the celibate "real widows" may have been an option for women who wanted to exercise their spiritual gifts within mainstream Christianity.

But sexual desire is not the only issue, for **in addition, [being] idle, they learn by going about from house to house** (5:13). The relationship between "idle" and "learn" is ambiguous. Most English translators insert an implied infinitive, "they learn *to be* idle" (KJV, NASB, NRSV, etc.), which suggests that young widows were picking up bad habits (NIV). The translation above supplies an implied participle, "being," which suggests that, *because* they are idle, the younger widows are going about (WYC, GNV, DRA). They are learning from one another in an informal way, whereas the approved way to learn would be "in full subordination" to the approved teachers of the church (2:11).

Idleness and industriousness were subjective value judgments. Roman elites associated idleness and luxury with moral decline (Columella, *On Agriculture* 12.pref. 9; see comments at 2:9–10). Normally, only a wealthy woman (cf. 1 Tim. 2:9–10) would have idle time, so she would not qualify as a "real widow." The wealthy widow Ummidia Quadratilla reported that, "with all a woman's idle hours to fill, she was in the habit of amusing herself playing draughts or watching her mimes" (Pliny the Younger, *Ep.* 7.24.5, trans. Radice, LCL). Stereotypical women of decorum were never idle, regardless of wealth. If not otherwise occupied, they were spinning and weaving. One element of imperial traditional values propaganda was that, except on special occasions, the emperor Augustus wore clothes made by his sister, wife, daughter, or granddaughters (Suetonius, *Augustus* 73; Winter 2003, 133–34).

And not only idle but also gossips and busybodies, saying what they ought not (5:13). Regarding those who waste time nosing in their neighbors' business (cf. 2 Thess. 3:6–15), Plutarch said one should attend to one's own vices (Plutarch, *Curios.* 5 [517c–d]). Our text criticizes women "going about from house to house," being "busybodies" (cf. 2 Thess. 3:11), and engaging in improper speech ("gossips," "saying what they ought not"). They are stereotypically bad widows (Winter 2003, 128–37; Kartzow 2009).

At issue is what exactly the younger widows were saying that they "ought not." Marianne Bjelland Kartzow (2009, 146–59) sees three possibilities. First, noting that the word "busybody" (*periergos*) connotes magic in Acts 19:19 and that widows were sometimes associated with witchcraft, she considers whether the young widows could have been using magic spells. But nothing else in this context points in that direction (though see 2 Tim. 3:8, 13).

Second, Kartzow offers the stronger possibility that "gossips" (*phlyaroi*) refers to uneducated or ignorant persons (Plutarch, *Rect. rat. aud.* 3 [39a]; *Superst.* 9 [169e]). Philip B. Payne takes "saying what they ought not" as the key indicator that some widows were influenced by and advancing the cause of false teachers (cf. Titus 1:11; Payne 2009, 299–304; a view challenged by Zamfir 2013, 179–95). That could explain the parallels between exhortations regarding widows here and those regarding "quiet" women in chapter 2. Both passages reject luxurious adornments (2:9; 5:6) and recommend "good deeds" (2:10; 5:3, 10). Perhaps Pastoral Paul also intended correspondences between "quietness" (2:11) and "busybodies" (5:13) and between "not to teach or presume authority" (2:12) and "saying what they ought not" (5:13).

Third, Kartzow (2009, 155–57) shows that, while the vocabulary in verse 13 fits the topos of the bad woman, the content of the frivolous talk is unspecified, and the whole verse turns on the rhetorical effect of a stereotype. Just because men label women's speech as frivolous, that doesn't make it so (Luke 24:11; John 4:42; Kartzow 2009, 168–72). We should beware of using a stereotype as the basis for a historical reconstruction of what women were actually doing or saying. In the context of concern about opponents "reviling" Christianity (5:14), Pastoral Paul "is concerned that their lifestyle *might* produce a negative reaction" (Bassler 2003, 141). To avoid being stereotyped by their society, widows should avoid gossiping as well as "behavior that might generate gossip *about* them" (Kartzow 2009, 161). Kartzow's second or third options are both plausible and not mutually exclusive.

I want younger widows, therefore, to marry, bear children, manage the household, give no opportunity for reviling to the opponent (5:14). This wish (cf. 2:15) is consistent with the principle that family should provide financial support (5:4–8) and with Roman law. Jouette M. Bassler describes the social pressures for women to marry (2003, 127–31), which could account for "reviling" opponents (D. MacDonald 1983). Adela Yarbro Collins reads "the opponent" as Satan, mentioned in verse 15 (2011, 160, citing *1 Clem.* 51.1;

Mart. Pol. 17.1). In my opinion, "reviling" points to a non-Christian, human opponent (cf. comments at 3:6–7 on the relation between a human "slanderer" and the devil).

The wish is surprising in two respects. First, the push for marriage runs contrary to Paul's preference for unmarried women to remain celibate (1 Cor. 7:8, 40). But both 1 Cor. 7 and 1 Tim. 5 offer advice for specific contexts, neither giving an absolute rule. The preference for celibacy in Corinth perhaps made sense in the context of "the present crisis" (1 Cor. 7:26; Winter 2001, 241–68), while the potential for "reviling" explains the preference for marriage here. Second, some have worried that a widow who remarried was no longer *univira* (5:9) and disqualified from being "enrolled" if her second husband should leave her destitute. But if a *chēra* is any unmarried woman (see comments at 5:3), it would be plausible to read this verse as recommending first marriages, not necessarily second marriages.

The verb "manage the household" (*oikodespotein*) reflects the cultural assumption that a wife managed internal affairs of the household as "mistress" (*despoina*), while her husband, the "master" (*despotēs*), was involved in political and business affairs outside the house (Osiek and M. MacDonald 2006, 144–52). The threefold wish to "marry, bear children, and manage the household" describes the ideal Roman *materfamilias*, a model of temperance as wife, mother and "mistress" of the household (Huizenga 2013, 201–13, 349–59).

For already some have turned aside after Satan (5:15). If those who "turned aside" are younger widows who have abandoned their "first pledge," then the association between sexual desire and Satan recalls the allusion to Eve (2:13–14). Following Satan included, but was not limited to, sexual sin. On this reading, outsiders "revile" young women for promiscuity, which would fit with the emphasis on modesty in 2:9–10.

On the other hand, the verb "turn aside" elsewhere describes rival teachers (1 Tim. 1:6; 6:20; 2 Tim. 4:4), so perhaps some women have "turned aside" to take a vow of celibacy, following teachers who "forbid marriage" (4:3). Pastoral Paul wants younger women to marry rather than live celibate lives. On this reading, outsiders revile Christian women who do not marry. This would fit with the emphasis on childbearing in 2:15.

5:16. *Women should care for widows.* **If any faithful woman has widows, let her aid them** (5:16). Although the pronouns of 5:3, 8 are gender neutral, meaning "anyone," it is easy to assume that those verses envision men caring for their families. So the reference to a "faithful woman" may be surprising. Some ancient scribes inserted words to make the verse read, "any *faithful man* or faithful woman." But we have examples of charitable women, including Tabitha (Acts 9:39), Lydia (Acts 16:15), Phoebe (Rom. 16:1–2), and Tryphaena (*Acts of Paul* 3.41). A tombstone from late second- or early third-century Scythia celebrates the life of Epiphania, the wealthy widow of a shipowner. Her epitaph includes this line: "And to friends abandoned, as woman to women, I provided much, with a view to piety [*eusebeia*]" (*SEG* 24 [1969] 1081 = *NewDocs* 2:§16; Osiek and M. MacDonald 2006, 75–76). The "faithful woman" could be the daughter of a widow or herself a widow of means who provides for other widows.

And let not the church be burdened, so that it may aid the real widows (5:16). "Burden" is a Pauline term for financial support (1 Thess. 2:9). The burden of caring for widows and orphans could be enormous. The church in Rome in the third century reportedly supported 1,500 needy widows (Eusebius, *Hist. eccl.* 6.43.11).

While limiting who is "enrolled" in the order, the passage does not forbid financial assistance. Early Christians took seriously their responsibility to assist destitute widows (Acts 6:1–7). Tertullian disapproved of a teenager in the order of "widows," but he did not oppose aid: "If the bishop had been bound to accord her any relief, he might, of course, have done it in some other way without detriment to the respect due to discipline" (Tertullian, *Virg.* 9.2, *ANF* 4:33; cf. *Didascalia apostolorum* 14; Beavis 2003). Pastoral Paul is discussing who represents the church in an official capacity, not who is worthy of aid.

Elders (5:17–25)

The passage alternates between directives about older men and exhortations about Timothy's conduct. Some see these verses as a disjointed jumble, with a break between 5:17–22 and 5:23–25 (Brox 1969, 203; Oberlinner 1994, 261) or a digression at 5:21–22 (Dibelius and Conzelmann 1972, 80–81). Most recent interpreters read 5:17–25 as a unit, though with uncertainty about the place of 5:23 in the argument. The following discussion identifies three coherent directives: honor for teaching elders (5:17–18), adjudication of charges against an elder (5:19–21), and ordination of elders (5:22–25).

5:17–18. *Honor for teaching elders.* The first directive deals with honor for teaching elders (5:17–18). **The elders who preside well are worthy of double honor, specifically** [or especially] **those who labor in word and teaching.** On "presiding," see comments at 3:4. The traditional translation of the adverb "especially" (*malista*) suggests that "those who labor in word and teaching" are a subset of the larger group "elders" (Poythress 2002) or, to multiply categories, "ruling elders" (Kim 2004). But the translation "specifically" (Skeat 1979) makes sense here in that "labor in word and teaching" (see comments at 1 Tim. 4:10) clarifies the meaning of "preside well." Either way, "double honor" goes to those who teach.

"Labor" is a Pauline metaphor for evangelism (4:10), so verse 17 suggests that some older men were ordained teachers. A second-century sermon illustrates the teaching function: "And let us not only seem to be faithful and paying attention now while being admonished by the elders, but also when we depart for home" (*2 Clem.* 17.3).

"Honor" (*timē*, 5:17) is a metaphor for financial support, as is clear from the context (5:3, 18; cf. 1 Cor. 9:1–17; Gal. 6:6). The cultural expectation was that "honor" went to benefactors. A club might honor its patron with a statue, crown, or office. A civic leader who paid for public works might receive the honor of a proclamation, a statue, or a funeral procession (*NewDocs* 2:§18). The archon of a Roman synagogue was remembered with "all honor" (*JIWE* 2:164). Pastoral Paul directs "honor" to those who "labor in word and teaching" (see comments at 5:10).

Some have thought "double honor" indicates elevation to a higher office (Campbell 1994a, 194–98), but the rationale in verse 18 indicates payment. Some have thought teaching elders were paid twice as much as "enrolled widows" (Tamez 2007, 16, 49). Possibly "double honor" indicates both financial honorarium and gestures of approval or respect, as in 6:1.

For the Scripture says, "You shall not muzzle an ox while it is threshing," and "the worker is worthy of his pay" (5:18). In support of paying teachers, Pastoral Paul quotes Torah (Deut. 25:4) and a saying of Jesus (Luke 10:7). The question is whether the word "Scripture" (*graphē*) applies to both or only the first. There are three possibilities: (1) *graphē* implies that both quotations have authoritative status as "Scripture"; (2) *graphē* refers to both quotations in a generic sense of written texts without implying special, authoritative status; or (3) *graphē* refers only to Deuteronomy as "Scripture."

If one assumes that Paul wrote 1 Timothy, then option 2 is difficult, because Paul uses *graphē* to refer to "Scripture," never to a generic "writing" (Rom. 1:2; 4:3; 9:17; 10:11; 11:2; 15:4; 16:26; 1 Cor. 15:3–4; Gal. 3:8, 22; 4:30). Option 1 is possible only if one assumes that Luke was written before the 60s. One might cite 2 Pet. 3:16 for comparison, assuming that Peter actually wrote that letter. But assuming such early dates for both Luke and 2 Peter is questionable. Option 3 is most compatible with Pauline authorship of the PE.

If one assumes that 1 Timothy is pseudonymous, then option 3 seems like special pleading. Option 2 is possible. Option 1, following the scholarly consensus that Luke was written in the 80s, offers evidence of a post-Pauline date for 1 Timothy, and 2 Pet. 3:16 offers evidence of a tendency in the late first century to refer to Christian writings as "Scripture." Further, our verse fits in the thought world of *Did.* 13.1, written around the turn of the second century and quoting Matt. 10:10.

5:19–21. *Adjudication of charges against elders.* The second directive concerns adjudicating charges against an elder (5:19–21). **Do not accept an indictment against an elder, except "upon two or three witnesses." Reprove before all those who sin, so that the rest may also have fear. I adjure you before God and Christ Jesus and the elect angels, that you should guard these things without prejudice, doing nothing with partiality** (5:19–21). If "elder" refers to any senior member of the community, this exhortation is about treating any older man "like a father" (5:1). But, situated between directives about honoraria (5:17–18) and ordaining elders (5:22–25), it reads more like guidelines for adjudicating charges against an ordained elder (5:17).

The instruction about how to conduct a hearing (5:19–21) contains judicial vocabulary. First, an "indictment" (*katēgoria*) is a formal accusation in court. Second, the phrase "two or three witnesses" alludes to Deut. 19:15 (cf. Matt. 18:16; John 8:17; 2 Cor. 13:1; cf. Deut. 17:6; Heb. 10:28; CD 9.16–10.3). Third, "reprove" (*elenchein*) is courtroom terminology for cross-examination (Gen. 31:37; James 2:9; cf. Titus 1:9, 13; MM 202, s.v. *elenchō*). Timothy is to "reprove those who sin," which could be either the elder or the accusers, depending on whether the charges are verified. He should point out the sin publicly (cf. Dio Chrysostom, *Or.* 77/78.41–42), so others will not emulate bad behavior. Fourth, "I adjure" (*diamartyromai*, 5:21) evokes a divine witness, as in English, "so help me" (cf. 2 Tim. 2:14; 4:1). Pastoral Paul invokes "God and Christ Jesus and the holy angels" to monitor Timothy's behavior. "That you guard . . ." (5:21) indicates not the purpose but the content of the admonition (Gk. *hina* in the sense of *hoti*, with verbs of praying or requesting, as in 1 Tim. 2:2; BDAG 476, s.v. ἵνα 2.a.γ). Fifth, "without prejudice" means not prejudging the case. And, sixth, "partiality" (*prosklisis*, lit., "leaning toward") is favoritism (Acts 5:36; 2 Macc. 14:24).

5:22–25. *Ordination of elders.* The third directive is about ordination (5:22–25). **Lay hands on no one hastily** (5:22). At first glance, this seems to belong with the previous paragraph. A few associate "laying on hands" with the restoration of sinners (Lock 1924, 63–64; Hanson 1983, 103), but that practice is not attested before the third century (Tertullian, *Pud.* 18.9; Eusebius, *Hist. eccl.* 7.2). Some understand "laying on hands" as the act of witnesses against the accused in a court (Lev. 24:14; Sus. 34; Irwin 2008), but Timothy is adjudicating charges, not acting as a witness, and it is unclear how witnesses against sinners would be "sharing in their sins."

Elsewhere in the NT, "laying on hands" is connected with ordination (1 Tim. 4:14; 2 Tim. 1:6; cf. Acts 6:6; 13:3; Aquinas, *Comm. 1 Tim.* 5.3.225 [Baer 2007]). Brian Irwin (2008) unwittingly bolsters the case for ordination by citing numerous LXX texts in which the idiom refers to sanctifying for a special purpose, such as designating an animal for sacrifice (LXX: Exod. 29:10, 15, 19; Lev. 1:4, 10; Num. 8:10, 12; 2 Chron. 29:23) or Moses commissioning Joshua as his successor (Num. 27:18, 23 LXX). In our text, "laying on hands" refers to ordination of some older men as official teachers (1 Tim. 5:17). Before ordaining an elder to teach, Timothy should be sure the elder's behavior is consistent with the faith.

The concern about sins, **nor share in the sins of others. Keep yourself holy** (5:22), is amplified in verses 24–25, so that 5:21–25 is a unit. To "share in the sins of others" does not imply that Timothy shares guilt (I. H. Marshall 1999, 622). The idea is that "evil companions corrupt good morals" (1 Cor. 15:33). Similarly, the point of 2 John 11 is not that saying "Hi" to a heretic makes you guilty of anything, but rather that one should not make friends with heretics. Christians should not seek fellowship with people who will be willing to "sin along with" them (Isocrates, *Demon.* 45). Not associating with sinners is one way to "keep yourself holy," a point elaborated in verse 23, before returning to the danger of acting "hastily."

No longer drink only water, but use a little wine on account of your stomach and your frequent illnesses (5:23; the following summarizes Hutson 2013). The exhortation "use a little wine" is a comment on being "holy" (5:22). Beside sexual chastity and separation from sinners (5:22, 24–25; cf. 2 Tim. 2:21), holiness entails abstinence from wine. In Greco-Roman culture, avoiding wine could be a matter of philosophical moderation (Diogenes Laërtius, *Lives* 10.11) or religious piety (Plutarch, *Cohib. ira* 16 [464b]; Apuleius, *Metamorphoses* 11.23). It was a mark of piety for Jews (Lev. 10:8–11; Num. 6:2–4; Jer. 35; Dan. 1:12; Philo, *Spec. Laws* 2.148; *Contempl. Life* 4 [37]; *m. Avot* 6.4, alluding to Ezek. 4:11). Clement of Alexandria (*Paed.* 2.2) interpreted "a little wine" as wine mixed with water in good Greco-Roman practice, though he preferred water only as the drink of temperance.

But the stated reason for using "a little wine" is its medicinal benefit. Physicians commonly suggested wine for stomach ills (Celsus, *On Medicine* 1.8.1–2; Pliny the Elder, *Nat.* 23.38; Seneca, *Ep.* 95.22; Dioscorides, *De materia medica* 5.7.1; Hutson 2013, 83).

The medical reference suggests a third reason for "a little wine," which stems from the larger context of a letter to a youthful minister (Hutson 2013, 83–86). According to the prevailing medical theory of the time, good health resulted from a balance of four bodily fluids, called "humors." These were blood, bile, black bile, and phlegm (Hippocrates, *Nat. hom.*; Nutton 2013, 78–86; Jouanna 2012, 335–59). Galen also emphasized balance between wet and dry, hot and cold. When combined with the old Pythagorean idea of the human life span divisible into four "seasons" (Diogenes Laërtius, *Lives* 8.10; Hippocrates, *Nat. hom.* 15; Galen, *PHP* 8.6.17–19), this humoral theory came to represent a sort of theory of everything. Children were thought to be warm and moist, with an excess of blood, but bodies cooled with age (Hippocrates, *Nat. hom.* 12; *Aph.* 1.13–15). Youths in the "summer of life" were hot and dry, with an excess of bile (*cholē*), which made them "choleric." Adult men were cool and dry, with an excess of black bile (*melaina cholē*), which made them "melancholy" (Epictetus, *Diatr.* 2.5; Plutarch, *Lys.* 2.3; ps-Aristotle, *Probl.* 30.1). And old men, being cold and moist (Hippocrates, *Vict. salubr.* 2), had an excess of phlegm (*phlegma*), which made them "phlegmatic" and irascible. The theory of humors applied only to men, as women were always considered cold and wet (Mattern 2008, 102–5).

Humors in Ancient Medical Theory

Humor	Age	Season	Characteristic
blood	child	spring	hot and wet
yellow bile	youth	summer	hot and dry
black bile	adult	autumn	cool and dry
phlegm	old man	winter	cool and moist

Philosophers dovetailed humoral theory with ethics, providing a physiological rationale for the tendency of youth toward excess (Eyben 1993, 28–41; Hutson 2013, 87–91; see "Addressees" in the general introduction). The logical response was training in self-control. Since youth were "hot" by nature, wine overheated them (Galen, *Bon. mal. suc.*, trans. Kühn 6:805, 809; cf. Aristotle, *Rhet.* 1389a; ps.-Aristotle, *Probl.* 3 [871–76]). Youths should drink water (ps.-Crates, *Ep.* 14). Galen cited Plato in support of his argument that children under eighteen should drink no wine, and young men under thirty should drink only in moderation (Galen, *Animi mores* 10, trans. Kühn 4:808–10; Plato, *Laws* 666a–b).

Moderation was a mark of maturity. "Access to wine represented the first step in the process of integration into the adult world, one of the most significant expressions of which was the symposium, or drinking party, from which women were excluded" (Cambiano 1995, 100). Sobriety is a mark of mature leadership in the PE (1 Tim. 3:2, 3, 8, 11; Titus 1:7; 2:2), so using "a little wine" is a way for Timothy to set an example (cf. 4:12) of moderation. The point of 5:21–23 is how youthful Timothy can maintain credibility as he administers his duties toward older men.

The sins of some people are obvious, leading to condemnation, but with others they follow after. Likewise also, their good deeds are obvious, and those that prove otherwise cannot be hidden (5:24–25). After the aside in 5:23, these verses expand on 5:22. They also recall that an overseer should not be a neophyte, because slanderers are looking for opportunities to malign Christian leaders (3:6–7; 5:14). The fact that some sins are not obvious explains why Timothy should not ordain an elder "hastily" (5:22). In addition, the matter of "obvious good deeds"—showing that they are obviously generous—echoes the similar concern regarding enrolled widows (5:10).

Slaves (6:1–2a)

6:1–2a. Instructions for masters in the NT usually complement instruction for slaves (Eph. 6:5–9; Col. 3:22–4:1; *Did.* 4.10–11), but not so here (nor Titus 2:9–10). For enslaved people to give "every honor" (6:1) to their masters for "benefactions" (6:2a) sounds like an endorsement of the cultural status quo, keeping the enslaved in their place (Verner 1983; Kartzow

2009, 139–40). Even so, this section suggests alternate ways for masters and enslaved to relate.

Whoever are slaves under a yoke must consider their own masters worthy of every honor (6:1). The image of a "yoke" is dehumanizing, as if enslaved people are trained animals. This is not at all the way Jesus used the metaphor. Being under Jesus's "yoke" is tantamount to being a disciple (Matt. 11:28–30). Or when Paul refers to Clement as "my true yokefellow" (Phil. 4:3), he is describing himself and Clement as two oxen working together, pulling a cart that Jesus is driving. But here, the metaphorical "yoke" highlights the status difference between literal slaves and masters. This "yoke" is consistent with descriptions of an enslaved person as an "animated tool" (Aristotle, *Pol.* 1253b) or a "musical instrument" that must be "tuned" with discipline (ps.-Theano, *Call.* 5.40–45). Roman law classified a slave as both a person and a thing (Glancy 2006, 6). A master could sell a slave's children on a whim (e.g., POxy 117).

The "yoke" in 6:1 describes slaves from the point of view of pagan masters who thought slaves should be controlled by force, like animals. When commenting on the rising numbers of slaves imported from so many nations with their "foreign cults," Tacitus advised, "You will never coerce such a medley of humanity except by terror" (Tacitus, *Annals* 14.44, trans. Jackson, LCL; Harrill 2006, 147–48, for examples of such terror). What if some slaves brought into the household the "foreign cult" of Christianity?

The command for enslaved people to consider masters "worthy of every honor" accords with the cultural expectation that inferiors owe deference in exchange for the beneficence of their superiors (Kidd 1990, 46–50, 111–15). The exhortation may elicit revulsion from modern readers, contemplating a society in which masters assumed sexual privileges with slaves (Horace, *Satire* 1.2.114–19; Seneca, *Ep.* 47.7–8; Petronius, *Satyricon* 75; Dio Chrysostom, *Or.* 15.5; Philo, *Spec. Laws* 3.69; Glancy 2006, 12–26, 50–57; 2015). No Roman law or social convention condemned a master for raping a slave. For an enslaved person to accord "every honor" to a master in such circumstances would be following Paul's advice in Rom. 12:9–21: "Outdo one another in showing honor. . . . Bless those who persecute you. . . . Repay no one evil for evil" (RSV). We do not usually consider the import of those words for enslaved Christians. Such exhortations leave room for abused slaves to be faithful followers of Jesus, who taught, "Love your enemies" (Matt. 5:44), but they do not condone abusive masters.

Likewise, in this context, where "honor" connotes financial payment (5:3, 17), modern readers may recoil at the idea of a master coercing a "gift" from a slave. Yet Seneca discusses whether a slave's gift to a master should be called a "duty," a "service," or a "benefit." Seneca argues that when a slave gives money or even his life to protect a master, such acts are "benefits" if motivated by genuine affection (*Ben.* 3.17–22). Stoics argued that bondage was a matter of indifference and real freedom was acting in accordance with one's moral purpose regardless of circumstances (Epictetus, *Diatr.* 3.22.38–44; 4.1.131; Dio Chrysostom, *Or.* 80). Though an action could be coerced, an attitude could not. Some slaves went to heroic lengths to protect their masters (Cassius Dio 47.9–10; Appian, *Civil Wars* 4.6.43; C. Martin 2007, 427–28). For the Stoics, then, a paragon of virtue would be a slave who "by his affection for his master has overcome the common hatred of being a slave" (Seneca, *Ben.* 3.17–22, trans. Basore, LCL; cf. Epictetus, *Diatr.* 3.24.58–77). Pastoral Paul sounds somewhat like Seneca, though he couches his exhortation in Christian language ("brother," "beloved"). Furthermore, the reversed polarity of slave as benefactor to the master is consistent with the ethic of Jesus (Matt. 5:43–47; Luke 22:25–27; John 13:3–7; Towner 2006, 387–90).

An enslaved Christian who gives "every honor" to a master—even an abusive master—makes it less likely that the master will "slander" Christianity, **so that the name of God and the teaching might not be blasphemed** (6:1). Outsiders might blaspheme, or "slander," Christianity, if they thought enslaved Christians were disrupting household order. On the other hand, "non-Christian masters of Christian slaves—upper-crust outsiders—would have been in a unique position to influence public opinion toward the Christian community" (Kidd 1999, 139; cf. "adorn the teaching," Titus 2:10). Thus, the enslaved could contribute to the evangelistic goal identified in 2:1–7. Pliny gained a favorable impression of Christianity after he tortured two enslaved Christian deaconesses (Pliny the Younger, *Ep.* 10.96; M. MacDonald 1996, 51–59). Even though he executed Christians for "stubbornness" in refusing to recognize the emperor as a god, he grudgingly admired their honesty and integrity.

If 6:1 regards enslaved people from the viewpoint of an unbelieving master, 6:2a views them from that of a believing master: **And those who have faithful masters must not despise them, because they are brothers** (6:2a). Epicurus included his slave Mys in his philosophical society (Diogenes Laërtius, *Lives* 10.9–10), and Seneca urged Lucilius to think of his slaves as humble friends (Seneca, *Ep.* 47.1, 16). Philosophically speaking, "friendship" was a relationship between equals, an idea first articulated by Pythagoras (Thom 1997, 77). But "friendship" could also be a euphemism for the unequal relation between ruler and ruled or master and slave (Seneca, *Ep.* 3.1–2). A cynical reading, therefore, might take "brothers" (6:2a) as a patronizing pat on the head, adopting the language of equality while treating the slave as inferior (Horrell 2001, 307; cf. Xenophon, *Oec.* 14.10, on "praise and honor" to diligent slaves). But Pastoral Paul is not discussing how masters treat slaves. He is discussing the attitude of slaves, which is under the slaves' control. Not only must slaves "not despise" their masters; they should also behave as if they were "brothers." Turning the tables on coercion by acting voluntarily in the best interest of one's tormentor is the factor that allows Seneca to say a slave can confer a "benefit" on a master (Seneca, *Ben.* 3.23–28). It is also what Jesus meant by "go the second mile" (Matt. 5:41; Wink 1992, 179–84).

Not only that, **but they must slave all the more, because they are faithful and beloved who assist in the benefactions** (6:2a). The exhortation to "slave all the more" runs counter to modern sensibilities. The Roman Empire was like the American South before the Civil War, when any talk of freeing slaves was viewed as sedition. Even though Paul encouraged slaves to take the opportunity for manumission when it came (1 Cor. 7:21 ESV; Bartchy 1973, 155–59), he also encouraged slaves to live out their Christian calling as slaves (1 Cor. 7:17–24; cf. Eph. 6:5–9; Col. 3:22–4:1; Titus 2:9; 1 Pet. 2:18–25; Ign. *Pol.* 4.2–3). We should not be surprised at a similar attitude here, considering the complexities of freeing slaves (in Roman society, Barclay 1991, 176–77; in antebellum America, Fife 1971, 46–49) and the likelihood that Christians freeing their slaves would bring greater attack upon Christianity.

The reason ("because") slaves should "slave all the more" is that masters make "benefactions." The verb *antilambanomai* means "assist" (Luke 1:54; Acts 20:35; cf. Luke 10:40; Rom. 8:26), but who is assisting whom? Perhaps the reasoning is as follows:

A. "because they (the masters) assist (the city) with benefactions" (by paying for public works projects; Danker 1982, §§34, 35), or
B. "because they (the masters) assist (the slaves) with benefactions" (food, clothing, shelter, medical care; Epictetus, *Diatr.* 4.1.37). On these first two interpretations, the motive for slaves would be that their masters are noble and virtuous, or
C. "because they (the slaves) assist (the masters) in the benefactions (to the city)," in which case the motive would be that slaves contribute to whatever benefactions the masters make. This would be true of all slaves, in that masters profited from slave labor, and especially of slaves who served as household managers and assisted directly in financial maneuvers (D. Martin 1990, 15–22).

All three interpretations are elitist in that they focus on the admirable benefactions of the masters, but option C gives credit to the slaves for helping make the benefactions possible.

Theological Issues

Structures of Power and Domination

Are Greco-Roman station codes in harmony with the basic principles of Christianity? Postmodern scholars critique that supposition as too convenient to the self-interests of the interpreters, who have nearly always been educated, affluent men. Or are the station codes post-Pauline retreats from the ideals of Jesus and Paul? Both readings concede too much to a worldly agenda because they assume that NT texts inscribe Greco-Roman social structures as normative for Christians.

Ancient elitist stereotypes of slaves as deceitful and dishonest may have had some basis in realities of resistance (Bradley 1987, 28–33). From the perspective of "infrapolitics" (see "James Scott and 'Infrapolitics'" in the general introduction), James Scott calls attention to "the ordinary weapons of relatively powerless groups: foot-dragging, dissimulation, false compliance, pilfering, feigned ignorance, slander, arson, sabotage, and so forth" (J. Scott 2013, 69; cf. Callahan and Horsley 1998). By explicitly rejecting that sort of thing, Pastoral Paul overtly supports the masters. He is, however, subversive in the ways he thinks about benefactions in 5:1–6:2a. While he seems to uphold Roman social expectations for slaves—loyalty (Lat. *fides*, "faithfulness") and obedience (Bradley 1987, 33–39), he ascribes "honor" to destitute widows and teachers rather than wealthy patrons. And, if we take interpretive option C for 6:2a, he recognizes the contributions of slaves to their masters' success. He adopts the terminology of the dominant culture but redefines it. This is not revolution, but it is quietly subversive. The PE reflect the cultural context in spite of which early Christians practiced their faith. But we must test this idea further in the case of slavery.

Slavery and the Gospel

Slavery is a persistent problem for modern believers. Texts like 1 Tim. 6:1–2 take for granted that Christian communities include slaves and masters, and they do not condemn slavery outright. Pastoral Paul assumes that Christian masters are beneficent and admonishes only the slaves (cf. Titus 2:9–10). Does this passage express God's word for the millions of people in the world today who have been trafficked as menial laborers and sex workers?

The idea that one person can keep another "under a yoke" is antithetical to the gospel, which teaches that God "was made evident in flesh" (3:16) and entered into the fleshly experience of the abused. Yet, not until the fourth century do we hear from Gregory of Nyssa a case for abolishing slavery (*Hom. Eccl.* 4 [see sidebar]). Gregory's passionate appeal is so well grounded in biblical theology that it is difficult to imagine how such arguments are not found before the fourth century. Perhaps early Christians picked their battles. Pastoral Paul asserts the sovereignty of the living God over all peoples and powers, a dangerous proposition in the Roman Empire. But after Constantine, Christianity moved from a "foreign" sect to the official religion. Having won the point that the lords of the world must submit to the lordship of Jesus Christ, Christians were freer to address the further implications of the gospel for oppressed people.

But even in the first century, Pastoral Paul was like a slave preacher before the American Civil War, who was ambiguously either a "force for accommodation to the *status quo* or a force for the exercise of slave autonomy"

Gregory of Nyssa: A Biblical Case for Abolition

Here Gregory comments on Ecclesiastes 2:7, "I obtained servants, maidens, servants born to me in my house."

"Do you see here a pride which makes false pretensions? Such words as these rise up against God. As prophecy has told us [Ps. 119:91], all things serve [God,] whose power is over them. As for the person who appropriates to himself what belongs to God and attributes to himself power over the human race as if he were its lord, what other arrogant statement transgressing human nature makes this person regard himself as different from those over whom he rules? 'I obtained servants and maidens.' What are you saying? You condemn man who is free and autonomous to servitude, and you contradict God by perverting the natural law. Man, who was created as lord over the earth, you have put under the yoke of servitude as a transgressor and rebel against the divine precept. You have forgotten the limit of your authority which consists in jurisdiction over brutish animals." (Homilies on Ecclesiastes 4, trans. McCambly)

(Raboteau 1978, 238). What the slave preacher said in secret did not necessarily match what he said in public (Botkin 1945, 26; C. Martin 1998, 223–28). Double meaning was a hallmark of slave preaching in the American South (Montgomery 1993, 32–33). Perhaps Pastoral Paul was like a white preacher who spoke with forked tongue, as recalled by a formerly enslaved eyewitness:

> One time when an old white man came along who wanted to preach, the white people gave him a chance to preach to the n—s. The substance of his sermon was this: "Now when you servants are working for your masters, you must be honest. When you go to the mill, don't carry along an extra sack and put some of the meal or the flour in for yourself. And when you women are cooking in the big house, don't make a big pocket under your dress and put a sack of coffee and a sack of sugar and other things you want in it." They took him out and hanged him for corrupting the morals of the slaves. (Botkin 1945, 26)

It turns out that preaching with a "hidden transcript" is dangerous. The message must be presented so the masters hear what they want to hear, and only ears tuned to the experience of oppression will catch the counterpoint. I have argued that 6:2a is deliberately ambiguous. Alas for interpreters who have been unable to hear anything other than an endorsement of slavery.

There are resources for the liberation of slaves embedded in the PE, if we tune our ears to hear them. Consider, for example, the story of the formerly enslaved Jeff Calhoun (see sidebar). As an old man remembering his childhood, Calhoun garbles the text, but Uncle Billy was likely quoting, "The laborer is

---

Jeff Calhoun Remembers Uncle Billy

"Uncle Billy was our preacher and the garden tender. Uncle Billy got in trouble once. He didn't like collards, and the missus had three big, fine collards in the garden, and she all time after Billy to take good care of these collards. So's one Saturday night after church, Billy slips out and cuts 'em down. The next mornin' the cook was sent to the garden for vegetables and some of these collards for the mistress, but they was gone. The cook hurries to the house and tells the missus. She tells master. He come in mad and say, 'Who done this?' The girl that is the cook says, 'Billy done it, 'cause he don't like collards.' He says to get Billy to come here. Billy come to the house. Master says, 'Billy, you preacher?' Billy say, 'Yassuh.' He says, 'Billy, you's cut them collards?' Billy says, 'Yassuh, I's got some greens.' He says, 'Now, Billy, you preacher, git me the Bible.' And he reads, 'Thou shalt not steal.' Then he handed Billy the Bible and said, 'Read this.' He sure hates to, but Master makes him do it. Then he sure tears loose on Billy 'bout stealin'. Finally, Billy says, 'Now, Master, I can show you in the Bible where I did not steal.' He tells Billy to find it, and Billy finds it and reads, 'You shall reap when you laboreth.' Master said to Billy, 'Get to hell out'n here.'" (Jeff Calhoun, interviewed Texas, n.d., *The American Slave*, ser. 1, vol. 4 [Tex., pt. 1], 188–90; repr., Berlin et al. 1998, 193–94, spelling and punctuation corrected from transcript)

---

worthy of his wages." Whether he was thinking of Jesus (Luke 10:7) or Paul (1 Tim. 5:18), his quotation was effective against his Christian master, because, even though both Jesus and Paul applied it to the principle of financial support for evangelists, the proverb struck at the essence of slavery. Uncle Billy shows how even Christian slaves who "give all honor" to their masters do not necessarily share the masters' viewpoint.

Theresa Urbainczyk describes two persistent themes in antiquity: the "natural animosity" between slaves and masters and the idea that slavery was not natural (Urbainczyk 2008, 76–80; Lysias, *Or.* 7.35). Aristotle was no egalitarian, but he knew of people "who maintain that for one man to be another man's master is contrary to nature, because it is only convention that makes the one a slave and the other a freeman and there is no difference between them by nature, and that therefore it is unjust, for it is based on force" (Aristotle, *Pol.* 1.2.3 [1253b], trans. Rackham, LCL). Roman law defined slavery as "a creation of the common law of peoples by which a person is subjected, contrary to nature, to ownership of another" (Justinian, *Digest* 1.5). In the mythological Golden Age there was no slavery (Plutarch, *Comp. Lyc. Num.* 1.5; Herodotus, *Histories* 6.137; Urbainczyk 2008, 76–80). Such a utopian ideal should resonate with Christian eschatology. The "eternal life" for which we "struggle" (1 Tim. 4:8–10; 6:11–12) is not merely a grand vision of the age to come. It is the vision that reorients behavior in the present age. There is no room for slavery in a Christian vision of heaven, and a Christian who owns slaves is playing by earthly rules (on slavery and Christian ethics, Swartley 1983, 31–64; Hutson 2005a).

Where he mentions it directly, Pastoral Paul seems to accept slavery; but he hedges it about, before and behind, with principles that undermine the position of the master: "a laborer is worthy of his wages" (5:18); a critique of how the rich use their money (6:6–10, 17–19); and the command to "take hold of eternal life" (6:12). His exhortation to slaves is two-sided, offering the possibility of viewing slaves not as animals to be exploited but as "brothers" who are "assisting" in their masters' "benefactions." The thoughtful minister must discern between earthly rules of domination and the gospel call for liberation. You cannot serve two masters (cf. comments and "Theological Issues" at 1 Tim. 2:8–15; Titus 2:1–15).

1 Timothy 6:2b–21

Third Charge to Timothy

Introductory Matters

We have seen how the ancient Household Management topos influenced the contents of our letter (see "The Household of God" in the general introduction). That topos discussed acquiring and maintaining wealth (Aristotle, *Pol.* 1.3–4 [1256a–59a]; Xenophon, *Oec.*; Philodemus, *Oec.*; Balch 1981, 33–59; Verner 1983, 84–86). Abraham J. Malherbe (2010, 387) views all of 5:3–6:19 as a single block unified around the topic of the use of money. Without denying that connection, I suggest that the shift to second-person imperatives in 6:2b–21 marks a new section and the letter closing. Given the correspondences between chapters 1 and 6 (see "Introductory Matters" for 1:3–20), it is appropriate to take 6:2b–21 together (similarly, Mihoc 2008, 138–39). This is the third and final charge to Timothy (cf. 1:3–20; 3:14–4:16). The material in this section pertains to ministerial formation.

Within this final charge and the letter closing are five imperatives: 6:2b, 11, 13, 17, and 20. There is a close connection between 6:3–10 and 6:11–12 as "reverse images of each other" (Kidd 1990, 94), and a similar correspondence between 6:17–19 and 6:20–21. The central imperative at 6:13–16 is the charge proper (see comments at 1:18–20; Craig Smith 2006). Reading 6:2b–21 this way, we find order in what might seem to be a disjointed chapter. Michel Gourgues (2016) reads the chapter as a chiasm —ABCB'A'—with 6:11–16 in the focal point. My analysis is similar—ABCA'B'— with 6:13–16 at the center. The focus is on what sort of teacher Timothy should be, defined christologically, in contrast to avaricious people of "the present age."

Timothy's "struggle" (6:12) is to live a moral life in anticipation of the age to come ("eternal life," 6:12; "until the manifestation of our Lord," 6:14). That struggle is grounded in a backward look at the life of Jesus, as Timothy's "good confession" (6:12) echoes the "good confession" of Jesus before Pilate (6:13). To those who are "rich in the present age" (6:17) or "desire to be rich" (6:9), Timothy should model how to live a life like that of Jesus, unspotted and oriented toward God's future.

Tracing the Train of Thought

Those Who Teach Otherwise (6:2b–10)

6:2b–10. Teach and exhort these things (6:2b). "These things" marks the transition to a new topic (cf. 3:14; 4:11). This paragraph distinguishes Timothy from those who "teach otherwise" (6:3). At issue are contrasting views of "piety" (6:3, 5, 6). The unethical practices of bad teachers (6:3–10, 17–21) contrast with the behavior of a "person of God" (6:11–12) whose confession is christological (6:13–16).

If anyone teaches otherwise and does not have recourse to healthy words, namely, the words about our Lord Jesus Christ, and to the teaching that is in accordance with piety, he is demented, understanding nothing, but sick with speculations and word battles, from which arise envy, strife, blasphemies, evil suspicions, constant frictions of people who are corrupt in mind and deprived of the truth, thinking of piety as means of profit (6:3–5). This long sentence echoes earlier criticisms of bad teachers (1:3–7; 4:1–5). Each of the three charges to Timothy (1:3–20; 3:14–4:16; 6:2b–21) describes the kind of teacher Timothy should not be, followed by an exhortation as to what he should be. In addition, this sentence recapitulates the theme of "piety" (*eusebeia*, 2:2; 3:16; 4:7, 8; cf. 2:10; 5:4), applied here in relation to money. In its attitude toward wealth, this letter is broadly consistent with the undisputed Pauline letters (Dahl 1977, 22–36).

The reliable teacher draws on "healthy words," defined in two ways. First, healthy

---

1 Timothy 6:2b–21 in the Rhetorical Flow

Letter opening (1:1–2)

Proem: First charge to Timothy (1:3–20)

First set of directives concerning the church (2:1–3:13)

Second charge to Timothy (3:14–4:16)

Second set of directives concerning the church (5:1–6:2a)

▶ Third charge to Timothy (6:2b–21)

    Those who teach otherwise (6:2b–10)

    Exhortation to flee . . . pursue (6:11–12)

    Exhortation to keep the commandment (6:13–16)

    The rich in this age (6:17–19)

    Exhortation to guard the deposit, and the letter closing (6:20–21)

words are "the teaching that is in accordance with piety." Second, they are "words of our Lord Jesus Christ," which could mean either words Jesus spoke (Gk. subjective gen.) or words about Jesus (Gk. objective gen.). The latter is more likely, because Pastoral Paul offers no arguments based on sayings of Jesus, except possibly 1 Tim. 5:18, which he does not attribute to Jesus. But he frequently cites tradition about Jesus (1 Tim. 1:15; 2:5–6; 3:16; 2 Tim. 1:9–10; 2:8–13; Titus 3:4–7), and that tradition constitutes "healthy words."

Ancient philosophers saw themselves as physicians of the soul, trying to cure people of the vices that clouded their judgment (Malherbe 1980; 2010, 388–92; see comments at 4:7, 15–16). Earlier, Pastoral Paul described immoral behavior as "contrary to healthy teaching" (1:10). Here, in contrast to those who teach "healthy words," false teachers are mentally ill: "demented," "knowing nothing," "sick with speculations and word battles," "corrupt in mind" in that they "think that piety is a means of profit" (cf. Titus 1:11). The results of unhealthy thinking are "envy, strife, blasphemies, evil suspicions, constant frictions."

Here Pastoral Paul does not pin any false doctrine on those who "teach otherwise." Nor does he mind that they get paid (see 5:17–18; cf. 1 Cor. 9). What is odious is their greed. Ancient teachers often had reputations as money-grubbers (Lucian, *Peregr.* 11–13, 16; *Fug.* 14, 17, 21, 24, 26; Malherbe 1989, 38–39; 2010, 388–89). Timothy should recognize and avoid unscrupulous teachers.

But there is great profit in piety with self-sufficiency (6:6). Timothy must cultivate a healthy understanding of money in relation to piety. The argument draws on the philosophical topos of self-sufficiency (Malherbe 2010, 392–400). Socrates said his meager possessions were "sufficient" for him, whereas wealth put constant strain on Critoboulos (Xenophon, *Oec.* 2.4–8). In our passage, the noun "self-sufficiency" (*autarkeia*, 6:6) and the verb "we shall be sufficed" (*arkēsometha*, 6:8) form brackets around 6:6–8 and indicate the difference between bad "profit" (6:5) and "great profit" (6:6). Pastoral Paul does not, like Jesus, advise selling all possessions, but he does warn against avarice, and he loathes greed. The "great profit" in piety is spiritual.

For we brought nothing into the world, [so] that we are not able to take anything out; and if we have food and covering, with these we shall be sufficed (6:7–8). If verse 7 is a proverb (Yarbrough 2009, 128–32; cf. 6:10), then verse 8 is a comment on it. In any case, the conjunction "for" marks 6:7–8 as explaining the claim in 6:6. Greed is unnatural. The awkward conjunction "that" (*hoti*) has caused consternation since antiquity. Some scribes clarified by adding words: "*it is evident* that . . ." (א[2] et al.; cf. KJV, YLT), or "*it is true* that . . ." (D et al.), or even omitting "that" and translating, "nor are we able . . ." (Jerome, RSV, CEV). But the simplest solution is to read "that" as meaning "*so* that" (BDAG 732, s.v. ὅτι 5.c; NASB, NRSV).

The second sentence, advocating self-sufficiency, complements the first. Rudimentary food and shelter should "suffice" (6:8). Most ancient philosophers would have agreed (Malherbe 2010), but they differed in perspective. Cynics renounced possessions, willing to "suffice" with simple food and water, only enough for the day (Philodemus, *Oec.* 12.39–40; cf. Matt. 6:11). They were mendicants who begged for daily bread (cf. Mark 6:7–11), having only the clothes on their backs: Diogenes famously slept in a huge pot. Stoics allowed for wealth, as long as one did not grab after it, cling to it, or mourn its loss. Seneca was enormously wealthy, but he taught that one should practice doing with bare necessities as preparation for the possibility of loss (Seneca, *Ep.* 18.5–6; 87; 123.2–3; cf. Epictetus, *Diatr.* 3.13.21; Plutarch, *Tu. san.* 3–4 [123b–f]). For Stoics, possessions were matters of indifference that should not interfere with freedom to act according to one's moral purpose. Epicureans rejected both Cynic poverty and Stoic splendor in favor of modest means. To be happy and self-sufficient, one should avoid the pains associated with great poverty or great wealth, being content with only "measured" or "natural" wealth (Philodemus, *Oec.* 12.18–19; 14.19; Asmis 2004). One should share generously with friends as a hedge against loss (Philodemus, *Oec.* 15.1–6; 25.3–4, trans. Tsouna 2012, 69; Fiore 2004, 275; cf. Tob. 4:9). In some ways, Pastoral Paul is closest to the Epicureans (Balch 2004), but he does not embrace their utilitarian motives.

But those who want to be rich fall into a trial and a snare and many mindless and harmful desires, which plunge people into ruin and destruction. For the root of all evils is devotion to money. By craving this, some have been seduced away from the faith and have pierced themselves with many pains (6:9–10). The centerpiece of this argument is verse 10a, which may be another proverb (Yarbrough 2009, 132–34). It was a commonplace that desire for wealth generates vice. The historian Sallust lamented how, as they encircled the Mediterranean, the Romans developed new appetites for wealth and power, which became the "basis of all evils" (Sallust, *Bellum Catalinae* 10.3). Philo bemoaned the newly rich, who "turn away [*ektrepontai*; cf. 1 Tim. 1:6; 6:20] into pathless wilds, because they do not see the road [of virtue] before them" (Philo, *Spec. Laws* 2.23). Wealth is not bad in itself, but "the root of all evils is devotion to money." On this point we find agreement among Stoics (Seneca, *Ep.* 87.31–34), Cynics (ps.-Diogenes, *Ep.* 50 [Malherbe 1977, 180]), Epicureans (Philodemus, *Oec.* 14.5–6), and Christians (Pol. *Phil.* 4.1, quoting 1 Tim. 6:10).

Exhortation to Flee . . . Pursue (6:11–12)

6:11–12. But as for you, person of God, flee these things, and pursue righteousness, piety, faithfulness, love, endurance, gentleness. Struggle the good struggle of the faith. Take hold of the eternal life to which you were called, even when you confessed the good confession in front of many witnesses (6:11–12). As a "person of God," Timothy should "flee these things"—namely, the "desire to be rich" (6:9). "Struggle the good struggle" (cf. 2 Tim. 4:7–8) echoes the opening charge, "fight the good fight" (1 Tim. 1:18). But the militaristic edge of that earlier metaphor was blunted by admonitions that men should avoid "anger and arguing" (2:8) and that the overseer should be "not violent but fair, not combative" (3:3). The "good struggle" is against passions and desires in one's own heart (2 Tim. 2:22; Phil. 1:30). We have seen hints throughout the letter that money, power, and status were problems. Women should decorate themselves with moral character, not the trappings of status (1 Tim. 2:9–10); "honor" goes to older people on the basis of service and teaching, not to benefactors (5:3–25); assistance by slaves is a kind of "benefaction" (6:2a); the "good struggle" is oriented toward eternal life (6:12; cf. 4:8–10). With such admonitions this letter undercuts the competitive spirit of Greco-Roman culture.

"Take hold of the eternal life to which you were called" (6:12b) orients Timothy's ministry toward the age to come. Timothy's "good confession before many witnesses" probably refers to his baptism. The correlation between Timothy's confession and that of Jesus (6:13) calls to mind Paul's understanding of baptism as a symbolic death-burial-resurrection in identification with the story of Jesus (Rom. 6:1–11).

Exhortation to Keep the Commandment (6:13–16)

6:13–16. At the center of 6:2b–21 is the sentence that most closely matches the form of a charge (see comments at 1:18–20; Craig Smith 2006). **I charge you before God, who gives life to everything, and Christ Jesus, who testified the good confession before Pontius Pilate, that you keep the commandment unspotted, unimpeachable, until the manifestation of our Lord Jesus Christ, which he will display when the times are right** (6:13–15a). The verb "I charge" (*parangellō*) echoes the noun "charge" (*parangelia*) in 1:18. The authority for the charge is twofold. Pastoral Paul appeals to "God, who gives life to everything," and to the story of Jesus's death, with an allusion to Pilate (6:13). This is not about anything Jesus said to Pilate but refers to Jesus's act of self-sacrifice. Jesus testified (cf. 2:6b; 2 Tim. 1:8) either "*in the time of* Pontius Pilate" (BDAG 367, s.v. ἐπί 18.a; Ign. *Smyrn.* 6.2) or "*before* Pontius Pilate" (BDAG 363–64, s.v. ἐπί 3). The latter reading is preferable as parallel to "in front of [*enōpion*] God" (6:13).

The charge itself is to "keep the commandment" (6:14). To "keep the commandments" (pl.) was a Jewish idiom for Torah observance (Matt. 19:17), adaptable to Christian contexts (1 Cor. 7:19; John 14:15, 21; 15:10; Rev. 12:17; 14:12). But "*the* commandment" (sg.) suggests some specific commandment (cf. Rom. 7:7–13). Nathan Eubank argues that "the commandment" here is shorthand for the Jewish commandment par excellence, to give alms (Eubank 2011, citing Sir. 29:8–13; *Lev. Rab.* 3.1; *T. Ash.* 2.8), though his examples are not all singular. Still, Eubank's approach explains how this exhortation could fit into the argument on the use of wealth (cf. Downs 2016, 147–52). Alternatively, the context offers explicit commands in 6:11–12 (Easton 1948, 166), though again not a single command. A third possibility is to take "the commandment" in a broad sense of "the gospel viewed as a rule of life"

(Knight 1992, 266–68), roughly equivalent to "I commit this charge to you" (1:18), "struggle the good struggle" (6:12), and "guard the deposit" (6:20).

Timothy is to keep the charge "unspotted" (cf. James 1:27; 2 Pet. 3:14), consistent with being "holy" (5:22) and "unimpeachable" (cf. 3:2). Pastoral Paul charges him to persevere until the "manifestation" of Jesus (6:14; see sidebar at Titus 2:13). The phrase "when the times are right" (6:15; see comments at 2:6) marks that manifestation as an eschatological event at the close of the age (Titus 2:13).

Finally, the subject of the verb "he will display" (6:15) is uncertain. It would be natural to fill in the subject from the previous clause, so that "our Lord Jesus Christ . . . will display" his own manifestation, taking the hymn that follows as a celebration of Jesus Christ. That would equate Jesus with God (see comments at Titus 2:13). The word "manifestation" appropriately applied to a deity, and a high Christology here would be consistent with the high ecclesiology at 3:15. On the other hand, a previous traditional quotation distinguished between the "one God" and the "human Christ Jesus" (2:5). In the hymn celebrating the resurrection (3:16) the verbs "was manifested" and "was taken up" are divine passives, implying that God is the agent. It is reasonable, therefore, to understand God as the one who "will display." The NRSV preserves the ambiguity nicely by inserting "he who is" before the hymn, leaving the reader to decide whether the hymn praises God or Christ-as-God.

> [He who is]
> The blessed and only Sovereign,
> The King of kings,
> And Lord of lords,
> The only One who has immortality
> Who inhabits unapproachable light,
> Whom no human has seen or is able to see
> To whom be honor and might forever, amen. (6:15–16)

This hymn (cf. 3:16; 2 Tim. 2:11–13) celebrates the "only" God and echoes the doxology in 1:17. The terms "only Sovereign," "King of kings," and "Lord of lords" reinforce that there is one God (cf. 2:5). Pagans might refer to an emperor (Plutarch, *Luc.* 14.5) or the chief deity (Dio Chrysostom, *Or.* 2.75) as "king of kings," whereas "Lord of lords" is more distinctively Jewish, since "LORD" was the standard circumlocution for the divine Name. "King of kings" could, therefore, be an instance of co-opting pagan terminology. It is consistent with an apocalyptic perspective that takes "as its starting point one of the central tenets of imperial propaganda: the equation of an imperial order with the order of the cosmos itself," and subverts it by claiming that both empire and cosmos will soon come crashing down (Lincoln 2000, 466–67; cf. Rev. 17–21; 1QM 12). This hymn challenges imperial ideology by subordinating the emperor to the one God (cf. 1 Tim. 2:1–7).

Transcending the limits of human experience, the one God "has immortality" and "dwells in unapproachable light." We might compare the vision of John of Patmos, who was transported in the spirit to the throne of God, found it difficult to describe, and resorted to similes (Rev. 4). Our hymn soars beyond John's vision to celebrate One "whom no one has seen or is able to see" (cf. 1 Tim. 1:17). "Honor and eternal dominion" (6:16) belong to one God and no other.

The Rich in This Age (6:17–19)

6:17–19. As for the rich in this age, charge them not to be arrogant nor to place hope in the uncertainty of riches, but in God who richly furnishes us with everything for enjoyment; to do good, to be rich in good deeds, to be generous, sharing, treasuring up for themselves a foundation for the future, so that they might take hold of the real life (6:17–19). After what appeared to be a grand finale in 6:15–16, this note seems like an afterthought. Lyn Kidson (2014, 115) puts it down to "the spontaneous nature of letters," repeating a key point for emphasis. But the balance among the five imperatives in 6:2b–21 (see "Introductory Matters") suggests careful composition.

The four terms in 6:18 are roughly synonymous, piled up to emphasize that giving money is a "good work." With "real life" we may compare Philo's description of "one who walks in the judgments and ordinances of God" as living a "true life," whereas godless people are "dead" (Philo, *Congr.* 87; cf. *Spec. Laws* 1.345; 1 Tim. 5:6; Downs 2016, 158–62). For Pastoral Paul, however, "real life" is not a better life in the present. Riches in "this age" are "uncertain" (6:17). One should lay up "treasure" for the "future" and "take hold of real life" in the age to come (6:12; cf. 2 Tim. 2:11; Matt. 5:19–21). Again, we find Christian ethics oriented toward the eschaton (cf. 1 Tim. 2:4, 6; 3:16; 4:8; 6:12, 14; Titus 2:13), an orientation that is deeply Pauline (2 Cor. 8–9; Phil. 4:10–20; Downs 2016, 162–73). Greek philosophers would agree that "God furnishes us with everything for enjoyment" on a daily basis, but they lacked the apocalyptic distinction between "this age" and "the future" with its "real life."

Exhortation to Guard the Deposit, and the Letter Closing (6:20–21)

These verses are tied closely to the preceding imperatives about wealth (see "Introductory Matters" for 6:2b–21). They serve both as the final exhortation of the larger unit 6:2b–21 and as the letter closing. Typical Greco-Roman letter closings were formulaic (Klauck 2006, 37–42; Weima 2010). The closing of this letter is unusually brief, only a final exhortation and a grace benediction.

6:20–21a. O Timothy, guard the deposit, turning aside from profane, empty talk and antitheses of what is falsely named "knowledge," by promising which some have deviated from the faith (6:20–21a). This final exhortation echoes earlier charges in chapters 1 and 4. The noun "deposit" (*parathēkē*, 6:20) is related to the verb "committed" (*paratithemai*, 1:18; cf. 2 Tim. 2:2), so these verses form an *inclusio* around the letter. A "deposit" (*parathēkē*) was anything of value entrusted to someone, who had a sacred obligation to protect it and return it on demand (Tob. 4:1–2; cf. 2 Tim. 1:12, 14). This directive reiterates Timothy's choice (4:1; cf. 2 Tim. 2–3). He should "turn aside from profane, empty talk" (cf. 1 Tim. 1:6–7; 4:7). The right focus will be the "healthy teaching" of Paul (see comments at 1:10; 4:6; 6:3).

The "antitheses of what is falsely named knowledge" (6:20) has been taken as evidence that the PE were composed to combat Gnosticism. In second-century struggles between mainstream Christians and gnostics, each side claimed true "knowledge" (*gnōsis*) and denigrated the other for failure to understand Jesus (Brakke 2010). Marcion wrote a book, now lost, called *The Antitheses*, which Irenaeus repudiated as "falsely named knowledge" (Irenaeus, *Haer.* 3.12.12), as he also repudiated other gnostics (Irenaeus, *Haer.* 1.23.4; 2.pref.1; 2.14.17; 3.11.1; cf. Eusebius, *Hist. eccl.* 5.7.1). Clement of Alexandria decried cowards who avoided martyrdom or rushed into it motivated by "falsely named knowledge" (*Strom.* 2.11; 3.4, 18; 4.4; 7.7). So it is tempting to read this verse as anti-gnostic polemic. But the PE can plausibly be dated to the first century (see "Date" in the general introduction), in which case it could be that church fathers found in passages like 1 Tim. 6:20 language they could use against the gnostics (B. White 2011).

This passage rejects oratorical display (cf. 1 Cor. 1:18–2:5; Winter 2002). Lucian depicts the god Hermes admonishing the dead to lay aside excess weight before stepping into Charon's boat to cross the Styx. He urges a philosopher to put aside "ignorance, contentiousness, vanity, unanswerable puzzles, thorny argumentations, and complicated conceptions—yes, and plenty of wasted effort, and no little nonsense, and idle talk, and splitting of hairs" (Lucian, *Dial. mort.* 20[10].369, trans. M. D. Macleod, LCL). He tells a rhetorician to "throw away your endless loquacity, your antitheses, balanced clauses, periods, foreign phrases, and everything else that makes your speeches so heavy" (Lucian, *Dial. mort.* 20[10].373–74; cf. Gray 2007, 313, on "antitheses" in philosophical debate). In Lucian's view, unscrupulous teachers used philosophical obfuscations and rhetorical embellishments to impress naive hearers and attract higher fees and invitations to dinner. In rejecting rhetorical razzle-dazzle, our verse recapitulates earlier exhortations (1:4, 6, 7; 4:6; cf. 2 Tim. 2:16; Titus 1:10; 1 Cor. 2:1–5). It also caps the immediate context, which rejects combative rhetoric and money-grubbing methods (6:3–5) and warns against worldly wealth (6:6–19).

6:21b. The benediction, **Grace be with you** (6:21b) seems abrupt. We expect a Pauline letter to end with travel plans (Titus 3:12–14) and personal greetings (2 Tim. 4:19–21; Titus 3:15a) before the final blessing. The benediction is more concise than we find at the end of most Pauline letters, though it appears in just this form in Col. 4:18.

The plural pronoun "you" is surprising at the end of a letter otherwise written entirely to "you," singular. The same benediction, appended to all three PE (2 Tim. 4:22b; Titus 3:15), gives the impression that they were composed together or edited into a collection intended for a secondary readership beyond the named addressees (Hutson 1998, 10–15; an "extended letter," Stirewalt 1993, 10–15). I take the secondary audience as any young minister who might benefit from this letter (and two others) of ministerial formation.

Theological Issues

Apophatic Theology

In the "Theological Issues" at 1:3–20, we considered the tradition of apophatic theology, which attempts to say only what God is not, such as "immortal, invisible" (1:17). Now Pastoral Paul extols God in terms of "immortality," "unapproachable light," "whom no human has seen or is able to see" (6:16). Once again, we soar upward to contemplate a God beyond human comprehension, as in the poem "I Entered Where I Did Not Know" by the sixteenth-century Spanish mystic St. John of the Cross (see sidebar).

Apophatic theology tends toward mysticism and is appropriate for one with long experience in contemplative prayer. Most believers find more engagement in "cataphatic" theology, which contemplates God in terms of some concrete metaphor. Our prayer employs the metaphor of monarch, expressed as "only Sovereign, King of kings, Lord of lords" (6:15). Contemplative prayer might explore a metaphor at length, dwelling on how such an understanding of God orients one's life. Only after exhausting all such metaphors is one able to move toward the more abstract apophatic theology. The hymn in 6:15–16 moves from concrete to abstract, suggesting the progression that one might follow through a lifetime of contemplative prayer.

> ### St. John of the Cross, "I Entered Where I Did Not Know" (*Entreme Donde No Supe*)
>
> *"I entered where I did not know,*
>
> ....
>
> *Unknowing where I was,*
> *I learned unheard of things,*
> *But what I heard I cannot say,*
> *For I remained unknowing,*
> *All reason now transcended."*
>
> (trans. Barnstone 1961)

Wealth, Poverty, and Ministry

It would be tempting to mine this passage for material with which to rail against the abuses of billionaires or browbeat affluent church members into giving generously. But before using this passage to pummel the powerful, the minister should make a careful self-evaluation. This passage informs the role of the minister in capturing the attention of people mesmerized by fool's gold and reorienting them to the throne of the transcendent God Almighty.

Consider how one draws people toward prayer in the first place. If cataphatic theology is about understanding God in concrete terms, then a life lived intentionally can become a concrete demonstration that turns people toward God. Consider the central imperatives for Timothy to "flee . . . pursue . . . struggle . . . take hold" (6:11–12). Just as Timothy once "made the good confession before many witnesses" (6:12), so now his whole life is an ongoing confession "before many witnesses." This is consistent with the "goal of our charge" (1:5) and the charge to "be an example to the believers" (4:12). Pastoral Paul is calling Timothy to live in a way distinct from "those who desire to be rich" (6:9) and who are "rich in the present age" (6:17). What does that look like?

Above we saw three approaches to wealth among the Greek philosophical traditions. At the high end, the Stoics thought a philosopher could be immensely wealthy, as long as he acquired wealth by just means, used it justly, and treated loss as a matter of indifference. This attitude dominates popular Christianity in America today. We can all name wealthy people whose philanthropy we admire, and we tell ourselves that wealth is a sign of God's blessing, that it does not change us in any negative way. But we should consider that the more affluent we are, the more difficult it is for nonbelievers to see how the faith we proclaim makes any difference. As a minister of Christ Jesus, you may "pursue justice, piety, faith, love, steadfastness, meekness," but how is that obvious?

A moderate position along Epicurean lines would be that there is pain both in great wealth and in great poverty. You should not strive after wealth but should be content with what you have and be generous toward friends. Regarding his collection for famine relief among Jewish Christians in Jerusalem (2 Cor. 8:11–13), Paul did not ask the Corinthians to impoverish themselves, but he exhorted them to recognize their surplus and share with those in need.

At the low end would be a Cynic decision to give up possessions and live as a mendicant, begging for food. Jesus lived this way and taught his disciples to pray, "Give us this day our daily bread" (Matt. 6:11). So also he instructed missionaries (Matt. 10:8–15//Luke 10:3–12) and challenged the rich (Mark 10:21//Matt. 19:21//Luke 18:22). But through the centuries few have been able to follow the path of poverty, and the ones who do, like Francis of Assisi, we call "saints."

Consider how the desert monk Macarius the Great responded to the theft of his few possessions (see sidebar). Most of us acknowledge the "uncertainty of riches" in the "present age," but we lack the faith to invest in God's future. From a present-age point of view, no matter how much we have, we feel insecure and think we need just a little more as a hedge against loss. But from the point of view of "treasure in heaven," we have more than we need and could do with a little less. Macarius was not a beggar, but he was downwardly mobile, content with a meager dwelling and minimal possessions. When a robber came, he realized he didn't really need those things either. Macarius's application of 1 Tim. 6:7 challenges interpreters who think the PE endorse accommodation to worldly establishments.

If you are not ready for Jesus's "get-rich-in-heaven-quick" scheme of selling everything, giving to the poor, and becoming a homeless preacher, then consider a "treasure-in-heaven" savings plan. Share your surplus. And no matter how much you give away, you are likely to discover that you still have more than you need, until, little by little, you have accumulated treasure in heaven, and people will see your good deeds and glorify God.

> **Macarius the Great, *On Possessions***
>
> *"The same Abba Macarius while he was in Egypt discovered a man who owned a beast of burden engaged in plundering Macarius' goods. So he came up to the thief as if he was a stranger and he helped him to load the animal. He saw him off in great peace of soul, saying, 'We have brought nothing into this world, and we cannot take anything out of the world.'* [1 Tim. 6:7] *'The LORD gave and the LORD has taken away; blessed be the name of the LORD'* [Job 1:21]." (*Sayings of the Desert Fathers*, Abba Macarius 18)

2 Timothy

Introduction to 2 Timothy

Genre

Like the other PE, 2 Timothy is paraenetic in content (see "Genre" in the general introduction), but it differs from them in form. In this letter Paul appears as an old man (Malherbe 1994; Hutson 1998, 25–32), pessimistic about the future (3:1–13) and contemplating death (4:6–8). Because Pastoral Paul expects to die soon and this letter comprises a literary passing of the torch to the next generation, 2 Timothy has frequently been read as a testament. It is true that 2 Timothy does not follow the form of the quintessential Jewish testamentary literature (e.g., *Testaments of the Twelve Patriarchs; Testament of Moses*; Richards 2002, 133–36). There is no deathbed around which the hero's children gather as he rehearses his life story and draws moral lessons. On the other hand, the testament is a subset of literature of moral exhortation. Mark Harding (1998, 146–53) highlights four features of 2 Timothy that are common to testaments: (a) imparting apostolic teaching (2:2; 3:14–17); (b) moral exhortation (throughout); (c) the author as model (3:10–12; 4:6–8); and (d) prediction of false teachers (3:1–9). John T. Fitzgerald (2003) identifies additional features of testaments that correlate with 2 Timothy, including (a) gratitude for assistance (1:3–5, 16–18; 4:11, 17–18); (b) consolation in knowing that one is enriching others by passing on a legacy (Paul's legacy is his teaching and example, 1:13; 2:2; 3:10–17); (c) moral judgment of those excluded from the legacy (1:15; 2:17–18; 3:6–9; 4:10, 14); and (d) frank speech and truth telling (2:17–21; 3:1–9; 4:2–4). Therefore, although formally it is not a testament, this letter does feel testamentary (similarly, Acts 20:17–38).

Second Timothy portrays Paul as imprisoned for the gospel, expecting to die, writing to his longtime, trusted coworker Timothy. Whereas in 1 Timothy Paul charges Timothy himself to "fight the good fight" (1:18) and "guard the deposit" (6:20), in 2 Timothy he guides his protégé to pass on that charge/ deposit to succeeding generations. The letter is a fitting sequel to 1 Timothy, and it would function nicely as the last in the PE series (see "The PE as a Letter Collection" in the general introduction).

One major difference between 2 Timothy and the other PE is the nature of the opposition. As in the other two letters, we read about rival Christian teachers (3:1–9; 4:4) and shame from outsiders (1:8). But in 2 Timothy the pressure is ratcheted up. Now Christian evangelists face governmental persecution (Hutson 2012, 171–77; see "Official Persecution" in the general introduction). Paul writes from prison (1:8, 16; 2:9). He has faced trial (4:16) and is contemplating execution (4:6–8).

Where Is Paul? Where Is Timothy?

Since there is no mention of events that led to Paul's arrest, it is not clear whether we should suppose house arrest in Rome (Acts 28) or a post-Acts imprisonment (*Acts of Paul* 10.3–5; Eusebius, *Hist. eccl.* 2.25.5; see "Chronology of Paul's Life" in the general introduction). Helmut Koester (2000, 302) considers a little-known tradition that Paul was martyred in Philippi and thinks the directions to coworkers in 4:9–21 would be consistent with a Philippian imprisonment. But the letter gives the impression that Paul is in Rome (1:17; see comments at 4:21).

If Timothy is in Ephesus (cf. 1 Tim. 1:3) and Paul sends greetings to Prisca and Aquila and the household of Onesiphorus (2 Tim. 4:19), not to mention Timothy himself, it's odd for him to say, "all who were in Asia turned away from me" (1:15), or to say, "I sent Tychicus to Ephesus" (4:12). According to the *Acts of Paul*, Onesiphorus lived in Iconium (*Acts of Paul* 2.1–7, 26). The same source identifies Demas (cf. Philem. 24; Col. 4:14) and Hermogenes as followers of Paul who later became opponents (*Acts of Paul* 1–2), though with no mention of Phygelus (2 Tim. 1:15). So we might imagine Timothy in Iconium along with Prisca and Aquila. Alternatively, we could suppose that the author of the *Acts of Paul* and/or a pseudonymous author of 2 Timothy preserved muddled memories about Paul's associates. Matthijs den Dulk argues that the author of the *Acts of Paul* mined the PE in order to highlight the Paul of 2 Timothy and throw shade on the Paul of 1 Timothy (den Dulk 2012). Certainly 2 Timothy reflects circumstances about which we have no other information. In any case, Timothy is somewhere other than Ephesus (Iconium?).

An Outline of 2 Timothy

Letter opening (1:1–5)

Author (1:1)

Addressee (1:2a)

Greeting (1:2b)

Proem: Thanksgiving (1:3–5)

Directive 1: Stir up the gift (1:6–18)

Exhortation (1:6–8)

Christological warrant (1:9–10)

Example of Paul (1:11–12)

Restatement of exhortation (1:13–14)

Negative and positive examples (1:15–18)

Directive 2: What you heard from me commit to others (2:1–13)

Exhortation (2:1–7)

Example of Paul (2:8–10)

Christological warrant (2:11–13)

Directive 3: Call to mind these things (2:14–3:9)

Model this behavior (2:14–15)

Beware of that behavior (2:16–21)

Model this behavior (2:22–26)

Beware of that behavior (3:1–9)

Directive 4: Remain in what you learned (3:10–17)

Example of Paul (3:10–12)

Negative counterexamples (3:13)

Remain in what you learned (3:14–15)

The benefit of Scripture (3:16–17)

Directive 5: Proclaim the word (4:1–8)

Exhortation (4:1–5)

Proclaim the word (4:1–2)

Warning: The time will come (4:3–4)

Do the work of an evangelist (4:5)

Pauline example (4:6–8)

Letter closing (4:9–22)

Travel reports and news (4:9–18)

Greetings (4:19–21)

Benediction (4:22)

2 Timothy 1:1–5

Letter Opening

Introductory Matters

Verses 1–4 follow the standard form of Greco-Roman letter opening: "Author(s) to Addressee(s), greeting," but each element is embellished, as is common in Pauline letters. Taking them in reverse order, the greeting is typically Pauline and consistent with 1 Timothy and Titus. The identification of Timothy is affectionate and, along with the affectionate thanksgiving prayer, is what we expect in a private letter to a close associate. But the self-identification of the author seems formal and inconsistent with a personal letter (see "Author" below).

Tracing the Train of Thought

Author (1:1)

1:1. Paul, an apostle of Christ Jesus through the will of God in accordance with the gospel of life that is in Christ Jesus (1:1). In other letters, Paul emphasizes his apostleship to a community he has never visited (Rom. 1:1, 5) and his commission "through the will of God" when addressees question his authority (1 Cor. 1:1; 2 Cor. 1:1; cf. Gal. 1:1, 4). But why assert his credentials to Timothy? Why not simply "Paul" (as in 1 Thess. 1:1; 2 Thess. 1:1)? Similarly, Paul, never having been to Rome, introduced himself to the Romans in terms of the contents of his gospel (Rom. 1:1–6). That message is here simplified to the good news about "life that is in Christ Jesus" (cf. 1:10; 2:11). But why would Paul need to remind Timothy about his basic message?

This rehearsal of credentials and doctrine create an air of artificiality, as if the letter is directed to readers who do not know Paul. Many have supposed that Paul expected Timothy to share this letter with his congregation, so they would acknowledge Paul's conferral of authority to his protégé (e.g., Johnson 2001, 91–99). William A. Richards classifies 2 Timothy as a "literary letter" aimed at readers who identify with Timothy as an evangelist (Richards 2002, 133). Richards's analysis is consistent with my reading of the PE as letters aimed at any "Timothy" (or "Titus") learning how to be an "evangelist" (4:5) in the Pauline tradition.

**2 Timothy 1:1–5
in the Rhetorical Flow**

▶ **Letter Opening (1:1–5)**

  Author (1:1)

  Addressee (1:2a)

  Greeting (1:2b)

  **Proem: Thanksgiving
  (1:3–5)**

Addressee (1:2a)

1:2a. The letter is addressed **to Timothy, my beloved child** (1:2a). The other two PE address "my true child" (1 Tim. 1:2; Titus 1:4). But the word translated "true" (*gnēsios*) connoted a "legitimate" child (MM 128–29), which would confuse matters in this letter with its references to Timothy's mother and grandmother (1:5; 3:14–15). "Beloved" (*agapētos*) strikes an affectionate chord. Paul was Timothy's mentor in ministry (3:10–12).

Greeting (1:2b)

1:2b. The opening greeting, **grace, mercy, and peace be to you from God our Father and Christ Jesus our Lord** (1:2b), is typical of Pauline letters, except that "mercy" appears in no other Pauline greeting except 1 Tim. 1:2 (see comments there) and as a textual variant in Titus 1:4. This is the sort of detail that links the PE together and distinguishes them from other Pauline letters.

Proem: Thanksgiving (1:3–5)

1:3–5. Paul typically opens a letter with a thanksgiving prayer, but his prayers usually begin with "I thank God" (*eucharistō tō theō*, Rom. 1:8; 1 Cor. 1:4; Phil. 1:3; Philem. 4; cf. plural, 1 Thess. 1:2; Col. 1:3) or "thanks to God" (Rom. 6:17; 7:25; 1 Cor. 15:57; 2 Cor. 2:14; 8:16; 9:15). The idiom **I am thankful** (lit., "I have thanks," 1:3; cf. 1 Tim. 1:12) is peculiar to the PE among Pauline letters.

The identification of God as the one **whom I serve with a pure conscience from the time of my ancestors** (1:3) calls to mind Paul's pride of pedigree (Phil. 3:5). Also familiar from Paul's opening prayers is his emotional connection with his reader, **as in my supplications night and day I hold unceasingly the memory of you, longing to see you** (1:3–4). In other letters, Paul remembers experiences with readers (1 Thess. 1:3) and longs to see them (Rom. 1:11; Phil. 1:8). We should take **as I remember your tears** (1:4) not as evidence that

Timothy was a sniveling kid (see comments at 1:7). Tears imply a strong emotional investment in a relationship (2 Cor. 2:4; Acts 20:19–20). Because of their bond, Pastoral Paul longs to see Timothy, **so that my joy may be made full, calling to mind your sincere faith, which dwelt first in your grandmother Lois and your mother Eunice, and I am persuaded dwells also in you** (1:4–5). And now we see one thing that connects them, a shared faith that each inherited from his forebears. Paul's opening prayer often introduces themes he will discuss in the body of a letter, and so here the identity of those who shaped Timothy's faith will appear again in 3:14.

John P. Meier (1999, 73–74) suggests that the pious Jewish household reflected in 1:5 is incompatible with Acts 16:1–3, where we read that Timothy had a gentile father and was uncircumcised. It is plausible, however, to imagine a gentile father forbidding circumcision as barbaric and indecent (Josephus, *Ag. Ap.* 2.137; T. Martin 2012), even as a Jewish mother taught her son the stories of Israel. It would also be plausible that, by the time Paul circumcised him (Acts 16:3), Timothy's father was deceased and/or Timothy was making his own religious choices apart from his father's wishes. Our text is consistent with Acts 16 in omitting Timothy's father as a religious influence. In this letter, Paul is the teacher ("in place of a parent," Pliny the Younger, *Ep.* 8.14) as a model for his "beloved child" (ps.-Isocrates, *Demon.* 9–15).

2 Timothy 1:6–18

Directive 1: Stir Up the Gift

Introductory Matters

This section consists of a charge to Timothy (1:6–8; cf. 4:1–8) supported by a christological statement (1:9–10) and presented as a summary of the gospel Paul was commissioned to proclaim (1:11–12). The example of Paul leads to a renewal of the exhortation (1:13–14), supported by negative and positive examples (1:15–18). The section contains several rhetorical devices typical of paraenesis, including reminder (1:6), example (1:13), and imperatives (1:8, 13, 14). Also, at least three themes bind the pieces into a coherent whole.

The first theme is shame. Honor and shame were important values in ancient Mediterranean cultures, in contrast with the greater emphasis on individual guilt in modern Western societies (Malina and Pilch 2006, 368–71; Dodds 1951, 1–63, shows that shame and guilt were not mutually exclusive in Greek religion). In ancient societies, honor resulted when people thought well of you because of birth (high-status family) and achievements (victories, benefactions). Shame resulted when people thought ill of you because of real or perceived low social status (low-status family, female, slave) and failures (defeats, needs, crimes). From a Greco-Roman point of view, the story of Jesus was shameful: a Jewish peasant from Galilee, a manual laborer, was convicted of insurrection, for which he was scourged, humiliated, and crucified. But early Christian evangelists flipped the categories (e.g., Neyrey 1994; Schmidt 1995), and so did Paul (P. Marshall 1983; Jewett 1999). Paul (1:12) and Onesiphorus (1:16) are examples of how one who is "not ashamed" of Jesus might proclaim the story as good news. This section challenges Greco-Roman assumptions of what is honorable or shameful.

The second theme is suffering. Pastoral Paul commands, ". . . share in suffering for the gospel . . ." (1:8). Again, Paul is the primary example (1:12). The expectation of suffering for the gospel is thematic (2:3, 11; 4:5; cf. persecution, 3:10–12).

The third theme is the transmission of tradition. Both Paul (1:3) and Timothy (1:5) inherited their faith from prior generations. In addition, Pastoral Paul has an apostolic commission to proclaim the gospel about Christ Jesus (1:11). Timothy has a "gift" that came through the "laying on of [Paul's] hands" (1:6) and is associated with his testimony about Jesus (1:8). He also has "heard healthy words" from Paul (1:13) and has received a "good deposit," which he must "guard" (1:13–14). This theme has to do with remembering basic doctrines and precepts (2:8, 11–13; 3:10–14; see "Genre" in the general introduction) and transmitting them to future generations (2:2; 4:2, 5).

> ### 2 Timothy 1:6–18 in the Rhetorical Flow
>
> Letter opening (1:1–5)
>
> ► Directive 1: Stir up the gift (1:6–18)
>
> Exhortation (1:6–8)
>
> Christological warrant (1:9–10)
>
> Example of Paul (1:11–12)
>
> Restatement of exhortation (1:13–14)
>
> Negative and positive examples (1:15–18)

The centerpiece of this section is a statement about what God has done in Christ Jesus (1:9–10). These verses appear to be an early Christian hymn in that they are theologically dense, and verse 9 begins in the style of a psalm by describing God as "the one who . . ." (Gk. participle). Also, the verses can be arranged into four couplets in such a way as to bring out the assonance (poetic repetition of sounds) in each couplet:

> Who saved [*tou sōsantos*] . . .
> and called [*kai kalesantos*] . . .
> Not in accordance with [*ou kata*] . . .
> but in accordance with [*alla kata*] . . .
> Which was given to us [*tēn dotheisan hēmin*] . . .
> and manifested now [*phanerōtheisan de nyn*] . . .
> Having destroyed [*katargēsantos men*] . . .
> and brought to light [*phōtisantos de*] . . .

Tracing the Train of Thought

Exhortation (1:6–8)

1:6–8. For which reason, I remind you connects the "gift in you" to the preceding prayer and the faith that "dwells in you" (1:5). That faith is a motivation **to fire up the gift of God that is in you through the laying on of my hands** (1:6). The word "fire up" (*anazōpyrein*) appears nowhere else in the

NT, but the Holy Spirit behaves like a flame (1 Thess. 5:19; Acts 2:3). To "fire up the gift of God" is Holy Spirit language.

Elsewhere in the NT, "laying on hands" accompanies healing (Matt. 9:18, 25; Mark 5:23; 6:5; 7:32; 8:23; 16:18; Luke 4:40; 13:13; Acts 28:8) or blessing (Matt. 19:13, 15), but those usages do not fit this context. The newly baptized sometimes received the Holy Spirit through "laying on of hands" (Acts 8:17; 19:6). But the word "gift" (*charisma*) does not appear in baptismal contexts, and when Paul imparted spiritual gifts, it was not necessarily at baptism (Rom. 1:11).

Most likely the reference is to ordination (1 Tim. 4:14; 5:22; Acts 13:3; cf. Acts 6:6). In Pauline vocabulary, "gifts" that connote some teaching function include prophecy (Rom. 12:6; 1 Cor. 12:10, 28; Eph. 4:11), ministry (*diakonia*, Rom. 12:7; Eph. 4:12), teaching (Rom. 12:7; 1 Cor. 12:28; Eph. 4:11), exhortation (Rom. 12:8), a word of wisdom (1 Cor. 12:8), a word of knowledge (1 Cor. 12:8), apostles (1 Cor. 12:28; Eph. 4:11), evangelists (Eph. 4:11), and pastors (Eph. 4:11). Of these, ministry (*diakonia*) is associated in the PE with Paul (1 Tim. 1:12; 2 Tim. 4:11) and Timothy (1 Tim. 4:6; 2 Tim. 4:5). Timothy is to teach (1 Tim. 4:11, 13 [but see comments on this verse]; 6:2b), charge (1 Tim. 4:11), exhort (1 Tim. 4:13 [but see comments on this verse]; 5:1; 6:2b; 2 Tim. 4:2), preach (2 Tim. 4:2), and rebuke (2 Tim. 4:2). Paul is reminding Timothy of the time when he laid hands on him and imparted the gift, whether that happened when he was ordained by the presbytery (1 Tim. 4:14) or on another occasion.

For God did not give us a spirit of cowardice but one of power and love and temperance (1:7). "Power" (*dynamis*) and "love" (*agapē*) are thematic in chapter 1. Paul was not ashamed, because he trusted in a God who is "powerful" (*dynatos*, 1:12). Timothy has seen love in Paul's life (1:13; 3:10; cf. 1 Tim. 1:14), and he is to cultivate it in himself (2 Tim. 2:22; cf. 1 Tim. 4:12; 6:11).

Despite the common canard that Timothy was timid (also sickly, 1 Tim. 5:23), this verse suggests nothing of the sort, and that allegation flies in the face of Paul's comments about him elsewhere. Timothy was one of Paul's closest associates (Phil. 2:19–24), trusted to handle the most difficult ministerial situations (1 Thess. 3:4–7; Acts 17:14; 1 Cor. 4:17; 16:10–11; Hutson 1997, 61–65; Alexander 1913).

We should understand "cowardice" in light of this letter's portrayal of Timothy as a youth (2:22; cf. 1 Tim. 4:12; Hutson 1997, 68–73; 1998, 351–63). According to Aristotle, youth are idealistic and motivated by shame (*Rhet.* 2.12.10–11 [1389a]). Epictetus shamed his students into doing what was right. "Aren't you ashamed to be more cowardly and ignoble than a runaway slave?" (*Diatr.* 3.26.1, trans. Oldfather, LCL; cf. *Diatr.* 1.24.1–10, 20; 2.1.8–13, 14, 38; 2.16.18; Plutarch, *Rect. rat. aud.* 17 [47b]).

Furthermore, one aspect of philosophical training (1 Tim. 4:6–16; see "Philosophical Training Regimen" in the general introduction) was anticipating calamities and meditating on how to respond from a philosophical point of view. One

---

Mental Preparation for Facing Threats as a Stoic

"If a man can behold with unflinching eyes the flash of a sword, if he knows that it makes no difference to him whether his soul takes flight through his mouth or through a wound in his throat, you may call him happy; you may also call him happy if, when he is threatened with bodily torture, whether it be the result of accident or of the might of the stronger, he can without concern hear talk of chains, or of exile, or of all the idle fears that stir men's minds, and can say, '. . . Today it is you who threaten me with these terrors; but I have always threatened myself with them, and have prepared myself as a man to meet man's destiny.' If an evil has been pondered beforehand, the blow is gentle when it comes." (Seneca, *Moral Epistles* 76.33–34, trans. R. M. Gummere, LCL)

---

should be prepared mentally to face arrest and execution (Seneca, *Ep.* 76.33–34 [see sidebar]; 4.5–9; Epictetus, *Diatr.* 3.10.1; Marcus Aurelius 2.1). "Cowardice" here is a rhetorical device to describe what Timothy *should not* be and to steel him against threats he might face as he does "the work of an evangelist" (2 Tim. 4:5).

The four "spirits" in 1:7 reflect Jewish piety, as, for example, the spirits of light and darkness in the *Community Rule* from Qumran (1QS 3–4). Especially helpful is *Testaments of the Twelve Patriarchs*, which gives moral instruction to young men. Scholars debate whether this is a Christian work or a Jewish work edited by Christians, but Christians were reading it in the second century (Origen, *Hom. Jes. Nav.* 15.6; Hollander and de Jonge 1985, 14–17, 82). The work describes virtues and vices as spirits from Beliar (aka Belial, "worthless," a derogatory term for Satan) to influence people toward good or bad (*T. Levi* 3.1–3). The "spirits of deceit" are "the sources of the deeds of youth" (*T. Reu.* 2.1; cf. *T. Sim.* 3.1). When Reuben admonishes his sons not to "walk in the ignorance and sexual promiscuity of youth" (*T. Reu.* 1.6), he is not calling them ignorant and promiscuous but warning that inexperience and libido pose constant threats to youth (cf. *T. Reu.* 2.9; *T. Jud.* 11.1–2). The human mind stands between the "spirit of truth" and the "spirit of error" and inclines toward one or the other (*T. Jud.* 20.1–2). This correlation between our internal inclinations and the spirits around us is reflected in a prayer for deliverance in the Dead Sea Scrolls: "Let not Belial dominate me, nor an unclean spirit; let pain and the evil inclination not possess my bones" (11QPs[a] 19.16, trans. Vermes 1997, 305; on similar correlation in Greek religion, Dodds 1951, 40–43).

Throughout *Testaments of the Twelve Patriarchs*, Jacob's sons warn against spirits of promiscuity, error, flattery, injustice, envy, and so on. They encourage attention to promptings from God. The "spirit of understanding from the Lord" resists deceit and injustice (*T. Levi* 2.3). The "spirit of holiness" resists Beliar (*T. Levi* 18.11). An "angel of power [*dynamis*]" followed Judah in combat (*T. Jud.* 3.10). "The spirit of hate cooperates with Satan in everything through faintheartedness for the death of humankind; but the spirit of love [*agapē*] cooperates with God's Torah in long-suffering for the salvation of humankind" (*T. Gad* 4.7, trans. Hutson). Joseph is a model of temperance (*sōphrosynē*, *T. Jos.* 4.1–2; 6.7; 9.2–3; 10.2–3).

The spirits from God in 2 Tim. 1:7 are divine resources. When opposition arises and a "spirit of cowardice" appears, Timothy should resist, knowing that God provides spirits of power, love, and temperance.

Do not be ashamed, therefore, of the testimony of our Lord nor of me, his prisoner, but share in suffering for the gospel, in accordance with the power of God (1:8). This verse introduces the theme of shame (1:8, 12, 16). On the word "testimony" (*martyrion*), see comments at 1 Tim. 2:6b. "The testimony of our Lord" could be Timothy's testimony *about* Jesus (Gk. objective gen.) or Jesus's testimony (Gk. subjective gen.). The difference is inconsequential because one who was ashamed of what Jesus did would likely be ashamed to tell the story. The call to "share in suffering" is a call to join Paul, who, without shame (2 Tim. 1:12) suffers for the message (1:12; 2:3, 9, 10; 3:11), to the point of persecutions (3:11), imprisonment (2:9), and possible death (4:6–8). This call is repeated in 4:5 and accords with the purpose of the letter: to entrust a dangerous mission to the next generation.

Christological Warrant (1:9–10)

1:9–10. Even though the "work of an evangelist" (4:5) is dangerous, the mission will succeed "in accordance with the power of God" (cf. 1:7). God's power is expressed in a hymn about what God did in Christ:

> **The one who saved us**
> **and called us with a holy calling,**
> > **not in accordance with our deeds**
> > **but in accordance with his own purpose and grace**
> > > **which was given to us in Christ Jesus before times eternal,**
> > > **and now is made evident through the manifestation of our**
> > > > **Savior Christ Jesus,**
> > > > **after he nullified death**
> > > > **and brought to light life and immortality through the gospel.**
> > > > > (1:9–10)

"Called us with a holy calling" (1:9) might sound like a "call" to evangelize (cf. Gal. 1:15) in this context of Paul's charge to Timothy and references to Timothy's ordination (1:6) and identity as an evangelist (4:5). But in the Pauline letters "calling" usually refers to the Christian life in general (Rom. 8:30; 9:24; 1 Cor. 7:17–24; Gal. 5:8), not to ordained ministry. God "calls" people away from allegiance to worldly powers into God's eternal kingdom (1 Tim. 6:12; 1 Thess. 2:12; 2 Thess. 2:14; cf. 1 Pet. 2:9; 5:10), away from self-indulgence (3:2–5) into holiness (1 Cor. 1:2; 1 Thess. 4:7). Such a calling is consistent with the need for Timothy to "purify himself" (2:21–22) and "be sanctified" (2:21; cf. 1 Tim. 5:22).

The phrases "not in accordance with our deeds, but in accordance with his own purpose and grace" (cf. Titus 3:5; Eph. 2:8) call to mind the basis on which God chose Israel (Deut. 7:6–8; 9:5; 10:14–15). Works are not a reason for God's grace but come in fulfillment of the covenant given by grace (4Q481; Dunn 2008, 391–92).

The idea that God's "purpose and grace" were given "before times eternal" (1:9; cf. Eph. 1:4) resembles a rabbinic tradition that "seven things were created before the world was made: Torah, repentance, the Garden of Eden, Gehenna, the throne of glory, the house of the sanctuary, and the name of the Messiah" (*b. Ned.* 39A, trans. Neusner 2006). That is, before creation God anticipated the problem of sin and a solution. Our passage differs from the rabbinic tradition in identifying the Messiah as "Jesus," who "nullified death" (see "Theological Issues," below).

The word "manifestation" (*epiphaneia*) here refers not to the anticipated second coming of Jesus (as in 4:1, 8) but to the Jesus who has already come "now" (cf. Titus 2:11; 3:4; "made evident," 1 Tim. 3:16). The God who "saved us" (1:9) is the God whose "purpose and grace are manifested through the appearing of the Savior Christ Jesus." An interesting contrast is an inscription from Ephesus, dated 48 CE, honoring Julius Caesar:

> The cities in Asia and the peoples and the nations [honor] Gaius Julius Caesar, son of Gaius, the High Priest and Emperor and Consul for the second time, the [offspring] of Ares and Aphrodite, God manifest [*epiphanē*], and the common Savior [*sōtēr*] of human life. (*SIG* 760)

Subject peoples in the Greek East of the Roman Empire acclaimed each new emperor in language they had previously applied to Hellenistic rulers—"savior" and "manifestation" of deity (see sidebar at Titus 2:13; Winter 2015, 61–74; Nock 1928, 1951). The PE present a significant counterclaim for Jesus (cf. 1 Tim. 2:1–7; Titus 2:11–15).

The christological climax of this hymn is that by his resurrection Jesus "nullified death" (1 Cor. 15:26; cf. 2 Thess. 2:8; cf. "Theological Issues" at 1 Tim. 3:14–16) and "brought to light life and immortality" (Rom. 6:1–11). The "good news" is the resurrection (1 Cor. 15:1–4), which grounds the "faithful saying" in 2 Tim. 2:11–13 (cf. 1 Tim. 3:16).

Example of Paul (1:11–12)

1:11–12. Pastoral Paul understands his mission in light of the christological statement in 1:9–10, **to which I was appointed a herald and apostle and teacher,**

for which reason I also suffer these things (1:11–12a). On Paul's apostolic commission, compare 1 Tim. 1:7; Rom. 1:1–6. In his suffering, Paul is a model for Timothy (2 Tim. 1:8). "These things" that Pastoral Paul suffers include imprisonment (1:8; 2:9), persecution (3:11), and possible death (4:6–8). He endures because he views his present sufferings from the perspective of life in the age to come (cf. 2:8–13).

But I am not ashamed, for I know in whom I have put my trust, and I am persuaded that he is able to guard my deposit until that day (1:12). Again, Pastoral Paul is not ashamed, because he views his present suffering from the perspective of "that day," when the Lord will come (4:6–8; cf. Phil. 1:20; 2 Thess. 1:5–12).

The identity of the one "in whom I have put my trust" is not obvious. The verb "believe/trust" (*pisteuō*) in the NT commonly expresses faith in God (Titus 3:8) or Christ (1 Tim. 3:16), so most interpreters assume that "whom" refers to God or Christ and illogically frame Christ as both depositor and guardian of the deposit. Stepp (2005, 153–54), for example, construes the syntax in just this way, but in spite of that he sees a chain of tradition from Christ to Paul to Timothy, which is on the right track. One could "believe/trust" a person (Mark 16:14; Acts 26:27; Tob. 2:14; BDAG 816–17, s.v. πιστεύω 1.b).

Here the one whom Pastoral Paul trusts "is able to guard my deposit," and at this point most interpreters lose track of who is depositing what with whom. The word "deposit" (*parathēkē*) commonly appears with a noun or pronoun identifying either the depositor (Gk. subjective gen.; "a neighbor's deposit," Exod. 22:7, 10 LXX; "deposits of widows and orphans," 2 Macc. 3:10) or the thing deposited (Gk. objective gen.; "deposit of silver drachmas," PRyl II.348; MM 483–84, s.v. *parathēkē*). In our passage, "my deposit" means "what I deposited." The translation "what has been entrusted *to me*" (RSV, CEB, ESV, HCSB) would require a different grammatical construction (Gk. dat., e.g., Lev. 5:23 LXX, or Gk. preposition *para*, MM 478–80).

"The one in whom I have put my trust" is Timothy. Paul was commissioned as an apostle of the story of Jesus ("entrusted with the gospel," 1 Tim. 1:11), and he himself "trusted" Timothy with that story as a "deposit" (2 Tim. 1:14; cf. 1 Tim. 1:18; 6:20). In 2:2 he directs Timothy to extend this chain to "trustworthy people," who will teach the next generation. When Jesus comes again, the faithfulness of Paul's converts will be the cause of his boasting, so he will not be "ashamed" to stand before the Judge (1 Thess. 2:19; Phil. 2:16; 4:1; 1 Cor. 1:8; 2 Cor. 1:14). Pastoral Paul has "put [his] trust" in Timothy to "guard the deposit," the gospel, "until that day" when Jesus comes again.

Restatement of Exhortation (1:13–14)

1:13–14. **Hold the example of healthy words that you heard from me in the faith and love that are in Christ Jesus** (1:13). Just as the passage exhibits a chain of tradition from Christ to Paul to Timothy, so each generation sets an example for the one to follow. "Faith and love" characterize both Jesus and people who are "in Christ" (Downs 2012, 154). Pastoral Paul's example is programmatic (3:10–13). Paul sent Timothy to Corinth so that the Corinthians could see Timothy and remember how to "imitate" Paul, who was imitating Christ (1 Cor. 4:16–17; 1 Cor. 11:1). For Timothy to "hold the example" entails behaving as Paul behaved in a life shaped by "the faith and love that are in Christ Jesus."

Guard the good deposit through the Holy Spirit, who dwells in us (1:14). This sentence recapitulates 1:6–13. The command "guard the deposit" (cf. 1 Tim. 6:20) subsumes "share in suffering" (2 Tim. 1:8) and "hold the example of the healthy words" (1:13). Similarly, "through the Holy Spirit" echoes the spirits given by God (1:7). For Paul, the community of believers constitutes a "temple" of the Holy Spirit (1 Cor. 3:16; 6:19; cf. 2 Cor. 6:16; Eph. 2:19–22; cf. Rom. 8:9–11; N. T. Wright 2013, 711–17). Timothy is a member of the community ("us") in whom the Spirit dwells, and that community will be guarding the deposit as they pass it from generation to generation. Chapters 2–4 amplify this command to perpetuate the tradition.

Negative and Positive Examples (1:15–18)

1:15–18. To illustrate faithfully following the leader (1:13), Pastoral Paul offers negative and positive examples (1:15–18). **You know this, that all who were in Asia turned away from me, including Phygelus and Hermogenes** (1:15). "All" is exaggeration (cf. Phil. 2:21) that heightens the sense of abandonment. Phygelus is otherwise unknown, and the apocryphal account of Hermogenes could be a fiction seeking verisimilitude by borrowing names from this letter (*Acts of Paul* 1–2; see the introduction to 2 Timothy). In any case, Paul comes across as a Christlike figure, whose disciples "all" abandoned him at his arrest (Mark 14:50). Whether that is a happy coincidence or an intentional allusion depends on how one dates the PE and Mark.

Ancient philosophers pointed to people who exemplified specific virtues (Seneca, *Ep.* 95.72). After Paul (1:12), Onesiphorus is the second example of one who was "not ashamed" (1:16). **May the Lord grant mercy to the household of Onesiphorus, because he often refreshed me and was not ashamed of my chains. But when he was in Rome he looked diligently for me and found me. May the Lord grant him to find mercy from the Lord in that day. And the ways in which he ministered to me in Ephesus, you know very well** (1:16–18). Onesiphorus "refreshed" (1:16) and "served" (1:18) Paul in Rome and Ephesus. The verb "serve" (*diakoneō*) implies serving food (Luke 4:39; 12:37). That idea here reflects the conditions of Roman prisons, in which prisoners received inadequate food and care unless friends or family brought relief (Wansink 1996, 64–65, 133–38). Whether or not Onesiphorus was the benefactor who paid for such provisions (Danker 1982, 450), he went to the trouble of delivering them personally (1:16–17).

This verse could support the common theory that Paul spent time in an Ephesian prison at some point.

"You know very well" (cf. 1:15) suggests the sort of thing that could go unexpressed between close associates (1:2–5; 3:10–17). If we assume Pauline authorship, it is easy to think Timothy knew the events to which Paul refers. But if this letter is pseudonymous, we must wonder whether this reference is a fiction or the pseudonymous author knew and assumed his readers knew details about Onesiphorus's life.

Theological Issues

Spiritual Warfare

Christian ethics can be construed as spiritual warfare. To cite one example from Orthodox tradition, in the fourteenth century St. Gregory of Sinai instructs novice monks on spiritual formation. At first, he sounds like a Stoic philosopher arguing that reason should control desires, but then he frames the matter as a spiritual battle:

> The demons fill our mind with images, or rather clothe themselves in images for our benefit and impinge on us (introduce a suggestion) according to the ruling passion habitually acting in the soul. For generally they make use of passionate habits to multiply in us passionate fantasies and even in sleep they fill our dreams with varied imaginings. (*Texts on Commandments and Dogmas* 1–2 [*WPh* 37])

Gregory names specific demons of lust, anger, cowardice, deceit, and others (*Texts on Commandments and Dogmas* 71–72 [*WPh* 49–50]). He does not let his monks off with the excuse that they are overpowered by demons beyond their control:

> The rising of passions and warfare of the flesh against the soul can be of five kinds in us. At times the flesh misuses what it has, at other times it seeks to do what is unnatural as if it were natural; sometimes it forms a close friendship with the demons who arm it against the soul; sometimes it happens that the soul acts lawlessly of itself, when pervaded by some passion; and, finally, the demons may sometimes be allowed to wage war against us to make us more humble. (*Text on Commandments and Dogmas* 124 [*WPh* 68])

For St. Gregory of Sinai, it is all the same whether you act for good or ill out of your own will or allow some spirit to drag you along. You must choose which spirits you invite into your life and entertain. For a similar approach to spiritual warfare in Roman Catholic monasticism, see Ignatius of Loyola, *Spiritual Exercises* 313–36 (Ganss 1991, 201–7).

173

People shaped by Western rationalism may struggle with talk of spiritual warfare, but we should recognize that it is deeply rooted in Jewish and Christian thought and resonates in many cultures today. Whether you think of spirits as real beings external to yourself, or the invisible forces of cultural systems, or metaphorical manifestations of your own desires, you should find some way to talk about them. You should neither dismiss such language as "superstition" nor get sucked into infatuation with the occult. You should take seriously that Christian ministry involves a spiritual struggle. (For various views, see Beilby and Eddy 2012; for a nuanced discussion of spiritual warfare in Pentecostalism, see Vondey 2013, 29–47; on this passage in the context of African Pentecostalism, see Nwankwo 2002; for help in talking about spiritual warfare in a Western, secular context, see R. Beck 2016).

Regardless of the language you use, you should recognize that Pastoral Paul is not encouraging Timothy to categorize people. When we label our enemies as demonic, we begin thinking of ourselves as angelic. We become blind to our own weaknesses and to any value or redeemable humanity in our enemies. We must recognize the struggle between good and bad spirits or inclinations *within ourselves*, martialing our own best impulses to meet and embolden the best impulses of our foes.

You would do well to heed the warnings of St. Gregory and the exhortations of Pastoral Paul. One who lives into the story of Jesus is likely to meet opposition from a world that acts out of self-indulgence. Worldly powers would rather co-opt Christian ministers than crush them. As God's servant you must nurture friendship with the spirits of power, love, and temperance that come from God. Do not be surprised when you draw hostile reactions, and do not flinch.

Hold the Example of Healthy Words

The term "healthy words" is not exactly "correct doctrine." It is not, for example, explaining the Trinity in a way that avoids Arianism or other heresies. Yes, it is important to think about such doctrines, but Pastoral Paul does not exhort Timothy to get some doctrine right. He exhorts him to "hold the example of healthy words . . . in faith and love" (2 Tim. 1:13; cf. 1 Tim. 4:12). He must internalize the story of Jesus and model it for others. The disciple unafraid of death can model faithfulness in the face of treachery, love in the face of aggression, temperance and holiness in a world of self-indulgence. The gospel is not about self-defense or self-satisfaction. It is about self-giving and self-denial. There is no more important thing a minister can do for a congregation than be an "example of healthy words." This is how the minister forms a community that is spiritually "healthy."

2 Timothy 2:1–13

Directive 2: What You Heard from Me Commit to Others

Introductory Matters

The first major section in the letter body (2:1–13) opens with the imperative "be strong" (2:1) and appears to continue the theme of suffering from the previous chapter (2:3, 9, 12). Pastoral Paul amplifies his opening commands (2:1–3) with three analogies (2:4–7), a reminder of the central tenet of the story for which he suffers (2:8–10), and a "faithful saying" that appears to be another early Christian hymn (2:11–13).

Despite its prominence, the theme of suffering is subordinate to a larger issue. In the opening charge the theme of suffering (1:8, 12) led up to the primary charge to "guard the good deposit" (1:14), which was the story of Jesus and instruction in following Jesus. The only way to guard this deposit is to teach it to others, so 2:2 is the topic sentence of this section. Suffering is not an end in itself but may be necessary for the sake of evangelism. The "deposit" must be passed on at all costs.

> **2 Timothy 2:1–13 in the Rhetorical Flow**
>
> Letter opening (1:1–5)
>
> Directive 1: Stir up the gift (1:6–18)
>
> ▶ Directive 2: What you heard from me commit to others (2:1–13)
>
> Exhortation (2:1–7)
>
> Example of Paul (2:8–10)
>
> Christological warrant (2:11–13)

Tracing the Train of Thought

Exhortation (2:1–7)

2:1–7. Timothy should pass along what he learned from Paul (2:1–2; cf. 3:10–4:8). **But as for you, my child, be strong in the grace that is in Christ Jesus** (2:1). The address "my child" (cf. 1:2) reminds us that this is a letter to an individual. Just as Pastoral Paul's suffering correlates with exhortations to Timothy to share in suffering, so also his endurance (2:10; cf. "the Lord . . . strengthened me," 4:17) correlates with the exhortation to "be strong . . . in Christ Jesus." The phrase "in the grace" should be understood as "by means of the grace" (Gk. instrumental dat.). On the relation between strength and grace, see 1 Tim. 1:12.

This command elaborates what it means to guard the "deposit" (*parathēkē*, 1:14): **and what you heard from me through many witnesses, commit to trustworthy people, who will be capable to teach others also** (2:2). The verb "commit" (or "deposit," *paratithēmi*) recalls 1 Tim. 1:18, where Paul "committed" (*paratithēmi*) a charge to Timothy to preach. The text envisions four generations—Paul, Timothy, "trustworthy people," and "others." If we read the PE as pseudonymous, this concern for the third and fourth generations is consistent with a date in the late first century.

The phrase "*through* [*dia*] many witnesses" is odd. If we read this as a real letter from Paul, we might think he is careless with prepositions. Perhaps he meant, "*with* [*epi*] many witnesses," referring to Timothy's ordination (1:6) or referring to "many" who could attest to his words (I. H. Marshall 1999, 725). On the other hand, "*through* [*dia*] many witnesses" implies a chain of transmission between Paul and Timothy. But this letter describes how Timothy learned from Paul directly, over an extended period of time (3:10–14). If we read this letter as pseudonymous, then for any young minister in a post-Pauline generation, Paul's teachings have been transmitted "*through* many witnesses."

Share in suffering as a good soldier of Christ Jesus (2:3). Since this letter associates evangelism with suffering (1:8, 12; 2:8–9; 4:5), "soldier" seems like an appropriate metaphor. It echoes the exhortation to "fight the good fight" (1 Tim. 1:18; cf. "contest the good contest," 1 Tim. 6:12; 2 Tim. 4:7). But "soldier" is one of three metaphors here, all familiar from the undisputed Pauline letters: soldier (Rom. 13:12; 1 Cor. 9:7; 2 Cor. 10:3–4; Phil. 2:25; 1 Thess. 5:18; Philem. 2), athlete (1 Cor. 9:24–27; Phil. 3:14), and farmer (1 Cor. 3:6–9; 9:7). We must consider how all three metaphors work together in this argument.

The first analogy explains the "good soldier" with a truism: **No one serving in the army gets entangled in the affairs of life, so that he might please his enlisting commander** (2:4). The "enlisting commander" (*stratologōn*) was the general who raised the army (Plutarch, *Caes.* 35.1). The analogy suggests that Timothy must please not Paul but Jesus (Ign. *Pol.* 6.2). By contrast with the "good soldier," Demas is a bad soldier (4:10).

Competing for a Lawful Crown

Dio Chrysostom told an anecdote about the Cynic philosopher Diogenes:

"Generally the managers of the Isthmian games and other honorable and influential men were sorely troubled and held themselves aloof whenever they encountered [Diogenes]. . . . But when he put the crown of pine upon his head, the Corinthians sent some of their servants to bid him lay aside the crown and do nothing unlawful [paranomos]. He asked why it was unlawful for him to wear the crown of pine. One of them said, 'Because you have won no victory, Diogenes.' He replied, 'Many and mighty antagonists have I vanquished, not like these slaves who are now wrestling here, hurling the discus and running, but more difficult in every way—I mean poverty, exile, and disrepute; yes, and anger, pain, desire, fear, and the most redoubtable beast of all, treacherous and cowardly, I mean pleasure, which no Greek or barbarian can claim he fights and conquers by the strength of his soul, but all alike have succumbed to her and have failed in this contest [agōn], . . . all, that is, save myself. It is I who am worthy of the pine.'" (Dio Chrysostom, *Isthmian Discourse*, Oration 9.10–13, trans. Cohoon, LCL, modified)

The "affairs of life" in which a soldier might become entangled could be financial (cf. 1 Thess. 2:5–9) or familial (cf. 1 Cor. 7:32–35). Alexander the Great burned the loot he plundered from Persia and encouraged his troops to do the same so they could march into India unencumbered (Plutarch, *Aem.* 12.11). Roman soldiers were prohibited from marrying (Cassius Dio 6.24.3), though the specific law and the terms are unclear (Phang 2001, 115–19). Some soldiers had conjugal relationships that functioned as marriages, and allowances may have varied among provinces and commanders (Phang 2001, 142–59). But soldiers lacked legal "wives" and were obliged to follow orders without regard for family. A soldier must display single-minded devotion to duty.

Second, **if anyone competes as an athlete, he is not crowned unless he competes according to the rules** (2:5). The "crown" was a metaphorical reward for winning the "struggle" (*agōn*) against vices, especially pleasure (Dio Chrysostom, *Or.* 8.11–35; 9.10–13 [see sidebar]). Paul thought of eternal life as the prize at the end the Christian "race" (cf. 1 Cor. 9:25; 1 Thess. 2:19; cf. 1 Tim. 6:12; 2 Tim. 4:7). But here the focus is less on the prize than on competing "according to the rules" (*nomimōs*). This verse does not specify the applicable rules for an evangelist, but ethical conduct is a theme of the PE. Vice lists in the PE (3:2–5; 1 Tim. 1:8–11; Titus 1:10–11) describe bad teachers, so we might read their vices as rules violations. But the only other NT occurrence of the adverb "according to the rules" (*nomimōs*) is at 1 Tim. 1:8, where it applies to the proper use of Torah (*nomos*) as the source of ethical instruction. We could read this adverb as a hint that the Christian "athlete" must play by the ethics of Torah. Indeed, the next analogy draws directly from Torah.

Third, **the farmer who labors must share in the first of the fruits** (2:6). The principle is from Deut. 25:4. Paul applied this verse to financial support for evangelists (1 Cor. 9:1–17; Gal. 6:6; cf. Luke 10:7). In the PE, a teaching elder receives double honor (1 Tim. 5:17–18). The verb "labor" (*kopiaō*) is a Pauline metaphor for evangelism (1 Tim. 4:10), so the third analogy invokes the principle that the church should support an evangelist.

Think about what I am saying; for the Lord will give you understanding in all things (2:7). At first, this verse seems banal. But philosophers taught students to meditate on what they learned, to internalize complex ideas and work out implications (see comments at 1 Tim. 4:13; Newman 1989). Similarly, Jewish wisdom offers "figures" and "riddles" that require "discerning" (Prov. 1:5–7 NRSV; Towner 2006, 496–98). So the analogies demand reflection.

Here are three considerations. First, none of the analogies focuses on suffering, as we might have expected from the context (2:3, 9, 12). Of course, soldiers and athletes suffer through self-denial and difficult training, not to mention pain endured in combat or competition, while farmers engage in backbreaking toil and are often thwarted by weather and pests. But Pastoral Paul does not make these points. Second, the three analogies are not parallel, so the relation among them is not obvious. Third, we should consider the possibility that Timothy might apply the analogies in more than one direction.

The three analogies amplify the command to "commit what you heard . . . to trustworthy people, who will be able to teach others also" (2:2). It is not only that Timothy should display in himself the qualities of a good soldier, athlete, and farmer but also that he should look for those qualities in the "trustworthy people" to whom he "commits" the teaching. The teaching will be preserved if it is "committed" to people who (a) are not distracted by family or financial affairs; (b) play by the rules, including not being "devoted to money" (3:2); and (c) can depend on financial support from the church. Not only does Timothy share in the suffering of Christ; he also joins with those to whom he commits the teaching and shares with them in the struggles of soldier, athlete, and farmer.

Example of Paul (2:8–10)

2:8–10. **Remember Christ Jesus, raised from the dead, from the seed of David, according to my gospel** (2:8). This summary (cf. 1:9–10) sounds Pauline: "seed of David" (Rom. 1:3); "according to my gospel" (Rom. 2:16); and emphasis on resurrection (Rom. 1:4; 6:4–5; 1 Cor. 15:3–4; 1 Thess. 1:10). The PE do not tell the Jesus story but assume it (see "The Fundamental Doctrine" in the general introduction).

Remembering prior instruction (3:14) was part of the philosophical training regimen (see "Genre: Philosophical Training Regimen" in the general introduction; Seneca, *Ep*. 16.1–3; cf. Epictetus, *Diatr*. 3.25; see comments at 4:13). Timothy should "remember" the resurrection of Jesus as a central tenet that orients his conduct. Verse 9 picks up the command to "share in suffering" from verse 3 and presents Paul as a model. The beginning point for reflection is the suffering of Jesus (Towner 2006, 496–98).

Verses 9–10 continue the exhortation from 2:3: **for which I suffer wrong as a wrongdoer to the point of bonds, but the word of God is not bound. I endure everything because of this: because of the elect, so that they may also attain salvation that is in Christ Jesus with eternal glory** (2:9–10). There is a parallel between 2:8–10 and 1:9–12. Paul suffers because he tells the Jesus story, and he suffers in order to tell it. The letter depicts Paul as a prisoner "in bonds" without specifying the charges against him "as a wrongdoer." Within the narrative world of these letters, we might imagine that outsiders perceived his affirmation of "one God" as seditious (see comments at 1 Tim. 2:1–7). But he "endures" abuse in the present age because he is oriented toward "eternal glory" in the age to come and shares in the "salvation that is in Christ Jesus."

Christological Warrant (2:11–13)

2:11–13. In further support of the command to "share in suffering" (2:3) is another compressed, poetic statement, possibly a hymn (cf. 1 Tim. 3:16) that encapsulates basic tenets of the faith:

> **Trustworthy is the saying, for**
> **If we share in dying, we shall also share in living;**
> **If we endure, we shall also share in reigning;**
>
> **If we deny [him], he will also deny us;**
> **If we are unfaithful, he remains faithful,**
> **for he cannot deny himself. (2:11–13)**

On the "trustworthy saying," compare 1 Tim. 1:15; 3:1; 4:9; Titus 3:8. This poem consists of four conditional sentences, arranged in two couplets. Two conditions are positive: "if we share in dying . . . if we endure" (2:11b–12a), while two are negative: "if we deny . . . if we are unfaithful" (2:12b–13a). This suggests that 2:13b might not be part of the hymn but a comment on it (cf. 1 Tim. 2:6b).

The conjunction "for" marks the hymn as an explanation of what precedes. The verbal connection is the word "endure" (2:10, 11), but there is also a logical connection from the resurrection of Jesus (2:8) and "I suffer wrong" (2:9) to "share in dying . . . share in living" (2:11). The hymn views suffering from the perspective of the age to come. Translators sometimes insert Jesus into the hymn, "if we die with *Him*, we will also live with *Him* . . . we will reign with *Him*" (NASB; cf. KJV, NIV, ESV, CEV). Adding "Him" makes the passage consistent with Pauline language of dying and living with Christ (Rom. 6:4, 8; cf. Eph. 2:5–6; Col. 2:12–13; 3:1).

In the larger context, however, the hymn supports the charge for Timothy to entrust the gospel to trustworthy people and "share in suffering" (2:3). Timothy is to "share in suffering" with Paul (2:9–10), which was in turn a sharing in the suffering of Christ. Timothy should "share in suffering" with "trustworthy people" and evangelists with each other. Just as Paul anticipated that he would "reign together" (*symbasileuō*) with the Corinthians (1 Cor. 4:8), this hymn expresses the solidarity of those who preserve the tradition, "if we have died together, we will also live together; . . . we will reign together" (CEB, YLT; Downs 2012, 155). The idea that believers die/live with one another does not replace but expands the idea that they die/live with Christ. As in Rom. 6:1–11, participation with Christ is a communal ("we") experience.

Theological Issues

Cultivating Leadership

A leader should cultivate other leaders. If you think of yourself as indispensable, you may cut off the creative energy that will keep the group going in the next generation. When a community is strong, a key leader—even you—may be removed unexpectedly, and the community will move forward because other leaders are functioning. As a Christian leader, you should seek "trustworthy people" to whom you commit the tenets of the faith.

Cultivating Life

Quotations and "trustworthy sayings" throughout the PE recall the core tenets of the faith. The hymn in 2:11–13 celebrates that Jesus was "raised from the dead" (2:8), so we shall "share in living" (2:11) and "share in reigning" (2:12). This is consistent with the statement that Jesus "abolished death and brought to light life and immortality" (1:10). But the hymn also warns that we should not "deny him." We should think of "denying" Jesus in terms of whether we embrace death, which Jesus abolished, or life, which is God's glorious future.

It is not the place of a minister of Christ Jesus to endorse any political party. All parties operate on worldly agendas oriented toward the present age dominated by death, whereas the reign of God is oriented toward the age to come and an agenda of life. A minister should help people think about whether their position on a given political issue promotes a culture of death or a culture of life. Are we playing by the rules of the worldly present or the heavenly future? Use this test to evaluate your position on such issues as abortion, adoption, banking regulation, capital punishment, child labor, criminal justice, domestic violence, education, fuel efficiency standards, gun sales, immigration, international trade agreements, sex trafficking, warfare, water rights, weapons manufacturing, or whatever issues are dominating the current election cycle. When we support (or fail to oppose) policies that embrace death, we deny the one who abolished death.

We should use the same test to evaluate how we spend our daily lives, how mundane activities promote a culture of death or life. Consider such activities as buying clothes, dining with neighbors, eating fast food, fishing, gardening, hiking in the woods, preparing a meal, reading alone, reading to children, playing sports, sewing, solving puzzles, studying a complex problem, teaching a teenager how to cook a family recipe or change the oil in a car, praying, surfing the internet, visiting a nursing home, watching movies, watching television, and so on. In most cases it is not a matter of *whether* we engage in an activity but *how* we engage in it. A Christian minister should set an example and help people think about how to engage everyday activities in ways that affirm life. When we participate in worldly systems that embrace death, turning a blind eye to the death implications of our behaviors, we are denying the one who abolished death.

2 Timothy 2:14–3:9

Directive 3: Call to Mind These Things

Introductory Matters

Whereas 2:1–13 developed the imperative to pass on the tradition in relation to suffering, this section develops that theme by appealing to honor and shame. The argument unfolds in four exhortations that alternate between the good behavior Timothy should model (2:14–15, 22–26) and the bad behavior of bad teachers (2:16–21; 3:1–9). On the coherence of 2:14–3:9, see Van Neste 2004, 201–3.

<table>
<tr><td>

**2 Timothy 2:14–3:9
in the Rhetorical Flow**

Letter opening (1:1–5)

Directive 1: Stir up the gift
(1:6–18)

Directive 2: What you heard from
me commit to others (2:1–13)

▶ Directive 3: Call to mind these
things (2:14–3:9)

  Model this behavior (2:14–15)

  Beware of that behavior (2:16–21)

  Model this behavior (2:22–26)

  Beware of that behavior (3:1–9)

</td></tr>
</table>

Tracing the Train of Thought

Model This Behavior (2:14–15)

2:14–15. Call to mind these things, as you are adjuring before God (2:14a). With the verb "call to mind," many interpreters insert a pronoun, "remind *them*" (NASB, NRSV, etc.; cf. Titus 3:1), meaning the "trustworthy people" (2:2). Verse 14 becomes, then, parallel to commands to "deposit" the tradition (2:2) and "preach the word" (4:2). On the verb "adjure," see comments at 1 Tim. 5:21; 2 Tim. 4:1. Timothy's "ministry" (4:5) is to carry on Paul's work as a "herald, apostle, and teacher"

(1:11) by teaching the tradition and equipping other teachers. Again, the content of this tradition is taken for granted. The emphasis is on the behavior of Christian teachers.

Not to engage in word battles, beneficial for nothing but the destruction of those who hear (2:14b). "Word battles" are characteristic of bad teachers (1 Tim. 6:4) and present a poor witness to outsiders (1 Tim. 2:8).

Be diligent to present yourself to God (2:15a). This is a favorite verse of Bible students, invariably quoted from the KJV, "Study to show thyself approved," taking "study" in its modern sense of hitting the books to investigate a matter. But "study" used to have a secondary sense, "to aim at, to set oneself deliberately to do something" (*OED*, s.v. "study" 4.a). That is the sense of the Greek verb (BDAG 939, s.v. σπουδάζω). Of course, Pastoral Paul endorses book learning (3:10, 15; see comments at 1 Tim. 4:13), but when he writes *spoudazō*, he means "be diligent/eager" (cf. 2 Tim. 4:9, 21; Titus 3:12). Epictetus (*Diatr.* 4.6.25–27) admonished that others might be diligent (*espoudakasin*) about status or wealth, but philosophy students should be diligent about the basic doctrines of philosophy. According to Epictetus, others "neglect" (*amelousin*; cf. 1 Tim. 4:14) what philosophers diligently attend to, and their craving (*oregountai*; cf. 1 Tim. 3:1) is misplaced. Again, we are in the thought world of the formation of young philosophers, now adapted to the formation of young Christian leaders.

That Timothy will "present [himself] to God" suggests a soldier on parade, as the commander reviews the troops (2:4; cf. Rom. 6:13). But references to salvation (2 Tim. 2:10) and to Christ who will not deny us (2:11–12) point toward the final review on "that Day" (1:12, 18).

As a worker unashamed, correctly interpreting the word of truth (2:15b). In Paul's vocabulary, "worker" (*ergatēs*) was a church worker (2 Cor. 11:13; Phil. 3:2; Rom. 16:3, 6, 9; 1 Tim. 5:18; Bassler 1996, 150). That usage is consistent with Timothy's goal to be a "person of God" (2 Tim. 3:17) and "evangelist" (4:5; cf. 1 Tim. 4:6). Continuing the theme of being "unashamed" (2 Tim. 1:8), if Timothy is "unashamed" like Paul (1:12) and Onesiphorus (1:16, who "*diligently* sought me," 1:17), he can tell the story of Jesus not as a shameful defeat but as the story of triumphant resurrection (2:8) and reign (2:12).

Interpreters toil over the phrase traditionally translated, "rightly dividing the word of truth" (2:15 KJV). First, this is not a statement about Scripture. Pastoral Paul is perfectly able to discuss Scripture (3:15–16; cf. 1 Tim. 5:18). In other Pauline letters, "the word of truth" is the gospel (Eph. 1:13; Col. 1:5; cf. 2 Cor. 6:7), also known as "the mystery of Christ" (Col. 4:3) or "the word of the cross" (1 Cor. 1:18). In this letter, "the word of truth" is found in oral instruction (1:13; 2:2; 3:10) and traditional quotations (1:9–10; 2:11–13, a "trustworthy *word*"). These texts focus on the death and especially the resurrection of Jesus. That was the essential story (1 Thess. 1:9–10; 1 Cor. 15).

Second, we should not get hung up on the etymology of the verb "rightly divide" (*orthotomeō*), literally, "cut straight." The idiomatic emphasis was more on "straight" than on "cut" (MM 456–57). In the Wisdom tradition, this was an idiom for "walk a straight line" (Prov. 3:6; 11:5). We might translate, "accurately delineate the word of truth" (Johnson 2001, 385), "correctly teach" (HCSB), or "interpret correctly" (CEB). While some split hairs over nonissues, Timothy should focus on proper application of the cross and resurrection of Jesus. The opponents' approach leads toward "impiety" (2:16), which is associated with immoral behavior (1 Tim. 1:9; Titus 2:12).

Beware of That Behavior (2:16–21)

2:16–21. But avoid profane, empty talk (2:16). Words like "profane" (*bebēlos*, cf. 1 Tim. 4:7) and "empty talk" (*kenophōnia*, cf. 1 Tim. 6:20) were often used to dismiss women (Kartzow 2009, 194). This language could imply that some false teachers were female, or it could be a rhetorical emasculation of the male teachers named in the next verse. "Profane, empty talk" could suggest glossolalia (1 Cor. 14) and/or the gibberish uttered by (gnostic) fake prophets (Irenaeus, *Haer.* 1.13.1–7; Origen, *Cels.* 7.9; Pietersen 2004, 120–21, 128–31). But we don't need to identify specific historical opponents in order to avoid types of behavior.

For they will progress all the more in impiety, and their word will spread like gangrene, among whom are Hymenaeus and Philetus, who have swerved around the truth (2:16–18a). The verb "progress" (2:16; see comments at 1 Tim. 4:15) is ironic. Those who "progress" in impiety have charted a course toward vice rather than "the truth" (2 Tim. 2:18; cf. 3:8). Verse 17 is grammatically awkward, since the pronouns "their" and "whom" have no antecedents (see comments at 2:21). Hymenaeus and Philetus (and Alexander, 1 Tim. 1:20) were bad teachers. As a physician of the soul (see comments at 1 Tim. 1:10; 4:16; 6:3–5), Timothy's task is to treat the infectious impiety of the false teachers.

Hymenaeus and Philetus taught an aberrant doctrine of resurrection, **saying that the resurrection has already happened, and they are upsetting the faith of some** (2:18b). Since the resurrection of Jesus had indeed "already happened," these opponents probably challenged the standard Christian apocalyptic expectation of a general resurrection at the close of the present age (cf. 1 Cor. 15:12, 35). Some gnostics taught a metaphorical resurrection (Irenaeus, *Haer.* 1.23.5; Justin Martyr, *1 Apol.* 26; cf. *Treat. Res.* 49.9–23; *Gos. Phil.* 19). The apocryphal *Acts of Paul* says Demas and Hermogenes taught resurrection as a metaphor either for a believer's present life or for offspring (*Acts of Paul* 3.14).

Whatever their precise doctrine, two quotations paint Hymenaeus and Philetus as heretics. **However, God's foundation stands firm, having this seal: "The LORD knows those who are His"** (2:19a). The first quotation is from the story of Korah's rebellion: "The LORD knows the ones who are his" (Num. 16:5 LXX, but changing "God" to "the LORD," following MT). The quotation places Hymenaeus and Philetus in the same category as Korah, who, having questioned the authority of God's chosen leaders Moses and Aaron, met a spectacular, seismic demise. In Num. 16:5, the verb "knows" is parallel to "chooses/elects" (cf. Hosea 5:3; 12:1 LXX; Amos 3:2; 1 Cor. 8:3; Gal. 4:9). William F. M. Arndt (1950, 302) concludes that this quotation speaks to the "indestructibility and permanence" of the church (cf. R. Collins 2002, 236), which would be consistent with the image of a firm foundation (see comments at 1 Tim. 3:15).

The second quotation, **and "Let everyone who names the name of the Lord stand aside from unrighteousness"** (2:19b), is uncertain. "The one who names the name of the Lord" sounds like Lev. 24:16, which prescribes death for anyone who says the divine name. But our context is not concerned about saying God's name. "Turn aside from unrighteousness" sounds like Sir. 17:26, while the idea, if not the exact language, of turning away from bad people suggests Num. 16:26. If we read "names the name of the Lord" as confessional (cf. Isa. 26:13 LXX), then Pastoral Paul is playing the role of Moses in Num. 16, calling followers to declare their loyalty to God and separate themselves from bad teachers before they are destroyed like Korah. On that reading, the second quotation is paraphrasing an idea from the Korah story.

Our text does not engage the alternative doctrine of resurrection. It simply condemns Hymenaeus and Philetus for "swerving around the truth." On the surface, this passage seems akin to 1 Cor. 3:12–15. But in 1 Corinthians, builders who use inferior materials and suffer loss will nevertheless be saved. Our passage, on the other hand, condemns Hymenaeus and Philetus as illegitimate teachers and implies that God will destroy them.

The word "unrighteousness" (2:19) provides a segue to the ethical considerations in the second part of the argument (2:20–25). **In a great house there are vessels not only of gold and silver but also of wood and pottery, some for honor, and some for dishonor** (2:20). The language echoes rabbinic discussions of uncleanness regarding household utensils (*m. Kelim* 2.1; 11.1; 15.1), but the application pertains to unclean persons (cf. Rom. 9:21).

Continuing the theme of shame (1:8, 12, 16; 2:15), Timothy can be unashamed by refraining from "word battles" (2:14), "rightly handling the word of truth" (2:15), and "standing clear of foolish and idle talk" (2:16).

If, therefore, one purifies oneself from these, one will be a vessel for honor, sanctified, useful to the master, prepared for every good work (2:21). The pronoun "these" is either neuter or masculine (the ambiguity is preserved in ASV, KJV, YLT). If the pronoun is masculine, one should "purify oneself" from "these *people*," teachers like Hymenaeus and Philetus (Knight 1992, 418). Several factors support this reading. First, chapters 2–3 present a choice between good and bad teachers. Second, the image of a holy or sanctified "vessel" is a metaphor for sexual chastity (1 Thess. 4:4; cf. 1 Sam. 21:6 LXX [21:5 Eng.]). Third, "sanctified" (*hēgiasmenon*, 2:21) calls to mind 1 Tim.

5:22, where being "holy" (*hagios*) includes avoiding fellowship with sinners (cf. 2 Cor. 6:14–7:1). Fourth, the nearest antecedent of "these" is "vessels" (implied) of wood and clay in 2:20. A few interpreters read the pronoun as neuter but the antecedent as "vessels for dishonor" (2:20; Johnson 2001, 388; so also CJB, NIV). This would be the functional equivalent of a masculine pronoun, because "vessel for honor" is a metaphor for a good teacher in 2:20, so "these" (vessels) from whom Timothy is to purify himself are dishonorable teachers. In other words, a pure vessel like Timothy will become impure by contact with bad teachers (see comments at 1 Tim. 5:22).

Alternatively, if the pronoun is neuter, one should "purify oneself" from "these *things*." But those who adopt this reading do not agree whether "these *things*" refers to "profane empty talk" (2:16; Spicq 1969, 763), or "all wickedness" (2:19; Johnson 1996, 78), or generally to all of 2:16–20 (I. H. Marshall 1999, 762; Towner 2006, 541). Whether the pronoun is masculine or neuter, the point is to denounce the words, actions, and/or character of bad teachers. But on the choice of language, see "Gentleness as Evangelistic Strategy," below. On "prepared for every good work," cf. 3:17.

Model This Behavior (2:22–26)

2:22–26. But flee youthful lusts, and pursue righteousness, faith, love, peace, along with those who call upon the Lord from a pure heart (2:22). On "fleeing" vices and "pursuing" virtues, compare 1 Tim. 6:11–12. A few scholars find the reference to "youthful lusts" (*neōterikas epithymias*) difficult and try to force an alternate translation: "flee passions for (theological) innovation" (Bassler 1996, 154; cf. Spicq 1969, 764; Richards 2002, 116), even though, as Jouette M. Bassler acknowledges, this usage for *neōterikos* is not attested before the third century. But the reference is clear if we keep in mind that this letter is addressed to a "young" minister. "Youthful lusts" reflects the Greco-Roman stereotype of youth as seeking pleasures, not least of which were women and wine (Eyben 1993, 98–112; Hutson 1998, 180–82, 243–51). Likewise in Jewish moral instruction, "youthful inclinations" are sexual (*T. Jud.* 11.1; cf. *T. Reu.* 5.5).

But avoid foolish and ignorant speculations, knowing that they generate fights (2:23). Bad teachers fight over foolish and ignorant (*apaideutos*) speculations (*zētēseis*). Lucian of Samosata illustrates the type in an anecdote about his teacher Demonax:

> And once, when he saw two philosophers very ignorantly [*apaideutōs*] quarreling about a speculation [*zētēsis*], one asking absurd questions, and the other responding with nothing that was to the point, he said, "Does it not seem to you, friends, that one of these is milking a he-goat, and the other is holding [*hypotithenai*] a sieve for him?" (Lucian, *Demon.* 28)

The two philosophers were fighting over pointless speculations, and Lucian punned that their "hypothesizing" wouldn't hold milk. Just as quarreling philosophers gave philosophy a bad name, so quarreling Christian teachers give Christianity a bad name (see comments at 1 Tim. 2:8).

But a slave of the Lord ought not to battle, but to be gentle toward all, didactic, tolerant, educating the opponents with meekness, that perhaps God may grant them repentance to a knowledge of truth (2:24–25). On "didactic" (*didaktikos*, 2:24), see 1 Tim. 3:2. The emphasis is on how the slave of the Lord engages opponents. The aim is to educate (2:25), not to score rhetorical points. Philosophers taught that effective teaching combines admonishment with "gentle words" (Plato, *Laws* 888a; Thom 1997, 88–89; cf. 1 Pet. 3:13–17 on "meekness" [*praütēs*] toward opponents).

Greco-Roman culture ascribed "honor" (2:20) to victory over rivals (Malina 1993, 34–37). Yet the slave of the Lord "must not battle" (2:24), should "pursue peace" (2:22) and avoid foolish speculations that "generate battles" (2:23), "educating his opponents with gentleness" (2:25). There is no honor in winning "word battles" (2:14) and no shame in suffering for the gospel (1:8, 12, 16). The real contest is one of endurance in the face of temptation and suffering (4:7; cf. 1 Tim. 1:18; 6:12). Against the prospect of shame from public censure, this letter reorients the youthful minister to a new sense of honor based on living in identification with the suffering of Christ and in pursuit of the consequent ethical ideals.

The key to gentleness and meekness is recognizing that opponents are themselves caught in a trap: **and they may come again to their senses from the snare of the devil/slanderer who captured them, that they might do His will** (2:26). "Come to senses" (*ananēphō*) is literally "sober up" (cf. 4:5; 1 Tim. 3:2, 11; Titus 2:2). We use the similar language "besotted" or "captivated" to describe how allurements cloud our judgment, entice and entrap us. It is not clear whether the trap is set by "the devil" or some human "slanderer" (cf. 3:3; see comments at 1 Tim. 3:6–7, 11; N. Beck 2010, 80). If Satan works through human agents, then the two ideas overlap. If a slanderer has ensnared people's minds so that they oppose Christianity, Timothy's task is, by "educating" them, to supply "the knowledge of the truth" that frees them.

The difficulty is compounded by the ambiguous pronouns in the final clause. A literal translation is "having been captured by him for his will," but captured by whom, for whose will? Typical English translations imply that the devil coerces people to do the devil's will (NIV; cf. KJV, NASB, NRSV, etc.). But in Greek, there are two different pronouns, so a more literal translation is "captured by this one [*autou*] for that one's [*ekeinou*] will," or idiomatically, "captured by the latter, for the will of the former." "The latter" refers to the nearest antecedent, which is *diabolos*. "The former" refers back to the main clause, "that God may grant them knowledge." The meaning is clearer in a paraphrase: "God will free them from the devil's snare, so that they can do his [God's] will" (GW; cf. Phillips, TLB). If opponents are ensnared by slanderous misinformation about Christianity, combativeness reinforces their misunderstanding, whereas gentleness and meekness confound the slander, and "knowledge of the truth" springs the trap.

Beware of That Behavior (3:1–9)

3:1–9. This section picks up from 2:16–21, presenting false teachers as negative counterexamples. Clearly, Pastoral Paul found some people reprehensible, but it is difficult to say who they were or what they taught, because the name-calling is boilerplate rhetoric (Karris 1973). This letter deplores bad behavior as evidence for lack of understanding.

But know this, that in the last days worse times will arise (3:1). Believers are in the "last days" (cf. Acts 2:17). Although the resurrection has not yet occurred (2 Tim. 2:18), the eschaton has begun with the epiphany of Christ (1:10). The typical apocalyptic perspective is that as the present age draws to a close, things will get worse before God intervenes, and Pastoral Paul sees evidence of this in a vice list: **for people will be devoted to themselves, devoted to money, pretenders, braggarts, blasphemers, disobedient to parents, ungrateful, irreligious, unaffectionate, implacable, slanderers, uncontrolled, uncivilized, undevoted to good, traitors, reckless, arrogant, devoted to pleasure rather than devoted to God, having a form of piety but denying its power. Turn away from these people** (3:2–5). This pile of overlapping terms suggests types of people. For rhetorical effect Pastoral Paul strings together adjectives with negative prefixes (English un- and in-) and compound words made up of "devoted to + noun" (Gk. *philo-*, traditionally translated "lovers of . . ."). In regard to the climactic "devoted to pleasure rather than devoted to God" (3:4), we have seen some correlation between Epicurean philosophers and Pastoral Paul regarding gentleness (1 Tim. 3:3–4), frank speech (1 Tim. 3:13), and wealth (1 Tim. 6:2b–21). But Pastoral Paul denies the fundamental tenet of Epicureanism. It is not the quest for "pleasure" (*hēdonē*) that orients the Christian life but the quest for God (Fiore 2004, 276–77). The whole stinking mess is summed up in the final phrase, "having a form of piety but denying its power." "Piety" (*eusebeia*) was an important Greco-Roman social value, entailing devotion to gods and family (1 Tim. 2:2 [see sidebar]; 3:16; 4:7–8; 5:4; 6:3, 5–6; cf. Titus 1:1; 2:12). Hypocrites pretend to piety while acting in their own interest. It would be unfair to suppose pagans lacked devotion to their families or gods. But for Pastoral Paul, the "power" of genuine piety is found "in Christ Jesus" (3:12).

The greater concern is teachers whose "pious" posturing is a cover for self-service. **For among these are those who enter into houses and capture little women who are piled up with sins, led by various lusts, always learning and never able to come to a knowledge of truth** (3:6–7). Philosophers criticized those who attended lectures without applying them to their own moral development (Seneca, *Ep.* 108). We might understand "little women" as a chauvinistic put-down of women in general for intellectual naivete. Some pagans criticized Christianity for appealing to "gullible women" and uneducated rabble (Minucius Felix, *Octavius* 8.4; cf. Malherbe 1985/86, 196–98). Or perhaps "little women" refers to younger women whose sexuality threatened the proper order of Christian households (1 Tim. 5:14; Streete 2009). Either way, these verses reflect a stereotype of women as unable to control their passions (cf. Eve in 1 Tim. 2:14; Medea in ps.-Theano, *Nik.* 7.62–66; Huizenga 2013, 311–12, 325).

The rhetoric is generally applicable. We could read these verses as a continuation of 3:3–5, further describing the moral decline before the end of the age (Tromp 2007, 222–23). Lucian satirized charlatans who seduced women (Lucian, *Fug.* 18). Our text might refer to some group that appealed especially to women, whether Montanists (see "Theological Issues" at 1 Tim. 2:8–3:1) or itinerant evangelists who advocated celibacy (e.g., *Acts of Paul*; *Acts of John*; Davies 1980, 50–94). If this passage refers to any such teachers, it is consistent with the charge that the apostates "prevent to marry" (1 Tim. 4:3). But if so, then "led by various lusts" suggests that their celibacy was a charade. Or perhaps we are too quick to point fingers. Pastoral Paul is not trying to refute a specific heresy but alerting Timothy to types of teachers who imperil the church.

In the way that Jannes and Jambres opposed Moses, so also these oppose the truth, people corrupt in mind, unproven about the faith (3:8). In Jewish tradition, Belial sent "Yoḥanah and his brother" to oppose Moses (CD 5.17–19). These characters appeared as Moses's antagonists in embellishments to several biblical stories: Pharaoh's court magicians, instigators of the golden calf at Sinai, aids to Balaam (Schürer 1986, 292; A. Pietersma, *ABD* 3:638–40; Tromp 2007). The legendary magicians became popular also among gentiles (Pliny the Elder, *Nat.* 30.2.11; Apuleius, *Apology* 90; Eusebius, *Praep. ev.* 9.8). And a Jewish *Apocryphon of Jannes and Jambres* from the Roman period survives only in fragments (*OTP* 2:427–42; Pietersma 1994). Pastoral Paul is appealing to some such tradition (see comments at 1 Tim. 2:15).

We need not assume that the opponents in 2 Timothy were Jewish magicians (Pietersen 2003). Magic was a stock rhetorical accusation against social deviants (Davies 1980, 37–40; cf. 1 Tim. 5:13), a charge leveled even against Paul in the apocryphal Acts (*Acts of Paul* 3.15). The point is that Jannes and Jambres "opposed Moses" just as some Christian teachers "oppose the truth" that Paul espoused. "Corrupt in mind" is consistent with mental illness as a metaphor for immorality (Malherbe 1980). **But they will not progress very far, for their mindlessness will be evident to all, as was that of those others** (3:9). Elsewhere, "mindlessness" leads to being "enslaved to lusts and various pleasures" (Titus 3:3). Here those who "oppose the truth" (2 Tim. 3:8) are "led by various lusts" (3:6). "Progress" is ironic (see comments at 2:16; 3:13; 1 Tim. 4:15).

Theological Issues

Gentleness as Evangelistic Strategy

Are Hymenaeus and Philetus broken sherds on the trash heap or dishonorable vessels who might yet repent (2:25) and be "purified" (2:21)? How do we square Pastoral Paul's vituperation (2:17–19; 3:1–9) with being "not combative but gentle toward all" (2:24) and the example of long-suffering Paul (3:10)? For one thing, what Pastoral Paul says *about* the false teachers is not the same as what he counsels Timothy to say *to* them. He is calling Timothy to choose between two options (cf. 1 Tim. 4:1–10). One option is a self-centered pseudo-piety (2 Tim. 3:2–5). It is like an infectious disease (2:17) from which Timothy must be purified (2:21). The other option is a life of faithful endurance in participation with the story of Christ (2:11–13). It is modeled by Paul (3:10–14) and grounded in a lifetime of Scripture study (3:14–16).

So what might Pastoral Paul say *to* his opponents? Would he engage them with an openness to learn from the encounter? Honest dialogue can help you see where your own arguments are weak. But what if the opponents are truly hostile and unwilling to engage in honest dialogue? These verses caution not to fight fire with fire, not to stoop to the opponents' level, but to meet hostility with gentleness and meekness. These are tactics both for survival in a hostile environment and for evangelism. Human tendency is to take an attack personally and fight back. But God's slave should not fight. It is easier to resist that temptation if you view your opponent as a victim of the devil (or duped by a human slanderer). "Be not overcome by evil, but overcome evil with good" (Rom. 12).

Finally, when deciding about the ambiguous "these" in 2:21, you should consider the rhetorical effect of labeling people "unclean." Such language will alienate rather than persuade. Humility is on the side of the neuter pronoun: you should purify yourself from unclean behaviors and call others to account for their unclean behaviors. When preaching this passage, consider a translation that treats the pronoun as neuter (e.g., ESV, NASB, NRSV). See also "Vilification of Enemies" among the "Theological Issues" at Titus 1:5–16.

2 Timothy 3:10–17

Directive 4: Remain in What You Learned

Introductory Matters

Some take 3:1–17 as a unit (e.g., Westfall 2010). Certainly the exhortation about good examples to follow (3:10–17) is closely related to examples of bad behaviors to avoid (2:16, 23; 3:5). And this section is tied to what precedes by such themes as "piety" (3:12; cf. 3:5) and "progress" (3:13; cf. 2:16; 3:9). Also, the verb "remain" (3:14) continues a string of imperatives (2:1, 2, 8, 14, 15, 16, 22, 23; 3:1, 5). Still, the emphatic, "but as for you" (3:10, 14) marks a shift from discussing bad teachers in the third person (3:1–9) to direct engagement with Timothy in the second person. This section calls Timothy to reflect on what he has learned from Paul. Ancient philosophers taught that one learned best not simply from books and lectures but from observing a master directly and participating in his life.

Tracing the Train of Thought

Example of Paul (3:10–12)

3:10–12. Verses 10–11 depict Paul as Timothy's teacher (1:13; 2:2) and model of endurance (1:8, 12–13; 2:3, 9–10). But as for you, you have followed my teaching, regimen, purpose, faith, long-suffering, love, steadfastness (3:10). In philosophical language, "regimen" (*agōgē*) could mean a "way of teaching," a program of philosophical instruction (Diogenes Laërtius, *Lives* 1.19; 2.86; 3.66; 4.51; 9.115; 10.138; ps.-Plutarch, *Lib. ed.*; Nock 1933, 167). But it could also mean a "way of living" (Diogenes Laërtius, *Lives* 9.83). Marcus Aurelius exploits the breadth of the word as he describes what he learned from his teacher Diognetus (see sidebar).

Diognetus's regimen included lectures, writing, and disciplined living. Pastoral Paul's regimen included intentional study and practice (see comments at 1 Tim. 4:12–16) and his personal example. His "purpose" echoes God's "purpose" that was "given to us in Christ Jesus" (1:9). Just as Paul was the beneficiary of God's "long-suffering" (1 Tim. 1:16) and "love" (1 Tim. 1:14), so he taught Timothy in "faith and love" (2 Tim. 1:13). Timothy is to model faith (1 Tim. 4:12), be long-suffering (2 Tim. 4:2), and pursue faith, love, and steadfastness (2:22; 1 Tim. 6:11).

Steadfastness in persecutions and sufferings, what happened to me in Antioch, Iconium, and Lystra, what persecutions I endured, and from all these the Lord delivered me (3:11). Most interpreters insert commas to demarcate

---

What Marcus Aurelius Learned from His Teacher

"From Diognetus, [I learned] not to be taken up with trifles; and not to give credence to the statements of wonder-workers and charlatans [goētai; cf. 2 Tim. 3:13] about incantations and the exorcizing of demons, and such-like marvels; . . . not to resent frank criticism; and to become familiar with philosophy; . . . and to write dialogues as a boy; and to set my heart on a pallet-bed and a pelt and whatever else tallied with the Greek regimen [agōgē]." (Marcus Aurelius 1.6, trans. Haines, LCL, modified)

"steadfastness, persecutions, sufferings" as three separate items (NA²⁸, KJV, NIV, NRSV, etc.). It is grammatically possible, however, to read "persecutions" and "sufferings" as the contexts in which Paul exercised steadfastness, as translated above (cf. NEB, Phillips). Pastoral Paul recalls persecutions and sufferings that we know from Acts 13–14. But according to Acts, Timothy was not present to observe Paul's endurance at Pisidian Antioch or Iconium, so we may ponder how Paul or pseudo-Paul arrived at this list. Nevertheless, the examples establish a pattern of persecution in Paul's career. Paul's letters include catalogs of hardships (1 Cor. 4:9–13; 2 Cor. 4:7–12; 6:3–10), which drew from philosophical traditions about the sage who demonstrates his wisdom by facing adversity with serenity (Fitzgerald 1988).

Paul's experiences of persecution lead to a warning: **All who wish to live pious lives in Christ Jesus will be persecuted** (3:12). Elsewhere we read a hint that Timothy was arrested (Heb. 13:23). The thing that would draw persecution was not Christian piety per se, for Greeks and Romans also valued piety (see comments at 1 Tim. 2:2 and the sidebar there; 4:8; 5:7–8). Christians garnered suspicion because they defined "piety" in terms of being "in Christ Jesus" rather than in terms of devotion to pagan gods, the emperor, or the "form of piety" (3:5) defined by the dominant society.

Negative Counterexamples (3:13)

3:13. But **evil people and charlatans will progress to the worse, deceiving and deceived** (3:13). Once again, "progress" is ironic (cf. 2:16; 3:9; see comments at 1 Tim. 4:5). The word translated "charlatan" (*goēs*) connotes a con artist who hoodwinks people by sleight of hand or misleading argument. Lloyd K. Pietersen (2004, 132–34, 144–58) translates "sorcerers" because of the reference to Jannes and Jambres in verse 8, but he assumes that the opponents viewed themselves as legitimate miracle workers whose charismatic expressions Pastoral Paul wanted to corral (see "Theological Issues" at 1 Tim. 2:11–3:1a). My translation focuses on the educational aims of the PE (Marcus Aurelius 1.6 [see sidebar]). Pastoral Paul rejected the rivals (cf. 2:18) with a rhetorical flourish implying that they did not have legitimate authority (Brown 2015).

Remain in What You Learned (3:14–15)

3:14–15. But **as for you, remain in what you learned and came to understand, knowing from whom you learned, and that from infancy you knew the sacred Scriptures that were able to make you wise to salvation through the faith that is in Christ Jesus** (3:14–15). The plural "whom" (3:14) indicates multiple teachers. Seneca suggested that a boy's teachers included his pedagogue, grandmother, and schoolmaster (Seneca, *Ep.* 94.9). Timothy learned under Paul (3:10–12) and "from infancy" under Lois and Eunice (1:5). "What" he learned included observations of Paul's behavior (3:10–12) as well as "the sacred Scriptures" of

Israel. From his mother and grandmother, Timothy learned the contents of those Scriptures, and from Paul a way of reading them christologically (3:15). The command to "remain in them" invites continued meditation on all these resources (see comments at 1 Tim. 4:13; 2 Tim. 2:8).

Interpreters generally take "through the faith that is in Christ Jesus" as an odd way of referring to Jesus as the object of faith, obscuring the oddity by translating "through faith in Christ Jesus" (e.g., Knight 1992, 444; NIV, NRSV). David Downs, however, points out that elsewhere in the letter, "life," "love," "grace," and "salvation" are all "in Christ Jesus" (1:1, 9, 13; 2:1, 10; 3:12, 15; cf. 1 Tim. 1:14; and Rom. 3:24; Gal. 2:4). He suggests that this is language of participation with Jesus, who is "faithful" (2:13; Downs 2012, 160; cf. comments at 2:11–13).

The Benefit of Scripture (3:16–17)

3:16–17. All Scripture is *theopneustos* and beneficial for teaching, for reproof, for correction, for education in righteousness, so that the person of God may be prepared for every good work (3:16–17). The opening words of this sentence are ambiguous. The word translated "Scripture" (*graphē*) was the common word for any written text (*T. Naph.* 5.8). In Jewish and Christian contexts it became a semi-technical term for holy writings (cf. 3:15; 4 Macc. 18:14; Acts 8:32; Rom. 10:11; 15:4; Gal. 3:8, 22; 2 Pet. 3:16, etc.). The adjective *theopneustos* is uncertain (see below). The conjunction "and" (*kai*) sometimes functions instead as an adverb, "also." As for syntax, Greek commonly leaves the verb "to be" implied, and scholars debate where to insert that implied verb here. The sentence could be translated either (1) "all Scripture *is theopneustos and* beneficial," or (2) "every *theopneustos* scripture *is also* beneficial." Option 1, overwhelmingly preferred in English translations, takes *graphē* in the technical sense of a religious text. Option 2 takes *graphē* in its generic sense of any written text, of which a subset are *theopneustos* and therefore beneficial (Theodore of Mopsuestia, *Comm. 2 Tim.* 222).

How much weight should we place on the use of the singular "Scripture" (*graphē*)? Paul refers to "the Scripture" (sg.) when citing a specific passage (Rom. 4:3; 9:17; 10:11; Gal. 4:30). Understood that way, the verse refers to "every [individual] Scripture text." The translation "all Scripture" implies some collection of texts, but it would be anachronistic to project a Christian or Jewish canon onto this verse. Certainly there was a consensus among Jews that "Scripture" included Torah, Prophets, and Writings (Luke 24:44; Sir. prologue; Josephus, *Ag. Ap.* 1.38). But even in the second century, rabbis were still debating whether to include Song of Songs and Ecclesiastes (*m. Yad.* 3.5; *t. Yad.* 2.14; J. P. Lewis, *ABD* 3:636). And the Christian canon was more tenuous. By the second century widespread tradition emphasized four Gospels and some collection of Pauline letters, but the Western canon of twenty-seven books did not coalesce until the late fourth century. Tertullian took "all Scripture" to include 1 Enoch (Tertullian, *Cult. fem.* 1.3). In short, while it is likely that Pastoral Paul had in mind a collection of Jewish texts, we cannot read "all Scripture" as referring to a sixty-six-book Protestant canon.

Even more problematic is the obscure word *theopneustos*. Etymologically, it is a compound of "God" (*theos*) and "spirit/breath" (*pneuma*). Pastoral Paul associated Scripture in some way with the breath or Spirit of God. A poet might seek divine assistance in artistic expression (Homer, *Iliad* 1.1; *Odyssey* 1.1; Hesiod, *Works and Days* 1–10) or a sibyl in uttering oracles (Plutarch, *Pyth. orac.*), but those texts do not use the word *theopneustos*, which appears only in the first century and later and in unexpected contexts. We can understand "*theopneustos* wisdom" (ps.-Phocylides 129) or "*theopneustos* breath" (*Sib. Or.* 5.407–8, trans. J. Collins, OTP 1:402), but what were *theopneustos* streams (*Sib. Or.* 5.308) or *theopneustos* ointments for burial (*T. Ab.* A.20.11)? We should be cautious about constructing a doctrine of Scripture from this obscure word.

In our passage, the English rendering "God-breathed" (NIV; "breathed out by God," ESV) suggests that the texts originated with God, as if human authors were mere passive recipients. There was an escalating tendency of Jewish writers from the Second Temple period through the early rabbinic period to ascribe divine origins first to Torah and then to all twenty-two scrolls of Scripture (Schürer 1979, 314–21). The traditional translation "inspired" (KJV, NASB, NRSV) implies that God "breathed into" the process and leaves room for human agency in composition. So prophets wrote by the "on-breathing" of God (*epipnoia*, Josephus, *Ag. Ap.* 1.37), which would be consistent with the understanding that the deity assists the poet's own expression (Pindar, *Nem.* 3.1–16; Plutarch, *Pyth. orac.* 21 [404e–f]; SEG 821.10–14 = *NewDocs* 1:§2).

Whatever Pastoral Paul intended by *theopneustos*, the word "beneficial" (*ōphelimos*) carries the weight of the sentence. According to Seneca, a true benefit must be (a) a thing of value, (b) freely given, (c) to one who is worthy, and (d) given for the sake of the recipient (Seneca, *Ben.* 4.29). Seneca said one could show gratitude for a benefit by repaying the benefit or by maintaining gratitude. If Scripture is a benefit bestowed by God, one could repay it by reading it and applying it to one's own life.

The expression "person of God" occasionally refers to a worshiper (2 Chron. 8:14; *Let. Aris.* 140; Philo, *Conf.* 41). If we took it in that broad sense in 3:17, we would understand Scripture as a source of preparation for any believer. That may be true, but the expression, traditionally rendered "man of God," usually designates an official functionary, especially a prophet (1 Kings 20:28; 2 Kings 1:13; Philo, *Gig.* 61; N. Bratsiotis, *TDOT* 1:233–35; J. Jeremias, *TDNT* 1:364–65), and in the PE it refers specifically to Timothy (1 Tim. 6:11). In the context of ministerial formation, this passage calls for Timothy, as a "person of God," to "remain in" the Scriptures and the teaching and example of Paul (3:10–15; cf. 1 Tim. 4:15). He should meditate on the Scriptures so that they will teach, reprove, correct, and educate *him*, so he will be "mature and prepared for every good work" (cf. 2:21; Titus 3:1).

Theological Issues

The Form of Piety

A minister must distinguish being a good follower of Christ from being a good citizen. We like to think good Christians are good citizens, especially when they use similar language to express their values. The PE co-opt the language of "piety" from Roman society (see sidebar at 1 Tim. 2:2), but our text distinguishes between "those who hold a form of piety" (3:5) and "those who wish to live piously in Christ Jesus" (3:12). We tend to read the Bible through the lenses of our own cultural contexts, so we do not notice when politicians co-opt biblical ideas to promote worldly agendas, especially if our society identifies itself as "Christian" (B. Scott 2016 offers an accessible discussion of the problem). A good minister must preach a piety defined "in Christ Jesus," even when that runs afoul of societal expectations.

Scripture and the Breath of God

Protestants frequently cite 2 Tim. 3:16–17 as a prooftext for the authority of Scripture, placing much weight on the obscure reference to the breath of God. The early Pietist leader Philipp Spener, however, emphasized the word "all." Because "all Scripture" is inspired, Christians should study the whole Bible and not merely their favorite sections (Spener 1675, §1). Spener focused on the Holy Spirit not as the author of Scripture but as the guide to its readers: "when pious hearts . . . continue to read the Scriptures with meditation and prayer, God the Holy Spirit will open their understanding more and more, so that they may also learn and understand the higher and more difficult matters as far as is necessary for strengthening of their faith, instruction in life, and comfort" (Spener, 1677, §34). From this perspective, regardless of one's theory of how God was involved in the production of the texts, what matters is how God "breathes" on the reader. Scripture is "beneficial" to one who is open to being taught, reproved, and corrected by the texts over a lifetime of prayerful study (see "A Regimen for Spiritual Formation" under "Theological Issues" at 1 Tim. 4:6–16).

2 Timothy 4:1–8

Directive 5: Proclaim the Word

Introductory Matters

The letter body concludes with a final charge to Timothy that nicely reflects all the formal elements of a charge proper: charge verb, person charged, and authority phrase (4:1); content of the charge (4:2–5); and implications (4:6–8; this analysis is slightly different from that of Craig Smith 2006, 152–53; cf. 1 Tim. 1:18–20).

References to Christ's "epiphany" and his role as judge (4:1, 8) orient the imperatives in this section christologically. Between these brackets, the section falls into two parts. First is the charge itself (4:1–5), in which "proclaim the word" (4:2) and "do the work of an evangelist" (4:5) bracket a warning about anticipated opposition from rival teachers (4:3–4). The likelihood of hostile opposition elicits the additional exhortation to "suffer wrong" (4:5). This leads to the second part of the section (4:6–8), which represents Paul as a model evangelist who, in anticipation of future reward, "kept the faith" amid difficult

---

**2 Timothy 4:1–8
in the Rhetorical Flow**

Letter opening (1:1–5)

Directive 1: Stir up the gift (1:6–18)

Directive 2: What you heard from me commit to others (2:1–13)

Directive 3: Call to mind these things (2:14–3:9)

Directive 4: Remain in what you learned (3:10–17)

▶ Directive 5: Proclaim the word (4:1–8)

  Exhortation (4:1–5)

    Proclaim the word (4:1–2)

    Warning: The time will come (4:3–4)

    Do the work of an evangelist (4:5)

  Pauline example (4:6–8)

---

circumstances. Some of those circumstances include opposition from fellow Christians (4:10, 14) and arrest (4:16). All this recapitulates the opening charge (1:6–18), underscoring the purpose of the whole letter, which exhorts Timothy to pass along the tradition to future generations, regardless of opposition.

Tracing the Train of Thought

Exhortation (4:1–5)

This section evokes the coming of Jesus for judgment at the end of the present age as motivation for the commands that follow.

4:1–2. *Proclaim the word.* **I adjure you before God and Christ Jesus, who is about to judge the living and the dead, and by his manifestation and his reign** (4:1). The verb "adjure" (*diamartyromai*) is a solemn charge, implying the invocation of divine witness (see comments at 1 Tim. 5:21; cf. 2 Tim. 2:14). On "manifestation" (*epiphaneia*), see the sidebar at Titus 2:13.

The substance of the charge is a series of five imperatives: **proclaim the word; stand forth in season and out of season, reprove, rebuke, exhort with all long-suffering and instruction** (4:2). The "word" that Timothy is to proclaim is the story of the death and resurrection of Jesus (2:15; cf. 1 Tim. 6:3; Titus 1:3, 9; "faithful sayings" and quotations throughout the PE). Timothy should seize the initiative, that is, "stand forth" (*ephistēmi*) against false teachers (LSJ 745, s.v. ἐφίστημι B.III.2). Abraham J. Malherbe (1984) shows how philosophers emphasized the importance of waiting for the opportune moment (*kairos*) to criticize or admonish. Except for a few harsh Cynics, who took pride in flouting social conventions and reviling their audiences, most philosophers thought speaking "out of season" (*akairōs*) was at best ineffective and at worst an indication that one was speaking out of passion rather than reason. Pastoral Paul is no harsh Cynic, since he discourages belligerence (2:14, 16, 23–24; cf. 1 Tim. 3:3; 6:4; Titus 3:9) and encourages gentleness, "all long-suffering and instruction" (cf. 2 Tim. 2:22, 24–26). According to Malherbe the exhortation to speak "out of season" implies that opponents are unwilling to listen to reason (3:1–9; 4:3–4). The commands to "reprove, rebuke, exhort" call to mind Paul's pastoral care, how like a good father he adjusted his corrections to each individual child and situation (1 Thess. 2:11–12).

4:3–4. *Warning: The time will come.* **For the time will come when they will not endure the healthy teaching, but because they have itching ears, they will pile up teachers for themselves in accordance with their own lusts, and they will turn their ears away from the truth, wandering off to the myths** (4:3–4). In keeping with the references to judgment and the reign of God (4:1), "the time will come" reflects an apocalyptic expectation that things will get worse before they get better. This letter earlier referred to women whose "lusts" (*epithymiai*) led them to false teachers (cf. 3:6–7). Now Pastoral Paul anticipates that the trend will continue and not only among women.

People will become like those Philo describes, whose "itchings" arise from "throbbing passions in the soul" and "from pleasure and lust," people who need the "curative [*sōtērios*] drug" of philosophy (Philo, *Worse* 110, trans. Colson and Whitaker, LCL, modified; cf. Plutarch, *Adul. amic.* 5, 12 [51d, 55e], on flatterers who tickle the ears). Seneca thought a physician who was entertaining or had a soothing bedside manner was delightful, but eloquence was no substitute for the right diagnosis and treatment (*Ep.* 75.6–7). The theater is where one goes to satisfy the "pleasure of the ear," but "the true hearer [of philosophy] is ravished and stirred by the beauty of the subject matter, not by the jingle of empty words" (Seneca, *Ep.* 108.6–7). As for the subject matter, if a philosopher speaks clearly about how to defy death or the vicissitudes of fortune, people are "impressed by such words, and become what they are bidden to be" (Seneca, *Ep.* 108.8; cf. Lucian, *Cal.* 21).

Pastoral Paul would say that the cure for such an itch is the "healthy teaching" (1 Tim. 1:10; Titus 1:9; 2:1), also known as the "healthy words," the essential teachings about Jesus (1 Tim. 6:3). Timothy learned those "healthy words" from Paul (2 Tim. 1:13). The evangelist, like a physician of the soul, must dispense words that promote spiritual health (see comments at 1 Tim. 1:10; cf. 1 Tim. 4:7, 15, 16; 6:3–5).

4:5. *Do the work of an evangelist.* **But as for you, be sober minded in everything, suffer wrong, do the work of an evangelist, fulfill your ministry (4:5).** To "be sober" (*nēphe*) is basically to be not drunk, but the verb could connote control of any physical appetites (cf. the adjective "sober," 1 Tim. 3:2, 11; Titus 2:2). In a context of a need for sleep, for example, it means, "be alert" (1 Thess. 5:6, 8; 1 Pet. 1:13; 4:7; 5:8). Here the qualifier "in everything" suggests a broad resistance to passions and emotions, and so "be sober minded." In particular, the command to "suffer wrong" suggests that Timothy must not yield to fear or intimidation as he does "the work of an evangelist." These commands recapitulate the letter opening, with its themes of resisting a spirit of cowardice and suffering for the gospel (2 Tim. 1:6–8). This is how Timothy will "fulfill [his] ministry."

The cumulative rhetorical effect of nine imperatives in verses 2 and 5 is a pounding, pounding, pounding urgency. Timothy must be relentless in challenging false teachers, patiently exposing their errors and correcting their followers, no matter the personal cost.

Pauline Example (4:6–8)

4:6–8. In this costly endeavor, Pastoral Paul offers himself as a model. **For already I am being poured out as a libation, and the time of my departure is at hand. I have struggled the good struggle, I have finished the course, I have kept the faith. At last there is set aside for me the crown of righteousness,**

with which the Lord will recompense me on that day, the judge who is just not only to me but also to all those who love his appearing (4:6–8). A "libation" was an offering of wine, or sometimes water, poured out to a god when making a request or a thanksgiving. Craig A. Smith (2006, 154) takes it here as a metaphor of Paul's preaching that was an offering pleasing to God (cf. Phil. 2:17). Michael Prior (1989) thinks the sentence refers to Paul's impending "release" from prison, but the context suggests impending execution: "my departure" (cf. Phil. 1:23; *1 Clem.* 44.5), "I have finished the course," "crown of righteousness," and "the Judge." Most interpreters, therefore, read it as a metaphor of Paul's life being "poured out" as his "departure" (from life) is at hand (Dibelius and Conzelmann 1972, 121). Ancient Greeks and Romans thought it was important to express gratitude at the end of life, especially in a will (Fitzgerald 2003, 658–63). Paul has few possessions, but he "pours out" his life in gratitude to God.

Verse 7 presents three images of Paul looking back on his life. First, the "good struggle" (*agōn*) corresponds to the "good struggle" enjoined upon Timothy (1 Tim. 6:12–14; Mihoc 2008, 138). The image of the race "course" with a "crown" for the winner recalls 1 Cor. 9:24–27, where the footrace in which one "struggles/competes" (*agōnizō*) is a metaphor for the Christian life. Second, "I have kept the faith" (*pistis*) recalls the gospel with which Paul was "entrusted" (1 Tim. 1:11; Titus 1:3), because God considered him "trustworthy" (*pistos*, 1 Tim. 1:12). Some might "be unfaithful" (2 Tim. 2:13), but Paul has "kept the faith" by continuing to proclaim the message entrusted to him. He is a model not only for Timothy, in whom he "has trusted" (1:12), but also for the "trustworthy" people to whom Timothy will commit what he learned from Paul (2:2).

Pastoral Paul does not say how God will "recompense" (cf. 4:14) him for his life, but presumably with a new life (2:11). The whole paragraph contemplates impending death and eternal reward. Paul models perseverance amid hardship (cf. 1:11–12; 2:10; 3:10–17), and his life is oriented toward the future appearance of Christ (1:12; 2:11–13; 4:1).

Theological Issues

Be Sober Minded

Pastoral Paul has little to say about the doctrines of other teachers. He criticizes their immoral methods. This final charge to Timothy focuses on the enticing tactics of bad teachers and warns against playing by their worldly rules. The problem is not that an evangelist might seek to manipulate the people. The danger Pastoral Paul presents is that the people might seek to manipulate the evangelist. The people have "itching ears" and "pile up teachers for themselves in accordance with their own lusts."

Your task as a physician of the soul is to preach "healthy doctrine." People will diagnose themselves and tell you what drugs to prescribe. If you say their pain can be cured through changes in habits and healthier spiritual diet, they will seek another opinion and demand doctors who provide the drugs they desire. People want you to baptize their greed with a prosperity "gospel." They want you to salve their ethnocentric itch with soothing assurance that God bestows special favor on their tribe. They want you to say that their favorite politicians are anointed, that politicians they oppose are full of gall and bitterness. They want to hear that their enemies are God's enemies on whom they are right to call down fire from heaven. They do not want to quit their self-serving habits and trust God. They want to be told that God trusts them to root out sinners from the land. "They will not endure the healthy teaching." People want you to give them a high, but your task is to cure their disease.

This calls for sober mindedness. Applause is intoxicating, and disapproval is painful. When you prepare your sermon, what is the ratio of time and effort you spend creating entertaining effects (images, videos, stunts) to the time you spend sweating over the details of your text, lest you misunderstand or misrepresent the point of the passage? The sober-minded evangelist will not play to the roar of the crowd but will attend to the cross and resurrection of Jesus, equipping people to live spiritually healthy lives in the present age by turning them away from earthly desires and exhorting them to live into a vision of God's glorious future. We may recall that Paul came to Corinth "not with eloquent words of wisdom, lest the cross be emptied of its power" (1 Cor. 1:17; cf. 2 Tim. 2:1–9).

2 Timothy 4:9–22

Letter Closing

Introductory Matters

On typical letter closings, see "Introductory Matters" for Titus 3:12–15. In lieu of a standard Greek farewell, this letter ends like other Pauline letters with a benediction (4:22). Paul typically described his own travel plans. This letter depicts Paul as a prisoner and with no plans for travel, but he offers news about his situation (4:16–18). He also directs Timothy's travel and reports on the movements of coworkers (4:9–15, 19–21). He sends personal greetings to Timothy's coworkers and from his own.

Tracing the Train of Thought

Travel Reports and News (4:9–18)

4:9–18. **See to it that you come to me quickly** (4:9). The request to "come quickly" is not jarring like the similar request in Titus 3:12, because the instructions in this letter are not tied to Timothy's location. The request is poignant for its urgency (cf. 4:21), prompted especially by the prospect of execution (4:18).

It is true that Paul feels lonely. **For Demas abandoned me, having loved the present age, and went to Thessalonica** (4:10). Elsewhere Paul identified Demas as a coworker (Philem. 24; cf. Col. 4:14). Here, however, Demas embodies the bad soldier who becomes "entangled in the affairs of life" (2 Tim. 2:4). He is "in love with the present age" (cf. 1 Tim. 6:17; Titus 2:12), which is to say not (any longer) oriented toward the messianic age to come. Hope in the realization of the reign of God serves to orient the faithful throughout this letter (1:9–12; 2:8–10; 4:1, 6–8; cf. 1 Tim. 6:12; Titus 2:11–14; 3:7). And repudiation of the "present age" (cf. Titus 2:12) is also Pauline (Rom. 12:2; 1 Cor. 1:20; 2:6–8; 3:18; 2 Cor. 4:4; Gal. 1:4; Eph. 1:21).

Crescens is otherwise unknown, though it was a common Latin name (*NewDocs* 3:§78). The report that he has gone **to Galatia** (4:10) seems at first like another abandonment. But it is also possible that Paul sent him away, just as he sent **Titus to Dalmatia** (4:10). There is no hint that Titus abandoned Paul. This report suggests that we should read this letter after the letter to Titus, in which Paul anticipates recalling Titus from Crete (Titus 3:12). Dalmatia was a

> ### 2 Timothy 4:9–22 in the Rhetorical Flow
>
> Letter opening (1:1–5)
> **Directive 1: Stir up the gift (1:6–18)**
> **Directive 2: What you heard from me commit to others (2:1–13)**
> **Directive 3: Call to mind these things (2:14–3:9)**
> **Directive 4: Remain in what you learned (3:10–17)**
> **Directive 5: Proclaim the word (4:1–8)**
> ▶**Letter closing (4:9–22)**
> Travel reports and news (4:9–18)
> Greetings (4:19–21)
> Benediction (4:22)

region northwest of Greece on the Adriatic coast, the southern part of the Roman province of Illyricum (Rom. 15:19), part of modern Croatia. When we read **Luke alone is with me** (4:11a), we should not think of Paul as totally abandoned; rather, he is still directing the movements of his coworkers. On the relation between this and "no one was with me" (4:16), see comments below.

Get Mark and bring him with you, for he is useful to me for ministry (4:11b). In this context, with Paul in prison and asking for a cloak and scrolls, it would be natural to take "useful for ministry" in its ordinary sense of providing food. Roman prisons were notorious for filth and inadequate food and care (Wansink 1996, 27–95). Christians who provided literal "ministry" to prisoners include Onesiphorus (1:16–18), Epaphroditus (Phil. 2:25; 4:10–20), Onesimus (Philem. 13; Wansink 1996, 175–99), Byrrhus (Ign. *Trall.* 2.1; *Magn.* 15.1; *Smyrn.* 12.1), and perhaps Luke in this passage.

On the other hand, Mark was an effective member of Paul's teaching team, along with the others named in 4:10–12, and tradition indicates that he had experience in Rome (1 Pet. 5:13; Eusebius, *Hist. eccl.* 2.15–16; 3.39.14–15). The Christians mentioned in 4:21 should have been able to provide for Paul's physical needs. So here we should probably think of Mark's "ministry" of evangelism.

As an afterthought, Pastoral Paul reports another deployment, **And I sent Tychicus to Ephesus** (4:12). Tychicus (cf. Titus 3:12) was from Asia (Eph. 6:21; Col. 4:7; Acts 20:4), which may explain why Paul sent him there.

Returning to directions for Timothy, **when you come, bring the cloak that I left in Troas with Carpus, and the scrolls, specifically the parchments** (4:13). Carpus is unknown. Paul passed through Troas several times on his travels between Asia and Macedonia (Acts 16:8, 11; 20:5, 6; 2 Cor. 2:12), but there is no correlation between this verse and any of those trips. The word "cloak" (*phailonēs*) appears only here in the NT, but it is known from papyri (Dibelius and Conzelmann 1972, 123). It was a heavy, woolen outer garment resembling a poncho. Some have imagined Paul shivering in a cold cell, although Luke and others might have brought warm clothing.

The word "scrolls" (*biblia*), strictly speaking, refers to relatively inexpensive papyrus rolls but could apply to other materials also. "Parchment" (*membrana*), made from finely tanned animal skins, was expensive and, just as today, was reserved for important documents produced by professional scribes. Whether we translate the adverb *malista* as "specifically" (Skeat 1979) or "especially" (Poythress 2002; Kim 2004) is of little consequence here (but cf. 1 Tim. 4:10; 5:17). Whether "parchments" are the only scrolls Pastoral Paul has in mind, they are clearly the primary objects of his concern. We can only speculate as to what parchment scrolls Paul might have owned—Torah? Psalms? Isaiah? other(s)? In any case, this passage presents Paul as a model of lifelong devotion to study (cf. 3:10–17; 1 Tim. 4:13).

Alexander the bronze-smith made a show of much harm to me. The LORD will recompense him in accordance with his work. You also guard against him, for he strenuously opposed our words (4:14–15). The identity of "Alexander" is unclear. If he was the same Alexander condemned in 1 Tim. 1:20 along with Hymenaeus, then he was at one time under Paul's guidance. Alternatively, he might have been the Jewish Alexander who tried in vain to address the Ephesian riot (Acts 19:33–34; Trebilco 2008, 160–61, 169–70). Although Acts neither refers to Alexander as a "bronze-smith" nor mentions that he took any action against Paul, the reference in 2 Tim. 4:14 would be compatible with the sort of synagogue opposition to Paul described in Acts and alluded to in 2 Tim. 3:11. Or this could be some other Alexander about whom we have no other information.

"The LORD will recompense him in accordance with his work" is a quotation (Pss. 62:12; 28:4; Prov. 24:12). This is a regular theme in early Christian eschatology (Matt. 16:27; 1 Pet. 1:17; Rev. 2:23; 18:6; 20:12–13; 22:12), reflecting a Jewish understanding of judgment (Pss. 28:4; 62:12; Prov. 24:12; Jer. 17:10; 32:19; 50:15, 29; Job 34:11; *T. Levi* 3.2; *Pss. Sol.* 9.5; N. T. Wright 2013, 1087). It is also Pauline (Rom. 2:6; 2 Cor. 5:10; 11:15) and calls to mind the accounting language in Philippians. When Paul entered into "partnership" with the Philippians, he could not repay their "investment" in him, but he expressed confidence that God would "fill every need" (Phil. 4:14–20; Sampley 1980). So also here, Pastoral Paul expects that in the end God will settle accounts, and Alexander will receive "payback" for his deeds. There is no need for

Timothy to take action against Alexander, but he should "guard" against a possible new attack.

Having described the movements of others, Pastoral Paul reports on his own circumstances. **In my first defense, not one was with me, but all abandoned me. May it not be counted against them. But the Lord was with me and empowered me, so that through me the proclamation was multiplied, and all the gentiles heard it, and I was delivered from the mouth of the lion. The Lord will deliver me from every evil work and will save me into his heavenly kingdom, to whom be glory forever and ever, amen** (4:16–18). These verses recall Phil. 1, where Paul contemplated possible execution with equanimity and expressed joy that his imprisonment afforded an opportunity for evangelism.

We should not take the "mouth of the lion" (4:17) literally. From the second and third centuries we read dramatic stories of Christians dying—or being miraculously delivered—in the arena (*Mart. Pol.*; *Acts of Paul* 3), including a fantastic tale about Paul's encounter with a lion at Ephesus (*Acts of Paul* 7). That tale is a fiction possibly inspired by this verse. There is no evidence that any Jesus followers were thrown to beasts in the first century. The "lion" is a figure of speech. In Jewish apocalyptic tradition, pagans who oppress the people of God are represented as wild animals (Dan. 7:2–8, 17; *1 En.* 85–90; Rev. 13). In this context pertaining to Paul's imprisonment and trial, the "lion" is a covert allusion to the Roman Empire (cf. 1 Pet. 5:8; Josephus, *Ant.* 18.228; N. Beck 2010, 80–81).

On the other hand, if "delivered from the mouth of the lion" means that Paul was acquitted, what happened next? On the basis of this reference to a "first defense," some have imagined that Paul was released (going west to Spain or east to Ephesus and Crete?) before being rearrested, and he wrote this letter from a supposed second Roman imprisonment, when he was finally executed (Eusebius, *Hist. eccl.* 2.22, 25). This would explain why he says Luke is with him now (4:11), although "at my first defense no one was with me" (4:16). Alternatively, "delivered" could mean he was not summarily executed, though he remained a prisoner. J. N. D. Kelly (1963, 218) suggests the first trial was inconclusive and required a second.

But we must notice the same verb in 4:18, where Paul clearly does not think he will escape death. He expects to be executed but is confident that "the Lord will deliver . . . and save me into his heavenly kingdom." A third possibility, then, is that "I was delivered" (4:17) is an ironic way of saying that the "lion" pronounced a death sentence, not realizing that Paul's death would be his eternal "salvation." On this interpretation, either "no one was with me" (4:16) is hyperbole, or "Luke alone is with me" (4:11) indicates that, though he was not with Paul at the trial, Luke is now with him as he awaits execution.

The hope of salvation gives rise to a doxology, "to whom be glory for ever and ever, amen" (4:18; cf. 1 Tim. 1:17; Rom. 11:36; 16:27; Gal. 1:5; Phil. 4:20;

Heb. 13:21; 4 Macc. 18:24; cf. Eph. 3:21; 1 Pet. 4:11; 2 Pet. 3:18; Jude 25; Rev. 1:6), which ends this part of the closing.

Greetings (4:19–21)

4:19–21. The second element of the letter closing is personal greetings, which are here mixed with additional travel reports. **Greet Prisca and Aquila and the household of Onesiphorus** (4:19). Prisca and Aquila were Jews from Pontus, who apparently converted to Christianity in Rome (Acts 18:2; Lampe 2003, 11–13) and became leaders of churches first in Corinth (Acts 18:2–3), later in Ephesus (1 Cor. 16:19; Acts 18:26), then back in Rome (Rom. 16:3–5). Onesiphorus is known in the NT only in this letter (1:16), but tradition identifies him as a resident of Iconium in Phrygia (*Acts of Paul* 3.1–7, 15, 26, 42). If this is a genuine letter from Paul, we must suppose that Prisca and Aquila have moved once again to wherever Timothy is now, perhaps Iconium (see "Introduction to 2 Timothy"). If the letter is pseudonymous, then for verisimilitude the author may have inserted names of associates of Paul known from other sources with or without accurate knowledge of their movements.

Erastus remained in Corinth, and I left Trophimus in Miletus, because he was sick (4:20). Paul had associates named Erastus in Corinth (Rom. 16:23) and Trophimus in Asia (Acts 20:4). The verse almost seems to reflect Paul's final trip to Jerusalem from Greece (Acts 20:2) by way of Miletus (Acts 20:15), except that Trophimus went on to Jerusalem with Paul (Acts 21:29). So once again we cannot correlate this letter with Paul's movements as recorded elsewhere in the NT.

See to it that you come before winter (4:21). The urgency (cf. 4:9) is not only a matter of receiving the cloak and scrolls (4:13) but also of receiving Timothy at all, because travel in winter would be difficult by land and practically impossible by sea.

Eubulus greets you, and Pudens and Linus and Claudia and all the brothers (4:21). It is not clear who these four people were, but later tradition may help. First, Eubulus is otherwise unknown. Second, the legendary *Acts of Pudentiana and Praxedis*, of uncertain date, recounts the martyrdom of two sisters, daughters of a wealthy Roman presbyter named Pudens, a disciple of Peter, who donated his house as the meeting place for a church in Rome. Third, early Christian tradition identifies one Linus as the second bishop of Rome after Peter, and Irenaeus was the first to connect our passage with that Linus (Irenaeus, *Haer.* 3.3.3; Eusebius, *Hist. eccl.* 3.2; 5.6). Fourth, later tradition identifies Claudia as a relative of Linus (*Apostolic Constitutions* 7.46). "All the brothers" suggests that these four were leaders of one or more congregations. The later traditions about these people, along with the reference to Prisca and Aquila, provide circumstantial evidence that Paul wrote this letter—or a pseudonymous author imagined Paul writing—from Rome, shortly before he died.

Benediction (4:22)

4:22. The final element of the closing is the benediction, **The Lord be with your** [sg.] **spirit** (4:22a). But there is a second benediction, **Grace be with you** [pl.] (4:22b). The plural "you" is surprising at the end of a letter written entirely to "you" in the singular. The same benediction, appended to all three PE (1 Tim. 6:21b; Titus 3:15), gives the impression that these letters were either composed as a collection or edited into a collection.

Titus

Introduction to Titus

Genre

The contents of this letter are paraenetic (see "Genre" in the general introduction) and significantly overlap with those of 1 Timothy. Even though the
following commentary will attend to the integrity of this letter, we shall notice
details that link it to 1 and 2 Timothy, so that the three letters form a distinct
collection within the NT.

In form, Titus somewhat resembles ancient administrative letters (see "Introduction to 1 Timothy"), but that form is truncated. An administrative
letter normally contained a description of the circumstances leading up to a
"therefore," followed by some directive(s) (see the introduction to 1 Timothy).
This letter lacks any real proem describing the circumstances, but the phrase
"as I ordered you" (1:5) suggests prior oral directives.

The body of the letter begins and ends with charges to Titus to deal with the
bad behavior of certain Christian teachers in Crete (1:5–16; 3:8b–11; similarly,
Van Neste 2004, 273–82). The opening charge directs Titus to "correct what
is lacking" and "appoint elders" (1:5) and to "reprove" bad teachers (1:13).
The closing charge directs him "to affirm" (3:3) correct doctrine that leads
to good behavior, to "avoid" (3:9) the sources of bad doctrine and behavior,
and to "reject" (3:10) anyone who does not abandon those bad sources and
bad practices. Between these two charges are directives to instruct about right
conduct of various members of the household of God (2:1–10) and submission
to authorities (3:1–2). Those instructions are grounded in a robust Christology,
expressed in two quotations of traditional (hymnic?) material (2:11–14; 3:4–8a).

Addressee

Like Timothy, Titus was one of Paul's trusted coworkers (2 Cor. 8:16, 23). He was the test case for a tense theological dispute over circumcision in Jerusalem (Gal. 2:1–10). And twice Paul sent him to deal with difficult situations in Corinth (2 Cor. 2:13; 7:6, 13–14; 8:6; 12:18). Although this letter does not explicitly describe Titus as youthful, Pastoral Paul addresses him as "my true child" (1:4; cf. 1 Tim. 1:2), and his peer group is the "younger men" (Titus 2:7). So, like 1 Timothy, this letter appears to be from an older mentor to a younger protégé.

Crete

The letter addresses Titus on Crete (1:5). We know little about early Christianity on Crete. The Romans administered Crete and Cyrenaica jointly as one province, with administrative centers at Gortyn and Cyrene. Crete was the more economically significant half of the two-part province (Chevrollier 2016; Lippolis 2016). The Romans colonized Knossos, but Roman culture did not overwhelm Greek culture on the island (Sweetman 2007; Baldwin Bowsky 2016). Some have argued that details in the letter resonate with the peculiar culture of Crete (Pietersen 2004; Wieland 2005; Spencer 2013; see comments at 1:5, 12), although most of the alleged connections are tenuous and seem broadly applicable to many geographical contexts. The letter fits comfortably in the hybrid cultural context of the Greek-speaking eastern half of the Roman Empire, including but not limited to Crete.

An Outline of Titus

Letter opening (1:1–4)

Directive 1: Community leaders (1:5–16)

Appoint elders (1:5–9)

Explanation of the need (1:10–16)

Directive 2: Instructions for the community (2:1–15)

Healthy teaching for the household of God (2:1–10)

Christological warrant (2:11–14)

Reiteration of directive (2:15)

Directive 3: More instructions for the community (3:1–11)

Submission to authorities (3:1–2)

Empathetic and christological warrants (3:3–8a)

Closing summative charge (3:8b–11)

Letter closing (3:12–15)

Titus 1:1–4

Letter Opening

Introductory Matters

Verses 1–4 follow the standard form of Greco-Roman letter opening: "Author(s) to Addressee(s), greeting," but here the author's self-identification is greatly expanded. In an administrative letter (see "Introduction to 1 Timothy"), we expect the author to include his official titles (Kidson 2014), but even so this opening is lengthy. Among the Pauline letters only Romans offers a longer author identification, since he had not yet visited Rome. When his authority was challenged, Paul emphasized his apostolic authority (1 Cor. 1:1; 2 Cor. 1:1; Gal. 1:1–2). When writing to friends, he did not explain who he was (1 Thess. 1:1; Phil. 1:1; Philem. 1). Here it is surprising that "Paul," in a personal letter to a longtime associate, belabors his apostolic commission (cf. 2 Tim. 1:1–2).

One explanation is that this letter aims at a secondary audience who did not know Paul, youthful ministers of later generations for whom the "Paul" of this letter functions as an epistolary mentor. Perhaps also this opening serves as the introduction to a three-letter collection, and the author expected us to read Titus before 1–2 Timothy (see "Genre" in the general introduction). These explanations are not mutually exclusive and not dependent on the question of authorship.

Missing from this letter is the thanksgiving that usually appears at the beginning of a Pauline letter. The overall tone is businesslike, certainly not as warm as 2 Timothy.

> **Titus 1:1–4**
> **in the Rhetorical Flow**
>
> ▶ Letter opening (1:1–4)

213

Tracing the Train of Thought

1:1–4. Paul, slave of God and apostle of Jesus Christ for the sake of the faith of God's elect and knowledge of truth that is in accordance with piety, for hope of eternal life, which the God who is not false promised before times eternal, and when the times were right he manifested his word in the proclamation, with which I was entrusted at the injunction of God our Savior (1:1–3). "For the sake of" indicates the purpose (BDAG 512, s.v. κατά B.4) of Paul's apostolic commission, to produce "faith" and "knowledge of the truth that is in accordance with piety." To the extent that the PE co-opt the Greco-Roman ideal of "piety" (see sidebar at 1 Tim. 2:2), this statement is apologetic. Christian truth is consistent with the Greco-Roman virtue of "piety" (2:12; see comments at 1 Tim. 2:2, 10) but distinct in that it is oriented toward the "hope of eternal life" (cf. 2:13) in the age to come (cf. 3:7; 1 Tim. 4:8; 6:12; 2 Tim. 2:9–13).

Reference to "the God who is not false" (*ho apseudēs theos*) sets an appropriate tone for the themes of truth, falsehood, and deception in the following section (1:5–16). Pastoral Paul denounces "deceivers" (1:10) and "liars" (*pseustai*, 1:12) and presents himself as champion of the truth (1:13–14). If this letter is pseudonymous, this appellation is highly ironic, a painfully "shrill"—but successful—attempt to appear authentic (J. Marshall 2008, 789; on transparent forgery, see "Author" in the general introduction).

The idea of being entrusted with a proclamation "at the injunction [*kat' epitagēn*] of God" is consistent with Paul's usage of this word for a divine command (1 Cor. 7:6, 25; 2 Cor. 8:8), here applied to Paul's apostolic commission (cf. 1 Tim. 1:1). Compare a second-century inscription dedicated to the goddess Nemesis "at (her) injunction" (*kat' epitagēn*; *NewDocs* 2:§49).

The second part of the letter opening is the identification of the addressee: **to Titus, a true child in accordance with a common faith** (1:4a). The appellation "true child" (cf. 1 Tim. 1:2) is not found in the undisputed Pauline letters but reflects how Paul related to his converts as a "father" to his "children" (1 Cor. 4:15; 2 Cor. 6:13; Gal. 4:19; 1 Thess. 2:11–12).

Finally, the letter opening contains a greeting: **grace and peace from God our Father and Christ Jesus our Savior** (1:4b). Some ancient scribes inserted "mercy" between "grace" and "peace" in an apparent attempt to make this greeting consistent with those of 1 Timothy and 2 Timothy. That change provides additional circumstantial evidence that scribes thought of the PE as a set.

Titus 1:5–16

Directive 1: Community Leaders

Introductory Matters

The overarching charge is "to correct what is lacking" (1:5), and all other directives in the letter are more specific, mainly instructions for the Christian community (2:1–3:8a).

The passage falls into two paragraphs that draw a contrast between the desirable behaviors expected of Christian elders (1:5–9) and the undesirable behaviors of bad teachers (1:10–16). Elders are needed because (*gar*, for, 1:10) the behavior of certain bad teachers (no mention of their doctrine) is creating havoc for the community. Elders must hew to the "faithful teaching" and be able to "exhort with sound doctrine and reprove" (1:9). Likewise, Titus is to "reprove them unceasingly, so that they may be sound in the faith" (1:13; cf. "exhort and reprove," 2:15). In other words, Titus will appoint elders who are equipped to do the same work he is doing and are able to carry on after he leaves.

> **Titus 1:5–16 in the Rhetorical Flow**
>
> Letter opening (1:1–4)
> ► Directive 1: Community leaders (1:5–16)
>   Appoint elders (1:5–9)
>   Explanation of the need (1:10–16)

The opening charge to Titus is balanced by the closing charge (3:8b–11). These two charges frame the instructions that Titus is to deliver to the community.

Tracing the Train of Thought

Appoint Elders (1:5–9)

1:5–9. For the sake of this, I left you in Crete (1:5). "I left you" seems to imply that Paul and Titus had been together in Crete, although this letter does not correlate with travels known from Acts or other Pauline letters. Also, the closing greetings (3:15) do not name any individuals, which is surprising if Paul had been there. Those who assume Paul wrote this letter must argue that we do not know many of Paul's movements over some three decades (Johnson 2001, 61–62) and/or that "I left you in Crete" expresses an administrative appointment by letter and not a recollection of prior travels (Porter 2013, 68). Those who read the letter as pseudonymous treat the Crete scenario as fictional.

The letter body opens with "for the sake of this," which points forward to the charge that follows. The reason for Titus to be in Crete is **so that you might further correct what is lacking and appoint elders in every city** [*kata polin*], **as I ordered you** (1:5). The phrase, "as I ordered you" points back to the charge just stated and suggests previous oral direction. The charge is "that you might further correct." The particular form of the verb "further correct" with its double prefixes (*epi-di-orthoō*) occurs only here in the NT, but the root "correct" (*ortho-*) is part of Pastoral Paul's vocabulary of instruction (2 Tim. 2:15; 3:16). The second prefix (*epi-*) has the force of "further," or "in addition" (Wackernagel 2009, 687), which is appropriate for this charge that supplements whatever charge Paul had previously given.

The phrase translated "in every city" (*kata polin*, 1:5) is ambiguous. The preposition *kata* could be a marker of relationship, "with respect to" (BDAG 513, s.v. κατά B.6). R. Alastair Campbell (1994a, 197) translates, "appoint elders *at the city level*," by which he understands a contrast with the majority of elders, whom he sees as the heads of families, leaders of churches "at the house level" (*kat' oikon*, Rom. 16:5; 1 Cor. 16:19; Col. 4:15; Philem. 2). For Campbell (1994a, 201–2), the new post of overseer "at the city level" places these letters on a trajectory toward the monepiscopacy that Ignatius takes for granted (cf. Aageson 2008, 123–40). But monepiscopacy is not otherwise attested before the time of Ignatius. Those who date this letter to the first century, therefore, may prefer to read *kata* as a marker of places viewed serially, "in every city" (BDAG 512, s.v. κατά B.1.d; Luke 8:1; Acts 15:36), which reflects the Pauline practice of traveling from town to town and appointing elders "in every church" (*kat' ekklēsian*, Acts 14:23).

The list of desirable qualities is rhetorically sophisticated. The antithetic style (not this, but that) is typical of paraenesis (Isocrates, *Demon.* 9–11; Seneca, *Ep.* 52.8; 1 Thess. 2:3–8; Malherbe 2005, 338). Pastoral Paul creates assonance by using prefixes, including *a-* (*asōtias, anypotakta*) and *phil-* (*philoxenon, philagathon*; for similar strings of *phil-* prefixes, cf. Dio Chrysostom, *Or.* 4.84 [in a vice list]; *CIJ* 1:321, 363 = *JIWE* 2:171, 127 [in virtue lists on tombstones]). Such a rhetorical device is effective for describing character types but not for describing the polity of the community.

Do we have two lists, one describing elders (1:6) and the other describing an overseer (1:7–8)? Or should we take all of 1:6–8 as a single list describing an overseer? A natural reading is to take 1:6 as describing an ideal elder, following the charge in 1:5, and to take the awkward switch from plural to singular as a quirk of the author's style (e.g., 1 Tim. 2:11–12, 15). Further, the analogy between father and household manager closely connects 1:7 with 1:6. We could understand "elders" and "overseer" as interchangeable terms (cf. Acts 20:17, 28; 1 Pet. 5:1–2) for which 1:6–8 constitutes a single list of desirable qualities. Comparison of this list with the one in 1 Tim. 3:2–7 supports such a reading. But we should note that 1 Tim. 5:17–25 treats elders as distinguishable from the overseer.

If anyone is blameless, husband of one wife, having faithful children, not susceptible to a charge of dissolution or insubordination. For it is necessary for the overseer to be blameless as God's household manager, not impudent, not irascible, not a drunkard, not violent, not after shameful gain, but devoted to guests, devoted to good, temperate, just, reverent, self-controlled, holding fast to the trustworthy word that is in accordance with the instruction, so that he may be able to exhort in the healthy teaching and to reprove those who speak against (1:6–9). This list of qualities is comparable primarily with the list in 1 Timothy for an overseer (1 Tim. 3:2–7), and to some extent with lists for deacons (1 Tim. 3:8–13) and widows (1 Tim. 5:9–10). Regarding overseers, both lists begin with a general idea that is repeated: "blameless . . . blameless" (Titus 1:6, 7) or "unimpeachable, . . . having a good reputation" (1 Tim. 3:2, 7), so these become the overarching ideas under which the other qualities are specific examples. Aquinas took "blameless" in a narrow legal sense, "without crime" (Aquinas, *Comm. Titus* 1.2.10, 13 [Baer 2007, 11, 12]). Surely an overseer should do nothing illegal, but the rest of the list suggests that Christian leaders should uphold higher standards. The specifics fall in no particular order but represent moral qualities of an exemplary head of God's metaphorical household (Titus 1:6–8; 1 Tim. 3:2–5), all aimed at an effective response to criticism from outsiders (Titus 1:9; 1 Tim. 3:6–7).

The two lists vary but with significant overlap. Below I list qualities in Titus 1 that are essentially equivalent to qualities in 1 Tim. 3. The two lists present qualities in different sequence, so we cannot discern an order of importance. Missing from the list in Titus are that an overseer should be a person of decorum (1 Tim. 3:2), tolerant (1 Tim. 3:3), dignified (1 Tim. 3:4, 8, 11), and experienced (1 Tim. 3:6, 10). Titus 1 includes some qualities not mentioned in 1 Tim. 3, which we shall examine below. These observations establish that each list is representative and neither is exhaustive.

Most of the following terms are identical between Titus 1 and 1 Tim. 3, and readers may consult the commentary on 1 Tim. 3 for discussion. Where the terms are not identical but synonymous, I have supplied the Greek, so that readers may judge whether the difference is significant.

Titus 1	1 Timothy 3
"without reproach" (*anenklētos*, 1:6)	"unimpeachable" (*anepilēmptos*, 3:2)
"husband of one wife" (1:6)	"husband of one wife" (3:2)
"not irascible" (*mē orgilos*, 1:7)	"not combative" (*amaxos*, 3:3)
"not given to wine" (1:7)	"not given to wine" (3:3; cf. 3:8)
"not violent" (1:7)	"not violent" (3:3)
"not after shameful gain" (*mē aischrokerdēs*, 1:7)	"not devoted to money" (*aphilargyros*, 3:3; cf. *mē aischrokerdēs*, 3:8)
"hospitable" (1:8)	"hospitable" (3:2; cf. 1 Tim. 5:10)
"temperate" (1:8)	"temperate" (3:2)
"self-controlled" (*enkratēs*, 1:8)	"sober" (*nēphalios*, 3:2, 11)

An additional point of comparison is the relation between a church leader and a good parent. The one who has "faithful" children, defined as "not open to a charge of dissolution, not insubordinate" (1:6), is prepared by analogy to serve as "God's household manager" (*oikonomos*, 1:7). God is the estate owner and head of household, while the overseer manages on the owner's behalf (see comments at 1 Tim. 1:4; 3:5; "Introductory Matters" at 1 Tim. 3:1–13; Malherbe 2012).

Titus 1 mentions four qualities not listed in 1 Tim. 3. The overseer should not be "impudent" (*authadēs*, 1:7), a word otherwise found in the NT only at 2 Pet. 2:10, where it is associated with "despising authority," "audacious," and "having no qualms about slandering the glorious ones." Josephus uses this word to criticize the insolent attitude of the slave Hagar toward Sarah (*Ant.* 1.189) and of a youth toward a parent (*Ant.* 4.263). An overseer who presumes authority, forgetting that God is the householder, will be a poor leader.

An overseer should be "devoted to good" (*philagathos*, 1:8). Although Pastoral Paul sometimes uses two Greek words for "good" interchangeably (see comments at Titus 3:1), here the focus is on what has intrinsic worth (*agathos*) and is not merely attractive in appearance (*kalos*). Elsewhere Pastoral Paul uses *agathos* when he exhorts young women (Titus 2:5), young men (Titus 2:10), the community in general (Titus 3:1), women (1 Tim. 2:10), widows (1 Tim. 5:10), rich men (1 Tim. 6:18), and Timothy (2 Tim. 2:21). Doing "every good work" is a mark of a "person of God" (2 Tim. 2:21; 3:17), and not doing "every good work" is a mark of a bad teacher (Titus 1:16).

An overseer should be "just" (*dikaios*; cf. 1 Tim. 1:9). The Christ story teaches believers to live "justly" (Titus 2:12). From a Jewish perspective, it might seem more apt to translate this word as "righteous," but the entire list in 1:7–9 seems calculated to resonate with a Greek sense of virtue. Certainly, any ancient rabbi would endorse every virtue in this list. It is not a matter of taking moral cues from Greek philosophy but of expressing ideals in language that gentiles will recognize and approve.

And the overseer should be "reverent" (*hosios*; cf. 1 Tim. 1:9; 2 Tim. 3:2). Some translate this as "holy" (cf. 1 Tim. 2:8), but the preferred word for "holy" in the LXX is *hagios*. The word *hosios* resonates with Greco-Roman sensibilities, being closely associated with piety (Hoklotubbe 2017, 170–72).

The "trustworthy word" (*pistos logos*) is the christological tradition quoted in 3:4–7, identified there as a "trustworthy saying" (*pistos logos*, 3:8; cf. 2 Tim. 2:11–13) and elsewhere as a "deposit" (1 Tim. 6:20; 2 Tim. 1:12, 14). The word "instruction" (*didachē*, cf. Rom. 6:17) calls to mind an ancient church manual titled *The Instruction* [*didachē*] *of the Lord to the Gentiles through the Twelve Apostles*, written about the end of the first century and known simply as the *Didache*. We need not assume Pastoral Paul had read the *Didache*, but the advice in Titus 1 fits comfortably into the social context reflected in that manual. And the phrase "in accordance with the instruction" suggests that the "trustworthy word" is a matter of tradition, as in 3:4–8a.

To "reprove" (*elenchō*, Titus 1:9) is to prove false by cross-examination and counterevidence (see comments at 1 Tim. 5:20). Elsewhere in the PE this is a duty of Paul's delegates (cf. 1 Tim. 5:20; 2 Tim. 4:2; Titus 1:13; 2:15), and only here is it the duty of an overseer. As to the identity of the opponents, literally, "those who speak against," the immediate context (1:10–11) suggests Christian teachers who are "insubordinate" (cf. comments on 1 Tim. 1:9) and "speak against" the approved leaders (cf. comments on 1 Tim. 2:12), while the larger context suggests outsiders who "speak against" Christianity (2:5, 8, 10; cf. 1 Tim. 3:7; 5:14; 6:1).

Pastoral Paul offers no logical proofs against the opponents. Instead, he emphasizes the source of correct doctrine (1:9) and the exemplary behavior of the elder/overseer (1:6–8), which we could take either as constituting the substance of the reproof or as the prerequisite, without which logical argument would be unconvincing. Either way, this verse is comparable to 1 Tim. 3:7, where the overseer's conduct is essential to refuting the slanderer.

Explanation of the Need (1:10–16)

1:10–16. For there are many insubordinate, worthless talkers and deceivers, especially [or specifically] those of the circumcision, whose mouths must be stopped, who are upsetting whole households, teaching what they ought not for the sake of shameful gain (1:10–11). The conjunction "for" (*gar*, 1:10) marks this paragraph as explaining the reason for the prior directives about elders. But it is also the context for the instruction to the community in the rest of the letter, as is clear from the closing charge (3:8b–11). Elders, and all faithful Christians, should avoid behaving like these "insubordinate" teachers whose shameful behavior invites criticism from outsiders.

Whether the adverb *malista* means "specifically" (Skeat 1979) or "especially" (Poythress 2002; Kim 2004) is of little consequence here (but cf. 1 Tim. 4:10; 5:17). Whether "those of the circumcision" are the only group Pastoral Paul opposes or one of several, they are his primary targets, and he does not identify others.

The appellation "those of the circumcision" could refer to advocates of circumcision (Gal. 2:12), regardless of their ethnicity, or it could refer to people who were ethnically Jewish (Col. 4:11), regardless of their doctrine. The translation "circumcision *party*" (RSV) may go too far in presuming the former. Jews were in Crete (Acts 2:11; Josephus, *Ant.* 17.327; *J.W.* 2.103; Philo, *Embassy* 282), probably since the mid-second century BCE (1 Macc. 15:23; van der Horst 1988, 183–86). So the community of Jesus followers likely included both gentiles and Jews. If this is intra-Jewish polemic, the verse reflects the hyperbolic rhetoric that groups often use to define themselves against others close to them (Dunn 1993, 460–61, 469). The point that the false teachers were "insubordinate" indicates that they were Christians, whether Torah-observant Jewish Christians or gentile Christians who held a muddled understanding of Jewish and/or Christian faith. Either way, polemical rhetoric does not easily translate across cultures, and this verse provides no justification for anti-Semitic prejudice on the part of modern-day Christians.

As for the "insubordinate" teachers, Pastoral Paul only hints at their sources (1:14; 3:9) and says nothing about their doctrine. The complaint is against their conduct. The accusation "insubordinate" (*anypotaktoi*, 1:10) recalls those in 2 Thess. 3:11 whose "disorderly" (*ataktōs*) walk entailed not working and expecting the community to feed them. The "insubordinate" teachers are motivated by "shameful gain" (Titus 1:11; cf. 1:7; 1 Tim. 6:5), so that their deeds belie their confession (1:16). In a similar vein, Seneca criticized those who studied philosophy "as if it were some marketable trade" and whose behavior did not correspond to their words (*Ep.* 108.36, trans. Gummere, LCL). The *Didache* warns that, if a traveling missionary "asks for money, he is a false prophet" (11.6; cf. 11.12). One may tell a true from a false prophet "from their behaviors" (*Did.* 11.8).

Interpreters understand the false teaching in different ways. The translation "teaching what is not necessary" (Genade 2011, 33) would imply that these things are optional, perhaps frivolous (cf. "worthless talk," 1:10; cf. 1 Tim. 5:13). But the majority translate Titus 1:11 as "teaching what they ought not," which implies teaching error (ESV, NIV, NRSV, etc.; cf. "swindlers," 1:10, and "whose mouths *must* be stopped," 1:11). Still, as to the nature of their error, we can only speculate.

One of their own, a prophet, said: "Cretans are always liars, evil beasts, lazy bellies." This testimony is true (1:12–13a). The source of the quotation is debated (Quinn 1990a, 107–9; I. H. Marshall 1999, 199–201). Theodore of Mopsuestia (*Comm. Titus* 243) attributed it to Callimachus (*Hymns* 1.4–9),

Figure 4. This photo shows the modern-day city of Heraklion, Crete, with Mount Juktas in the background.

but Callimachus was quoting Epimenides (Hopkinson 1984, 140). Clement of Alexandria (*Strom.* 1.14 [59]; cf. Augustine, *Leg.* 2.4, 13) identified the "prophet" as Epimenides, a sixth-century-BCE poet and religious figure, the subject of legendary lore, who came to Athens from Crete, hence, "one of their own" (Dodds 1951, 141–42; Rothschild 2014, 37–49). Epimenides's poem has survived only in Syriac translation, from which J. Rendel Harris reconstructed a hypothetical Greek text and English translation (J. Harris 1907; cf. Acts 17:28). Epimenides accused the Cretans of being "liars"

"Cretan Liars"

"They fashioned a tomb for thee, O holy and high one
The Cretans, always liars, evil beasts, idle bellies!
But thou art not dead: thou livest and abidest forever,
For in thee we live and move and have our being."
　　(Epimenides, *Cretica* 1–4, trans. J. Rendel Harris)

"'Cretans are ever liars.' Yea, a tomb, O Lord, for thee
The Cretans builded; but thou didst not die, for thou art forever."
　　(Callimachus, *Hymn to Zeus* 8–9, trans. Mair and Mair, LCL)

---

because they perpetrated a myth that Zeus had died and that they had built a tomb for him (Lucian, *Timon* 6; Callimachus, *Hymns* 1.8–9; Clement of Alexandria, *Protr.* 2; Origen, *Cels.* 3.34). Indeed, the Bronze-Age Minoans venerated Mount Juktas, near Knossos, as the head of Zeus in repose. Callimachus extended the Cretan lie beyond the claim that Zeus died on Crete to the claim that he was born on the island rather than on the mainland in Arcadia (Hopkinson 1984), which makes his claim of Cretan "liars" a slur in a game of ethnic one-upmanship.

To add to the rhetorical complexity, Pastoral Paul is deploying the famous "liar's paradox": If a Cretan says all Cretans are liars, is he telling the truth or lying? We must consider how proverbial liars, beasts, and lazy bellies fit into the argument. This famous conundrum confounded philosophical novices in antiquity (Seneca, *Ep.* 45.10; Epictetus, *Diatr.* 2.17.34; 2.18.18; 2.21.17; 3.9.21; Plutarch, *Comm. not.* 2 [1059d]).

George M. Wieland (2005, 347–49) argues that "beasts" (*thēria*) is particularly apt since Cretans organized young men into "herds" for military training, and those youths were devoted to Artemis, the "Mistress of Beasts" (*thērōn*). This reading is tenuous, however, because (a) Crete was "beastless" (*atheros*, Plutarch, *Inim. util.* 1 [86c]; cf. Pliny the Elder, *Nat.* 8.83); (b) the word "herd" (*agelē*) normally referred to domestic animals, which suggests that Cretans viewed their youths like "herds" of horses or oxen, not wild beasts; (c) "Mistress of Beasts" was a standard epithet of Artemis hardly unique to Crete (Homer, *Iliad* 21.470); and (d) Wieland's interpretation of votive figurines of youthful soldiers found in Gortyn is speculative. Furthermore, (e) information about the Cretan "herds" of youths comes from Strabo (*Geography* 10.4.16), who was describing the origins of some Cretan customs in the Bronze Age under the legendary Minos and admits that society was different in the Roman era (Strabo, *Geography* 10.4.22). In short, our passage would have been understandable to a Greek reader anywhere in the ancient Mediterranean world.

The better course is to read the quotation not within the cultural context of Crete but within the rhetorical argument of the letter as a whole. For Anthony C. Thiselton (1994) and Patrick Gray (2007), "this testimony is true" (1:13) is ironic, and the liar's paradox illustrates the sort of "worthless talk" (1:10; cf. 1 Tim. 1:6) and "foolish controversies" (3:9; cf. 1 Tim. 1:4; 6:3; 2 Tim. 2:23) that were the hallmark of bad philosophy teachers. For Troy Martin (2000, 13), the Epimenides quotation is a cipher to mark the opponents as any who "misrepresent the true nature of deity" (though I disagree with his conception that this letter promotes Marcionism). Riemer Faber (2005) offers the most straightforward reading, that the problem is not what the false teachers say but their rapacious greed and self-indulgence. A true prophet manifests the "ways of the Lord" (*Did.* 11.8), while a false prophet expects to benefit personally from the charity of the church (*Did.* 11.9).

Regrettably, many have taken "this testimony is true" as permission to perpetuate ancient stereotypes of Cretans as untrustworthy (Plutarch, *Lys.* 20.2) and greedy (Polybius, *Histories* 6.46.2–3, 9; 6.47.4–5). But taking 1:10–12 as an empirical statement on the nature of all Cretans leaves Pastoral Paul engaging in just the sort of speech that he decries—falsehood (1:12) and slander (2:3). It also urges upon Titus a slanderous stereotype that would hardly enhance his effectiveness among Cretans. Both "Jewish myths" and the Epimenides quotation reflect the sorts of stereotypes that ancient people routinely used to denigrate "others" (Stegemann 1996; cf. "gentile sinners," Gal. 2:15). Furthermore, "beasts" was a metaphor among philosophers for any people who lived according to their passions and desires (Lucian, *Fug.* 4; a crab's "whole body is a belly," Plutarch, *Adul. amic.* 9 [54b]). Harrill (2017) reads this passage in the context of second-century rhetorical debates: a one-liner from popular culture distinguishes Paul as an oracle of truth and purveyor of "healthy teaching" (1:9) as opposed to "worthless talkers" (1:10) whose pseudo-intellectual babble belies their self-serving motives (1:10).

Finally, we might recognize the quotation of a Cretan prophet as Cretan self-criticism in the way that the prophets of Israel offered ethical critiques of Israel. On that reading, the proverb would suggest an admirable "Cretan social and ethical consciousness" (Kidd 1999, 192). Before we get too judgmental, we might consider how we are all a little bit "Cretan" sometimes (see comments at 3:3).

For which reason, reprove them unceasingly, so that they may be healthy in the faith, not giving attention to Jewish myths and commandments of people who pervert the truth (1:13b–14). On the verb "reprove," see comments at 1:9; 1 Tim. 5:20. As Titus appoints elders, he is to reprove false teachers (1:11) "so that they may be healthy in the faith." This verse recalls "correct what is lacking" (1:5) and calls to mind instruction to Timothy on disciplining elders (1 Tim. 5:20–25). Despite the negative things said about them, Pastoral Paul assumes that Cretans can be corrected (cf. 2 Tim. 2:25).

The fact that some teachers are following "Jewish myths" (cf. "myths," 1 Tim. 1:4; 4:7; 2 Tim. 4:4) does not indicate whether they were Jewish (see comments at Titus 1:10; 1 Tim. 1:7) or what texts they were reading. The concern is not about false doctrines, only immoral behaviors.

"To the pure, all things are pure, but to those who are polluted and unfaithful nothing is pure," however [*alla*] their mind and conscience are polluted. They confess to know God, but by their deeds they deny him, because they are abominable and disobedient and counterfeit with regard to every good deed (1:15–16). The quotation (1:15) resembles an ancient maxim (Spicq 1969, 612; Dibelius and Conzelmann 1972, 138; Malherbe 2004, 305). The closest parallel is from the third century, "Nothing is bad for the good person, and nothing good for the bad" (Plotinus, *Enneads* 3.2.6), but similar proverbs appear in the first century: "The evil man turns everything into evil" (Seneca, *Ep.* 98.3; cf.

Philo, *Spec. Laws* 3.208–9); "The good man does everything right" (Seneca, *Ben.* 5.12.4). With this last example, Seneca cautions that we should not treat a proverb as an absolute truth.

Because of the word "pure," this proverb resembles a saying of Jesus on cups and plates (Luke 11:41) and a saying of Paul on kosher food (Rom. 14:20). Some have supposed, therefore, that Pastoral Paul is opposing dietary restrictions, perhaps a *kosher* diet in light of the reference to "Jewish myths and human commandments" (1:14). But, apart from the ambiguous 1 Tim. 4:3, diet is not an issue in the PE. Troy Martin suggests that the proverb does not represent Pastoral Paul's view but that the false teachers used it to justify libertinism and that the rebuttal begins with "however" (1:15c). He argues that Pastoral Paul presents the correct ethical perspective in 2:12 (T. Martin 2000, 16n40). Understood this way, our passage resembles 1 Cor. 6:12–20; 10:23–24, in which Paul quotes maxims that his opponents use as pseudo-philosophical justification for licentious behavior.

Theological Issues

Church Leadership

This passage, along with 1 Tim. 3:1–13, is a locus classicus for questions of church polity (see "Theological Issues" at 1 Tim. 3:1–13). A major issue is whether we should understand "overseer" and "elder" as interchangeable designations for the same function (Clement of Alexandria, *Quis div.* 42) or as two different offices (Ign. *Magn.* 3.1; *Trall.* 3.1). Interpreters from congregational traditions generally favor the former interpretation, while those from episcopal traditions favor the latter. But Pastoral Paul was not writing a handbook on church organization. This is a letter of exhortation on ministerial formation.

A hot topic in churches and seminaries these days is leadership. What makes a good leader? How do you develop good leaders? If you're interested in leadership development, take a long look at this chapter. First, make an honest assessment of yourself to be sure your ethics fit what Pastoral Paul is looking for. Second, as you seek to develop leaders in your church, do not look first for people with skills. Look first for people whose ethics are exemplary. Then teach them the skills they need.

Vilification of Enemies

A number of passages in the PE resort to invective against opponents (cf. 1 Tim. 1:3–11; 4:1–2; 6:3–5; 2 Tim. 4:3–4; Karris 1973). Anyone who has been the victim of negative stereotyping should wince (C. Martin 2007, 415–16, 433). Scholars spend much energy trying to identify some specific heretical movement and debating whether the PE unfairly stereotype that group. Is the present passage fair to Cretans, or for that matter, to the false teachers?

Beruriah Teaches: Hate the Sins, Not the Sinners

"There were some thugs in R. Meir's neighborhood, who gave him a lot of trouble. R. Meir prayed for mercy for himself so that they would die.

"His wife, Beruriah, said to him, 'What is on your mind? [Do you pray that they should die] *because it is written* [at Ps. 104:35], *"Let sins die"? Is it written "sinners"? What is written is "sins." And at the end of the verse, moreover, it is written, "And let wicked men be no more"* [Ps. 104:35]. *Since my sins will stop, there will be no more wicked men. Rather, pray for mercy concerning them that they will revert in repentance and not be wicked any more.'*

"He prayed for mercy concerning them, and they did revert in repentance."
(Babylonian Talmud, *Berakoth* 1.7 [10A], trans. Neusner)

On this point, the words of Beruriah are instructive. Beruriah was the wife of Rabbi Meir, a rabbi of the second century frequently quoted in the Mishnah. Beruriah was legendary for erudition, and later tradition embellished her legend for good and for ill (Ilan 1996, 197–200; Baskin 2002, 82–83). The Talmud (see sidebar) recounts when R. Meir prayed for God to have mercy on him by killing his tormentors. He prayed Psalm 104:35, "Let sinners [*ḥaṭṭāîm*] be consumed from the earth, and let wicked men be no more." The two clauses of this verse are traditionally understood as parallel. But Beruriah construed the Hebrew letters differently and prayed, "Let sins [*ḥěṭāîm*] be consumed from the earth." She interpreted the second clause not as parallel but as a result clause, "and (as a result) wicked men will be no more."

If, like Beruriah, we prayed for an end to sins rather than sinners, what would it mean to pray for God to have mercy on us? Elsewhere in the PE we read that Paul was shown mercy when he was a blasphemer, a persecutor, insolent, and "the foremost of sinners" (1 Tim. 1:13–16). In this letter, God's saving grace appeared to "us," even when we were characterized by impiety and worldly desires (Titus 2:11–12); and God saved "us," acting "in accordance with his mercy" (3:5), when we were "foolish, disobedient, deceived, slaves to desires and various pleasures, continuing in evil and envy, despicable, hating one another" (3:3). A vice list is not for fingering others but for self-examination.

As Titus appoints elders, he should look for those who exhibit the behaviors described in 1:6–9 and avoid those who exhibit behaviors described in 1:10–16. He should emulate the former and reprove the latter, so that those who practice such things "may become healthy in the faith" (1:13).

Alas, "liars, evil beasts, lazy gluttons" are not confined to Crete. When church leaders abuse their trust for sexual gratification or financial gain, they deny the very God they confess. Individuals and communities experience trauma from which they may never fully recover. Such leaders create a climate of self-indulgence that robs the cross of its power. The letter to Titus offers a timely critique of today's "prosperity gospel" (Bonnah 2008), not to mention clergy sexual predators. Good ministers should seek to cultivate in themselves and demand of church leaders a morality that is clearly seen to be and is in fact "blameless."

Titus 2:1–15

Directive 2: Instructions for the Community

Introductory Matters

After discussing church leaders, Pastoral Paul turns to the community as a whole in 2:1–3:11. The moral and christological language of this letter resembles that of 1 Peter, Ephesians, and Colossians, so as to suggest that all three letters were drawing from a common, early Christian tradition of baptismal catechesis (Hanson 1968, 78–96).

The Titus material is arranged in two parallel sections:

Titus 2:1–15	Titus 3:1–11
Command: "Tell" (2:1)	Command: "Remind" (3:1a)
Moral exhortations (2:2–10)	Moral exhortations (3:1b–3)
Christological tradition: Grace appeared Await the manifestation, . . . Jesus (2:11–14)	Christological tradition: Kindness and philanthropy appeared Heirs of eternal life (3:4–7)
Commands: Tell, exhort, reprove (2:15)	Commands: Affirm, avoid, turn away (3:8–11)

Chapter 2 unfolds in two closely linked sections. The first is a "station code" (2:1–10; Verner 1983) that offers instruction to specific groups in the community and resembles a Household Code (Eph. 5:21–6:9; Col. 3:18–4:1; 1 Pet. 2:18–3:7; Balch 1981). The second section (2:11–15) provides the theological warrant for the instruction in 2:2–10, as is clear from the explanatory "for" (2:11). The dense christological statement in 2:11–14 may be drawing on early Christian tradition (I. H. Marshall 1999, 263–64). The imperative "tell" (*lalei*) forms an inclusio (2:1, 15) that binds the two parts together (compare also *parakalei* in 2:6, 15). Two themes run through this section. First, "temperance" (*sōphro-*) that Titus is to instill in the community (2:2, 4, 6) reflects divine instruction (2:12). Second, concern for outsider criticism is expressed in three purpose clauses, "so that" (*hina*, 2:5, 8, 10). This concern is less obviously repeated in the second part, but see comment at 2:15.

Tracing the Train of Thought

*Healthy Teaching for the Household of God
(2:1–10)*

2:1–10. But as for you, tell what befits the healthy teaching (2:1). The verb "tell" governs all of 2:1–10, which is a checklist of groups in the community. The umbrella topic is "healthy teaching," elaborated in terms of appropriate behavior for each group. Some have argued on the basis of the matriarchal culture of Crete (Spencer 2013) or on the basis of patristic evidence (Ramelli 2010a) that "older men . . . older women" in 2:2–3 may refer to ordained male and female "elders/ presbyters." Among similar age groups in 1 Tim. 5:1–25 the "real widows" and "elder men" seem to refer to ordained functionaries, so we might keep the possibility in mind here. But the juxtaposition with younger women (2:4), younger men (2:6), and slaves (2:9) suggests that the primary referents are to age groups within God's "household" (1 Tim. 5:1–2; and see "Introductory Matters" for 5:1–6:2).

[Tell] **older men [or male elders?] to be sober, dignified, temperate, healthy in faith, love, steadfastness** (2:2). Elsewhere Pastoral Paul applies "sober" to the ideal overseer (1 Tim. 3:2). The basic idea is being not drunk (1 Tim. 3:11; cf. wine in 1 Tim. 3:3, 8; Titus 1:6; 2:3), but here it carries a larger connotation of sober mindedness (cf. 2 Tim. 4:5). Additional qualities desirable of church leaders are that they be "dignified" (1 Tim. 3:4, 8, 11) and "temperate" (1 Tim. 3:2; 2 Tim. 1:7), though temperance is also impressed upon all members of the community (Titus 2:4, 5, 6, 12; see comments at 1 Tim. 2:9, 15).

[Tell] **older women [or female elders?] likewise to be in their demeanor as is befitting priests, not slanderers, not enslaved to much wine, teaching what is admirable** (2:3). Again the issue is the demeanor of women (see comments on "order" and "decorum" at 1 Tim. 2:9). The point of the adjective "befitting priests" (cf. 4 Macc. 9:25) is that women who held priestly offices were expected to be paragons of virtue. Young Christian women should aspire to the highest moral ideals. The opposite of priestly women were stereotypical wealthy widows who had idle time for slanderous gossip and wine (see comments at 1 Tim. 3:11; 4:7; 5:13; cf. slander associated with apostates, 2 Tim. 3:2). Christian women should not provide opportunities for outsiders to cast them in that stereotype.

"Teaching what is admirable" (2:3) describes the duty of older women, **that they should train the younger women in temperance: to be devoted to husbands, devoted to children, temperate, holy, good homemakers, subordinated to their own husbands** (2:4). Annette Bourland Huizenga (2013, 271–72) argues that verse 4 is steering Titus away from dealing directly with the younger women, though given the social realities of the time, he would hardly have been in a position to deal with them anyway.

The common assumption was that older women had a duty to train younger women (e.g., Grapte in *Herm. Vis.* 2.4.3; Cyprian, *Hab. virg.* 24; Osiek and Balch 1997, 167–73; Osiek and M. MacDonald 2006, 90–92). Such training was sometimes institutionalized in religious cults of Venus (D'Ambra 2007, 172–76), but for a systematic statement of beliefs, the philosophers are more helpful. Five pseudonymous letters purportedly written by prominent Pythagorean women philosophers offer instruction to younger women in their roles as wives, mothers, and household managers (Huizenga 2009; 2013, 11–17, 117–27; Pomeroy 2013; see also sidebars at 1 Tim. 2:9 and 5:8). The letters make explicit that

> teaching ought to come from the older women [*presbyterai*] because they are forever giving advice about household management [*oikonomia*]. For it is good first to learn the things you do not know and to consider the counsel of the older women [*presbyterai*] the most suitable; for a young soul must be brought up in these teachings from girlhood. (ps.-Theano, *Call.* 1, trans. Huizenga 2013, 73)

And what do older women teach younger women? The verb "train in temperance" (*sōphronizō*, 2:4) is a heading for the list that follows. The qualities in 2:4–5 add up to an ancient ideal of a temperate woman (see comments at 1 Tim. 2:9). These topics read almost like a table of contents for the *Pythagorean Letters to Women*: older women teach younger women to be "devoted to their husbands" (ps.-Melissa, *Cl.*), even when the husbands cheat (ps.-Theano, *Nik.*); to be "devoted to their children"—that is, by choosing good nurses (ps.-Myia, *Phyl.*) and training children toward virtues such as temperance (ps.-Theano, *Eu.*); to be "temperate" (*sōphrōn*, ps.-Melissa, *Cl.*; cf. Xenophon, *Oec.* 7.14); to be "holy," a trope for sexual purity (Huizenga 2013, 339–43); to be "good homemakers," as in managing slaves well (ps.-Theano, *Call.*); and to be "submissive to their own husbands" (cf. 1 Tim. 2:11), or, as ps.-Melissa puts it, "completing his desires," which are a temperate woman's "unwritten law" (ps.-Melissa, *Cl.* 2).

Finally, the gravestone of a Jewish woman named Regina (see sidebar) illustrates Jewish assimilation to Roman culture. The epitaph adopts Latin

> ### Epitaph of a Virtuous Jewish Woman
> ### (Rome, late 3rd/early 4th cent. CE)
>
> *"Here is buried Regina, covered by such a tomb,*
> *which her spouse set up in accordance with [his] love of her [?].*
> *After twice ten [years], she spent with him a year*
> *and a fourth month with eight days remaining.*
> *She will live again, return to the light again.*
> *For she can hope therefore that she may rise into the age*
> *promised for both the worthy and the pious,*
> *she, a true pledge, who deserved to have an abode in the venerable country.*
> *Your piety [pietas] has achieved this for you, your chaste life [pudica],*
> *your love of your people [family?] also, your observance of the law,*
> *the merit of your marriage, whose honour was your concern.*
> *From these deeds there is future hope for you,*
> *and your grieving spouse seeks his comfort in that."*
>
> (*JIWE* 2:103 = *CIJ* 1:476, trans. Chester 2013, 115)

terminology to express the essence of Regina's "love of [her] people" and "observance of the Law." The epitaph also affirms an afterlife in an "age" to come. The criteria of behavior are Jewish, but by embracing Latin terms for Jewish values, Regina's husband affirms that Jews are good Roman citizens.

So that the word of God might not be blasphemed (2:5; cf. 1 Tim. 6:1). This list of virtues shows how early Jesus followers could thwart the suspicions of outsiders regarding the behavior of Christian women (cf. 3:2; see comments at 1 Tim. 2:9–15; 5:14).

The younger men, likewise, exhort to be temperate, in every respect presenting yourself as an example of good deeds, [and presenting] incorruptibility in the teaching, dignity, a healthy word not open to condemnation, so that the one from the opposition may be turned back, having nothing ill to say about us (2:6–8). Titus's peer group is younger men, for whom he serves as a model. The thrust is similar to that of 1 Tim. 4:12–16. The call for temperance continues the theme from verses 2, 3, 5.

Depending on whether one places a comma before or after it, the phrase "in every respect" modifies either "to be temperate" (2:6) or "presenting yourself" (2:7). Pastoral Paul may have placed the phrase so it could function both ways. "Presenting yourself as an example of good deeds" describes how Titus should comport himself, and the next three items amplify what his example should look like. "Incorruptibility in the teaching" suggests integrity—that is, not teaching only what is popular or avoiding what is unpopular (cf. impartiality in dealing with elders, 1 Tim. 5:21; avoiding itching ears, 2 Tim. 4:1–8). "Dignity" is a quality desired of elders (2:2; cf. 1 Tim. 3:4, 8). "Not open to condemnation" is a desirable quality of church leaders ("unimpeachable," 1 Tim. 3:2; 5:7). A "healthy word" recapitulates the primary command in this section (2:1; cf. "healthy teaching," 1:9, 13; 2:2; 1 Tim. 1:10; 6:3; 2 Tim. 1:13; 4:3).

Against a youthful tendency toward rashness (Aristotle, *Rhet.* 2.12 [1388b–89b]; Dio Chrysostom, *Or.* 22.1–2; Hutson 1998, 157–59), Titus should be circumspect. "Not open to condemnation" calls to mind similar exhortations to Timothy (1 Tim. 6:13), an overseer (1 Tim. 3:2), and elders (Titus 1:6). If Titus were careless in speech, outsiders would be emboldened to attack, but a "healthy word" accompanied by exemplary behavior will deflect criticism.

Finally, Titus should tell **slaves to be subordinate to their own masters in everything, to be well pleasing, not back-talking, not stealing, but displaying all good faith, so that in everything they may adorn the teaching about God our Savior** (2:9–10). In this passage we face tension between modern revulsion toward slavery as antithetical to the gospel and ancient acceptance of slavery as an unquestioned fact of life. Pastoral Paul is picking his battles (see "Theological Issues" below and comments and "Theological Issues" at 1 Tim. 6:1–2). The main point is that Christians of all stripes should present a public image that will not attract criticism.

The translation "back-talking" reflects the social reality that any slave who said what he really thought *to* a master would likely face harsh punishment. The alternative translation "talking against" (cf. 1:9) would suggest that a slave might talk *about* a master behind his back. We should not assume that enslavers and enslaved heard this exhortation the same way. "Stealing" (*nosphizomenos*) reflects a common stereotype of slaves as untrustworthy, but "stealing" might also be the masters' disapproving term for the way slaves managed their own money (Malherbe 2010, 387n50). Still, the point is that the behavior of the enslaved could "adorn the teaching about God our Savior" (Gk. objective gen.). If non-Christian masters perceived—rightly or wrongly—their slaves engaging in bad behavior and associated that behavior with the slaves' foreign religion, there could be implications for the entire Christian community.

Although the passage calls attention to critics of Christianity with particular reference to the behavior of younger women (2:5), slaves (2:10), and Titus himself (2:7–8), all of 2:2–10 speaks to a concern for cultivating a positive public image. By way of comparison, numerous inscriptions illustrate how Jews presented themselves as good citizens through the virtues they named on their tombstones. In addition to the epitaph of Regina (see sidebar), the tombstone of a Jewish man named Lazar who died in Rome in the third or fourth century remembered him as "religious, just, devoted to children, devoted to the brothers, devoted to the synagogue" (*hosios, dikaios, philoteknos, philadelphōn, philosynagōgos*, JIWE 2:171 = CIJ 1:321; cf. JIWE 2:127, 240 = CIJ 1:363, 203). "Jews show, to the public gaze, that they intend themselves to be model citizens, pillars of society, responsible, liked, contributing to the good of the city (and local community) as a whole" (Chester 2013, 130). This does not mean that Jews adopted Greco-Roman standards of morality (Chester 2013, 139–42). They expressed their own values in language that outsiders could recognize and respect.

Christological Warrant (2:11–14)

2:11–14. The conjunction "for" (*gar*) in 2:11 indicates that what follows is explanatory. A single sentence in Greek, comprising all of 2:11–14, provides the theological warrant for the ethical instruction in 2:1–10.

Verses 11–14 allude to the story of Jesus. Pastoral Paul assumes knowledge of the fundamental Christian narrative without telling it (see "Not telling the story" in the general introduction). This dense theological statement focuses on the ethical implications of the Christ story, framed in Greco-Roman language of temperance, justice, piety, and good deeds. But the motivation is distinctively Christian: behavior "in the present age" is grounded in anticipation of the parousia of Christ. Christians live in the present age but play by the rules of the age to come. Pastoral Paul also appropriates the language of Greco-Roman religion to express his eschatological theology in terms of two "epiphanies" (2:11, 13; see sidebar at Titus 2:13) that mark the turning point(s) of the ages.

For the grace of God has been manifested as salvific to all people (2:11). Some ancient manuscripts read "grace of God our Savior," which would be in line with 1:3; 2:10; and 3:4 (cf. 1 Tim. 2:3). To say the "grace of God" is "salvific," where "grace of God" is a metaphor for Christ, is tantamount to referring to Christ as Savior (1:4; 2:13; 3:6; cf. 2 Tim. 1:10). This clause alludes to the first "manifestation" of Christ and is parallel to 3:4 (cf. 2 Tim. 1:10). This use of "grace" as an abstract metaphor for the Christ event is peculiar to this letter. Similar metaphorical uses of "kindness" and "philanthropy" occur in 3:4, and the whole of 2:11–14 and 3:4–7 are densely christological, perhaps quotations from catechetical tradition. On the phrase "to all people," see comments at 1 Tim. 2:1–7.

Educating us that, denying impiety and worldly lusts, we should live temperately and justly and piously in the present age (2:12). Soteriology in this passage is instructional, "salvation as a moral conversion" (Malherbe 2005, 354). Pastoral Paul does not cite any ethical teachings of Jesus (except possibly at 1 Tim. 5:18). To say, therefore, that the saving grace of God "educates us" invites reflection on how the death and resurrection of Jesus exemplify temperance, justice, and piety.

Reggie M. Kidd (1999, 193) overreaches when he suggests that the triad of quintessentially Greek virtues—temperance, justice, and piety—are exact counterparts to the triad of Cretan vices in 1:12. The vicious counterparts to "piety" and "temperance" are expressed as "impiety" and "lusts." Kidd (1999, 203–9) is correct, however, that this triad of virtues (Lucian, *Somn.*

Two Ages

Jewish eschatology anticipates a time when the present age dominated by evil, an "age of wickedness" (1QpHab 5.7–8., trans. Vermes 1997, 480), will give way to the age to come (*1 En.* 71.15; *4 Ezra* 7.45–61; *2 Bar.* 83.4–9; *m. Avot* 4.17, 22; *m. Sanh.* 10), when God's reign will be undeniable and "every knee shall bow" (Isa. 45:23). That will be the messianic age (*2 Bar.* 25–30; *t. Arakh.* 2.7).

The Christian twist on this posits a two-stage turning of the ages. On the one hand, the earthly life, death, and resurrection of Jesus mark the beginning of the age to come. On the other hand, the present age continues until the second coming (parousia) of Jesus, when the reign of God will be finally and fully realized.

10; cf. Plato, *Republic* 427e, 435b; *Prot.* 349b) is programmatic for the apologetic aims of the letter. By expressing their values in the terminology of the dominant culture (temperance, justice, piety), Christians could deflect some of the suspicion with which Romans viewed new religions, even if their ethical values were rooted in Jewish thought (wisdom, *mishpat*; "fear of the Lord").

The expression "the present age" reflects the Jewishness of Pauline theology (Rom. 12:2; 1 Cor. 1:20; 2:6, 8; 3:18; 2 Cor. 4:4; Gal. 1:4; Eph. 2:2; see sidebar). Here Jewish eschatology has its familiar, Christian twist into a two-stage eschaton that began with the incarnation of Jesus (2:11; cf. 3:4) and will be consummated with the parousia of Christ (2:13; cf. 1 Tim. 6:14; 2 Tim. 1:10; 4:1, 8). Christians must choose whether to follow the "impiety and worldly lusts" of the present age or to follow the way of the cross and live into the age to come.

As we await the blessed hope and manifestation of the glory of our great God and Savior, Jesus Christ (2:13). The motivation for living temperately and justly in the present age is anticipation of the age to come (cf. Phil. 3:20). What we "await" is stated as a hendiadys, with one article ("the") governing two related nouns, "the blessed hope and manifestation" (BDF §442[16]; cf. 1 Tim. 1:4; 2:12). In a hendiadys, the second noun is often explanatory, so that, "we await the blessed hope, namely, the manifestation . . ." (I. H. Marshall 1999, 274; K. Smith and Song 2006, 285). On the "manifestation" (*epiphaneia*, cf. 1 Tim. 6:14), see sidebar.

Exactly what will appear, according to this verse, depends in part on how we understand "glory." Do we await "the glorious manifestation of" (CEV, ISV, Phillips; "glory" as Gk. adjectival gen., Zerwick 1963, §40), or do we await "the manifestation of the glory of" (ESV, NIV, NRSV; "glory" as Gk. objective gen., Zerwick 1963, §36)? The latter is more likely in light of the parallel between "the grace of God was manifested" (Titus 2:11) and "the

Epiphany

In Greek religion an *epiphaneia* (manifestation, appearance; epiphany) referred to the manifestation of a deity to a human being, bestowing some special favor or disfavor. A god might "appear" in a vision or some natural phenomenon (e.g., Herodotus, *Histories* 6.61; Pausanias 4.27.2; Platt 2015; Lau 1996, 179–89). When applied to a king, the epithet *epiphanēs* could mean simply "distinguished" or could suggest that a king's opportune appearance was godlike in producing "some striking result," especially a military victory. Seleucid rulers used the epithet "God manifest" (*theos epiphanēs*) on their coins (Nock 1928, 38–41). Roman emperors adopted their practice (*SIG* 760 [on which, see comments at 2 Tim. 1:10]; Philo, *Embassy* 346).

Hellenistic Jews used the word *epiphaneia* (2 Macc. 2:21; 3:24–28; 5:2–4; 12:22; 14:15; 15:27) in pointed response to claims that Antiochus IV Epiphanes was "God manifest" (Lau 1996, 189–225). In the NT, the noun *epiphaneia* occurs only once outside the PE (2 Thess. 2:8). In the PE it refers either to the first coming of Jesus (2 Tim. 1:10) or the second (1 Tim. 6:14; 2 Tim. 4:1, 8; Titus 2:13). The related verb "appear, be manifested" (*epiphainō*) similarly applies to Jesus (Titus 2:11; 3:4; cf. Luke 1:79; Acts 2:20). By his vocabulary, Pastoral Paul presents Jesus as the "manifestation" of the one true God over against the claims of Hellenistic and Roman rulers (see comments at 1 Tim. 2:1–7).

kindness and philanthropy of God was manifested" (Titus 3:4). But we await the manifestation of whose glory? Things get sticky, depending on whether we read "God and Savior" as another hendiadys and on how we understand "Jesus Christ" in relation to "God and Savior." There are three options:

1. "The manifestation of the glory [or glorious manifestation] of our great God and Savior, Jesus Christ" (Gk. "glory" as objective [or adjectival] gen.; "God and Savior" as hendiadys; "Jesus Christ" as appositional to "God and Savior"). On this translation, Pastoral Paul refers to Jesus explicitly as "God" (CEB, CEV, ESV, NET; Quinn 1990a; Knight 1992; Lau 1996, 247–50; I. H. Marshall 1999; R. Collins 2002).
2. "The manifestation of the glory of our great God and Savior, Jesus Christ" (Gk. "glory" as objective gen.; "God and Savior" as hendiadys; "Jesus Christ" as appositional to "glory"). On this translation, Pastoral Paul refers to Jesus as the "glory" of God but not explicitly as "God" (NLT; Fee 1988; Towner 2006). This would be consistent with Titus 3:4–7, which celebrates Jesus as a manifestation of God's "kindness and philanthropy" and the one "through" whom God "poured out" the Holy Spirit.
3. "The manifestation of the glory [or glorious manifestation] of the great God and of our Savior Jesus Christ" (Gk. "glory" as objective [or

adjectival] gen.; "God" and "Savior" as two separate objective genitives with "manifestation"; "Jesus Christ" as appositional to "Savior"). On this translation Pastoral Paul anticipates the "manifestation" of two separate persons, "God" and "our Savior Jesus Christ" (KJV, NABRE, Phillips; Dibelius and Conzelmann 1972; Edwards 2011).

The main issue is whether Pastoral Paul intends to describe Jesus as "God." The deity of Jesus is affirmed strongly in option 1, weakly in option 2, and not in option 3.

J. Christopher Edwards (2011) argues for option 3 on the basis of parallels between Titus 2:11–14 and 1 Tim. 2:1–7, where Jesus is referred to as a "human being" (1 Tim. 2:5), but the supposed parallels seem forced. Besides, it is hardly surprising that a NT writer should affirm both the humanity and the divinity of Jesus. And in terms of grammar, option 3 ignores the hendiadys construction in "our God and Savior" (BDF §276[3]; Wallace 1996, 270–77). On balance, option 3 seems the weakest.

A good translation strategy would be to preserve the ambiguity between options 1 and 2 (NASB, NIV, NRSV). To decide between these options, we must look closely at how Pastoral Paul argues. In favor of option 2, elsewhere in the PE God and Jesus are two distinct persons (1 Tim. 5:21; 2 Tim. 4:1). On the other hand, the NT nowhere else refers to Jesus as the "glory of God" (M. Harris 2011, 150). And the use of the noun *epiphaneia* implies the "manifestation" of a deity. Martin Dibelius and Hans Conzelmann try to explain away the force of *epiphaneia*. After acknowledging that the "formulation of the expression" suggests that Jesus is "God," they argue that early Christians watered down the word *epiphaneia* by applying it to a human agent of God, so in the PE it came to imply the "subordination of Christ to God" (Dibelius and Conzelmann 1972, 143; cf. 104). That argument seems upside down.

Option 1 is the most straightforward reading grammatically. Option 1 might seem to put Titus in tension with 1 Timothy: Jesus as a manifestation of deity in contrast with the assertion that no one is able to see God (see "Theological Issues: The Immortal, Invisible, Only God" after the comments on 1 Tim. 1:3–20; and "Theological Issues: Apophatic Theology" after the comments on 6:2b–21), but we could say God is invisible *except* as "manifested in flesh" (1 Tim. 3:16). The word *epiphaneia* implies the "manifestation" of a deity, and every other instance of this word in the PE refers to the appearing of Jesus, not of God. Further, option 1 is consistent with the ascription of "Savior" in this letter to both God (Titus 1:3; 2:10; 3:4; cf. 1 Tim. 1:1; 2:3; 4:10) and Jesus (Titus 1:4; 3:6; cf. 2 Tim. 1:10). It is also consistent with the traditional understanding of Rom. 9:5 (N. T. Wright 2013, 707–8) and 2 Pet. 1:1 and with references to Jesus as "God" in the Apostolic Fathers (Ign. *Eph.* inscr.; 1.1; 7.2; 15.3; 18.2; 19.3; *Rom.* inscr.; 3.3; *Smyrn.* 1.1; Pol. *Phil.* 8.3; cf. 2 *Clem.* 12.1; 17.4). And it is the traditional interpretation (as a statement against Arianism, e.g., Aquinas, *Comm. Titus* 2.3.72 [Baer 2007]; Calvin on Titus 2:13). In my opinion, option 1 makes the best sense of the passage.

Who gave himself for us, so that he might ransom us from all lawlessness and purify for himself a special people, zealous for good deeds (2:14). The goal of Jesus's sacrifice was to "ransom" people from "lawlessness" (cf. 1 Tim. 1:8–10) and to "purify a people" for "good deeds" (Titus 2:7; 3:8, 14; cf. 1:16; 3:1). The verbs "gave himself" and "ransom" call to mind Mark 10:45 (see comments at 1 Tim. 2:6; cf. 1 Pet. 1:18; Ps. 130:8; Edwards 2009). Mark does not indicate from whom or what Jesus "ransomed" people, but here Pastoral Paul says it was "from lawlessness," which anticipates "slaves to lusts and . . . pleasures" (Titus 3:3; cf. Rom. 1:24–32; 6:19). When ancient people were "ransomed," they usually made an offering to some god (*NewDocs* 3:§46); whereas in this passage the divine savior "gave himself" (cf. 1 Tim. 2:6; Eph. 5:2). Jesus "educates us" (Titus 2:12) by modeling what it means to renounce "worldly lusts" and live "temperately" (2:12) or even self-sacrificially (cf. Kidd 1999, 204).

The verse also echoes OT sentiments about God's relationship with Israel ("purify for himself a . . . people," Ezek. 37:23 LXX; "special people," Exod. 19:5; Deut. 7:6; 14:2; 26:18 LXX). The allusion to Exod. 19:5 is instructive: "and now, if you really heed my voice and keep my covenant, you will be for me a special people from among all the nations, for the whole earth is mine." Pastoral Paul pulls "special people" from the context of the covenant at Sinai and ties it to "good deeds." This is consistent with the function of Torah as moral formation (see comments at 1 Tim. 1:8–11; cf. 4 Macc. 5:16–24; *T. Dan* 5.1–3; etc.). Taking his cue from the final clause of Exod. 19:5, "the whole earth is mine," Pastoral Paul insists that the grace of God appeared not only to Israel at Sinai but "to all people" (Titus 2:11). Similarly, 1 Tim. 2:4–6 appropriates Sinai imagery—the Shema and the Mediator—in making a case for God's interest in "all people." And 1 Pet. 2:9 alludes to Exod. 19:6 as a theological warrant for similar station code material. This passage offers a Jewish ethical perspective shaped by the Christ story and applied in language that would make sense in a Greco-Roman context.

Reiteration of Directive (2:15)

2:15. Tell these things and exhort and reprove (2:15). This sentence forms the closing bracket of an inclusio around chapter 2 by recapitulating the commands to "tell" (2:1) and "exhort" (2:6). The phrase "these things" includes both moral exhortation (2:2–10) and the christological warrant (2:11–14). The command to "reprove" is new but makes sense in terms of the three purpose clauses (2:5, 8, 10). If outsiders blaspheme the word of God (2:5) and speak ill of the Christian community (2:8), Titus should cross-examine and refute false claims ("reprove" at 1:9, 13b; 1 Tim. 5:20). Exemplary behavior will allay suspicions (2:2–10), and Titus must frame the Christ story so outsiders hear it not as a shameful execution for insurrection but as a divine epiphany that "instructs" people in virtue (2:11–14).

Titus is to do these things **with all authority** (2:15). The noun "authority" (*epitagē*) appeared previously, in 1:3, where by divine "injunction" (*epitagē*) Pastoral Paul was entrusted with a message. So here Paul passes on that injunction to proclaim the message about Christ.

Finally, **Let no one despise you** (2:15) calls to mind the imperative regarding Timothy's "youth" (1 Tim. 4:12). Although this letter does not mention Titus's age, it does imply that he is relatively young, in that Pastoral Paul addresses him as "my true child" (1:4; cf. 1 Tim. 1:2), and his peer group is "younger men" (2:6–7; cf. 1 Tim. 5:1).

Theological Issues

Ethics and Eschatology

It is important to distinguish Pastoral Paul's social agenda and his theological orientation, discerning which is the cart and which the horse. The social agenda laid out in 2:1–10 includes a well-ordered, patriarchal household with women, youths, and enslaved in proper subordination to free, male householders. The purpose of maintaining this social structure is defensive, "so that the word of God might not be slandered" (2:5). The theological warrant is that "the saving grace of God was manifested to all people, . . . educating us" (2:11–12). The epiphany of God's grace has universal implications (cf. 1 Tim. 2:4–6). But it was not the purpose of that epiphany to educate all peoples that they should forever conform to Greco-Roman social expectations regarding an ideal household (see "The Subordination of Women" in the general introduction). The educational aim of God's epiphany was "so that, renouncing impiety and worldly desires, we should live temperately and justly and piously in the present age" (2:12). Temperance, justice, and piety took specific forms in Greco-Roman culture, including assumptions about honor and shame, domestic hierarchies, and so forth. But we must not confuse the foundational doctrines with the precepts by which Pastoral Paul applied those doctrines in a particular cultural context (see "Doctrines and Precepts" in the general introduction).

Christology and apocalyptic eschatology, not Greco-Roman culture, are the theological drivers of Titus 2. We live in the "present age" (2:12), cognizant of an epiphany past (2:11), when the earthly Jesus "gave himself for us" (2:14). Jesus's death had ethical implications, to "redeem us from all lawlessness and purify for himself a special people, zealous for good deeds" (2:14). And at the same time, we live, "expecting the blessed hope and glorious manifestation of the Great God and our Savior Jesus Christ" (2:13), an epiphany future, the coming (parousia) of Jesus. Christian ethics, regardless of cultural context, are defined by the manifestations of Jesus, past and future.

237

Those two epiphanies undermine the presumptions of patriarchal domination that were taken for granted in Greco-Roman society. What would it mean, for example, if a *paterfamilias* identified himself as a follower of Jesus, when the essential fact about Jesus is that "he gave himself for us" (2:14)? What are the ethical implications for living in "the present age" (2:12) if Jesus died "to redeem us from all lawlessness" (2:14)? Jesus's resurrection liberates us from bondage to the tyranny of sin and death (Rom. 5–7). Indeed, all forms of domination and coercion are instances of that larger problem of the tyranny of sin. If the "lawlessness" from which Jesus redeems us includes sexual exploitation and domination (1 Tim. 1:10), what are the implications for how an older man relates to women, younger men, and slaves? The eschatology of the PE is countercultural (Kidd 1990, 159–94; Witherington 2006, 146–51; see "Theological Issues" at 1 Tim. 2:8–3:1a).

Slavery and the Gospel

But isn't Pastoral Paul upholding an exploitative social order by commanding "slaves to submit to their masters in all things"? The American experience with slavery sheds light on the ancient social situation. Before the late eighteenth century, few American slave owners were interested in the religious lives of enslaved people (Montgomery 1993, 5–6). They had a sense that Christianity would upset the dynamics of domination. Francis Le Jau, an Anglican missionary in South Carolina, found varying attitudes among planters as to the desirability of Christianizing the enslaved. In a letter of December 11, 1712, he wrote that some masters refused to allow enslaved people to attend church on the "old pretext that Baptism makes the Slaves proud and Undutifull [*sic*]" (Klingberg 1956, 125). He never taught or baptized any enslaved person without the master's consent, and in a letter of October 20, 1709, he described his policy:

> To remove all pretence [*sic*] from the Adult Slaves I shall baptise [*sic*] of their being free upon that Account, I have thought fit to require first their consent to this following declaration *You declare in the Presence of God and before this Congregation that you do not ask for the holy baptism out of any design to free yourself from the Duty and Obedience you owe to your Master while you live, but meerly [sic] for the good of Your Soul and to partake of the Graces and Blessings promised to the Members of the Church of Jesus Christ.* (Klingberg 1956, 60; cf. Montgomery 1993, 6)

Le Jau was anxious to convert English and French settlers, Native Americans, and Africans, but in colonial South Carolina, he had to choose. He could teach enslaved people to accept their status, or he could not introduce Christianity to them at all. He fought to introduce Christianity.

Once the enslaved learned Christianity, all attempts by the masters to interpret the Bible for them were futile. They could read for themselves that God was consistently on the side of oppressed people against their oppressors and that deliverance was sure to come in God's glorious future (Thomas 2013; C. Martin 1998, 223–25).

We have considered what James Scott calls the "arts of resistance" among oppressed peoples (see "James Scott and 'Infrapolitics'" in the general introduction). William E. Montgomery (1993) describes one tactic, the use of double meaning to say one thing to masters and something else to the enslaved. Former slave Lewis Favor described attending church on a Georgia plantation. The white preacher told the enslaved in the rear, "Don't steal your master's chickens or his eggs and your backs won't be whipped." Afterward, the black exhorter rose to say, "Obey your masters and mistresses and your backs won't be whipped." While the white preacher was urging submission, the black preacher was advising on how to avoid punishment (Montgomery 1993, 32–33). When the enslaved met in their "hush arbors" away from white eyes, the message was worded differently (Powery and Sadler 2016; cf. D. Walker 1830, 51; C. Martin 1998).

When we read a passage like Titus 2, we should not assume the viewpoint of the dominant society. After all, even relatively affluent Christians were still on the margins of Greco-Roman society. If a free, male citizen who owned a house and slaves should convert to Christianity, that conversion per se marginalized him in a society in which all aspects of civil, commercial, and social life were involved with obligatory rituals honoring pagan deities. If the majority of Christians in any town were artisans, subsistence workers, freed persons, and enslaved, we should attempt to hear the text from their point of view.

And what do we hear when Pastoral Paul argues that by their behavior slaves may "adorn the teaching about God our Savior" (2:10)? Listening from above, we may hear in the station code (2:1–10) a call for order and submission and in the christological warrant (2:11–14) that God has appeared as a champion of temperance, justice, and piety in the present age. But listening from below, we should hear that God will appear again (2:13); that the Messiah gave himself to ransom us from the tyranny of lawlessness to become God's special people (2:14); that the present social order is not God's order; that God has acted, is acting, and will act to overthrow it.

The Greco-Roman household is not normative for Christians. Pastoral Paul clothes Christian values in garb that will be recognizable to the dominant society, but he does not adopt the double standards of Greco-Roman patriarchalism. We must apply temperance, justice, and piety in ways consistent with the cross of Christ and with an expectation of a blessed future. When we do that, not only our households but also God's household must shatter all forms of domination and exploitation that prevail in the present age (see "Theological Issues" after 1 Tim. 2:11–3:1a and after 5:1–6:2a).

Titus 3:1–11

Directive 3: More Instructions for the Community

Introductory Matters

Titus 3:1–11 is tightly connected to chapter 2 in content and form (see "Introductory Matters" for 2:1–15). The directive in 3:1–2 continues the station code from 2:2–10. And the passage continues the themes of "manifestation" (3:4; 2:11) and "good deeds" (3:1, 8; 1:16; 2:7, 14; 3:14).

The thrust of 3:1–11 is ethical exhortation. References to "good deeds" (3:1, 8) form an inclusio, and between these brackets the passage reminds us that "deeds" are not the basis on which God saves us. References to "battles" (3:2, 9) form a second inclusio, and between these brackets the hymn reminds us that God has acted toward us out of "kindness and philanthropy." Taken together, 3:1–11 describes how believers should behave in response to the divine epiphany (3:1, 3–8) and how they should not behave (3:2, 9–11).

Supporting these exhortations are two warrants, one from basic human empathy (3:3) and the other from Christology (3:4–7). Verses 4–7 contain another condensed statement of the foundational doctrine taken for granted throughout the PE (cf.

> **Titus 3:1–11
> in the Rhetorical Flow**
>
> Letter opening (1:1–4)
>
> Directive 1: Community leaders (1:5–16)
>
> Directive 2: Instructions for the community (2:1–15)
>
> ▶ Directive 3: More instructions for the community (3:1–11)
>
>   Submission to authorities (3:1–2)
>
>   Empathetic and christological warrants (3:3–8a)
>
>   Closing summative charge (3:8b–11)

1 Tim. 2:5–6; 3:16; 2 Tim. 1:9–10; 2:11–13). These verses are a single sentence in Greek, identified as a "faithful saying" (1 Tim. 1:15; 3:1; 4:9; 2 Tim. 2:11). It is not quite correct to say that "poetic elements are entirely lacking" in this passage (I. H. Marshall 1999, 307). Because of its compressed Christology and its quasi-poetic style, it seems to be a quotation of traditional material, perhaps a hymn (cf. 1 Tim. 3:16; 2 Tim. 1:9–10; 2:11–13; R. Martin 1983, 19, 292) or baptismal liturgy (Knight 1992, 350) that celebrates the "washing of regeneration."

Tracing the Train of Thought

Submission to Authorities (3:1–2)

3:1–2. Remind them to submit to ruling authorities, to obey rulers, to be prepared for every good work, to blaspheme no one, to be uncombative, tolerant, displaying all gentleness toward all people (3:1–2). Some ancient scribes inserted "and," creating a reminder to submit "to rulers *and* authorities," which brought this verse in line with Eph. 1:21; 3:10; Col. 1:16; 2:10, 15 (cf. Eph. 2:2; 6:12), but the difference in sense is negligible. The reminders in 3:1–2 resemble those in 1 Tim. 2: "submit to ruling authorities" (1 Tim. 2:1–2; also Rom. 13:1–8; 1 Pet. 2:13–14); concern for "all people" (cf. 1 Tim. 2:4, 6); "uncombative" (cf. "without anger or argument," 1 Tim. 2:8); and "good deeds" (cf. 1 Tim. 2:10). We should not be concerned about the difference between deeds that are "good" (*kalos*, "beautiful," Titus 2:7, 14; 3:14; cf. 1 Tim. 3:1; 5:10, 25; 6:18) and those that are "good" (*agathos*, "noble," Titus 1:16; 3:1; cf. 1 Tim. 2:10; 5:10): Pastoral Paul uses the two adjectives interchangeably.

Christian behavior bears witness to outsiders. If outsiders "blaspheme" Christian women (Titus 2:5), Christians should "blaspheme no one" (3:2) in return. Pastoral Paul expects Christian leaders to model uncombative and gentle behavior (overseer, 1 Tim. 3:3; Titus 1:7; Timothy as "God's slave," 2 Tim. 2:24). In this letter Titus's "good deeds" and "healthy word" deflect any bad things opponents might say (2:7–8). Now all believers contribute to the defense by being "prepared for good deeds," "uncombative," and "gentle," and by "displaying all gentleness toward all people."

Empathetic and Christological Warrants (3:3–8a)

3:3–8a. The first warrant for gentleness toward all is human empathy born of self-reflection. For once we also were mindless, disobedient, deceived, slaves to lusts and various pleasures, continuing in evil and envy, despicable, hating one another (3:3). Regarding the capacity of music to soothe the savage soul, Clement of Alexandria likened human beings to "wild beasts" (*agriōtata thēria*) and quoted Titus 3:3–5 with the comment that God's "new song" has "made men from beasts" (Clement of Alexandria, *Protr.* 1.4). We are all a little bit like "evil beasts" (Titus 1:12). If Christians recognize that they used to suffer from a sort of mental illness (1 Tim. 6:4–5; 2 Tim. 3:8–9), being "foolish and disobedient," it is easier to respond with gentleness toward those who suffer the same affliction. If Christians recognize themselves as freed from the tyranny of sin (Rom. 6–7; Eph. 2), it is easier to see their abusers as "slaves to lusts and pleasures" (cf. 2 Tim. 3:4; 4:3).

The second warrant for gentleness toward critics grows out of the first. Believers should recognize their own former sorry state and God's gracious intervention to regenerate, renew and reorient them. The reminder comes in the form of a dense, quasi-poetic statement, probably quoted from early liturgical tradition:

> **But when was manifested the kindness and philanthropy of God our Savior,**
>> **not by deeds that we did in righteousness,**
>> **but in accordance with his mercy,**
> **[God] saved us**
>> **through a washing of regeneration and renewal of the Holy Spirit,**
>> **which [God] poured out upon us richly through Jesus Christ our Savior,**
> **So that we might become heirs**
>> **having been justified by his grace,**
>> **in accordance with the hope of eternal life.**
>
> **Trustworthy is the saying.** (3:4–8a)

This is one sentence with three clauses, arranged above in three triplets, so the main line of thought is clear in the first line of each triplet: "When was manifested the kindness and philanthropy of God . . . [God] saved us . . . so that we might become heirs." The other lines expand on these three points. The main clause is at the center: "[God] saved us." The first clause explains when God saved, while the third explains why.

The first clause (3:4) alludes to the story of Jesus (cf. 2 Tim. 1:10; on the verb "manifested" [*epephanē*], see sidebar at Titus 2:13). In Pauline thought, God's "kindness" (*chrēstotēs*) was expressed in the grafting of gentiles as wild branches into God's olive tree (Rom. 11:22; cf. Eph. 2:7). "Philanthropy" could describe the attitude of any higher-status person toward inferiors (Acts 27:3), but, as here, it originally described the attitudes of gods toward humans (U. Luck, *TDNT* 9:107–12). Two phrases explain the basis for God's saving work, which was "not by deeds that we did" (cf. 2 Tim. 1:9; Eph. 2:8–9) but "in accordance with [God's] mercy" (cf. Eph. 2:4; 1 Pet. 1:3).

The second clause is the main point: "[God] saved us." This central clause invites contemplation of the meaning of baptism, the work of the Holy Spirit, and trinitarian theology. "Washing" (cf. 1 Cor. 6:11; Eph. 5:26; Acts 22:16)

"The Bath of Regeneration"

Writing about 180 CE, Theophilus of Antioch offered a spiritual interpretation of Gen. 1, including this meditation on the Fifth Day:

"On the fifth day came into existence the living creatures from the waters, through which the 'manifold wisdom of God' [Eph. 3:10] is made plain. For who would be able to count their multitude and variety? Moreover, the things that came from the waters were blessed by God, in order that this might be a sign that people were going to receive repentance and forgiveness of sins through water and the 'bath of regeneration' [palingenēsias, Titus 3:5], namely all those who come to the truth and are born again [anagennōmenous] and received a blessing from God." (Theophilus of Antioch, *To Autolycus* 2.16, from Ferguson 2009, 247)

reflects the earliest baptismal practice of immersion in water, following the Jewish practice of immersion as a symbolic purification. More to the point, when a gentile converted, after instruction in Torah and circumcision for men, immersion in water was the point at which the gentile became an Israelite (*b. Yevam.* 47A–B).

Some gentile readers may have associated "regeneration" (*palingenēsia*, 3:5) with the mystery religions (Dibelius and Conzelmann 1972, 148–50) or the Stoic "regeneration" of the earth after its destruction by fire (Philo, *Aet.* 89–93, who rejected this Stoic doctrine). The latter would resonate with an apocalyptic idea of the age to come (Matt. 19:28). But the more immediate resonance for Christians was to baptism as the symbolic death, burial, and resurrection of the individual to "newness of life" in Christ (Rom. 6:4–5). That is how Theophilus of Antioch understood this verse when he glossed "regeneration" with "being born again" (see sidebar; cf. Irenaeus, *Haer.* 3.17.2; 5.15.3; Tertullian, *Bapt.* 20.5, etc., all discussed in Ferguson 2009). "Regeneration" and "renewal" describe what the Holy Spirit does at baptism (Knight 1979, 96–102).

The Holy Spirit "which he poured out upon us" (Titus 3:6) recalls the day of Pentecost (Acts 2:17–18, quoting Joel 2:28–32), on which Jesus Christ "poured out" (Acts 2:33) the Holy Spirit. This suggests a close association between the Holy Spirit and baptism (Acts 2:38). At the same time, the idea that God sent the Holy Spirit "through Jesus Christ" has affinity with Johannine theology (John 7:38–39; 14:15–17; 20:22).

Putting all the parts together, the phrase, "through a washing of regeneration and renewal of the Holy Spirit" (3:5) is still grammatically ambiguous. The phrase could mean either (1) "through a washing that can be characterized as a regeneration and renewal, [both effected] by the Holy Spirit," or (2) "through a washing of regeneration and [through] a renewal of the Holy Spirit." The question is whether Pastoral Paul understood salvation in terms of (1) a single baptismal event in which the work of the Holy Spirit is integral (Knight 1979, 96–103) or (2) two closely related but distinguishable events—baptism and the renewal of the Holy Spirit (Knight 1992, 342–44). The book of Acts seems to distinguish them. Those who are baptized should expect to receive the Holy Spirit (Acts 2:38; 19:1–7), and those who receive the Spirit should expect to be baptized (10:44–48), and either one without the other is problematic (10:44–48; 19:1–7). Paul assumes that all believers have been symbolically buried and resurrected to new life in Christ (Rom. 6:1–11) and have the Spirit dwelling in them (8:9–11). All in all, option 1 seems preferable, taking "regeneration" and "renewal" as synonyms, both describing what the Holy Spirit does at baptism. Either way, God and the Holy Spirit are active in baptism.

The third clause expresses the aim of God's saving work, "so that we might become heirs" (Titus 3:7; cf. Rom. 8:17; Gal. 3:29; Eph. 1:18; Col. 3:24). Two phrases describe this salvation. The first identifies the cause of salvation, "justified by his grace." The verb "justify" (3:7), so important in Romans and Galatians, appears in the PE only in quotations of traditional liturgy (here and 1 Tim. 3:16). This passage does not develop a law-court metaphor but seems to use "justified" as a generic equivalent to "saved" in 3:5. The emphasis is on "grace," which ties this liturgical celebration of the manifestation of God's kindness and philanthropy back to the earlier manifestation of God's grace (2:11).

The second phrase orients salvation toward an eschatological promise "in accordance with the hope of eternal life" (3:7), which orients all "who have believed in God" (3:8) in their responses to hostile outsiders (cf. 1 Pet. 1:3–9). This same hope defines Paul's apostleship (Titus 1:2). Elsewhere, the prospect that "we shall live together" sustains every "soldier of Christ" (2 Tim. 2:3, 11; cf. 1 Tim. 4:10).

"Trustworthy is the saying" (3:8a). Pastoral Paul affirms that the established tradition about Christ is a "trustworthy saying" (*pistos logos*, cf. 1 Tim. 1:15; 2 Tim. 2:11). Elsewhere he asserts that God considered him "trustworthy" (*pistos*) to be a minister of that tradition (1 Tim. 1:12), the content of which he "deposited" with Timothy (1 Tim. 1:18; 6:20), and he directed Timothy to "deposit" what he had learned with "trustworthy" (*pistos*) people who would be able to teach others (2 Tim. 2:2). Similarly, an overseer must "hold forth the trustworthy message [*pistos logos*] that is in accordance with the teaching" (1:9).

Closing Summative Charge (3:8b–11)

3:8b–11. The closing charge to Titus recapitulates the opening charge (1:10–16). Titus is to "affirm" (3:8) the doctrine summarized in chapters 1–2.

Bad teachers start from the wrong places (3:9; cf. 1 Tim. 4:1; 2 Tim. 4:3–4). Good teaching results in "good deeds" that are "beneficial to people" (3:8), whereas the "deeds" of the insubordinate teachers belie their confession (1:16). Titus should "admonish" (3:10; cf. "reprove," 1:2) with the goal of turning them in the right direction (3:8, 10; 1:13). Those who refuse to heed are "self-condemned" (3:11; cf. "by their deeds," 1:16).

Because the Christ story is "trustworthy" and has been passed down through a succession of "trustworthy" teachers, people can "put their trust" in it: **And I want you to affirm these things, so that those who have put their trust in God may have in mind to take the lead in good deeds. These things are good and beneficial to the people** (3:8b). Those who "put their trust" in this tradition behave a certain way. The purpose of God's manifestation (3:4) was that believers might "take the lead in good deeds" (cf. 2:14; 3:1). This purpose is consistent with a Jewish understanding of covenantal relationship. Deeds come in response to the covenant given by God's grace and are not a condition of that grace (3:5; cf. Eph. 2:10; *Sifre Num.* 115.5; Dunn 2008, 391–92).

At first glance, it might seem that these things are "good and beneficial" to insiders. Surely believers should act with "good deeds" toward one another (1 Tim. 5:10). But in this letter "good deeds" bear witness to hostile outsiders (2:7–8; 3:1). The context emphasizes "all people" (3:2) and bad teachers (3:9–11). How believers behave both toward one another and toward their persecutors bears witness to the manifestation of God's kindness and philanthropy. "Good deeds" can change the world.

The next directive continues the theme of avoiding belligerent behavior, with the focus on errant Christians. **But stay away from foolish speculations and genealogies and contentions and legal fights; for they are unbeneficial and empty** (3:9). This admonition resembles others regarding errant teachers (1 Tim. 1:3–7; 2 Tim. 2:22–26). It is unclear whether "legal fights" refers to quarrels about interpretation of Torah, as hinted perhaps at 1:10, 14 (cf. 1 Tim. 1:7) or to civil litigation, the sort of thing denounced in 1 Cor. 6:1–8. The other occurrence of the adjective "legal" (*nomikos*) in this context is similarly ambiguous (3:13). Either way, fights are to be avoided, as are those who stir up controversies.

After a first and second admonition, avoid a factious person, knowing that such a one is perverted and is sinning, being self-condemned (3:10–11). The word "factious" (*haeretikos*) in later centuries came to have the sense of "heretic," a purveyor of unsound doctrine, but the idea here is simpler. A "party" (*haeresis*) was a clearly defined subgroup, for example, Sadducees (Acts 5:17), Pharisees (Acts 15:5; 26:5), Nazarenes (Acts 24:5) or Jesus followers (Acts 24:14; 28:22). Much like our word "denomination," it identified a school of thought. This passage fits with Paul's disapproval of a "party spirit" that was competitive and divisive (1 Cor. 11:19; Gal. 5:20; cf. "schism," 1 Cor. 1:10; 11:18; 12:25). The "factious" person could be doctrinally correct and still divisive, insisting on conformity to some pet phrase or practice. Just as Titus is to "speak and exhort and refute" (2:15), so also now he is to "admonish." But he should not be combative. After a second admonition, he has nothing to do with the factious person.

Theological Issues

Regeneration

The comments above suggest that "regeneration" could apply to the regeneration of the individual at baptism or to an apocalyptic idea of the regeneration of the cosmos in the age to come. These are not mutually exclusive ideas. We are living in the present age and awaiting the beginning of the age to come at the parousia of Christ (Titus 2:12–13). At the same time the death and resurrection of Jesus Christ already marks the beginning of the age to come. So we are living between two epiphanies (Titus 2:11–14), in the overlap of the two ages, and we must decide to live according to the rules of the one or the other.

Renouncing Satan

Before you can embrace the age to come, you must recognize the hold Satan has over the present age and renounce worldly ways. That means not treating enemies with belligerence (3:1–2). Satan does not care whom you hate or why you hate them, as long as you hate somebody. It also means being aware of your tendency toward self-deception (3:3). As Ann Lamott (2000, 22) puts it, "You can safely assume you've created God in your own image when it turns out that God hates all the same people you do." The greatest self-deception is that God sees things just as you see them, which is to create an idol named "God." The corrective to this idolatrous self-deception is the acknowledgment that God might be against us (see sidebar). If baptism is the point at which one

---

Making God into an Idol

"This capacity for prophetic imagination, that God is free to be against us, is the great weapon against idolatry. Whenever and wherever the people of God lose this capacity, God becomes enslaved. When the prophetic imagination is eclipsed—when God can no longer be imagined as being against us and for those we oppress, exclude, stigmatize, marginalize, ignore, or aggress against—God is no longer free but a slave. In that event, with the silencing of the prophetic voice within the faith community (or those voices of critique from the outside), God is no longer God but a principality and power—a tool of the devil—leading us into sin." (R. Beck 2014, 121)

decides to participate in the age to come, we could think of the exhortations in 3:1–3 in terms of the traditional Catholic pre-baptismal question, "Do you renounce Satan and all his works?"

A Trinitarian Rite of Baptism

In terms of a theological trajectory from the undisputed Paul to the Nicene Creed, we might ponder whether Titus 3 reflects proto-trinitarian or full-blown trinitarian thought. Pastoral Paul draws on a tradition that in his time was already a poetic liturgy contemplating how the Savior God, the Messiah Jesus, and the Holy Spirit all act for the renewal and regeneration of the believer. Later church fathers would develop the baptismal rite more fully along trinitarian lines. They understood baptism as a believer's physical experience of divine action within the larger drama that is the conflict between Satan and God.

A Lenten sermon of John Chrysostom from the year 388 illustrates how the baptismal ritual developed by the fourth century. After discussing the

---

St. John Chrysostom, Lenten Sermon

"After the renunciation of the devil and the covenant with Christ, inasmuch as you have henceforth become his very own and have nothing in common with that evil one, he straightway bids you to be marked and places on your forehead the sign of the cross. That savage beast is shameless and, when he hears those words, he grows more wild—as we might expect—and desires to assault you on sight. Hence, God anoints your countenance and stamps thereon the sign of the cross. In this way does God hold in check all the frenzy of the Evil One; for the devil will not dare to look upon such a sight. Just as if he had beheld the rays of the sun and had leaped away, so will his eyes be blinded by the sight of your face and he will depart; for through the chrism the cross is stamped upon you. The chrism is a mixture of olive oil and unguent; the unguent is for the bride, the oil is for the athlete. . . . After he anoints all your limbs with this ointment, you will be secure and able to hold the serpent in check; you will suffer no harm.

"After the anointing, then, it remains to go into the bath of sacred waters. After stripping you of your robe, the priest himself leads you down into the flowing waters. But why naked? He reminds you of your former nakedness, when you were in Paradise and you were not ashamed. For Holy Writ says: Adam and Eve were naked and were not ashamed, until they took up the garment of sin, a garment heavy with abundant shame.

"Do not, then, feel shame here, for the bath is much better than the garden of Paradise. There can be no serpent here, but Christ is here initiating you into the regeneration that comes from the water and the Spirit." (*The Eleventh Instruction* 27–29, Papadopoulos-Kerameus, no. 3, trans. P. W. Harkins, as quoted in Whitaker 1970, 35–38)

relationship between the physical actions and the spiritual experience of baptism, Chrysostom tells the story of Jesus's baptism. Then he describes a typical baptismal ritual, detailing to his catechumens what will happen and the spiritual significance of each physical action. The catechumens are led into the church. They drop to their knees, lift their hands, and offer thanks to God. The liturgy includes the declarations, "I renounce thee, Satan," and "I enter into thy service, O Christ." This is the point at which the excerpt begins (see sidebar).

Chrysostom's sermon resonates with Titus 3. He understands baptism as the spiritual experience of the Trinity at work on the believer in a bath of regeneration. As for anointing the whole body and baptizing the initiate naked, Chrysostom does not explain here, but for the sake of propriety women deacons assisted in the baptism of women (*Apostolic Constitutions* 3.16; cf. comments at 1 Tim. 3:11).

As a minister of the gospel, you should take baptismal liturgy seriously. Consider how a wedding ceremony has a direct effect on the happy couple and an indirect effect on witnesses, reminding them of their own vows. So also, a baptismal ceremony has a direct effect on the initiate, transferring her from the clutches of Satan to the kingdom of God, and an indirect effect on witnesses, reminding them of their baptismal commitments to the lordship of Jesus. Whether or not your denomination has a fixed baptismal liturgy, you should articulate the spiritual significance of each action in the process. You should perform it every time as if for the first time and explain it with passion. In narrating and performing a drama, you create a physical memory of a spiritual experience, and you remind the congregation who they are in Christ.

Titus 3:12–15

Letter Closing

Introductory Matters

Ancient letter closings were formulaic (Klauck 2006, 37–42; J. White 1986, 193–213). Paul's letter closings followed a general pattern with variation (Weima 2010; Murphy-O'Connor 1995, 98–113). This closing is relatively brief, consisting of notes on the travel plans of associates (3:12–13); a final exhortation (3:14); general greetings to and from (3:15); and a benediction (3:15b).

> **Titus 3:12–15 in the Rhetorical Flow**
>
> Letter opening (1:1–4)
>
> Directive 1: Community leaders (1:5–16)
>
> Directive 2: Instructions for the community (2:1–15)
>
> Directive 3: More instructions for the community (3:1–11)
>
> ►Letter closing (3:12–15)

Tracing the Train of Thought

3:12–15. Whenever I send Artemas or Tychicus to you, be diligent to come to me at Nicopolis, for I have decided to winter there (3:12). Artemas is otherwise unknown. Tychicus was from the province of Asia (Acts 20:4), a "beloved brother and faithful minister," who delivered Paul's letters to Ephesus (Eph. 6:21–22) and Colossae (Col. 4:7–9). One of these coworkers will come to replace Titus in Crete. If the letter is not fictional, we might guess that the replacement turned out to be Artemas, since we read that Paul sent Tychicus to Ephesus (2 Tim. 4:12).

Nicopolis was on the western coast of Greece. "Victory City" was so named by Augustus, who built it on the site where his army camped during the Battle of Actium, where he won his decisive victory over Antony and Cleopatra in 31 BCE. In the late first century, Epictetus would establish his school of Stoic philosophy there. This note, recalling Titus from Crete to Nicopolis, places this letter chronologically prior to 2 Tim. 4:10, which mentions that Titus has gone up the Adriatic coast to Dalmatia.

On the request to come (cf. 2 Tim. 4:9, 21), it is surprising to hear an urgent request for Titus to come to Nicopolis rather than staying in Crete to carry out the instructions in the letter. Those who read this letter as genuinely Pauline might find evidence that its instruction was meant for the churches in Crete rather than for Titus, who would soon depart (Mounce 2000, 457). But in that case, why didn't Paul address the letter to the churches in Crete? Those who read this letter as pseudonymous might see here a clumsy insertion for verisimilitude, the sort of thing that "would make a literary editor wince" (Pervo 2016, 7). But the letter seems artfully composed. Neither explanation is entirely satisfactory.

Send Zenas the law expert and Apollos along the way diligently, so that nothing may be lacking to them (3:13). Zenas is not otherwise known, and it is not clear how we should understand "law expert" (*nomikos*). If Zenas was a professional rhetor who argued in civic courts (Epictetus, *Diatr.* 2.13.6–8; Plutarch, *Cic.* 26.6), that would suggest Paul was anticipating a trial. But the reference to Nicopolis suggests he was not in prison or facing trial. Alternatively, if Zenas was a Torah scholar (cf. Luke 7:30; 10:25; 11:45–46, 52; 14:3; Matt. 22:35 var.), that would suggest an endorsement of Zenas and Apollos ("mighty in the Scriptures," Acts 18:24) as trustworthy guides to Jewish Scriptures over against the false teachers who misinterpreted the texts (1:14; cf. 1 Tim. 1:4, 7). To "send them along the way" is to provision them for the next leg of their journey (cf. Rom. 15:24; 1 Cor. 16:6; 2 Cor. 1:16). It would be reasonable to read Zenas and Apollos as the couriers of this letter.

And let our people also learn to take the lead in good deeds for the urgent necessities, so that they may not be fruitless (3:14). This sentence is a final, summative exhortation, recapitulating the theme of "good deeds" so prominent throughout the letter. On the relation between "good deeds" and bearing fruit, cf. Col. 1:10. It is not clear what other people Pastoral Paul has in mind when he says, "our people *also*" should learn. We might take "also" in the sense of "and once again [let me repeat myself]" (Mounce 2000, 458). The phrase "to take the lead in good deeds" echoes 3:8. One example of a good deed would be providing for traveling missionaries (3:13).

The closing greeting is general. **All those with me greet you. Greet those who are devoted to us in faith** (3:15a). "All those with me" might include Artemas and/or Tychicus (3:12) and who knows what others. There is no sense of abandonment here as in 2 Tim. 4:16, so again, we might think of this letter as falling chronologically before 2 Timothy. The omission of names raises the question whether Paul had ever actually been to Crete (see comments at 1:5). On the other hand, Paul offers similarly general greetings to the Thessalonians (1 Thess. 5:26), even though he had been there very recently and certainly knew names. "Devoted to us in faith" has to do not so much with personal affection for Paul as with adherence to the gospel Paul preached.

The benediction, **Grace be with you** (3:15b), is addressed to "you" in the plural, which is surprising at the end of a letter written entirely to "you" in the singular. The same benediction, appended to all three PE (1 Tim. 6:21b; 2 Tim. 4:22b; Titus 3:15b), gives the impression that all three letters were either composed as or edited into a collection with a secondary audience in mind.

That secondary audience now includes readers of this commentary. And so I add my own benediction for my readers:

May you take to heart what Pastoral Paul wrote to Timothy and Titus.

May your own Christian ministry become more effective as you consider this ancient advice.

And may grace be with you.

Bibliography

Aageson, James W. 2008. *Paul, the Pastoral Epistles, and the Early Church*. Peabody, MA: Hendrickson.

Abraham, William J. 2009. "Christian Perfection." Pages 587–601 in *The Oxford Handbook of Methodist Studies*. Edited by W. J. Abraham and J. E. Kirby. New York: Oxford University Press.

Adewuya, J. Ayodeji. 2016. *Holiness in the Letters of Paul: The Necessary Response to the Gospel*. Eugene, OR: Cascade.

Alexander, J. P. 1913. "The Character of Timothy." *Expository Times* 25:277–85.

Alford, Henry. 1871. *The Greek New Testament*. Vol. 3. 5th ed. London: Rivingtons.

Ames, Frank Ritchel, and J. David Miller. 2011. "Prayer and Syncretism in 1 Timothy." Pages 94–111 in vol. 2 of *Women in the Biblical World: A Survey of Old and New Testament Perspectives*. Edited by E. A. McCabe. Lanham, MD: University Press of America.

Anderson, J. G. C. 1937. "An Imperial Estate in Galatia." *Journal of Roman Studies* 27:18–21.

Armstrong, Karen. 2009. *The Case for God*. New York: Knopf.

Arndt, William F. M. 1950. "ἔγνω, 2 TIM 2:19." *Concordia Theological Monthly* 21.4:299–302.

Arzt, Peter. 1994. "'The Epistolary Introductory Thanksgiving' in the Papyri and in Paul." *Novum Testamentum* 36.1:29–46.

Asmis, Elizabeth. 2004. "Epicurean Economics." Pages 133–76 in *Philodemus and the New Testament World*. Edited by J. T. Fitzgerald, D. Obbink, and G. S. Holland. Supplements to Novum Testamentum 111. Leiden: Brill.

Aulén, Gustav. 1969. *Christus Victor: An Historical Study of the Three Main Types of the Idea of the Atonement*. Translated by H. G. Hebert. New York: Macmillan, 1931.

Baer, Chrysostom, trans. 2007. *Thomas Aquinas: Commentaries on St. Paul's Epistles to Timothy, Titus, and Philemon*. South Bend, IN: St. Augustine's Press.

253

Balch, David L. 1981. *Let Wives Be Submissive: The Domestic Code in 1 Peter*. Society of Biblical Literature Monograph Series 26. Atlanta: Scholars Press.

———. 2004. "Philodemus, 'On Wealth' and 'On Household Management': Naturally Wealthy Epicureans against Poor Cynics." Pages 177–96 in *Philodemus and the New Testament World*. Edited by J. T. Fitzgerald, D. Obbink, and G. S. Holland. Supplements to Novum Testamentum 111. Leiden: Brill.

Baldwin, Henry Scott. 2005. "An Important Word: Αὐθεντέω in 1 Timothy 2:12." Pages 39–51, 195–204 in *Women in the Church: An Analysis and Application of 1 Timothy 2:9–15*. Edited by Andreas J. Köstenberger and Thomas R. Schreiner. 2nd ed. Grand Rapids: Baker Academic.

Baldwin Bowsky, Martha W. 2016. "A Context for Knossos: Italian Sigillata Stamps and Cultural Identity across Crete." Pages 27–41 in *Roman Crete: New Perspectives*. Edited by Jane E. Francis and Anna Kouremenos. Philadelphia: Oxbow.

Barclay, J. M. G. 1991. "Paul, Philemon and the Dilemma of Christian Slave-Ownership." *New Testament Studies* 37:161–86.

Barnstone, Willis, trans. 1961. *An Anthology of Spanish Poetry*. Edited by Angel Flores. New York: Doubleday.

Barrett, C. K. 1963. *The Pastoral Epistles*. New Clarendon Bible. Oxford: Oxford University Press.

Bartchy, S. Scott. 1973. *ΜΑΛΛΟΝ ΧΡΗΣΑΙ: First-Century Slavery and 1 Corinthians 7:21*. Society of Biblical Literature Dissertation Series 11. Missoula, MT: Scholars Press.

Bartman, Elizabeth. 2001. "Hair and the Artifice of Female Adornment." *American Journal of Archaeology* 105.1:1–25.

Baskin, Judith R. 2002. *Midrashic Women: Formations of the Feminine in Rabbinic Literature*. Hanover: Brandeis University Press.

Bassler, Jouette M. 1984. "The Widow's Tale: A Fresh Look at 1 Timothy 5:3–16." *Journal of Biblical Literature* 103.1:23–41.

———. 1988. "Adam, Eve, and the Pastor: The Use of Genesis 2–3 in the Pastoral Epistles." Pages 43–65 in *Genesis 1–3 in the History of Exegesis: Intrigue in the Garden*. Edited by Gregory A. Robbins. Lewiston, NY: Mellen.

———. 1996. *1 Timothy, 2 Timothy, Titus*. Abingdon New Testament Commentaries. Nashville: Abingdon.

———. 2003. "Limits and Differentiation: The Calculus of Widows in 1 Timothy 5:3–16." Pages 122–46 in *A Feminist Companion to the Deutero-Pauline Epistles*. Edited by Amy-Jill Levine. Cleveland: Pilgrim.

Bateman, John J., trans. 1993. *Paraphrases on the Epistles to Timothy, Titus, and Philemon*. Collected Works of Erasmus. Edited by R. D. Sider. Vol. 44. Toronto: University of Toronto Press.

Batten, Alicia J. 2009. "Neither Gold nor Braided Hair (1 Tim. 2.9; 1 Pet. 3.3): Adornment, Gender and Honour in Antiquity." *New Testament Studies* 55:484–501.

———. 2014. "The Paradoxical Pearl: Signifying the Pearl in East and West." Pages 233–50 in *Dressing Judeans and Christians in Antiquity*. Edited by K. Upson-Saia, C. Daniel-Hughes, and A. J. Batten. Farnham, UK: Ashgate.

Baugh, S. M. 2005. "A Foreign World: Ephesus in the First Century." Pages 13–38, 181–95 in *Women in the Church: An Analysis and Application of 1 Timothy 2:9–15*. Edited by Andreas J. Köstenberger and Thomas R. Schreiner. 2nd ed. Grand Rapids: Baker Academic.

Baur, Ferdinand Christian. 1835. *Die sogennanten Pastoralbriefe des Apostels Paulus aufs neue kritisch untersucht*. Stuttgart: Cotta.

Beavis, Mary Ann. 2003. "'If Anyone Will Not Work, Let Them Not Eat': 1 Thessalonians 3.10 and the Social Support of Women." Pages 29–36 in *A Feminist Companion to the Deutero-Pauline Epistles*. Edited by Amy-Jill Levine. Cleveland: Pilgrim.

Beck, Norman A. 2010. *Anti-Roman Cryptograms in the New Testament: Hidden Transcripts of Hope and Liberation*. Rev. ed. New York: Peter Lang.

Beck, Richard. 2014. *The Slavery of Death*. Eugene, OR: Cascade.

———. 2016. *Reviving Old Scratch: Demons and the Devil for Doubters and the Disenchanted*. Minneapolis: Fortress.

Beilby, James K., and Paul Rhodes Eddy. 2012. *Understanding Spiritual Warfare: Four Views*. Grand Rapids: Baker Academic.

Belleville, Linda L. 2005a. "Ἰουνίαν . . . ἐπίσημοι ἐν τοῖς ἀποστόλοις: A Re-examination of Romans 16.7 in Light of Primary Source Materials." *New Testament Studies* 51.2:231–49.

———. 2005b. "Teaching and Usurping Authority: 1 Timothy 2:11–15." Pages 205–23 in *Discovering Biblical Equality: Complementarity without Hierarchy*. Edited by Ronald W. Pierce and Rebecca Merrill Groothuis. Downers Grove, IL: InterVarsity.

———. 2013. "Christology, the Pastoral Epistles, and Commentaries." Pages 317–36 in *On the Writing of Commentaries: Festschrift for Grant R. Osborne on the Occasion of His 70th Birthday*. Edited by Stanley E. Porter and Eckhard J. Schnabel. Leiden: Brill.

Berding, Kenneth. 1999. "Polycarp of Smyrna's View of the Authorship of 1 and 2 Timothy." *Vigiliae Christianae* 53.4:349–60.

Berlin, Ira, Marc Favreau, and Steven F. Miller, eds. 1998. *Remembering Slavery: African Americans Talk about Their Personal Experiences of Slavery and Emancipation*. New York: New Press.

Bird, T. E. 1940. "Exegetical Notes: Self-Control (ΣΩΦΡΟΣΥΝΗ)." *Catholic Biblical Quarterly* 2:259–63.

Blackburn, Barry L. 1993. "The Identity of the 'Women' in 1 Timothy 3:11." Pages 303–19 in vol. 1 of *Essays on Women in Earliest Christianity*. Edited by Carroll D. Osburn. Joplin, MO: College Press.

Bonhoeffer, Dietrich. 1954. *Life Together: A Discussion of Christian Fellowship*. Translated by John W. Doberstein. San Francisco: Harper & Row. Original German edition 1938.

Bonnah, George Kwame Agyei. 2008. "The Responsibilities of Titus on the Island of Crete: A Replica for the Leadership of the Church in the contemporary West African Society." Pages 213–31 in *Ein Meisterschüler: Titus und sein Brief*. Edited by Hans-Ulrich Weidemann and Wilfried Eisele. Stuttgart: Verlag Katholisches Bibelwerk.

Botkin, B. A., ed. 1945. *Lay My Burden Down: A Folk History of Slavery*. Chicago: University of Chicago Press.

Bradley, K. R. 1987. *Slaves and Masters in the Roman Empire: A Study in Social Control*. New York: Oxford University Press.

Brakke, David. 2010. *The Gnostics: Myth, Ritual, and Diversity in Early Christianity*. Cambridge, MA: Harvard University Press.

Bremmer, Jan N. 2014. *Initiation into the Mysteries of the Ancient World*. Boston: Walter de Gruyter.

Brooten, Bernadette J. 1982. *Women Leaders in the Ancient Synagogue: Inscriptional Evidence and Background Issues*. Brown Judaic Studies 36. Atlanta: Scholars Press.

Brown, Aaron. 2015. "ΓΟΗΤΕΣ not ΜΑΓΟΙ: The Use of the Jannes and Jambres Tradition in 2 Timothy 3:1–13." Unpublished paper.

Brox, Norbert. 1969. *Die Pastoralbriefe: Timotheus I, Timotheus II, Titus*. Regensburger Neues Testament 7.2. Regensburg: Pustet.

Burtchaell, James T. 1992. *From Synagogue to Church: Public Services and Offices in the Earliest Christian Communities*. Cambridge: Cambridge University Press.

Bush, Peter G. 1990. "A Note on the Structure of 1 Timothy." *New Testament Studies* 36:152–56.

Callahan, Allen Dwight, and Richard A. Horsley. 1998. "Slave Resistance in Classical Antiquity." Pages 133–51 in *Slavery in Text and Interpretation*. Semeia 83/84. Edited by A. D. Callahan, R. A. Horsley, and Abraham Smith. Atlanta: SBL Press.

Cambiano, Giuseppe. 1995. "Becoming an Adult." Pages 86–119 in *The Greeks*. Edited by Jean-Pierre Vernant. Translated by C. Lambert and T. L. Fagan. Chicago: University of Chicago Press.

Campbell, R. Alastair. 1994a. *The Elders: Seniority within Earliest Christianity*. New York: T&T Clark.

———. 1994b. "Identifying the Faithful Sayings in the Pastoral Epistles." *Journal for the Study of the New Testament* 54:73–86.

———. 1995. "ΚΑΙ ΜΑΛΙΣΤΑ ΟΙΚΕΙΩΝ—A New Look at 1 Timothy 5.8." *New Testament Studies* 41:157–60.

Campenhausen, Hans von. 1963. "Polykarp von Smyrna und die Pastoralbriefe." Pages 197–252 in *Aus der Frühzeit des Christentums*. Tübingen: Mohr Siebeck.

Chester, Andrew. 2013. "The Relevance of Jewish Inscriptions for New Testament Ethics." Pages 107–45 in *Early Christian Ethics in Interaction with Jewish and Greco-Roman Contexts*. Edited by Jan Willem van Henten and Joseph Verheyden. Boston: Brill.

Chevrollier, François. 2016. "From Cyrene to Gortyn. Notes on the Relationship between Crete and Cyrenaica under Roman Domination (1st century BC–4th century AD)." Pages 11–26 in *Roman Crete: New Perspectives*. Edited by J. E. Francis and Anna Kouremenos. Philadelphia: Oxbow.

Clark, Ron. 2006. "Family Management or Involvement? Paul's Use of προΐστημι as a Requirement for Church Leadership." *Stone-Campbell Journal* 9:243–52.

Clifton, Shane. 2009. "Empowering Pentecostal Women." *Asian Journal of Pentecostal Studies* 12.1:171–79.

Cohn, Naftali S. 2014. "What to Wear: Women's Adornment and Judean Identity in the Third Century Mishnah." Pages 21–36 in *Dressing Judeans and Christians in Antiquity*. Edited by K. Upson-Saia, C. Daniel-Hughes, and A. J. Batten. Farnham, UK: Ashgate.

Collins, Adela Yarbro. 2011. "The Female Body as Social Space in 1 Timothy." *New Testament Studies* 57:155–75.

———. 2016. "Opportunities and Limits for Women in Early Christianity." Pages 197–229 in *Bodies, Borders, Believers: Ancient Texts and Present Conversations*. Edited by Anne Hege Grung, Marianne Bjelland Kartzow, and Anna Rebecca Solevåg. Cambridge: James Clarke.

Collins, Raymond F. 2002. *I and II Timothy and Titus: A Commentary*. Louisville: Westminster John Knox.

Cooley, Alison E., and M. G. L. Cooley. 2004. *Pompeii: A Sourcebook*. New York: Routledge.

Corley, Kathleen E. 1993. *Private Women, Public Meals: Social Conflict in the Synoptic Tradition*. Peabody, MA: Hendrickson.

Corrington, Gail Paterson. 1992. "The Defense of the Body and the Discourse of Appetite: Continence and Control in the Greco-Roman World." *Semeia* 57:65–74.

Cotter, Wendy. 1994. "Women's Authority Roles in Paul's Churches: Countercultural or Conventional?" *Novum Testamentum* 36.4:350–72.

Countryman, L. William. 1980. *The Rich Christian and the Church of the Early Empire: Contradictions and Accommodations*. New York: Edwin Mellen.

Crook, Zeba. 2009. "Honor, Shame, and Social Status Revisited." *Journal of Biblical Literature* 128.3:591–611.

Crouch, James E. 1972. *The Origin and Intention of the Colossian Haustafel*. Göttingen: Vandenhoeck & Ruprecht.

Cukrowski, Kenneth L. 2006. "An Exegetical Note on the Ellipsis in 1 Timothy 2:9." Pages 232–38 in *Transmission and Reception: New Testament Text-Critical and Exegetical Studies*. Edited by J. W. Childers and D. C. Parker. Piscataway: Gorgias.

Cunningham, Mary B. 2012. "The Place of the Jesus Prayer in the *Philokalia*." Pages 195–202 in *The Philokalia: A Classic Text of Orthodox Spirituality*. Edited by Brock Bingaman and Bradley Nassif. New York: Oxford University Press.

Dahl, Nils A. 1977. *Studies in Paul: Theology for the Early Christian Mission*. Minneapolis: Augsburg.

———. 1978. "The Origin of the Earliest Prologues to the Pauline Letters." *Semeia* 12:233–77.

D'Ambra, Eve. 2007. *Roman Women*. Cambridge: Cambridge University Press.

Danby, Herbert. 1933. *The Mishnah: Translated from the Hebrew with Introduction and Brief Explanatory Notes*. Oxford: Oxford University Press.

D'Angelo, Mary Rose. 2003. "Εὐσέβεια: Roman Imperial Family Values and the Sexual Politics of 4 Maccabees and the Pastorals." *Biblical Interpretation* 11.2:39–65.

Daniel-Hughes, Carly. 2016. "The Perils of Idolatrous Garb: Tertullian and Christian Belongings in Roman Carthage." Pages 15–26 in *Religious Competition in*

257

the Greco-Roman World. Edited by Nathaniel P. DesRosiers and Lily C. Vuong. Atlanta: SBL Press.

Danker, Frederick W. 1982. *Benefactor: Epigraphic Study of a Graeco-Roman and New Testament Semantic Field*. St. Louis: Clayton.

Davies, Stevan L. 1980. *The Revolt of the Widows: The Social World of the Apocryphal Acts*. Carbondale, IL: Southern Illinois University Press.

Dehandschutter, Boudewijn. 2010. "The Epistle of Polycarp." Pages 117–33 in *The Apostolic Fathers: An Introduction*. Edited by Wilhelm Pratscher. Waco: Baylor University Press.

de Jonge, Marinus. 1978. *The Testaments of the Twelve Patriarchs: A Critical Edition of the Greek Text*. Leiden: Brill.

den Dulk, Matthijs. 2012. "I Permit No Woman to Teach Except for Thecla: The Curious Case of the Pastoral Epistles and the 'Acts of Paul' Reconsidered." *Novum Testamentum* 54.2:176–203.

Deseille, Placide. 2008. *Orthodox Spirituality and the Philokalia*. Translated by Anthony P. Gythiel. Wichita: Eighth Day.

de Villiers, Pieter G. R. 2003. "'Empty Talk' in 1 Timothy in the Light of Its Graeco-Roman Context." *Patristica et Byzantina* 14:136–55.

Dibelius, Martin, and Hans Conzelmann. 1972. *The Pastoral Epistles*. 4th ed. Translated by P. Buttolph and A. Yarbro. Hermeneia. Philadelphia: Fortress.

Dodds, E. R. 1951. *The Greeks and the Irrational*. Sather Classical Lectures 25. Berkeley: University of California Press.

Donelson, Lewis R. 1986. *Pseudepigraphy and Ethical Argument in the Pastoral Epistles*. Hermeneutische Untersuchungen zu Theologie 22; Tübingen: Mohr Siebeck.

Douglass, Jane Dempsey. 2009. "Calvin and the Church Today: Ecclesiology as Received, Changed, and Adapted." *Theology Today* 66:135–53.

Downs, David J. 2012. "Faith(fulness) in Christ Jesus in 2 Timothy 3:15." *Journal of Biblical Literature* 131.1:143–60.

———. 2016. *Alms: Charity, Reward, and Atonement in Early Christianity*. Waco: Baylor University Press.

Duff, Jeremy. 1998. "$\mathfrak{P}^{46}$ and the Pastorals: A Misleading Consensus?" *New Testament Studies* 44:578–90.

Dunn, James D. G. 1993. "Echoes of Intra-Jewish Polemic in Paul's Letter to the Galatians." *Journal of Biblical Literature* 112.3:459–77. Repr., Dunn 2008, 227–45.

———. 2008. *The New Perspective on Paul*. Rev. ed. Grand Rapids: Eerdmans. Original edition Tübingen: Mohr Siebeck, 2005.

Easton, Burton Scott. 1948. *The Pastoral Epistles: Introduction, Translation, Commentary and Word Studies*. London: SCM.

Edwards, J. Christopher. 2009. "Reading the Ransom Logion in 1 Timothy 2,6 and Titus 2,14 with Isaiah 42,6–7; 49,6–8." *Biblica* 90.2:264–66.

———. 2011. "The Christology of Titus 2:13 and 1 Timothy 2:5." *Tyndale Bulletin* 62.1:141–47.

Ehrman, Bart D. 2013. *Forgery and Counterforgery: The Use of Literary Deceit in Early Christian Polemics*. New York: Oxford University Press.

Eisen, Ute E. 2000. *Women Officeholders in Early Christianity: Epigraphical and Literary Studies*. Translated by L. M. Maloney. Collegeville, MN: Liturgical Press.

Elliott, Neil. 2004. "Strategies of Resistance and Hidden Transcripts in Pauline Communities." Pages 97–122 in *Hidden Transcripts and the Arts of Resistance: Applying the Work of James C. Scott to Jesus and Paul*. Edited by R. A. Horsley. Semeia Studies 48. Atlanta: SBL Press.

Engberg-Pedersen, Troels. 2000. *Paul and the Stoics*. Louisville: Westminster John Knox.

Epp, Eldon Jay. 2002. "Issues in the Interrelation of New Testament Textual Criticism and Canon." Pages 485–515 in *The Canon Debate*. Edited by L. M. McDonald and J. A. Sanders. Peabody, MA: Hendrickson.

———. 2005. *Junia: The First Woman Apostle*. Minneapolis: Fortress.

Erasmus. *See* Bateman 1993.

Estep, James Riley, Jr. 2011. "Women in Greco-Roman Education and Its Implications for 1 Corinthians 14 and 1 Timothy 2." Pages 80–93 in vol. 2 of *Women in the Biblical World: A Survey of Old and New Testament Perspectives*. Edited by E. A. McCabe. Lanham, MD: University Press of America.

Eubank, Nathan. 2011. "Almsgiving as 'the Commandment': A Note on 1 Timothy 6.6–19." *New Testament Studies* 58:144–50.

Evans, Rachel Held. 2015. *Searching for Sunday: Loving, Leaving, and Finding the Church*. Nashville: Nelson.

Eyben, Emiel. 1993. *Restless Youth in Ancient Rome*. London: Routledge.

Faber, Riemer A. 2005. "'Evil Beasts, Lazy Gluttons': A Neglected Theme in the Epistle to Titus." *Westminster Theological Quarterly* 67.1:135–46.

Fantham, Elaine, Helene Peet Foley, Natalie Boymel Kampen, Sarah B. Pomeroy, and Alan H. Shapiro. 1994. *Women in the Classical World*. New York: Oxford University Press.

Fatum, Lone. 2005. "Christ Domesticated: The Household Theology of the Pastorals as Political Strategy." Pages 175–207 in *The Formation of the Early Church*. Edited by Justein Ådna. Wissenschaftliche Untersuchungen zum Neuen Testament 183. Tübingen: Mohr Siebeck.

Fee, Gordon H. 1988. *1 and 2 Timothy, Titus*. Rev. ed. Peabody, MA: Hendrickson.

Ferguson, Everett. 1960. "Ordination in the Ancient Church (I)." *Restoration Quarterly* 4.3:117–38.

———. 1968. "Church Order in the Sub-Apostolic Period: A Survey of Interpretations." *Restoration Quarterly* 11.4:225–48.

———. 1975. "Laying on of Hands: Its Significance in Ordination." *Journal of Theological Studies* 2/26.1:1–12.

———. 1991. "Τόπος in 1 Timothy 2.8." *Restoration Quarterly* 33:65–73.

———. 1992. "Ordain, Ordination." *Anchor Bible Dictionary* 5:37–40.

———. 1996. *The Church of Christ: A Biblical Ecclesiology for Today*. Grand Rapids: Eerdmans.

———. 2009. *Baptism in the Early Church: History, Theology, and Liturgy in the First Five Centuries*. Grand Rapids: Eerdmans.

Fife, Robert O. 1971. *Teeth on Edge*. Grand Rapids: Baker.

Fiore, Benjamin. 1986. *The Function of Personal Example in the Socratic and Pastoral Epistles*. Analecta Biblica 105. Rome: Biblical Institute Press.

———. 2004. "The Pastoral Epistles in the Light of Philodemus' 'On Frank Criticism.'" Pages 271–93 in *Philodemus and the New Testament World*. Edited by J. T. Fitzgerald, D. Obbink, and G. S. Holland. Supplements to Novum Testamentum 111. Leiden: Brill.

Fitzgerald, John T. 1988. *Cracks in an Earthen Vessel: An Examination of the Catalogues of Hardships in the Corinthian Correspondence*. Society of Biblical Literature Dissertation Series 99. Atlanta: Scholars Press.

———. 1995. "The Problem of Perjury in Greek Context: Prolegomena to an Exegesis of Matthew 5:33; 1 Timothy 1:10; and *Didache* 2.3." Pages 156–77 in *The Social World of the First Christians: Essays in Honor of Wayne A. Meeks*. Edited by L. M. White and O. L. Yarbrough. Minneapolis: Fortress.

———. 2003. "Last Wills and Testaments in Greco-Roman Perspective." Pages 637–72 in *Early Christianity and Classical Culture: Comparative Studies in Honor of Abraham J. Malherbe*. Edited by J. T. Fitzgerald, T. H. Olbricht, and L. M. White. Atlanta: SBL Press.

Ford, J. Massyngberde. 1971. "A Note on Proto-Montanism in the Pastoral Epistles." *New Testament Studies* 17.3:338–46.

Frede, Michael. 2010. "The Case for Pagan Monotheism in Greek and Graeco-Roman Antiquity." Pages 53–81 in *One God: Pagan Monotheism in the Roman Empire*. Edited by Stephen Mitchell and Peter van Nuffelen. New York: Cambridge University Press.

Fredrickson, David E. 1996. "Παρρησία in the Pauline Epistles." Pages 163–83 in *Friendship, Flattery, and Frankness of Speech: Studies on Friendship in the New Testament World*. Edited by J. T. Fitzgerald. Supplements to Novum Testamentum 82. Leiden: Brill.

Freese, John H. 1926. *Aristotle: The "Art" of Rhetoric*. Loeb Classical Library. Cambridge, MA: Harvard University Press.

Friesen, Steven J. 1999. "Ephesian Women and Men in Public Office during the Roman Imperial Period." Pages 107–13 in *100 Jahre Österreichische Forschungen in Ephesos: Akten des Symposions Wien 1995*. Edited by Barbara Brandt and K. R. Krierer. Vienna: Verlag der Österreichischen Akademie der Wissenschaften.

———. 2001. *Imperial Cults and the Apocalypse of John: Reading Revelation in the Ruins*. New York: Oxford University Press.

———. 2014. "Junia Theodora of Corinth: Gendered Inequalities in the Early Empire." Pages 203–26 in *Corinth in Contrast: Studies in Inequality*. Edited by S. J. Friesen, S. A. James, and D. N. Schowalter. Leiden: Brill.

Galinsky, Karl. 1996. *Augustan Culture*. Princeton: Princeton University Press.

Ganss, George E., ed. 1991. *Ignatius of Loyola: The Spiritual Exercises and Selected Works*. Classics of Western Spirituality. Mahwah, NJ: Paulist Press.

Genade, Alfred A. 2011. *Persuading the Cretans: A Text-Generated Persuasion Analysis of the Letter to Titus*. Eugene, OR: Wipf & Stock.

Glad, Clarence E. 1995. *Paul and Philodemus: Adaptability in Epicurean and Early Christian Psychagogy*. Supplements to Novum Testamentum 81. Leiden: Brill.

Glancy, Jennifer A. 2006. *Slavery in Early Christianity*. Minneapolis: Fortress. Original edition, Oxford University Press, 2002.

———. 2015. "The Sexual Use of Slaves: A Response to Kyle Harper on Jewish and Christian *Porneia*." *Journal of Biblical Literature* 134.1:215–29.

Gloer, Hulitt. 1984. "Homologies and Hymns in the New Testament: Form, Content and Criteria for Identification." *Perspectives in Religious Studies* 11.2:115–32.

Goodwin, Mark J. 2001. *Paul, Apostle of the Living God*. New York: T&T Clark.

Goulder, Michael. 1996. "The Pastor's Wolves: Jewish Christian Visionaries behind the Pastoral Epistles." *Novum Testamentum* 38.3:242–56.

Gourgues, Michel. 2016. "Jesus' Testimony before Pilate in 1 Timothy 6:13." *Journal of Biblical Literature* 135.3:639–48.

Gray, Patrick. 2007. "The Liar Paradox and the Letter to Titus." *Catholic Biblical Quarterly* 69:302–14.

Greene-McCreight, Kathryn. 2000. *Feminist Reconstructions of Christian Doctrine: Narrative Analysis and Appraisal*. New York: Oxford University Press.

Gummere, Richard A. 1925. "Appendix A." Pages 451–52 in *Seneca VI: Epistulae Morales III*. Loeb Classical Library 77. Cambridge, MA: Harvard University Press.

Gundry, Robert H. 1970. "The Form, Meaning and Background of the Hymn Quoted in Timothy 3:16." Pages 203–22 in *Apostolic History and the Gospel*. Exeter: Paternoster.

Hadot, Pierre. 1995. *Philosophy as a Way of Life*. Cambridge, MA: Blackwell.

Häfner, Gerd. 2007. "Das Corpus Pastorale als literarisches Konstrukt." *Theologische Quartalschrift* 187:258–73.

Ham, Clay. 2000. "The Christ Hymn in 1 Timothy 3:16." *Stone-Campbell Journal* 3:209–28.

Handy, Lowell K. 1997. *The Educated Person's Thumbnail Introduction to the Bible*. St. Louis: Chalice.

Hanson, Anthony T. 1968. *Studies in the Pastoral Epistles*. London: SPCK.

———. 1983. *The Pastoral Epistles*. New Century Bible Commentary. Grand Rapids: Eerdmans.

Hardin, Justin K. 2008. *Galatians and the Imperial Cult: A Critical Analysis of the First-Century Social Context of Paul's Letter*. Wissenschaftliche Untersuchungen zum Neuen Testament 2/237. Tübingen: Mohr Siebeck.

Harding, Mark. 1998. *Tradition and Rhetoric in the Pastoral Epistles*. New York: Peter Lang.

———. 2017. "Apocalypticism in the Pastoral Epistles." Pages 259–74 in *The Jewish Apocalyptic Tradition and the Shaping of New Testament Thought*. Edited by B. T. Reynolds and L. T. Stuckenbruck. Minneapolis: Fortress.

Harrill, J. Albert. 2006. *Slaves in the New Testament: Literary, Social, and Moral Dimensions.* Minneapolis: Fortress.

———. 2017. "'Without Lies or Deception': Oracular Claims to Truth in the Epistle to Titus." *New Testament Studies* 63.3:451–72.

Harris, J. Rendel. 1907. "A Further Note on the Cretans." *Expositor* 3:332–37.

Harris, Murray J. 2011. "A Brief Response to 'The Christology of Titus 2:13 and 1 Timothy 2:5.'" *Tyndale Bulletin* 62.1:149–50.

Harrison, P. N. 1921. *The Problem of the Pastoral Epistles.* London: Oxford University Press.

———. 1936. *Polycarp's Two Epistles to the Philippians.* Cambridge: Cambridge University Press.

Hartog, Paul. 2002. *Polycarp and the New Testament.* Wissenschaftliche Untersuchungen zum Neuen Testament 2/134. Tübingen: Mohr Siebeck.

Hengel, Martin. 1980. "Hymn and Christology." Pages 173–97 in *Studia Biblica III: Sixth International Congress on Biblical Studies . . . 1978.* Sheffield: JSOT Press.

Herzer, Jens. 2008. "Rearranging the 'House of God': A New Perspective on the Pastoral Epistles." Pages 547–66 in Empsychoi Logoi—*Religious Innovations in Antiquity: Studies in Honour of Pieter Willem van der Horst.* Edited by Alberdina Houtman, Albert de Jong, and Magdalena Wilhelmina Misset-van de Weg. Leiden: Brill.

Hoag, Gary G. 2015. *Wealth in Ancient Ephesus and the First Letter to Timothy: Fresh Insights from "Ephesiaca" by Xenophon of Ephesus.* Winona Lake: Eisenbrauns.

Hodge, Archibald A., and Benjamin B. Warfield. 1881. *Inspiration.* Philadelphia: Presbyterian Board of Publication.

Hoklotubbe, T. Christopher. 2017. *Civilized Piety: The Rhetoric of Pietas in the Pastoral Epistles and the Roman Empire.* Waco: Baylor University Press.

Holladay, Carl R., John T. Fitzgerald, Gregory E. Sterling, and James W. Thompson, eds. 2014. *Light from the Gentiles: Hellenistic Philosophy and Early Christianity; Collected Essays, 1959–2012, by Abraham J. Malherbe.* Supplements to Novum Testamentum 150. Leiden: Brill.

Hollander, H. W., and M. de Jonge. 1985. *The Testaments of the Twelve Patriarchs: A Commentary.* Leiden: Brill.

Holmes, Michael W. 2006. *The Apostolic Fathers in English, after the Earlier Version of J. B. Lightfoot and J. R. Harmer.* 3rd ed. Grand Rapids: Baker Academic.

Hopkinson, Neil. 1984. "Callimachus' *Hymn to Zeus.*" *Classical Quarterly* 34.1:139–48.

Horrell, David G. 1993. "Converging Ideologies: Berger and Luckman and the Pastoral Epistles." *Journal for the Study of the New Testament* 50:85–103.

———. 2001. "From ἀδελφοί to οἶκος θεοῦ: Social Transformation in Pauline Christianity." *Journal of Biblical Literature* 120.2:293–311.

———. 2008. "Disciplining Performance and 'Placing' the Church: Widows, Elders and Slaves in the Household of God (1 Tim. 5,1–6,2)." Pages 109–34 in *1 Timothy Reconsidered.* Edited by K. P. Donfried. Colloquium Oecumenicum Paulinum 18. Leuven: Peeters.

Horsley, Richard A., ed. 2004. *Hidden Transcripts and the Arts of Resistance: Applying the Work of James C. Scott to Jesus and Paul.* Semeia Studies 48. Atlanta: SBL Press.

Huizenga, Annette Bourland. 2009. "Advice to the Bride: Moral Exhortation for Young Wives in Two Ancient Letter Collections." Pages 232–47 in *Jewish and Christian Scripture as Artifact and Canon.* Edited by Craig A. Evans and H. Daniel Zacharias. New York: T&T Clark.

———. 2010. "*Sōphrosynē* for Women in Pythagorean Texts." Pages 379–99 in *Women and Gender in Ancient Religions: Interdisciplinary Approaches.* Edited by S. P. Aherne-Kroll, P. A. Holloway, and J. A. Kelhoffer. Wissenschaftliche Untersuchungen zum Neuen Testament 263. Tübingen: Mohr Siebeck.

———. 2011. "Epitomizing Virtue: Clothing the Christian Woman's Body." Pages 261–81 in *Christian Body, Christian Self: Concepts of Early Christian Personhood.* Edited by Clare K. Rothschild and Trevor W. Thompson. Wissenschaftliche Untersuchungen zum Neuen Testament 284. Tübingen: Mohr Siebeck.

———. 2013. *Moral Education for Women in the Pastoral and Pythagorean Letters: Philosophers of the Household.* Supplements to Novum Testamentum 147. Leiden: Brill.

Hutson, Christopher R. 1996. "Laborers in the Lord: Romans 16 and the Women in Pauline Churches." *Leaven* 4.2:1–3, 40.

———. 1997. "Was Timothy Timid? On the Rhetoric of Fearlessness (1 Cor. 16:10–11) and Cowardice (2 Tim. 1:7)." *Biblical Research* 42:58–73.

———. 1998. "My True Child: The Rhetoric of Youth in the Pastoral Epistles." PhD diss., Yale University.

———. 2004. "The Cross as Canon: Galatians 6.16." *Leaven* 12.1:49–53.

———. 2005a. "Middle Ground? Alexander Campbell on Slavery and Carroll Osburn on Gender." Pages 335–54 in *Restoring the First-Century Church in the Twenty-First Century: Essays on the Stone-Campbell Restoration Movement (in Honor of Don Haymes).* Edited by Warren Lewis and Hans Rollmann. Eugene, OR: Wipf & Stock.

———. 2005b. Review of Van Neste 2004. *Review of Biblical Literature,* posted October 22, 2005. https://www.bookreviews.org/pdf/4529_4908.pdf.

———. 2007. "A Good Minister of Christ Jesus (1 Timothy 3:14–4:16)." *AME Zion Quarterly Review* 95.1:2–7.

———. 2012. "Ecclesiology in the Pastoral Epistles." Pages 164–88 in *The New Testament Church: The Challenge of Developing Ecclesiologies.* Edited by John Harrison and James D. Dvorak. McMaster Biblical Studies Series. Eugene, OR: Wipf & Stock.

———. 2013. "'A Little Wine': 1 Timothy 5:23 and Greco-Roman Youth." *Lexington Theological Quarterly* 45:79–98.

———. 2014. "'Saved through Childbearing': The Jewish Context of 1 Timothy 2:15." *Novum Testamentum* 56.4:392–410.

Ilan, Tal. 1996. *Jewish Women in Greco-Roman Palestine.* Peabody, MA: Hendrickson.

Instone-Brewer, David. 2002. *Divorce and Remarriage in the Bible: The Social and Literary Context.* Grand Rapids: Eerdmans.

Irwin, Brian. 2008. "The Laying on of Hands in 1 Timothy 5:22: A New Proposal," *Bulletin of Biblical Research* 18.1:123–29.

Jepsen, Gary R. 2006. "Dale Martin's '*Arsenokoités* and *Malakos*' Tried and Found Wanting." *Currents in Theology and Mission* 33.5:397–405.

Jewett, Robert. 1999. *Saint Paul Returns to the Movies: Triumph over Shame*. Grand Rapids: Eerdmans.

Johnson, Luke Timothy. 1989. "The New Testament's Anti-Jewish Slander and the Conventions of Ancient Polemic." *Journal of Biblical Literature* 108.3:419–41.

———. 1996. *Letters to Paul's Delegates: 1 Timothy, 2 Timothy, Titus*. Valley Forge, PA: Trinity.

———. 2001. *The First and Second Letters to Timothy*. Anchor Bible 35A. New York: Doubleday.

Jouanna, Jacque. 2012. *Greek Medicine from Hippocrates to Galen: Selected Papers*. Edited by P. van der Eijk. Translated by Neil Allies. Leiden: Brill, 2012.

Judge, E. A. 1960. *The Social Pattern of the Christian Groups in the First Century: Some Prolegomena to the Study of the New Testament Ideas of Social Obligation*. London: Tyndale. Repr., pages 1–56 in *Social Distinctives of the Christians in the First Century: Pivotal Essays by E. A. Judge*. Edited by David M. Scholer. Peabody, MA: Hendrickson, 2008.

Kahl, Brigitte. 2010. *Galatians Re-Imagined: Reading with the Eyes of the Vanquished*. Minneapolis: Fortress.

Kaiser, Walter C., Jr. 2000. *Mission in the Old Testament: Israel as a Light to the Nations*. Grand Rapids: Baker Academic.

Kaminsky, Joel, and Anne Stewart. 2006. "God of All the World: Universalism and Developing Monotheism in Isaiah 40–66." *Harvard Theological Review* 99.2:139–63.

Karris, Robert J. 1973. "The Background and Significance of the Polemic of the Pastoral Epistles." *Journal of Biblical Literature* 92.4:549–64.

Kartzow, Marianne Bjelland. 2009. *Gossip and Gender: Othering Speech in the Pastoral Epistles*. Beihefte zur Zeitschrift für die neutestamentliche Wissenschaft 164. New York: de Gruyter.

Kearsley, R. A. 1999. "Women in Public Life in the Roman East: Iunia Theodora, Claudia Metrodora, and Phoebe, Benefactress of Paul." *Tyndale Bulletin* 50.2:189–211.

Keble, John. 1833. "Adherence to the Apostolical Succession the Safest Course." *Tracts for the Times*, no. 4. Oxford. Online at http://anglicanhistory.org/tracts/tract4.html.

Keener, Craig S. 1992. *Paul, Women & Wives*. Peabody, MA: Hendrickson.

Kelly, J. N. D. 1963. *The Pastoral Epistles: I Timothy, II Timothy, Titus*. Black's New Testament Commentaries. London: A&C Black. Repr., Grand Rapids: Baker.

Kent, John Harvey, ed. 1966. *Corinth VIII.3: The Inscriptions, 1926–1950*. Princeton: American School of Classical Studies at Athens.

Kenyon, Frederic G. 1936. *The Chester Beatty Biblical Papyri, Fasciculus III Supplement, Pauline Epistles: Text*. London: Emery Walker.

Kidd, Reggie M. 1990. *Wealth and Beneficence in the Pastoral Epistles*. Society of Biblical Literature Dissertation Series 122. Atlanta: Scholars Press.

———. 1999. "Titus as *Apologia*: Grace for Liars, Beasts, and Bellies." *Horizons in Biblical Theology* 21:185–209.

Kidson, Lyn. 2014. "1 Timothy: An Administrative Letter." *Early Christianity* 5:97–116.

Kim, Hong Bom. 2004. "The Interpretation of ΜΑΛΙΣΤΑ in 1 Timothy 5:17." *Novum Testamentum* 46.4:360–68.

Kittredge, Cynthia Briggs. 2004. "Reconstructing 'Resistance' or Reading to Resist: James C. Scott and the Politics of Interpretation." Pages 145–55 in *Hidden Transcripts and the Arts of Resistance: Applying the Work of James C. Scott to Jesus and Paul*. Edited by R. A. Horsley. Semeia Studies 48. Atlanta: SBL Press.

Klauck, Hans-Josef. 2006. *Ancient Letters and the New Testament: A Guide to Context and Exegesis*. Waco: Baylor University Press.

Kline, A. S. 2003. "Horace: The Odes." https://www.poetryintranslation.com/PITBR/Latin/Horacehome.php.

———. 2008. "Propertius: The Elegies. Book IV." https://www.poetryintranslation.com/PITBR/Latin/PropertiusBkFour.php.

Klingberg, Frank J. 1956. *The Carolina Chronicle of Dr. Francis Le Jau, 1706–1717*. Berkeley: University of California Press.

Knight, George W. 1979. *The Faithful Sayings in the Pastoral Letters*. Grand Rapids: Baker. Original edition Kampen: Kok, 1968.

———. 1992. *Commentary on the Pastoral Epistles*. New International Greek Testament Commentary. Grand Rapids: Eerdmans.

Koester, Helmut. 2000. *History and Literature of Early Christianity*. Vol. 2 of *Introduction to the New Testament*. 2nd ed. Minneapolis: Fortress.

Konstan, David, Diskin Clay, Clarence E. Glad, Johan C. Thom, and James Ware. 1998. *Philodemus on Frank Criticism: Introduction, Translation, and Notes*. Society of Biblical Literature Texts and Translations 43. Atlanta: Scholars Press.

Köstenberger, Andreas J. 2005. "A Complex Sentence: The Syntax of 1 Timothy 2:12." Pages 53–84, 204–7 in *Women in the Church: An Analysis and Application of 1 Timothy 2:9–15*. Edited by Andreas J. Köstenberger and Thomas R. Schreiner. 2nd ed. Grand Rapids: Baker Academic.

Kraemer, Ross S. 1985. "A New Inscription from Malta and the Question of Women Elders in the Diaspora Jewish Communities. *Harvard Theological Review* 78:431–38.

———. 1988. *Maenads, Martyrs, Matrons, Monastics: A Sourcebook on Women's Religions in the Greco-Roman World*. Philadelphia: Fortress.

———. 1992. *Her Share of the Blessings: Women's Religions among Pagans, Jews, and Christians in the Greco-Roman World*. New York: Oxford University Press.

Krause, Deborah. 2016. "Construing and Containing an Imperial Paul: Rhetoric and the Politics of Representation in the Pastoral Epistles." Pages 203–20 in *An Introduction to Empire in the New Testament*. Edited by Adam Winn. Atlanta: SBL Press.

Kroeger, Richard Clark, and Catherine Clark Kroeger. 1992. *I Suffer Not a Woman: Rethinking 1 Timothy 2:11–15 in Light of Ancient Evidence*. Grand Rapids: Baker.

Lacey, W. K. 1968. *The Family in Classical Greece*. Ithaca: Cornell University Press.

Lamott, Anne. 2000. *Traveling Mercies: Some Thoughts on Faith*. New York: Anchor Books.

Lampe, Peter. 2003. *From Paul to Valentinus: Christians at Rome in the First Two Centuries.* Translated by M. Steinhauser. Edited by M. D. Johnson. Minneapolis: Fortress.

Lau, Andrew Y. 1996. *Manifest in Flesh: The Epiphany Christology of the Pastoral Epistles.* Wissenschaftliche Untersuchungen zum Neuen Testament 2/86. Tübingen: Mohr Siebeck.

Lefkowitz, Mar R., and Maureen Fant. 1992. *Women's Life in Greece and Rome: A Source Book in Translation.* 2nd ed. Baltimore: Johns Hopkins University Press.

Le Saint, William P., trans. 1951. *Tertullian, Treatises on Marriage and Remarriage: "To His Wife" and "Exhortation to Chastity, Monogamy."* Ancient Christian Writers 13. Westminster, MD: Newman.

Lienhard, Joseph T., trans. 1996. *Origen: Homilies on Luke; Fragments on Luke.* Fathers of the Church 94. Washington, DC: Catholic University of America Press.

Lightfoot, J. B. 1868. *St. Paul's Epistle to the Philippians.* London: Macmillan. Repr., Peabody, MA: Hendrickson, 1991.

———. 1889–90. *The Apostolic Fathers.* 2 parts in 5 vols. London: Macmillan.

Lightman, Marjorie, and William Zeisel. 1977. "Univira: An Example of Continuity and Change in Roman Society." *Church History* 46:19–32.

Lincoln, Bruce. 2000. "Apocalyptic Temporality and Politics in the Ancient World." Pages 457–75 in *The Origins of Apocalypticism in Judaism and Christianity.* Vol. 1 of *The Encyclopedia of Apocalypticism.* Edited by J. J. Collins. New York: Continuum.

Lippolis, Enzo. 2016. "Roman Gortyn: From Greek Polis to Provincial Capital." Pages 155–74 in *Roman Crete: New Perspectives.* Edited by Jane E. Francis and Anna Kouremenos. Philadelphia: Oxbow.

Lock, Walter. 1924. *A Critical and Exegetical Commentary on the Pastoral Epistles.* International Critical Commentary. Edinburgh: T&T Clark.

Luibheid, Colm, trans. *Pseudo-Dionysius: The Complete Works.* Mahwah, NJ: Paulist Press, 1987.

MacDonald, Dennis Ronald. 1983. *The Legend and the Apostle: The Battle for Paul in Story and Canon.* Philadelphia: Westminster.

MacDonald, Margaret Y. 1988. *The Pauline Churches: A Socio-Historical Study of Institutionalization in the Pauline and Deutero-Pauline Writings.* Society of New Testament Studies Monograph Series 60. Cambridge: Cambridge University Press.

———. 1996. *Early Christian Women and Pagan Opinion: The Power of the Hysterical Woman.* Cambridge: Cambridge University Press.

MacLeod, David J. 2006. "Christology in Six Lines: An Exposition of 1 Timothy 3:16." *Bibliotheca Sacra* 159.635:314–48.

MacLeod, M. D. 1961. *Lucian with an English Translation.* Loeb Classical Library. Cambridge, MA: Harvard University Press.

MacMullen, Ramsay. 1980. "Women in Public in the Roman Empire." *Historia: Zeitschrift für alte Geschichte* 29.2:208–18.

———. 1981. *Paganism in the Roman Empire.* New Haven: Yale University Press.

————. 1982. "Roman Attitudes to Greek Love." *Historia: Zeitschrift für alte Geschichte* 31.4:484–502.

Madigan, Kevin, and Carolyn Osiek. 2005. *Ordained Women in the Early Church: A Documentary History.* Baltimore: Johns Hopkins University Press.

Malherbe, Abraham J. 1977. *The Cynic Epistles: A Study Edition.* Sources for Biblical Study 12. Atlanta: Scholars Press.

————. 1980. "Medical Imagery in the Pastoral Epistles." Pages 19–35 in *Texts and Testaments: Critical Essays on the Bible and Early Christian Fathers.* Edited by W. E. March. San Antonio: Trinity University Press. Repr., Holladay et al. 2014, 117–34.

————. 1983. *Social Aspects of Early Christianity.* 2nd ed. Philadelphia: Fortress.

————. 1984. "'In Season and Out of Season': 2 Timothy 4:2." *Journal of Biblical Literature* 103:235–43. Repr., Holladay et al. 2014, 187–96.

————. 1985/86. "Not in a Corner." *Second Century* 5.4:193–210. Repr., Holladay et al. 2014, 209–27.

————. 1986. *Moral Exhortation: A Greco-Roman Sourcebook.* Philadelphia: Westminster.

————. 1988. *Ancient Epistolary Theorists.* Society of Biblical Literature Sources for Biblical Study 19. Atlanta: Scholars Press. Originally in *Ohio Journal of Religious Studies* 5 (1977): 3–77.

————. 1989. *Paul and the Popular Philosophers.* Minneapolis: Fortress.

————. 1994. "*Paulus Senex.*" *Restoration Quarterly* 36.4:197–207. Repr., Holladay et al. 2014, 277–88.

————. 2004. "Paraenesis in the Epistle to Titus." Pages 297–317 in *Early Christian Paraenesis in Context.* Edited by James Starr and Troels Engberg-Pedersen. Beihefte zur Zeitschrift für die neutestamentliche Wissenschaft 125. New York: de Gruyter. Repr., Holladay et al. 2014, 407–30.

————. 2005. "'Christ Jesus Came into the World to Save Sinners': Soteriology in the Pastoral Epistles." Pages 331–58 in *Salvation in the New Testament: Perspectives on Soteriology.* Edited by Jan G. van der Watt. Supplements to Novum Testamentum 121. Leiden: Brill. Repr., Holladay et al. 2014, 431–58.

————. 2007. "The *Virtus Feminarum* in 1 Timothy 2:9–15." Pages 45–65 in *Renewing Tradition: Studies in Texts and Contexts in Honor of James W. Thompson.* Edited by M. W. Hamilton, T. H. Olbricht, and J. Peterson. Eugene, OR: Pickwick. Repr., Holladay et al. 2014, 459–78.

————. 2008. "How to Treat Old Women and Old Men: The Use of Philosophical Traditions and Scripture in 1 Timothy 5." Pages 263–90 in *Scripture and Traditions: Essays on Early Judaism and Christianity in Honor of Carl R. Holladay.* Edited by Patrick Gray and Gail R. O'Day. Supplements to Novum Testamentum 129. Leiden: Brill. Repr., Holladay et al. 2014, 479–506.

————. 2010. "Godliness, Self-Sufficiency, Greed, and the Enjoyment of Wealth: 1 Timothy 6:3–19, Part I." *Novum Testamentum* 52.4:376–405. Repr., Holladay et al. 2014, 507–34.

———. 2011. "Godliness, Self-Sufficiency, Greed, and the Enjoyment of Wealth: 1 Timothy 6:3–19, Part II." *Novum Testamentum* 53.1:73–96. Repr., Holladay et al. 2014, 535–58.

———. 2012. "Overseers as Household Managers in the Pastoral Epistles." Pages 72–88 in *Text, Image, and Christians in the Greco-Roman World: A Festschrift in Honor of David Lee Balch*. Edited by A. C. Niang and C. Osiek. Pittsburgh Theological Monograph Series 176. Eugene, OR: Wipf & Stock. Repr., Holladay et al. 2014, 559–73.

Malherbe, Abraham J., and Everett Ferguson, trans. 1978. *Gregory of Nyssa: The Life of Moses*. Mahwah, NJ: Paulist Press. Repr., San Francisco: HarperOne, 2006.

Malina, Bruce M. 1993. *The New Testament World: Insights from Cultural Anthropology*. Rev. ed. Louisville: Westminster John Knox.

Malina, Bruce M., and J. Pilch. 2006. *Social-Science Commentary on the Letters of Paul*. Minneapolis: Fortress.

Marshall, I. Howard. 1999. *The Pastoral Epistles*. International Critical Commentary. New York: T&T Clark.

Marshall, John W. 2008. "'I Left You in Crete': Narrative Deception and Social Hierarchy in the Letter to Titus." *Journal of Biblical Literature* 127.4:781–803.

Marshall, Peter. 1983. "A Metaphor of Social Shame: ΘΡΙΑΜΒΕΥΕΙΝ in 2 Corinthians 2:14." *Novum Testamentum* 25.4:302–17.

Martin, Clarice J. 1998. "'Somebody Done Hoodoo'd the Hoodoo Man': Language, Power, Resistance, and the Effective History of Pauline Texts in American Slavery." Pages 203–33 in *Slavery in Text and Interpretation*. Semeia 83/84. Edited by A. D. Callahan, R. A. Horsley, and Abraham Smith. Atlanta: SBL Press.

———. 2007. "1–2 Timothy, Titus." Pages 409–36 in *True to Our Native Land: An African American New Testament Commentary*. Edited by B. K. Blount et al. Minneapolis: Fortress.

Martin, Dale B. 1990. *Slavery as Salvation: The Metaphor of Slavery in Pauline Christianity*. New Haven: Yale University Press.

———. 2006. *Sex and the Single Savior: Gender and Sexuality in Biblical Interpretation*. Louisville: Westminster John Knox.

———. 2010. "When Did Angels Become Demons?" *Journal of Biblical Literature* 129.4:657–77.

Martin, Ralph P. 1983. *Carmen Christi: Philippians 2:5–11 in Recent Interpretation and in the Setting of Early Christian Worship*. Rev. ed. Grand Rapids: Eerdmans.

Martin, Troy W. 2000. "Entextualized and Implied Rhetorical Situations: The Case of First Timothy and Titus." *Biblical Research* 45:5–24.

———. 2012. "Poets, Playwrights, Plastic Artists, Physicians, Physiologists, Philo, and Paul on *Peritomē*." Paper delivered at the Christian Scholars Conference in Nashville, Tennessee.

Martyn, J. Louis. 1998. *Galatians: A New Translation with Introduction and Commentary*. Anchor Bible 33A. New York: Doubleday.

Mattern, Susan P. 2008. *Galen and the Rhetoric of Healing*. Baltimore: Johns Hopkins University Press.

Mbuwayesango, Dora R. 2014. "Feminist Biblical Studies in Africa." Pages 71–85 in *Feminist Biblical Studies in the Twentieth Century: Scholarship and Movement*. Edited by Elisabeth Schüssler Fiorenza. The Bible and Women 9.1. Atlanta: SBL Press.

McGowan, Andrew. 2001. "Marcion's Love of Creation." *Journal of Early Christian Studies* 9.3:295–311.

McKee, Elsie. 2009. "Calvin and Praying for 'All People Who Dwell on Earth.'" *Interpretation* 63.2:130–40.

Meeks, Wayne A. 1983. *The First Urban Christians: The Social World of the Apostle Paul*. New Haven: Yale University Press.

Meier, John P. 1999. "The Inspiration of Scripture: But What Counts as Scripture? (2 Tim. 1:1–14; 3:14–17; cf. 1 Tim. 5:18." *Mid-Stream* 38.1–2:71–78.

Meritt, Benjamin Dean, ed. 1931. *Corinth VIII.1: Greek Inscriptions, 1896–1927*. Cambridge, MA: Harvard University Press for the American School of Classical Studies at Athens.

Merz, Annette. 2004. *Die fictive Selbstauslegung des Paulus: Intertextuelle Studien zur Intention und Rezeption der Pastoralbriefe*. Novum Testamentum et Orbis Antiquus 52. Göttingen: Vandenhoeck & Ruprecht.

Methuen, Charlotte. 1997. "The 'Virgin Widow': A Problematic Social Role for the Early Church?" *Harvard Theological Review* 90.3:285–98.

Metzger, Bruce M. 1972. "Literary Forgeries and Canonical Pseudepigrapha." *Journal of Biblical Literature* 91.1:3–24.

Mihoc, Vasile. 2008. "The Final Admonition to Timothy (1 Tim 6,3–21)." Pages 135–52 in *1 Timothy Reconsidered*. Edited by K. P. Donfried. Colloquium Oecumenicum Paulinum 18. Leuven: Peeters.

Miller, James D. 1997. *The Pastoral Letters as Composite Documents*. Society of New Testament Studies Monograph Series 93. Cambridge: Cambridge University Press.

Mitchell, Margaret M. 1992. "New Testament Envoys in the Context of Greco-Roman Diplomatic and Epistolary Conventions: The Example of Timothy and Titus." *Journal of Biblical Literature* 111.4:641–62.

———. 1999. "'Speaking of God as He Was Able': A Response to Luke Timothy Johnson and Jerry L. Sumney." *Horizons in Biblical Theology* 21.2:124–39.

———. 2002. "PTebt 703 and the Genre of 1 Timothy: The Curious Career of a Ptolemaic Papyrus in Pauline Scholarship." *Novum Testamentum* 44.4:344–70.

———. 2008. "Corrective Composition, Corrective Exegesis: The Teaching on Prayer in 1 Timothy 2,1–15." Pages 41–62 in *1 Timothy Reconsidered*. Edited by Karl P. Donfried. Colloquium Oecumenicum Paulinum 18. Leuven: Peeters.

Montgomery, William E. 1993. *Under Their Own Vine and Fig Tree: The African-American Church in the South, 1865–1900*. Baton Rouge: Louisiana State University Press.

Moo, Douglas. 2006. "What Does It Mean Not to Teach or Have Authority over Men? 1 Timothy 2:11–15." Pages 179–93 in *Recovering Biblical Manhood and Womanhood: A Response to Evangelical Feminism*. Edited by John Piper and Wayne Grudem. Wheaton: Crossway.

Mounce, William D. 2000. *Pastoral Epistles*. Word Biblical Commentary 46. Nashville: Nelson.

Murphy-O'Connor, Jerome. 1991. "2 Timothy Contrasted with 1 Timothy and Titus." *Revue biblique* 98:403–18.

———. 1995. *Paul the Letter Writer: His World, His Options, His Skills.* Collegeville, MN: Liturgical Press.

Nadar, Sarojini. 1991. "A South African Indian Womanist Reading of the Character of Ruth." Pages 159–75 in *Other Ways of Reading: African Women and the Bible.* Edited by Musa W. Dube. Atlanta: SBL Press.

Neusner, Jacob. 2006. *The Babylonian Talmud: Translation and Commentary.* 22 vols. Peabody, MA: Hendrickson.

Nevett, Lisa. 2002. "Continuity and Change in Greek Households under Roman Rule." Pages 81–97 in *Greek Romans and Roman Greeks.* Edited by E. N. Osternfeld. Aarhus: Aarhus University Press.

Newman, R. J. 1989. "*Cotidie meditare*: Theory and Practice of the *meditatio* in Imperial Stoicism." *Aufstieg und Niedergang der römischen Welt: Geschichte und Kultur Roms im Spiegel der neueren Forschung* 2.36.3:1473–1517.

Neyrey, Jerome H. 1994. "Despising the Shame of the Cross: Honor and Shame in the Johannine Passion Narrative." *Semeia* 68:113–37.

———. 2003. "Teaching You in Public and from House to House (Acts 20.20): Unpacking a Cultural Stereotype." *Journal for the Study of the New Testament* 26.1:69–102.

———. 2005a. "'First,' 'Only,' 'One of a Few,' and 'No One Else': The Rhetoric of Uniqueness and the Doxologies of 1 Timothy." *Biblica* 86:59–87.

———. 2005b. "God as Benefactor and Patron: The Major Cultural Model for Interpreting the Deity in Greco-Roman Antiquity." *Journal for the Study of the New Testament* 27.4:465–92.

Ng, Esther Yue L. 2008. "Mirror Reading and Guardians of Women in the Early Roman Empire." *Journal of Theological Studies* 2/59.2:679–95.

Nock, Arthur Darby. 1928. "Notes on Ruler-Cult III: Ptolemy Epiphanes." *Journal of Hellenic Studies* 48:38–41. Repr., Nock 1972, 1:152–56.

———. 1933. *Conversion: The Old and the New in Religion from Alexander the Great to Augustine of Hippo.* Oxford: Clarendon.

———. 1951. "*Soter* and *Euergetes*." Pages 127–48 in *The Joy of Study: Papers on New Testament and Related Subjects Presented to Honor Frederick Clifton Grant.* Edited by S. E. Johnson. New York: Macmillan. Repr., Nock 1972, 2:720–35.

———. 1972. *Essays on Religion and the Ancient World.* Edited by Zeph Stewart. 2 vols. Cambridge, MA: Harvard University Press.

North, Helen. 1966. *Sophrosyne: Self-Knowledge and Self-Restraint in Greek Literature.* Ithaca: Cornell University Press.

Nutton, Vivian. 2013. *Ancient Medicine.* 2nd ed. New York: Routledge.

Nwankwo, Lawrence. 2002. "'You Have Received the Spirit of Power . . .' (2 Tim. 1:7): Reviewing the Prosperity Message in the Light of a Theology of Empowerment." *Journal of the European Pentecostal Theological Association* 22:56–77.

Oberlinner, Lorenz. 1994. *Kommentar zum ersten Timotheusbrief.* Vol. 1 of *Die Pastoralbriefe.* Herders theologischer Kommentar zum Neuen Testament. Freiburg im Breisgau: Herder.

O'Neill, J. C. 2004. "Paul Wrote Some of All, but Not All of Any." Pages 169–88 in *The Pauline Canon*. Edited by S. E. Porter. Atlanta: SBL Press.

Osborn, Eric F. 2001. *Irenaeus of Lyon*. Cambridge: Cambridge University Press.

Osburn, Carroll D. 1982. "ΑΥΘΕΝΤΕΩ (1 Tim. 2:12)." *Restoration Quarterly* 25.1:1–12.

———. 2001. *Women in the Church: Reclaiming the Ideal*. 2nd ed. Abilene, TX: Abilene Christian University Press.

Osiek, Carolyn, and David L. Balch. 1997. *Families in the New Testament World: Households and House Churches*. Louisville: Westminster John Knox.

Osiek, Carolyn, and Margaret Y. MacDonald. 2006. *A Woman's Place: House Churches in Earliest Christianity*. Minneapolis: Fortress.

Oulton, John E., and Henry Chadwick. 1954. *Alexandrian Christianity: Selected Translations of Clement and Origen*. Library of Christian Classics 2. Philadelphia: Westminster.

Padgett, Alan. 1987. "Wealthy Women at Ephesus: 1 Timothy 2:8–15 in Social Context." *Interpretation* 41.1:19–31.

Page, Sydney. 1993. "Marital Expectations of Church Leaders in the Pastoral Epistles." *Journal for the Study of the New Testament* 50:105–20.

Pagels, Elaine. 1979. *The Gnostic Gospels*. New York: Random House.

———. 1995. *The Origin of Satan*. New York: Random House.

Pao, David W. 2010. "Gospel within the Constraints of a Literary Form: Pauline Introductory Thanksgivings and Paul's Theology of Thanksgiving." Pages 101–27 in *Paul and the Ancient Letter Form*. Edited by S. E. Porter and S. A. Adams. Leiden: Brill.

Parkin, Tim G. 2003. *Old Age in the Roman World: A Cultural and Social History*. Baltimore: Johns Hopkins University Press.

Paulsell, Stephanie. 2001. "'The Inscribed Heart: The Spirituality of Intellectual Work'; Reading as a Spiritual Practice." *Lexington Theological Quarterly* 36.3:139–54.

Payne, Philip B. 2009. *Man and Woman, One in Christ: An Exegetical and Theological Study of Paul's Letters*. Grand Rapids: Zondervan.

Peterson, Erik. 2012. *ΕΙΣ ΘΕΟΣ: Epigraphische, formgeschichtliche und religionsgeschichtliche Untersuchungen*. Edited by Christoph Markschies. Würtzburg: Echter. Repr. of Forschungen zur Religion und Literatur des Alten und Neuen Testaments 24. Göttingen: Vandenhoeck & Ruprecht, 1926.

Pervo, Richard I. 1994. "Romancing an Oft-Neglected Stone: The Pastoral Epistles and the Epistolary Novel." *Journal of Higher Criticism* 1:25–47.

———. 2010. *The Making of Paul: Constructions of the Apostle in Early Christianity*. Minneapolis: Fortress.

———. 2015. "Acts in Ephesus (and Environs) c. 115." *Forum*, 3rd series, 4.2:125–51.

———. 2016. *The Pastorals and Polycarp: Titus, 1–2 Timothy, and Polycarp to the Philippians*. Salem, OR: Polebridge.

Pfitzner, V. C. 1967. *Paul and the Agon Motif*. Leiden: Brill.

Phang, Sara Elise. 2001. *The Marriage of Roman Soldiers (13 BC–AD 235): Law and Family in the Imperial Army*. Leiden: Brill.

Pietersen, Lloyd K. 2003. "Magic/Thaumaturgy and the Pastoral Epistles." Pages 157–67 in *Magic in the Biblical World: From the Rod of Aaron to the Ring of Solomon.* Edited by T. E. Klutz. New York: T&T Clark.

———. 2004. *The Polemic of the Pastorals: A Sociological Examination of the Development of Pauline Christianity.* Journal for the Study of the New Testament Supplement Series 264. New York: T&T Clark.

Pietersma, Albert. 1994. *The Apocryphon of Jannes and Jambres the Magicians.* Leiden: Brill.

Pitts, Andrew W. 2013. "Style and Pseudonymity in Pauline Scholarship: A Register Based Configuration." Pages 113–52 in *Paul and Pseudepigraphy.* Edited by S. E. Porter and G. P. Fewster. Leiden: Brill.

Platt, Verity. 2015. "Epiphany." Pages 491–504 in *Oxford Handbook of Ancient Greek Religion.* Edited by Esther Eidinow and Julia Kent. New York: Oxford University Press.

Pomeroy, Sarah B. 1975. *Goddesses, Whores, Wives, and Slaves: Women in Classical Antiquity.* New York: Schocken.

———. 1984. *Women in Hellenistic Egypt from Alexander to Cleopatra.* New York: Schocken.

———, trans. 1994. *Xenophon, Oeconomicus: A Social and Historical Commentary.* Oxford: Clarendon.

———. 2013. *Pythagorean Women: Their History and Writings.* Baltimore: Johns Hopkins University Press.

Portefaix, Lilian. 2003. "'Good Citizenship' in the Household of God: Women's Position in the Pastorals Reconsidered in the Light of Roman Rule." Pages 147–58 in *A Feminist Companion to the Deutero-Pauline Epistles.* Edited by Amy-Jill Levine. Cleveland: Pilgrim.

Porter, Stanley E. 2013. "Pauline Chronology and the Question of Pseudonymity of the Pastoral Epistles." Pages 65–88 in *Paul and Pseudepigraphy.* Edited by S. E. Porter and G. P. Fewster. Leiden: Brill.

Powell, Mark A. 2008. "Canonical Theism and the Challenge of Epistemic Certainty: Papal Infallibility as a Case Study." Pages 195–209 in *Canonical Theism: A Proposal for Theology and the Church.* Edited by W. J. Abraham, J. E. Vickers, and N. Van Kirk. Grand Rapids: Eerdmans.

Powers, Janet Everts. 2001. "Recovering a Woman's Head with Prophetic Authority: A Pentecostal Interpretation of 1 Corinthians 11:2–16." *Journal of Pentecostal Theology* 10.1:11–37.

Powery, Emerson B., and Rodney S. Sadler Jr. 2016. *The Genesis of Liberation: Biblical Interpretation in the Antebellum Narratives of the Enslaved.* Grand Rapids: Eerdmans.

Poythress, Vern Sheridan. 2002. "The Meaning of μάλιστα in 2 Timothy 4:13 and Related Verses." *Journal of Theological Studies* 2/53.2:423–532.

Price, S. R. F. 1980. "Between Man and God: Sacrifice in the Roman Imperial Cult." *Journal of Roman Studies* 70:28–43.

———. 1984. *Rituals and Power: The Roman Imperial Cult in Asia Minor.* Cambridge: Cambridge University Press.

Prior, Michael. 1989. *Paul the Letter Writer and the Second Letter to Timothy.* Journal for the Study of the New Testament Supplement Series 23. Sheffield: JSOT Press.

Purvis, Sally B. 1993. *The Power of the Cross: Foundations for a Christian Feminist Ethic of Community.* Nashville: Abingdon.

Quasten, Johannes. 1950. *Patrology I: The Beginnings of Patristic Literature; From the Apostles Creed to Irenaeus.* Repr., Westminster, MD: Christian Classics, 1986.

Quinn, Jerome D. 1990a. *The Letter to Titus: A New Translation with Notes and Commentary.* Anchor Bible 35. New York: Doubleday.

———. 1990b. "Paraenesis and the Pastoral Epistles: Lexical Observations Bearing on the Nature of the Sub-genre and Soundings on Its Role in Socialization and Liturgies." *Semeia* 50:189–210.

Raboteau, Albert J. 1978. *Slave Religion: The "Invisible Institution" in the Antebellum South.* New York: Oxford University Press.

Ramelli, Ilaria L. E. 2009. "The Pastoral Epistles and Hellenistic Philosophy: 1 Timothy 5:1–2, Hierocles and the 'Contraction of Circles.'" *Catholic Biblical Quarterly* 73:562–81.

———. 2010a. "Theosebia: A Presbyter of the Catholic Church." *Journal of Feminist Studies in Religion* 26.2:79–102.

———. 2010b. "1 Timothy 5:6 and the Notion and Terminology of Spiritual Death: Hellenistic Moral Philosophy in the Pastoral Epistles." *Aevum* 84.1:237–50.

———. 2011. "Spiritual Weakness, Illness, and Death in 1 Corinthians 11:30." *Journal of Biblical Literature* 130.1:145–63.

Rawson, Beryl. 1986. "The Roman Family." Pages 1–57 in *The Family in Ancient Rome: New Perspectives.* Edited by Beryl Rawson. Ithaca, NY: Cornell University Press.

Reed, Jeffrey T. 1996. "Are Paul's Thanksgivings 'Epistolary'?" *Journal for the Study of the New Testament* 61:87–99.

Reumann, John Henry Paul. 1959. "*Oikonomia* = "Covenant": Terms for *Heilsgeschichte* in Early Christian Usage." *Novum Testamentum* 3.4:282–92.

Richards, William A. 2002. *Difference and Distance in Post-Pauline Christianity: An Epistolary Analysis of the Pastorals.* New York: Peter Lang.

Robinson, John A. T. 1976. *Redating the New Testament.* London: SCM.

Rohrbaugh, Richard L. 2001. "Gossip in the New Testament." Pages 239–59 in *Social Scientific Models for Interpreting the Bible: Essays by the Context Group in Honor of Bruce J. Malina.* Edited by J. J. Pilch. Leiden: Brill.

Rollins, Peter. 2006. *How (Not) to Speak of God: Marks of the Emerging Church.* Brewster, MA: Paraclete.

Rothschild, Clare K. 2014. *Paul in Athens: The Popular Religious Context of Acts 17.* Wissenschaftliche Untersuchungen zum Neuen Testament 341. Tübingen: Mohr Siebeck.

Rowe, C. Kavin. 2009. *World Upside Down: Reading Acts in the Graeco-Roman Age.* New York: Oxford University Press.

Ruden, Sarah. 2010. *Paul among the People: The Apostle Reinterpreted and Reimagined in His Own Time.* New York: Random House.

Saller, Richard P. 1999. "*Pater Familias, Mater Familias*, and the Gendered Semantics of the Roman Household." *Classical Philology* 94.2:182–97.

Sampley, J. Paul. 1980. *Pauline Partnership in Christ: Christian Community and Commitment in Light of Roman Law.* Philadelphia: Fortress.

Sanders, Jack T. 1962. "The Transition from Opening Epistolary Thanksgiving to Body in the Letters of the Pauline Corpus." *Journal of Biblical Literature* 81.4:348–62.

Schmidt, Thomas E. 1995. "Mark 15:16–32: The Crucifixion Narrative and the Roman Triumphal Procession." *New Testament Studies* 41.1:1–18.

Schreiner, Thomas R. 2005. "An Interpretation of 1 Timothy 2:9–15: A Dialogue with Scholarship." Pages 85–120, 207–29 in *Women in the Church: An Analysis and Application of 1 Timothy 2:9–15.* Edited by Andreas J. Köstenberger and Thomas R. Schreiner. 2nd ed. Grand Rapids: Baker Academic.

Schürer, Emil. 1979. *The History of the Jewish People in the Age of Jesus Christ: A New English Edition.* Vol. 2. Revised by G. Vermes, F. Millar, and M. Black. Edinburgh: T&T Clark.

———. 1986. *The History of the Jewish People in the Age of Jesus Christ: A New English Edition.* Vol. 3.1. Revised by G. Vermes, F. Millar, and M. Goodman. Edinburgh: T&T Clark.

Schüssler Fiorenza, Elisabeth. 1983. *In Memory of Her: A Feminist Theological Reconstruction of Christian Origins.* New York: Crossroad.

———. 1998. *The Book of Revelation: Justice and Judgment.* 2nd ed. Minneapolis: Fortress.

———, ed. 2014. *Feminist Biblical Studies in the Twentieth Century: Scholarship and Movement.* The Bible and Women 9.1. Atlanta: SBL Press.

Scott, Brian DeWayne. 2016. *Kyle and Yeshua: How American Interests Hijacked the Messiah's Religion.* 2nd ed. Gallatin, TN: Blacksheep.

Scott, James C. 1990. *Domination and the Arts of Resistance: Hidden Transcripts.* New Haven: Yale University Press.

———. 2013. *Decoding Subaltern Politics: Ideology, Disguise, and Resistance in Agrarian Politics.* New York: Routledge.

Sherrard, Philip. 1989. "The Revival of Hesychast Spirituality." Pages 417–31 in *Christian Spirituality: Post-Reformation and Modern.* Edited by Louis Dupré and D. E. Saliers, with John Meyendorff. New York: Crossroad.

Skeat, T. C. 1979. "Especially the Parchments: A Note on 2 Timothy 4:13." *Journal of Theological Studies* 2/30.1:173–77.

Smail, T. A., trans. 1964. *The Second Epistle of Paul to the Corinthians, and the Epistles to Timothy, Titus and Philemon.* By John Calvin. Calvin's New Testament Commentaries 10. Edited by D. W. Torrance and T. F. Torrance. Grand Rapids: Eerdmans.

Smith, Christian. 2011. *The Bible Made Impossible: Why Biblicism Is Not a Truly Evangelical Reading of Scripture.* Grand Rapids: Brazos.

Smith, Craig A. 2006. "A Study of 2 Timothy 4:1–8: The Contribution of Epistolary Analysis and Rhetorical Criticism." *Tyndale Bulletin* 57.1:151–54.

Smith, James K. A. 2016. *You Are What You Love: The Spiritual Power of Habit.* Grand Rapids: Brazos.

Smith, Kevin, and Arthur Song. 2006. "Some Christological Implications in Titus 2:13." *Neotestamentica* 40.2:284–94.

Smyth, Herbert Weir. 1956. *Greek Grammar.* Revised by Gordon M. Messing. Cambridge, MA: Harvard University Press.

Sørensen, Søren Lund. 2015. "A Re-examination of the Imperial Oath from Vezirköprü." *Philia* 1:14–32.

Spencer, Aída Besançon. 2013. "Leadership of Women in Crete and Macedonia as a Model for the Church." *Priscilla Papers* 27.4:5–15.

Spener, Philipp Jakob. 1675. *Pia Desideria.* Translated by T. G. Tappert. Excerpted on pages 31–49 in *Pietists: Selected Writings.* Edited by Peter C. Erb. Mahwah, NJ: Paulist Press, 1983.

———. 1677. *The Spiritual Priesthood Briefly Described according to the Word of God in Seventy Questions and Answers.* Translated by Peter C. Erb. Pages 50–64 in *Pietists: Selected Writings.* Edited by Peter C. Erb. Mahwah, NJ: Paulist Press, 1983.

Spicq, Ceslas. 1969. *Saint Paul: Les épîtres pastorales.* 4th ed. Études bibliques. Paris: Lecoffre.

Standhartinger, Angela. 2000. "The Origin and Intention of the Household Code in the Letter to the Colossians." *Journal for the Study of the New Testament* 79:117–30.

Stegemann, Wolfgang. 1996. "Anti-Semitic and Racist Prejudices in Titus 1:10–16." Pages 271–94 in *Ethnicity and the Bible.* Edited by Mark G. Brett. Leiden: Brill.

Stephens, Janet. 2008. "Ancient Roman Hairdressing: On (Hair)Pins and Needles." *Journal of Roman Archaeology* 21:110–32.

Stepp, Perry L. 2005. *Leadership Succession in the World of the Pauline Circle.* Sheffield: Sheffield Phoenix.

Stewart-Sykes, Alistair. 1999. "The Original Condemnation of Asian Montanism." *Journal of Ecclesiastical History* 50.1:1–22.

Stiefel, Jennifer H. 1995. "Women Deacons in 1 Timothy: A Linguistic and Literary Look at 'Women Likewise . . .' (1 Tim. 3:11)." *New Testament Studies* 41:442–57.

Stirewalt, M. Luther. 1993. *Studies in Ancient Greek Epistolography.* Society of Biblical Literature Resources for Biblical Study 27. Atlanta: Scholars Press.

———. 2003. *Paul, the Letter Writer.* Grand Rapids: Eerdmans.

Streete, Gail Corrington. 1999. "*Askesis* and Resistance in the Pastoral Letters." Pages 299–316 in *Asceticism and the New Testament.* Edited by L. E. Vaage and V. L. Wimbush. New York: Routledge.

———. 2009. "Bad Girls or Good Ascetics? The *Gynaikaria* of the Pastoral Epistles." Pages 155–64 in *Women in the Biblical World: A Survey of Old and New Testament Perspectives.* Edited by E. A. McCabe. Lanham, MD: University Press of America.

Sumney, Jerry L. 1999a. *"Servants of Satan," "False Brothers," and Other Opponents of Paul.* Journal for the Study of the New Testament Supplement Series 188. Sheffield, UK: Sheffield Academic.

———. 1999b. "'God Our Savior': The Fundamental Operational Theological Assertion of 1 Timothy." *Horizons in Biblical Theology* 21.2:105–23.

275

Swartley, Willard M. 1983. *Slavery, Sabbath, War, and Women: Case Issues in Biblical Interpretation.* Scottdale, PA: Herald Press.

Sweetman, Rebecca J. 2007. "Roman Knossos: The Nature of a Globalized City." *American Journal of Archaeology* 111.1:61–81.

Tabbernee, William. 2007. *Fake Prophecy and Polluted Sacraments: Ecclesiastical and Imperial Reactions to Montanism.* Leiden: Brill.

Tamez, Elsa. 2007. *Struggles for Power in Early Christianity: A Study of the First Letter to Timothy.* Translated by Gloria Kinsler. Maryknoll, NY: Orbis Books.

Thiselton, Anthony C. 1994. "The Logical Core of the Liar Paradox in Titus 1:12, 13: A Dissent from the Commentaries in the Light of Philosophical and Logical Analysis." *Biblical Interpretation* 2.2:207–23.

Thom, Johan C. 1997. "'Harmonious Equality': The *Topos* of Friendship in Neopythagorean Writings." Pages 77–103 in *Greco-Roman Perspectives on Friendship.* Edited by J. T. Fitzgerald. Society of Biblical Literature Resources for Biblical Study 34. Atlanta: Scholars Press.

Thomas, Rhondda Robinson. 2013. *Claiming Exodus: A Cultural History of Afro-Atlantic Identity, 1774–1903.* Waco: Baylor University Press.

Thompson, Cynthia L. 1988. "Hairstyles, Head-Coverings, and St. Paul: Portraits from Roman Corinth." *Biblical Archaeologist* 51.2:99–115.

Thurston, Bonnie Bowman. 1989. *The Widows: A Women's Ministry in the Early Church.* Minneapolis: Fortress.

Tolmie, D. Francois. 2005. "Salvation as Redemption: The Use of 'Redemption' Metaphors in Pauline Literature." Pages 247–69 in *Salvation in the New Testament: Perspectives on Soteriology.* Edited by J. G. van der Watt. Leiden: Brill.

Torjesen, Karen Jo. 1998. "The Early Christian *Orans*: An Artistic Representation of Women's Liturgical Prayer and Prophecy." Pages 42–56 in *Women Preachers and Prophets through Two Millennia of Christianity.* Edited by B. M. Kienzle and P. J. Walker. Berkeley: University of California Press.

Towner, Philip H. 1989. *The Goal of Our Instruction: The Structure of Theology and Ethics in the Pastoral Epistles.* Journal for the Study of the New Testament Supplement Series 34. Sheffield: JSOT Press.

———. 2006. *The Letters to Timothy and Titus.* New International Commentary on the New Testament. Grand Rapids: Eerdmans.

Trebilco, Paul. 1991. *Jewish Communities in Asia Minor.* Society of New Testament Studies Monograph Series 69. Cambridge: Cambridge University Press.

———. 2008. *The Early Christians in Ephesus from Paul to Ignatius.* Grand Rapids: Eerdmans. Original edition Tübingen: Mohr Siebeck, 2004.

Trevett, Christine. 1996. *Montanism: Gender, Authority and the New Prophecy.* Cambridge: Cambridge University Press.

Trobisch, David. 1994. *Paul's Letter Collection: Tracing the Origins.* Minneapolis: Fortress.

Tromp, Johannes. 2007. "Jannes and Jambres (2 Tim. 3,8–9)." Pages 211–26 in *Moses in Biblical and Extra-Biblical Traditions.* Edited by Axel Graupner and Michael Wolter. Berlin: de Gruyter.

Tsouna, Voula, trans. 2012. *Philodemus: On Property Management*. Writings from the Greco-Roman World. Atlanta: Society of Biblical Literature.

Upson-Saia, Kristi. 2011. *Early Christian Dress: Gender, Virtue, and Authority*. New York: Routledge.

Urbainczyk, Theresa. 2008. *Slave Revolts in Antiquity*. Berkeley: University of California Press.

van der Horst, Pieter. 1988. "The Jews of Ancient Crete." *Journal of Jewish Studies* 39:183–200.

van Nes, Jermo. 2013. "The Problem of the Pastoral Epistles: An Important Hypothesis Reconsidered." Pages 153–69 in *Paul and Pseudepigraphy*. Edited by S. E. Porter and G. P. Fewster. Leiden: Brill.

———. 2018. *Pauline Language and the Pastoral Epistles: A Study of Linguistic Variation in the Corpus Paulinum*. Linguistic Biblical Studies 16. Leiden: Brill.

Van Neste, Ray. 2004. *Cohesion and Structure in the Pastoral Epistles*. Journal for the Study of the New Testament Supplement Series 280. London: T&T Clark.

Vermes, Géza. 1997. *The Complete Dead Sea Scrolls in English*. New York: Penguin Books.

Verner, D. C. 1983. *The Household of God: The Social World of the Pastoral Epistles*. Society of Biblical Literature Dissertation Series 71. Chico, CA: Scholars Press.

Volf, Miroslav. 2011. *Allah: A Christian Response*. New York: HarperOne.

Vondey, Wolfgang. 2013. *Pentecostalism: A Guide for the Perplexed*. New York: Bloomsbury T&T Clark.

Wackernagel, Jacob. 2009. *Lectures on Syntax with Special Reference to Greek, Latin, and Germanic*. Translated (from 2nd German ed., 1928) and edited by David Langslow. New York: Oxford University Press.

Walker, David. 1830. *Walker's Appeal, in Four Articles, together with a Preamble, to the Colored Citizens of the World, But in Particular, and Very Expressly to Those of the United States of America*. 2nd ed. Boston: D. Walker. Repr., North Stratford, NH: Ayer 2008.

Walker, Peter. 2012a. "Revisiting the Pastoral Epistles—Part I." *European Journal of Theology* 21.1:4–16.

———. 2012b. "Revisiting the Pastoral Epistles—Part II." *European Journal of Theology* 21.2:120–32.

Walker, William O. 2004. "Interpolations in the Pauline Letters." Pages 189–235 in *The Pauline Canon*. Edited by Stanley E. Porter. Atlanta: SBL Press.

Wall, Robert W. 2004. "The Function of the Pastoral Letters within the Pauline Canon of the New Testament: A Canonical Approach." Pages 27–44 in *The Pauline Canon*. Edited by Stanley E. Porter. Atlanta: SBL Press.

Wallace, Daniel B. 1996. *Greek Grammar beyond the Basics*. Grand Rapids: Zondervan.

Wallace-Hadrill, Andrew. 2008. *Rome's Cultural Revolution*. Cambridge: Cambridge University Press.

Wansink, Craig S. 1996. *Chained in Christ: The Experience and Rhetoric of Paul's Imprisonments*. Journal for the Study of the New Testament Supplement Series 130. Sheffield, UK: Sheffield Academic.

Ware, Kallistos. 2012. "St. Nikodimos and the *Philokalia*." Pages 9–35 in *The Philokalia: A Classic Text of Orthodox Spirituality*. Edited by Brock Bingaman and Bradley Nassif. New York: Oxford University Press.

Warfield, Benjamin B. 1915. "Inspiration." *International Standard Bible Encyclopedia* 3:1473–83. Edited by James Orr. Chicago: Howard-Severance. Repr. as "The Biblical Idea of Inspiration." Pages 129–66 in *The Inspiration and Authority of the Bible*. By B. B. Warfield. Edited by S. G. Craig. Phillipsburg, NJ: Presbyterian & Reformed Publishing, 1948.

Waters, Kenneth L., Sr. 2004. "Saved through Childbearing: Virtues as Children in 1 Timothy 2:11–15." *Journal of Biblical Literature* 123.4:703–35.

Weber, Max. 1963. *The Sociology of Religion*. 4th ed. Translated by Ephraim Fischoff. First ed. in Eng., Boston: Beacon, 1956. Original German edition 1922.

Weima, Jeffrey A. D. 2010. "Sincerely Paul: The Significance of the Pauline Letter Closings." Pages 307–45 in *Paul and the Ancient Letter Form*. Edited by Stanley E. Porter and Sean A. Adams. Pauline Studies 6. Leiden: Brill.

Welles, C. Bradford. 1934. *Royal Correspondence in the Hellenistic Period: A Study in Greek Epigraphy*. New Haven: Yale University Press. Repr., Chicago: Ares, 1974.

Wesley, John. 1777. "A Plain Account of Christian Perfection as Believed and Taught by The Reverend Mr. John Wesley, From the year 1725, to the year 1777." Pages 366–446 in vol. 11 of *The Works of John Wesley*. Edited by Thomas Jackson (1872). Online at http://wesley.nnu.edu/john-wesley/a-plain-account-of-christian-perfection/.

Westfall, Cynthia Long. 2010. "A Moral Dilemma? The Epistolary Body of 2 Timothy." Pages 213–52 in *Paul and the Ancient Letter Form*. Edited by Stanley E. Porter and Sean A. Adams. Pauline Studies 6. Leiden: Brill.

Whitaker, E. C. 1970. *Documents of the Baptismal Liturgy*. 2nd ed. London: SPCK.

White, Benjamin L. 2011. "How to Read a Book: Irenaeus and the Pastoral Epistles Reconsidered." *Vigiliae Christianae* 65:125–49.

———. 2014. *Remembering Paul: Ancient and Modern Contests over the Image of the Apostle*. New York: Oxford University Press.

White, John L. 1986. *Light from Ancient Letters*. Philadelphia: Fortress.

White, L. Michael. 1990. *Building God's House in the Roman World: Architectural Adaptation among Pagans, Jews and Christians*. Vol. 1 of *The Social Origins of Christian Architecture*. Baltimore: Johns Hopkins University Press. Repr., Harvard Theological Studies 42. Valley Forge, PA: Trinity, 1996.

———. 1997. *Texts and Monuments for the Christian Domus Ecclesiae in Its Environment*. Vol. 2 of *The Social Origins of Christian Architecture*. Harvard Theological Studies 42. Valley Forge, PA: Trinity.

Wieland, George M. 2005. "Roman Crete and the Letter to Titus." *New Testament Studies* 55.3:338–54.

Wilken, Robert L. 1984. *The Christians as the Romans Saw Them*. New Haven: Yale University Press.

Williams, Margaret H. 1998. *The Jews among the Greeks and Romans: A Diaspora Sourcebook*. Baltimore: Johns Hopkins University Press.

Willis, John T. 2001. "The Lifting Up of Hands in the Bible and the Church." *Stone-Campbell Journal* 4:81–106.

———. 2003. Review of *Mission in the Old Testament: Israel as a Light to the Nations*, by Walter Kaiser. *Restoration Quarterly* 45:280–81.

Wink, Walter. 1992. *Engaging the Powers: Discernment and Resistance in a World of Domination*. Minneapolis: Fortress.

Winter, Bruce W. 2001. *After Paul Left Corinth: The Influence of Secular Ethics and Social Change*. Grand Rapids: Eerdmans.

———. 2002. *Philo and Paul among the Sophists: Alexandrian and Corinthian Responses to a Julio-Claudian Movement*. 2nd ed. Grand Rapids: Eerdmans.

———. 2003. *Roman Wives, Roman Widows: The Appearance of New Women and the Pauline Communities*. Grand Rapids: Eerdmans.

———. 2015. *Divine Honours for the Caesars: The First Christians' Responses*. Grand Rapids: Eerdmans.

Witherington, Ben, III. 1988. *Women in the Earliest Churches*. Cambridge: Cambridge University Press.

———. 2006. *Letters and Homilies for Hellenized Christians I: A Socio-Rhetorical Commentary on Titus, 1–2 Timothy and 1–3 John*. Downers Grove: IVP Academic.

Wood, George O. 2001. "Exploring Why We Think the Way We Do about Women in Ministry." *Enrichment Journal* 5.2 (Spring). Online at http://enrichmentjournal. ag.org/200102/index.cfm.

Wright, N. T. 1992. *The Climax of the Covenant: Christ and the Law in Pauline Theology*. Minneapolis: Fortress.

———. 2003. *The Resurrection of the Son of God*. Christian Origins and the Question of God 3. Minneapolis: Fortress.

———. 2013. *Paul and the Faithfulness of God*. Christian Origins and the Question of God 4. Minneapolis: Fortress.

Wright, Richard A. 2007. "Plutarch on Moral Progress." Pages 136–50 in *Passions and Moral Progress in Greco-Roman Thought*. Edited by J. T. Fitzgerald. New York: Routledge.

Yarbrough, Mark M. 2009. *Paul's Utilization of Preformed Traditions in 1 Timothy: An Evaluation of the Apostle's Literary, Rhetorical, and Theological Tactics*. Library of New Testament Studies 417. London: T&T Clark.

Young, Frances. 1994. *The Theology of the Pastoral Letters*. Cambridge: Cambridge University Press.

Zamfir, Korinna. 2013. *Men and Women in the Household of God: A Contextual Approach to Roles and Ministries in the Pastoral Epistles*. Göttingen: Vandenhoeck & Ruprecht.

Zamfir, Korinna, and Joseph Verheyden. 2008. "Text-Critical and Intertextual Remarks on 1 Timothy 2:8–10." *Novum Testamentum* 50.4:376–406.

Zerwick, Maximilian, SJ. 1963. *Biblical Greek Illustrated by Examples*. Translated by Joseph Smith. 4th ed. Rome: Biblical Institute Press.

Index of Subjects

Index of Modern Authors

Index of Scripture and Ancient Sources

Page numbers in italic for 1 Timothy, 2 Timothy, and Titus indicate where the primary discussion of the verses occurs in the commentary.